PENGUIN BOOKS

RISE TO GLOBALISM

Stephen E. Ambrose was born in Decatur, Illinois, in 1936. He received a B.A. from the University of Wisconsin in 1956, an M.A. from Louisiana State University in 1957, and a Ph.D. in history from the University of Wisconsin in 1963. Formerly E. J. King Professor of Maritime History at the Naval War College and Eisenhower Professor of War and Peace at Kansas State University, he is currently the Boyd Professor of History at the University of New Orleans. He has written twenty books on military affairs and foreign policy in the nineteenth and twentieth centuries, including biographies of Dwight Eisenhower and Richard Nixon. His most recent books—*D-Day* and *Undaunted Courage*—were mainstays on *The New York Times* bestseller list. Among his hobbies, Professor Ambrose counts gardening, biking, jogging, and woodworking.

Douglas G. Brinkley was born in Atlanta, Georgia, in 1960. He received a B.A. from Ohio State University in 1982. He earned an M.A. in 1983, as well as a Ph.D. in diplomatic history from Georgetown University in 1989. Formerly a teacher at the U.S. Naval Academy, Princeton University, and Hofstra University, he is currently professor of history and director of the Eisenhower Center for American Studies at the University of New Orleans. He has authored, coauthored, and edited ten books on U.S. foreign policy including biographies of Jimmy Carter, Franklin Roosevelt, Dean Acheson, and James For___ ___ ___ *The Majic Bus: An American Odyssey*—v___ ___ ___ untry college histo___ ___ accolades from arou___ ___ tor on National Pu___ ___ ys writing poetry, ca___

Works by Stephen E. Ambrose

Upton and the Army

Halleck: Lincoln's Chief of Staff

Ike's Spies: Eisenhower and the Espionage Establishment

Crazy Horse and Custer: The Parallel Lives of Two American Warriors

Eisenhower and Berlin, 1945: The Decision to Halt at the Elbe

Duty, Honor, Country: A History of West Point

The Supreme Commander: The War Years of Dwight D. Eisenhower

Eisenhower: Soldier, General, President-Elect, 1890–1952

Eisenhower: The President

Pegasus Bridge: June 6, 1944

Nixon: The Education of a Politician, 1913–1962

Nixon: The Triumph of a Politician, 1962–1972

Nixon: The Ruin and Recovery of a Politician, 1973–1990

Eisenhower: Soldier and President

*Band of Brothers: E Company, 506th Regiment, 101st Airborne
from Normandy to Hitler's Eagle Nest*

D-Day

Undaunted Courage

Works by Douglas G. Brinkley

Jean Monnet: Path to European Unity (ed.)

Dean Acheson: The Cold War Years

Dean Acheson and the Making of U.S. Foreign Policy

Driven Patriot: The Life and Time of James Forrestal (coauthor)

The Majic Bus: An American Odyssey

FDR and the Creation of the United Nations (coauthor)

The Atlantic Charter (ed.)

Jimmy Carter: The Post-Presidential Years

For Alexander, Corina,
and Stephen Riley.
May they know
only peace.

Contents

List of Maps

Maps by Ahmad Massasati, University of New Orleans

Introduction

In 1939, on the eve of World War II, the United States had an army of 185,000 men with an annual budget of less than $500 million. America had no entangling alliances and no American troops were stationed in any foreign country. The dominant political mood was isolationism. America's physical security, the *sine qua non* of foreign policy, seemed assured, not because of American alliances or military strength but because of the distance between America and any potential enemy.

A half century later the United States had a huge standing Army, Air Force, and Navy. The budget of the Department of Defense was over $300 billion. The United States had military alliances with fifty nations, over a million soldiers, airmen, and sailors stationed in more than 100 countries, and an offensive capability sufficient to destroy the world many times over. It had used military force to intervene in Indochina, Lebanon, the Dominican Republic, Grenada, Central America, and the Persian Gulf, supported an invasion of Cuba, distributed enormous quantities of arms to friendly governments around the world, and fought costly wars in Korea and Vietnam. But despite all the money spent on armaments and no matter how far outward America extended her power, America's national security was constantly in jeopardy.

By 1993, however, the Soviet Union was gone, there were no military threats to the United States, and the American armed forces were shrinking. America's overseas concerns were no longer the armies and missiles of the communist superpower, but access to raw materials and markets and concern over small nations causing major upheavals, plus the trade policies of its World War II enemies, Germany and Japan. America had won the Cold War and was once again, as in 1939, turning away from the world.

Shifts in attitudes accompanied these bewildering changes in policy. Before World War II most Americans believed in a natural harmony of interests between nations, assumed that there was a common commitment to peace, and argued that no nation or people could profit from a war. These beliefs implied that peace was the normal condition between states and that war, if it came, was an aberration resulting from the irrational acts of evil or psychotic men. It was odd that a nation that had come into existence through a victorious war, gained large portions of its territory through war, established its industrial revolution and national unity through a bloody civil war, and won a colonial empire through war could believe that war profited no one. Yet most Americans in the 1930s did so believe.

During and after World War II, Americans changed their attitudes. They did not come to relish war, but they did learn to accept it. They also became aware of their own vulnerability, which supported the post–Pearl Harbor belief that threats had to be met early and overseas. After World War I, the United States had adopted a policy of unilateral disarmament and neutrality as a way to avoid another war. After World War II, the nation adopted a policy of massive rearmament and collective security as a way to avoid another war. That meant stationing troops and missiles overseas.

Technological change, especially in military weapons, gave added impetus to the new expansionism. For the first time in its history the United States could be threatened from abroad. High-speed ships, long-range bombers, jet aircraft, atomic weapons, and eventually intercontinential missiles all combined to endanger the physical security of the United States.

Simultaneously, America became vulnerable to foreign economic threats. An increasingly complex economy, coupled with the tremendous economic boom of the postwar years maintained by cheap energy, made America increasingly dependent on foreign sources.

And so, the irony. America had far more military power in the early 1990s than she had had in the late thirties, but she was less secure. America was far richer in the nineties than she had been during the Depression, but also more vulnerable to economic blackmail.

It was an unexpected outcome. At the conclusion of World War II, America was on a high. In all the world only the United States had a healthy economy, an intact physical plant capable of mass production of goods, and excess capital. American troops occupied Japan, the only important industrial power in the Pacific, while American influence was dominant in France, Britain, and West Germany, the industrial heart of Europe. The Pacific and the Mediterranean had become American lakes. Above all, the United States had a monopoly on the atomic bomb.

Yet there was no peace. The Cold War came about because the United States and the U.S.S.R. were deeply suspicious of each other, and with good reason. Economic rivalry and ideological differences helped fuel the rivalry, but another important factor was the pace of scientific and technological change in the postwar period. Nuclear weapons and the missiles to deliver them became the pivot around which much of the Cold War revolved. The fear that its opponents would move ahead on this or that weapons system drove each nation to make an all-out effort in the arms race. In the United States the resulting growth of the armed services and their suppliers—the military-industrial complex—gave generals, admirals, and industrialists new sources of power, leading to a situation in which Americans tended to find military solutions to political problems. Not until the late sixties did large numbers of Americans learn the costly lesson that the power to destroy is not the power to control.

The United States of the Cold War period, like ancient

Rome, was concerned with all political problems in the world. The loss of even one country to Communism, therefore, while not in itself a threat to American physical security, carried implications that officials in Washington found highly disturbing. In the early sixties, few important officials argued that South Vietnam was essential to the defense of the United States, but the attitude that "we have to prove that wars of national liberation don't work" (a curious attitude for the children of the American Revolution to hold) did carry the day.

America's rise to globalism was by no means mindless, nor was it exclusively a reaction to the Communist challenge or a response to economic needs. A frequently heard expression during World War II was that "America has come of age." Americans had a sense of power, of bigness, of destiny. They had saved the world from Hitler; now they would save the world from Stalin. In the process, American influence and control would expand. During World War II, Henry Luce of *Life* magazine spoke for most political leaders as well as American businessmen, soldiers, and the public generally when he said that the twentieth century would be "the American century." Politicians looked for areas in which American influence could dominate. Businessmen looked for profitable markets and new sources of cheap raw materials; the military looked for overseas bases. All found what they wanted as America inaugurated a program of expansion that had no inherent limits.

Americans launched a crusade for freedom that would be complete only when freedom reigned everywhere. Conservatives like Senator Robert Taft doubted that such a goal was obtainable, and old New Dealers like Henry Wallace argued that it could only be achieved at the cost of domestic reform. But most politicians and nearly all businessmen and soldiers signed on as crusaders.

While America's businessmen, soldiers, and politicians moved into South and Central America, Europe, and Southeast Asia, her leaders rarely paused to wonder if there were limits to American power. The disorderly expansion and the astronomical growth of areas defined as constituting a vital American interest seemed to Washington, Wall Street, and the Pentagon to be entirely normal and natural. Almost no important public figure argued that the nation was overextended, just as no one could suggest any attitude toward Communism other than unrelieved hostility.

But ultimately, military reality put limits on American expansion. At no time after 1945 was the United States capable of destroying Russia or her allies without taking on totally unacceptable risks herself; at no time was the United States able to establish an imperial dominion. The crusade against Communism, therefore, took the form of containment rather than attack. As a policy, containment, with its implication of an acceptance of a permanently divided world, led to widely felt frustration. These frustrations were deepened by self-imposed constraint on the use of force in Korea, Vietnam, and elsewhere.

The failure of containment in Indochina led to another basic shift in attitude toward America's role in the world. It was not a return to isolationism, 1939 style— the pendulum did not swing that far. It was a general realization that, given the twin restraints of fears of provoking a Russian nuclear strike and America's reluctance to use her full military power, there was relatively little the United States could accomplish by force of arms. President Reagan showed an awareness of these limits in Poland, Afghanistan, and even Central America, and in withdrawing from Lebanon.

Following the involvement in Vietnam there was also a shift in the focus of American foreign policy, especially after 1973, when the Arab oil boycott made Americans suddenly aware that the Middle East was so important to them. Nixon's 1972 trip to China, the emergence of black Africa, and the discovery of abundant raw materials in both Africa and South America helped turn American eyes from the northern to the southern half of the globe. This shift emphasized the fundamentally changed nature of the American economy, from self-sufficiency to increasing dependency on others for basic supplies. America in the 1990s was richer and more powerful—and more vulnerable—than at any other time in her history.

Rise to Globalism

I returned and saw under the sun that the race is not to the swift, nor the battle to the strong, neither yet bread to the wise nor riches to men of understanding, but time and chance happeneth to them all.

ECCLESIASTES

We are willing to help people who believe the way we do, to continue to live the way they want to live.

DEAN ACHESON

The biggest thing that has happened in the world in my life, in our lives, is this: By the grace of God, America won the Cold War.

GEORGE BUSH

[1]

The Twisting Path to War

I hate war.

FRANKLIN DELANO ROOSEVELT

The United States felt fairly secure in the world of 1938. Neither of the great totalitarian political forces of the century, Fascism nor Communism, was a threat. So long as Britain and France continued to stand against Hitler and the Nazis, the United States had nothing to fear militarily from Germany. Elsewhere, anti-Communism was triumphing in Spain, while in central and eastern Europe governments hostile to the Soviet Union continued to contain Communism.

On the other side of the world the United States, in combination with the British, French, and Dutch, still ruled the Pacific. American control of Hawaii and the Philippines, Dutch control of the Netherlands East Indies (N.E.I., today's Indonesia), French control of Indochina (today's Laos, Cambodia [Democratic Kampuchea], and Vietnam), and British control of India, Burma, Hong Kong, and Malaya gave the Western powers a dominant position in Asia. Japan, ruled by her military, was aggressive, determined to end white man's rule in Asia, and thus a threat to the status quo. But Japan lacked crucial natural resources, most notably oil, and was tied down by her war in China.

On the great land mass connecting Europe and Asia, Russia was relatively weak and nonexpansive. In the Middle East and Africa, European colonialism dominated. In Latin America, American economic imperialism guaranteed cheap raw materials for American industries and a dependable market.

The United States in 1938 saw no pressing need to play any great role in the world. Isolationism reigned in the Congress, reflecting a national mood. The Nye Committee, conducting a Senate investigation, had "proved" that Wall Street had dragged the United States into World War I. The aftermath led many to believe that entering World War I had been a mistake—so many as to make disarmament and neutrality the dominant factors in American foreign policy in the 1920s and 1930s.

The attitude of the President himself reinforced isolationism. Unlike Winston Churchill, Hitler, or the Japanese leaders and unlike his cousin Theodore Roosevelt, Franklin D. Roosevelt saw neither glory nor romance in war, nor did he feel that it strengthened the national fiber. If not a pacifist, FDR was certainly no militarist. On a number of occasions he declared, with deep emotion, "I hate war."

American foreign policy in 1938 was to support the status quo, but only through vaguely worded statements. Roosevelt, Secretary of State Cordell Hull, and a majority of the American people did not want a German domination of Europe or a Japanese domination of Asia, but neither were they ready to do much to stop it. Least of all were they willing to improve the armed forces so that the United States could threaten to punish aggression.

In mid-March of 1939 Hitler's armies overran Czechoslovakia. Roosevelt failed to support a Senate resolution that would have repealed the arms embargo (required in case of war by the neutrality acts of the mid-thirties) and allowed American industries to sell war goods to France and Britain on a cash-and-carry basis. Although FDR and a majority of the people had declared that their sympathies lay with the democracies, they had also demonstrated to Hitler that in the immediate future he had nothing to fear from the United States. On August 23, 1939, Hitler announced the Nazi-Soviet Pact, which provided for the division of Poland between Russia and Germany and relieved Germany of the nightmare of a two-front war. On September 1, 1939, the Nazis struck

Poland; two days later Britain and France declared war on Germany, and World War II was under way.

Americans split sharply over the question of how to react. Isolationists resisted any steps that might lead to aid for the democracies, fearing that the United States would thereby become so committed to an Allied victory that, as in 1917, she would be drawn into war against her will. Interventionists, meanwhile, wanted to abandon neutrality and give military aid to Britain and France. Roosevelt took a middle ground. In a speech to a special session of Congress, FDR declared four times that his policy was designed to keep the United States out of war. He then asked for repeal of the embargo on arms and approval of a cash-and-carry system. Congress agreed in November 1939.

Cash-and-carry symbolized much that was to follow. It aligned the United States with the democracies, reiterated American concern and friendship for Western Europe, and made it clear that the country would resist any attempt to upset the balance of power in Europe. But it also indicated that the United States was unwilling to pay a high price to stop Hitler. America would sell arms to the democracies as long as the democracies picked them up and carried them off. America was taking uncommonly large risks by not doing more.

Just how great those risks were, Roosevelt knew as did few others in the world. On October 11, 1939, world-renowned physicist Albert Einstein, a Jewish refugee from the Nazis, warned FDR that the Germans were working on the problem of harnessing atomic energy into a bomb. If Hitler got an atomic bomb, he would surely conquer Europe. Roosevelt was impressed by Einstein's message. He conferred privately with key congressional leaders and together they started the Manhattan Project. This secret project was designed to build an atomic bomb capable of being dropped from an airplane, and to get it built before Hitler could complete his own plans.

The Manhattan Project was the beginning of the mar-

riage between science and government in the United
States, and thus one of the most important legacies of
World War II. It was also the first use of extreme secrecy
about government activities, justified on the grounds of
national security. In the case of the Manhattan Project,
most members of Congress did not even know where
the funds they had appropriated were going.

But although Roosevelt was willing to act decisively in
the race for an atomic bomb, there was otherwise a distinct limit on the American contribution to stopping Hitler. After German armies overran Poland in the fall of
1939, a period of stagnation set in on the western front.
Americans called it a "phony war" and saw no pressing
reason to strain themselves to build up their stength.
FDR increased the regular army from 210,000 to
217,000 and asked for an army budget of $853 million,
which the Congress cut by nearly 10 percent. These pal-
try figures constituted an announcement to Hitler that
the United States did not intend to fight in Europe in
the near future.

The German spring offensive of 1940 brought forth
a tough verbal but limited practical response from the
United States. The President asked for a supplemental
appropriation to raise troop strength to 255,000; Congress, after hearing Army Chief of Staff George C. Marshall's desperate appeals, raised the force to 375,000.
The Nazis, meanwhile, rolled on. On May 15 the new
British Prime Minister, Winston Churchill, urgently requested forty or fifty American destroyers to protect
Britain's Atlantic supply line. Churchill called it a matter
of "life or death." Roosevelt was reluctant to act. On June
5, with the fall of France imminent and Britain about to
be left standing alone, he told a Cabinet official that it
would require an act of Congress to transfer the destroyers to England and implied that he was not ready to ask
for such a bill.

He was ready to speak out. On June 10, 1940, the
President told the graduating class of the University of
Virginia that the United States would follow "two ob-

vious and simultaneous courses," extending to France and Britain "the material resources of this nation" and speeding up the development of these resources so that the American armed forces could be strengthened. The speech was hailed by interventionists in the United States as setting a new course, but the French quickly discovered its limits. On June 14 French Premier Paul Reynaud appealed to Roosevelt to send American troops to Europe in France's hour of need. Roosevelt refused. Even had he wanted to act, he had no troops available to send overseas. Within the week the French signed an armistice with Germany.

The fall of France was a shattering blow. No one had forecast it. The United States now faced an entirely new situation. No longer could the nation comfortably expect that the British and French would stop the Germans. The British, standing alone, might survive, although even that was questionable, but would never be able to roll back the Nazis by themselves. The best-disciplined and most highly educated and productive nation in Europe now dominated the Continent. The balance of power was gone. Hitler posed no immediate military threat to the New World, but if he could conquer England and get control of the British fleet, then overrun Russia—suddenly real possibilities—he would command the greatest military might the world had ever known. What could happen then was anyone's guess, but it was becoming increasingly apparent that it behooved Americans to do something more than sit by and watch. Hitler could be stopped and some kind of balance could be restored in Europe only if others came to Britain's aid.

Isolationism was obviously an obstacle to forthright presidential action, but FDR had an inner conflict that reflected the public confusion. He was very much of his time and place, sharing general attitudes on the mistake of entering World War I. In a famous campaign speech in Boston on October 30, 1940, FDR declared: "And while I am talking to you mothers and fathers, I give you one more assurance. I have said this before, but I shall say it again and again and again: Your boys are not going to be sent into any foreign wars."

Neither, it seemed, was a great deal of American equipment. The British still obtained supplies only on a cash-and-carry basis and they lacked the destroyers necessary to protect the convoys transporting those goods they could afford to purchase. On July 21, 1940, Churchill made another eloquent plea for destroyers: "Mr. President, with great respect I must tell you that in the long history of the world this is a thing to do *now*." The British were losing merchant shipping in the Battle of the Atlantic in appalling numbers, the Battle of Britain was reaching its peak, and the German General Staff was preparing plans for an invasion of the British Isles. The President allowed private groups to work out the details of a destroyer-for-bases deal, which eventually (September 2) gave the British fifty overage American destroyers in return for rent-free bases on British possessions from Bermuda to British Guiana.

There was, meanwhile, a growing tension between the War Department and the White House. General Marshall reasoned that the only way to defeat Hitler was to fight and defeat the German army in northwestern Europe. To do that Marshall needed a mass army; to get that he needed conscription. But given the tenor of Roosevelt's third-term campaign, there was no possibility that the President could give public support to a conscription bill.

Congress proved more willing to act than the President. Private groups, led by Republicans Henry L. Stimson and Elihu Root, Jr., persuaded Congressmen favoring intervention to introduce a selective-service bill in both houses of Congress. Roosevelt remained aloof, but he did give General Marshall permission to support the bill; the President also helped by appointing Stimson, an interventionist, Secretary of War. In late August of 1940, Congress authorized the President to call the National Guard and other reserves to active duty for one year, and on September 16 it provided for selective service for one year. Both measures limited the employment of troops to the Western hemisphere.

In November 1940 Roosevelt won the election. Churchill, among others, thought that the reelected President would be willing to assume a more active role in the struggle against Hitler. The Prime Minister sent FDR a lengthy and bleak description of the British situation, emphasizing that his nation was running out of money. Cash-and-carry would no longer suffice, for "the moment approaches when we shall no longer be able to pay cash for shipping and other supplies."

Roosevelt responded sympathetically. On December 7, 1940, he called in the press, outlined the British dilemma, and said he believed that "the best defense of Great Britain is the best defense of the United States." Seeking to avoid the mistakes of Woodrow Wilson and the long controversy over World War I war debts, Roosevelt said he wanted to simply lend or lease to England the supplies she needed. He compared his scheme to the idea of lending a garden hose to a neighbor whose house was on fire.

In a radio address to the nation a few days later, Roosevelt justified lend-lease as essential to national security. If England fell, "all of us in the Americas would be living at the point of a gun." He said the best way to keep the United States out of the war was to "do all we can now to support the nations defending themselves against attack by the Axis." He declared again that he had no intention of sending American boys to Europe; his sole purpose was to "keep war away from our country and our people." He would do this by making America the "great arsenal of democracy."

The isolationists were furious. They charged that lend-lease was a most unneutral act, placing the United States squarely on the British side. Senator Robert Taft found the idea of loaning military equipment absurd. He said it was rather like loaning chewing gum: "Once it had been used, you didn't want it back."

By early March 1941, however, the Administration

had overcome the opposition, and the lend-lease bill went through Congress with an initial appropriation of $7 billion. Secretary Stimson correctly called it "a declaration of economic war." But it was hardly enough to sustain a Britain on the defensive, much less give Hitler cause for concern.

What was needed was a more extensive American involvement. Realizing this, Roosevelt declared an Atlantic neutrality zone that extended almost to Iceland, ordering the Navy to patrol the area and report the location of German submarines to the British. In April 1941 American troops moved into Greenland. In July, following Hitler's invasion of Russia, his first big mistake, American troops occupied Iceland, which released British troops for the Middle East, and the U.S. Navy began escorting convoys as far as Iceland. By September the U.S. Navy was fully at war with Germany in the Atlantic. When a German submarine fired a torpedo at the American destroyer stalking it, FDR brazenly denounced the "rattlesnakes of the Atlantic" for the supposedly unprovoked act and ordered the Navy to shoot on sight at all German submarines they encountered. In October FDR persuaded Congress to remove nearly all restrictions on American commerce; henceforth, American merchant vessels could carry goods to British ports. He also extended lend-lease to Russia.

Roosevelt's tone, in public and private, was by November of 1941 one of unrestrained belligerency. German advances to the gates of Moscow made it impossible to underestimate the threat. Roosevelt seems to have reasoned that Hitler could not long permit American ships to transport goods to Britain. The Germans would have to order their submarine captains to sink the American vessels. FDR could then overcome isolationist opposition in Congress and obtain a declaration of war.

Whether he was right or not will never be known. It is clear that by December 1941 American foreign policy in Europe had failed to make any significant contribution to stopping—much less overcoming—Hitler. In retrospect, the steps the President and Congress took to protect American interests in Europe were halting and limited. Everything hinged on Russia and Britain. If they kept going, America could—eventually—supply them with the tools and men to do the job. The United States, in the meantime, was taking great risks.

The American ship of state was drifting, without a rudder or power, in a storm. The world's greatest industrial democracy could not stem the tide of Fascism. Roosevelt's caution was so great that in September 1941, when the original selective service bill ran out and had to be repassed if the soldiers already partly trained were to be retained in the Army, he refused to pressure Congress, either privately or publicly. Working behind the scenes, General Marshall was able to get the draft bill passed—by one vote. Even this left the U.S. Army ridiculously small (1.6 million men) if the nation ever intended to play a role in the conflict raging in Europe.

Fortunately for the United States, the British and Russians held out against Germany, making it possible for America to later exert her power to help win the war. Fortunately, too, the Japanese solved Roosevelt's problem of how to get fully involved in the war.

Japan was the aggressor in the Pacific, as Mussolini was in the Mediterranean and Hitler was in Europe. Since the mid-thirties, Japan had been involved in a war of conquest in China. From the beginning the United States had protested, but because FDR had not supported his demands with action, the Japanese ignored him.

The overall Japanese program called for Asia for the Asians (although some Asians were going to be more equal than others). The Japanese proposed to substitute themselves for the white rulers in China, Indochina, Malaya, Burma, the Philippines, and the N.E.I. It was essential to the Japanese that they control these areas if Japan were to be a great power, for despite her human resources Japan was almost devoid of critical raw materials, especially oil, which was available in Southeast Asia.

The American colony of the Philippines lay directly athwart the Japanese proposed line of advance. Whether correctly or not, the Japanese were convinced that the United States would never allow them to advance into Malaya or the N.E.I. without striking against their lines of communications. More fundamentally, they believed that the United States would never willingly allow them to become a great power and would consistently oppose their advance southward. Thus, although the Japanese realized that they were doomed if they goaded the United States into war and the United States chose to fight it to a finish, they felt they were also doomed without war. "Japan entered the war," a prince of the Japanese imperial family later wrote, "with a tragic determination and in desperate self-abandonment."

The fall of France in 1940 and Britain's preoccupation with Germany opened the door to Southeast Asia for Japan. Bogged down in her war with China, Japan decided to overcome her crippling shortage of oil through a program of southward expansion. Only the Soviet Union and the United States were potentially strong enough in the Pacific to interfere; Japan moved politically to minimize these threats. In the late summer of 1940 she signed a five-year nonaggression pact with the Soviets, an agreement that Stalin, fearing Hitler, was happy to sign.

Japan also entered into the Tripartite Pact with the Germans and Italians, a defensive alliance that pledged mutual support if any one of the three signatories were attacked. The German invasion of Russia in June 1941 opened new possibilities for Japan, and a great debate within Japan ensued. Should Japan take advantage of Russia's desperate position vis-à-vis Germany and attack the Soviets through Siberia? Some military leaders thought so. Others argued that because of Hitler's involvement in Russia, Germany no longer posed so much of a threat to England; this strengthened the Anglo-American position in the Pacific because Churchill was now free to send part of the fleet from the home isles to Britain's Asian colonies (as he in fact did do in 1941). Japan, therefore, should seek to reach an agreement with the United States, making such concessions as were necessary to stave off war. Still others held out for the long-planned conquest of Southeast Asia.

Roosevelt listened in on the debate through the medium of MAGIC,* the code name applied to intercepted and decoded Japanese messages, and characterized it as "a real drag-down and knock-out fight . . . to decide which way they were going to jump—attack Russia, attack the South Seas [or] sit on the fence and be more friendly with us." The decision was to reject war with Russia and instead move south immediately, meanwhile trying to avoid war with the United States by carrying on negotiations as long as possible. The first step was the unresisted occupation of French Indochina, which gave Japan possession of air and naval bases stretching from Hanoi to Saigon.

The U.S. Navy did not wish to provoke the Japanese. It wanted time, not only to bring about Hitler's defeat but also to build a first-class striking force. The Chief of Naval Operations, Admiral Harold R. Stark, advised the President to do nothing when the Japanese moved into French Indochina. But whatever the military realities, FDR also had political realities to deal with. The polls indicated that nearly 70 percent of the people were willing to risk war in the Pacific rather than let Japan continue to expand. FDR froze all Japanese assets in the United States. The British and Dutch supported his

---

*While the Americans were listening in on the Japanese, the British had broken the German code (they called their system ULTRA) and the Germans had broken the British code. And while the Japanese were decoding American messages, the Russians were reading Japanese radio traffic. On balance the Americans got more useful information from MAGIC and the British from ULTRA than the Axis got from their monitoring systems.

move. The effect of the freeze was to create an economic blockade of Japan. She could not buy oil, steel, or other necessities without Roosevelt's permission.

The embargo made it clear to the Japanese that they either had to pull back from Indochina and China and thereby reach an agreement with the United States that would provide them with access to oil, or go to war. The one slim hope remaining was that America's fear of a two-ocean war would impel Roosevelt to compromise. From August until November 1941, the Japanese sought some form of acceptable political compromise, all the while sharpening their military plans and preparations. If the diplomatic offensive worked, the military offensive could be called off, including the planned attack on the U.S. fleet at Pearl Harbor.

In essence, the Japanese demanded from the United States a free hand in Asia. There were variations through a series of proposals, but the central points always included an Anglo-American promise not to "meddle in nor interrupt" a settlement between Japan and China, a recognition of Japan's "special position" in French Indochina, an agreement not to reinforce Singapore and the Philippines, and a resumption of commercial relations with Japan, which included selling oil.

Although the Americans were willing to go part way to compromise, they would not consider giving the Japanese a free hand in China. Since it was precisely on this point that the Japanese were most adamant, conflict was inevitable. Neither side wanted war in the sense that each would have preferred to gain its objectives without having to fight for them, both were willing to move on to a showdown. In Japan it was the military who pressed for action, over the protests of the civilians, while in America the situation was reversed. Prime Minister Fumimaro Konoye of Japan resigned in October when he was unable to secure military approval of a partial withdrawal from China in order to "save ourselves from the crisis of a Japanese-American war." His successor,

General Hideki Tojo, was willing to continue negotiations with the United States, but only until late November. If no progress was made by then, Japan would strike.

In the United States, Roosevelt stood firm, even though his military advisers strongly urged him to avoid a crisis with Japan until he had dealt with Germany. Secretary Hull made one last effort for peace, suggesting on November 21 that the United States should offer a three months' truce. Japan might have accepted, but Chiang Kai-shek, the Chinese leader, protested vehemently, and Roosevelt would not allow Hull to make the offer. "I have washed my hands of the Japanese situation," Hull told Stimson on November 27, "and it is now in the hands of . . . the Army and Navy."

A little over a week later, on Sunday, December 7, 1941, the Japanese launched their attack, hitting Pearl Harbor, the Philippines, Malaya, and Thailand.* They soon added the N.E.I. to the list. On December 8 the Anglo-Americans declared war on Japan, but the United States still had no more reason to go to war with Germany than it had had on December 6, so even in the excitement over Pearl Harbor, FDR did not ask Congress for a declaration of war on Germany. All earlier war plans had assumed that the United States and the United Kingdom would concentrate their efforts against Germany; suddenly it seemed that the war would take an entirely unexpected course, with the Americans fighting only the

---

*One of the most persistent myths in American history is that FDR knew the attack on Pearl Harbor was coming but refused to give the commanders in Hawaii advance notice. In fact, Washington gave the military in Hawaii plenty of warning about the imminent outbreak of hostilities. There was no specific warning about an attack on Pearl Harbor because no one imagined the Japanese were capable of such a daring raid. MAGIC was no help because the Japanese fleet maintained radio silence.

Japanese. On December 11 Hitler ended the uncertainty by declaring war on the United States.*

The United States was finally at war with the Axis. The status quo in Europe and in Asia had been challenged and was being upset. America had been unable to preserve it short of war. The need now was to defeat the Axis on the field of battle, a task of staggering proportions but one that carried with it great opportunities for the extension of American power and influence. The United States was quick to grasp them, even while saving the world from the unimaginable horror of being ruled by Hitler and the Japanese Army.

*An inexplicable action. No one has ever explained why Hitler did it. He was not required to do so by the terms of the Tripartite Pact; he did not discuss his actions with his own military leaders or foreign office, nor indeed with anyone else. Thus Hitler, after a long string of successes, made two fatal errors between June and December of 1941—the invasion of Russia and the declaration of war against the United States.

2

The War in Europe

Give me allies to fight against!

NAPOLEON

There is only one thing worse than fighting with allies, and that is fighting without them.

WINSTON CHURCHILL

The Grand Alliance of World War II, sometimes called the "Strange Alliance," joined together Britain, the world's greatest colonial power, led by Churchill; with Russia, the world's only Communist nation, led by Stalin; with the United States, the world's greatest capitalist power, led by Roosevelt. Only Hitler could have brought them together, and only the threat of Nazi Germany could have held them together through four years of war. The Big Three mistrusted each other, but each of the partners knew he needed both of the others. No combination of two was powerful enough to defeat Germany. It took all three to do the job.

So the Grand Alliance was successful. Despite many stresses and strains, it held together to the end, a great achievement. In the process, however, nerves and resources were stretched almost to the breaking point.

The process began in January 1942 when Churchill and his military leaders came to Washington to discuss strategy. Churchill advocated a series of operations around the periphery of Hitler's European fortress, combined with bombing raids against Germany itself and encouragement to Resistance forces in the occupied countries, but no direct invasion. He called this "closing the ring."

The American military opposed Churchill's policy. Marshall felt that the concept was risky rather than safe, and that it would waste lives and material rather than save them. To leave the Red Army to face the bulk of the Wehrmacht, as Churchill advocated in effect, was to court disaster. Marshall was not at all sure that the Russians could survive unaided, and he thought it would be the greatest military blunder in all of history to allow an army of eight million fighting men to go down to defeat without doing anything to prevent it. For the Allies to avoid a confrontation with the Germans on the Continent in 1942 and 1943 might save British and American lives in the short run, but it might also lead to a complete victory for Hitler. Even if Churchill was right in supposing that the Red Army would hold out, Marshall believed that the effect would be to let the war drag on into 1944 or even 1945. The end result would be higher, not lower, Anglo-American casualties.

Marshall therefore proposed that the Anglo-Americans set as a goal for 1942 a buildup of American ground, air, and naval strength in the United Kingdom, with the aim of launching a massive cross-Channel invasion in the spring of 1943. Only thus, he argued, could the Americans bring their power to bear in a decisive manner, the Allies give significant help to the Russians, and the final aim of victory be quickly achieved.

There were two specific problems with Marshall's program of a 1942 buildup and a 1943 invasion. First, it would be of little help to the Russians in 1942, and second, it would mean that the United States would spend the whole year without engaging in any ground fighting with the Germans. The second point worried Roosevelt, for he wanted to get the American people to feel a sense of commitment in the struggle for Europe (well into 1942 public-opinion polls revealed that Americans were more eager to strike back at the Japanese than fight the Germans). The fastest way to do it was to get involved in the European fighting. The President therefore insisted that American troops engage German troops somewhere in 1942. But Roosevelt was also drawn to

Churchill's concept of closing the ring, with its implication that the Russians would take the bulk of the casualties, and he was determined that the first American
offensive should be successful, all of which made the
periphery more tempting as a target than northwestern
Europe.

Marshall proposed, as an addition to his program for
a 1943 invasion, an emergency landing on the French
coast in September 1942. The operation, code name
SLEDGEHAMMER, would be a suicide mission designed to take pressure off the Russians. It would go
forward only if a Russian collapse seemed imminent. But
although Marshall had no intention of starting SLEDGE-
HAMMER except as a last resort, he could and did hold
it out to FDR as an operation that would satisfy the
President's demand for action in 1942. The obvious difficulty with SLEDGEHAMMER was the risk, and
Churchill countered with a proposal, code name
TORCH, to invade French North Africa. This was certainly much safer than a cross-Channel attack in either
1942 or 1943, especially since it would be a surprise
assault on the territory of a neutral nation. (North Africa
was ruled by the French government at Vichy, under
Marshal Henri Pétain; it was Fascist and pro-Nazi, but
had declared its neutrality in the war.) TORCH dove-
tailed nicely with British political aims, since it would
help the British reestablish their position in the
Mediterranean.

Roosevelt had to choose between Marshall's and
Churchill's proposals. The pressures on him, from all
sides, were as tremendous as the stakes. Soviet Foreign
Minister V. M. Molotov had visited him in the spring.
Although the President had tried not to be specific about
where it would be opened, Molotov, like the rest of the
world, thought of a second front only in terms of the
plains of northwestern Europe. Roosevelt also knew that
the hard-pressed Russians—facing nearly 200 German
divisions on a front that extended from Leningrad to
the Caucasus, with huge areas, including their prime
industrial and agricultural lands, under occupation, with

ICELAND

0   250   500
     Miles

North
Sea

D

IRELAND   UNITED
           KINGDOM

NETHERLAN

*Atlantic
Ocean*

BELGIUM   G

LUXEMBO

FRANCE

SWITZERLANI

PORTUGAL

SPAIN

EUROPE IN 1997   *Medite*

millions of dead already, and with a desperate need for time in which to rebuild their industry and their army— regarded a second front as absolutely essential and as a clear test of the Western democracies' good faith. If the Anglo-Americans did nothing soon to draw off some German divisions, the Russians might conclude that it meant the Allies were willing to see Hitler win, in the East at least.

Roosevelt was never foolish enough to believe that anyone but the Nazis would benefit from a German victory over Russia, but he did have other concerns and pressures. America was far from full mobilization. Whatever Marshall's plans, the U.S. Army could not invade France alone. Even in combination with the British the United States would have taken heavy casualties. Churchill and his military were insistent about not going back onto the Continent in 1942, or indeed until everything had been well prepared, and they made North Africa sound attractive to the President. Churchill was willing to go to Moscow himself to explain TORCH to Stalin, and said he could convince the Soviets that TORCH did constitute a second front. Given British intransigence, it seemed to FDR that for 1942 it was TORCH or nothing. He picked TORCH.

On July 28 Roosevelt gave his orders to Marshall. General Dwight D. Eisenhower, commander of the American forces in Britain, commented bitterly that it could well go down as the "blackest day in history." Eisenhower and Marshall were convinced that the decision to launch a major invasion of French North Africa in November 1942 would have repercussions that would shape the whole course of the war, with implications that would stretch out far into the postwar world.

They were right. Once TORCH was successful, the temptation to build up the already existing base in Algeria and Tunisia and use it as a springboard for further operations was overwhelming. By far the greater part of the Anglo-American effort in 1942 and 1943 went into the Mediterranean, first in North Africa, then Sicily (July 1943), and finally Italy (September 1943). Impressive gains were made on the map, but there was no decisive or even significant destruction of German power.

The practical problems involved in launching a 1942 or even a 1943 invasion were enormous, perhaps insurmountable. It is quite possible that the British were right in arguing that a premature cross-Channel attack would simply result in a bloodbath. But political motives were paramount in the TORCH decision. Churchill wanted a strong British presence in the Mediterranean, while Roosevelt wanted a quick and relatively safe American involvement to boost morale at home. Both got what they needed from TORCH.

When TORCH was launched (November 8, 1942), the Americans scarcely knew what to anticipate. Because they believed that the French Army in Algeria, Morocco, and Tunisia was at heart anti-German, they hoped the invasion would be unopposed. American spies and secret agents had been operating in North Africa for two years. They were members of the Office of Strategic Services (OSS), an organization created by FDR at the beginning of the war, modeled after the British Secret Service. In setting up the OSS, Roosevelt told the man he selected to head the organization, William Donovan, that this was a no-holds-barred war and that the OSS must fight the Gestapo with Gestapo techniques. Roosevelt then gave Donovan an unlimited budget (literally) from blind Congressional appropriations. Nevertheless, by European standards the OSS was woefully amateur in its methods, techniques, ideology, and politics. Its agents represented a political rainbow of reactionary Ivy League sportsmen, radical Jewish intellectuals, members of the Communist Party, U.S.A., and every shade in between. All they had in common was a hatred of Hitler.

Later in the war the OSS did do much good work, especially in combination with the British and Resistance behind German lines in Europe. But in 1942, in North Africa, the OSS was out of its depth in the complexity of French politics. When Pétain had surrendered to the Germans, General Charles de Gaulle had refused to obey the Vichy government and instead had flown to London, where he denounced Pétain as a traitor and claimed that he, de Gaulle, was now head of a new French government that would continue the war. De Gaulle called his organization the Free French. Few Frenchmen in the colonial armies of France rallied to de Gaulle, however, because it was easier and safer for them to remain loyal to Pétain.

The Americans, although they were invading North Africa, did not want to fight the French. They preferred to make a deal. But Pétain had ordered resistance to any invasion, from whatever direction.

Admiral Jean Darlan, the commander in chief of Vichy's armed forces, was in Algiers when the invasion began. Thanks to clumsy OSS work, his own secret service was fully informed of the American plans. Darlan was bitterly anti-British, author of Vichy's anti-Semitic laws, and a willing collaborator with the Germans, but he was ready to double-cross Pétain. He agreed to a deal, which required the French to lay down their arms, in return for which the Allies would make Darlan Governor General of all French North Africa. General Henri Giraud would become head of the North African army. Within a few days the French officers obeyed Darlan's order to cease fire, and a week after the invasion Eisenhower flew to Algiers to approve the agreement. FDR gave his approval to the Darlan deal on the basis of military expediency.

The result was that in its first major foreign-policy venture in World War II, the United States gave its support to a man who stood for everything Roosevelt and Churchill had spoken out against. Darlan was the antithesis of the principles the Allies said they were defending.

The Darlan deal raised a storm of protest. Critics raised serious questions: Did it mean that when the Allies went into Italy they would make a deal with Mussolini? If the opportunity presented itself, would they deal with Hitler or the German generals? Roosevelt rode out the storm by stressing the temporary nature of the deal.

Darlan, increasingly indignant, complained that the Americans regarded him as a lemon to be squeezed dry then thrown away when its usefulness was over.

The controversy ended on Christmas Eve 1942, when a young Frenchman in Algiers assassinated Darlan. The assassination was part of a widespread conspiracy that involved more than two dozen men, but no positive evidence exists to show who was ultimately behind the plot to kill Darlan.

Whoever did it, the embarrassment of dealing with Darlan was over. As Eisenhower's deputy, General Mark Clark, put it, "Admiral Darlan's death was . . . an act of Providence . . . His removal from the scene was like the lancing of a troublesome boil. He had served his purpose, and his death solved what could have been the very difficult problem of what to do with him in the future."

But deep-rooted Russian suspicions about American political intentions for liberated Europe increased. At the conclusion of the Casablanca Conference in January 1943, Roosevelt tried to allay them. He announced that the Allied policy toward Germany and Japan—and by implication toward Italy—would be to demand unconditional surrender.

What did this mean? Roosevelt did not spell out the details. Presumably, unconditional surrender meant the Allies would fight until such time as the Axis governments put themselves unconditionally into the hands of the Allies, but beyond that nothing was known. What kind of governments would replace those of Mussolini, Tojo, and Hitler? Obviously there would be a period of military occupation, with control invested in an allied military governor, but then what? FDR did not say.

He did not because in all probability he did not know himself. A self-confident pragmatist, he was sure that he could handle situations as they arose. He would continue to make most of his decisions on the basis of military expediency. Meanwhile, he had assured Stalin and the world that there would be no deals with Hitler and his gang, and that the Allies would fight on until the Axis governments surrendered, at which time he would settle

everything and satisfy everyone. It was a brilliant stroke.
By keeping war aims vague, he prevented bickering
among the Allies.

Roosevelt's self-confidence was immense, but not always justified, as Franco-American relations soon demonstrated. At the beginning of 1943, Giraud was still
leader of France's North African forces but even with
American support he would not remain so for long. With
British encouragement, de Gaulle came to Algiers, organized the French Committee of National Liberation,
and joined Giraud as co-President. Giraud was a political
innocent, however, and despite Roosevelt's efforts de
Gaulle soon squeezed Giraud out of the French North
African government altogether. By the end of 1943,
FDR's French policy was a shambles and de Gaulle was
in power.

The major Anglo-American military operations in
1943 were directed against Italy. The invasion of Sicily
began in July; the assault on the Italian mainland followed in September. Even though Italy quit the war, it
was not until mid-1944 that the Allies reached Rome,
and the spring of 1945 before they controlled the whole
of Italy. Heavy military commitments had been made
for limited results. The Allies had tied down twenty German divisions in Italy, and they had obtained some additional airfields from which to send bombers against
Germany.

Two weeks after the landings at Sicily, the Allies
bombed Rome for the first time. As a result of the raid,
and because of the deteriorating military situation, the
Fascist Grand Council overthrew Mussolini. Marshal Pie-
tro Badoglio replaced him. Badoglio's sole objective was
to double-cross the Germans. The Anglo-Americans
were willing enough to oblige.

The Italians wanted protection against the Germans
for the government in Rome, and to be allowed to declare
war on Germany and join the Allies as a cobelligerent,
thus avoiding the humiliation of signing an unconditional surrender.

Churchill and Roosevelt gradually gave Eisenhower permission to concede the central Italian demands. They wanted both stability in Italy and a neutral Italian army and were thus willing to deal with Badoglio to avoid social upheaval and possibly chaos. They finally allowed the Italian government to surrender with conditions, to stay in power, to retain administrative control of Italy, to retain the Italian monarchy, and eventually to join the Allies as cobelligerent.

The result was that by 1945 the same political groups that had run Italy before and during the war were still in power, backed by an Allied Control Council from which the Russians had been systematically excluded. Stalin had protested initially but did not press the point, for he recognized the value of the precedent—those who liberated a country from the Nazis could decide what happened there. He was more than willing to allow the Allies to shape the future in Italy in return for the same right in Eastern Europe.

American foreign policy in World War II was too complex and diverse to be encompassed by any generalization, no matter how sweeping. In lieu of a policy, most political decisions were dictated by military necessity. If, for example, the Americans tried to promote a right-wing government in French North Africa and Italy, and allowed the British to do the same in Greece, it was equally true that the United States dropped arms and equipment to the Resistance in France, which was decidedly left wing, and to Marshal Tito in Yugoslavia, who was leading a Communist revolution. Within occupied France the Americans had to deal with the Resistance, since there was no one else fighting the Nazis, but in Yugoslavia there was an alternative to Tito in the form of a guerrilla force under General Draja Mikhailovitch, who supported the monarchy and the London-based Yugoslav government-in-exile. Eisenhower and the Americans followed the British lead in giving aid to Tito, however, because he was supposedly more effective than Mikhailovitch in fighting the Nazis. Actually the civil war was as much Croatians versus Serbians as it was Nazis versus Communists.

In January 1944 the confusion and drift that had characterized American policy came to an end. America was more fully mobilized than it had ever been. Eisenhower took command of the Allied Expeditionary Force (AEF) in the United Kingdom and began the preparations for Operation OVERLORD, the cross-Channel assault. From that point on, a single question dominated American thought: Will this proposal help or hurt OVERLORD? OVERLORD had top priority and subsidiary operatons geared to it. America was now concentrating exclusively on the defeat of Germany. Postwar problems, for the most part, could be decided in the postwar period. In general, this was true until the very last day of the war.

And rightly so. OVERLORD was not only the supreme military act of the war by the Anglo-Americans, it was also the supreme political act. It was the ultimate expression of a permanent and fundamental goal of American foreign policy—to maintain the balance of power.

Examples of America's newly developed leadership and single mindedness abound. Most involved the British, practically none the Russians, partly because the Americans had a close working relationship with the British and almost no contact with the Red Army, and partly because the British were more concerned with long-range questions than were the Americans. Three issues were especially important: What to do in the Mediterranean, what form the advance into Germany should take, and whether the objective should be Berlin or the German Army. On all three issues the Americans had their way. American preponderance in the Allied camp had become so great that, if necessary, the Americans could insist upon their judgment, while the British simply had to accept the decision with the best grace possible, for their contribution to Anglo-American resources was down to 25 percent of the whole.

American domination of the Alliance reflected, in

turn, a new era in world history. The United States had replaced Great Britain as the dominant world power. By 1945 American production had reached levels that were scarcely believable. The United States was producing 45 percent of the world's arms and nearly 50 percent of the world's goods. Two-thirds of all the ships afloat were American-built.

On the question of what to do in the Mediterranean, the Americans insisted on slowing down operations in Italy and using the troops instead to invade the south of France in order to provide a covering force for OVERLORD's right flank. The British objected, advocating instead operatons into Austria and Yugoslavia, but they dared not argue their case on political grounds for they realized that Roosevelt would turn a deaf ear to their political case. As FDR told Churchill, "My dear friend, I beg you to let us go ahead with our plan. For purely political reasons over here, I should never survive even a slight setback in OVERLORD if it were known that fairly large forces had been diverted to the Balkans." (That year, 1944, was an American presidential election year; FDR was running for a fourth term.) On June 6, 1944, OVERLORD was launched. It was staggering in scope, with 5,000 ships, 6,000 airplanes, and 175,000 men landing in France. The warriors came from 12 nations, led by American, British, and Canadian forces. It was a grand show of Allied unity, and for that reason successful.

Churchill hoped to secure the British position in the Mediterranean by taking all of Italy and the Adriatic coast. He later declared that he was also interested in forestalling the Russians in central Europe, but he never used such an argument at the time. To the contrary, he repeatedly told Eisenhower—who bore the brunt of the argument on the American side—that he wanted an extended offensive in the Adriatic strictly as a military proposition. Eisenhower was convinced Churchill had Britain's postwar position in mind and told the Prime Minister that if he wished to change the orders (which

directed Eisenhower to strike at the heart of Germany),
he should talk to Roosevelt. On military grounds Eisenhower insisted on a landing in the south of France.

Churchill could not persuade Roosevelt to intervene,
and the landing took place in August 1944, ending the
Allies' opportunities to extend operations into Eastern
Europe or the Balkans. The Americans had been willing
to go as far east in the Mediterranean as Italy, but no
farther. The possibility of the Soviet Union's postwar
expansion into the Balkans or Eastern Europe did not
seem to the Americans to be important enough at the
time to justify a diversion from Germany.

A second great issue, fought out in September 1944,
was the nature of the advance into Germany. Eisenhower
directed an offensive on a broad front, with the American and British armies moving toward Germany more
or less abreast. General Bernard L. Montgomery, commanding the British forces, argued for a single thrust
into Germany, insisting that his plan promised a quick
end to the war. Churchill supported Monty, partly
because he wanted the British to have the glory of
capturing Berlin, mainly because he wanted the Anglo-
Americans as far east as possible when they linked up
with the Red Army.

Eisenhower insisted on his own plan. He was absolutely convinced that the broad front was militarily correct. Whether he was right or not depended upon one's
priority. If the main goal were to ensure a German defeat, Eisenhower's cautious approach was correct. But if
the goal were to forestall a Russian advance into central
Europe by an Allied liberation of Berlin, Prague, and
Vienna, Monty's audacious program was better. Roles
had been reversed. Eisenhower and Marshall, who in
1942 had been willing to accept any risk to go across the
Channel, now adopted a dull, unimaginative campaign.
The British, who earlier had hesitated at the thought of
confronting the Wehrmacht on the Continent, were now
ready to take great risks to get the war over with and
occupy Berlin.

In the early spring of 1945 the Allies moved across

the Rhine into Germany on a broad front. As immediate objectives Eisenhower ordered the encirclement of the industrial Ruhr and a drive to Dresden to link up with the Red Army in central Germany, which would cut Germany into two parts. Montgomery and Churchill objected. They wanted Eisenhower to give priority to supplies and air support for the British drive to Berlin, in order to get there before the Russians.

There has been much confusion about Churchill's advocacy of Berlin as a target. It is commonly asserted that he wanted to keep the Russians out of eastern Germany, to retain a united Germany, and to maintain Berlin's status as the capital, and that if only the Allies had captured the city there would have been no Berlin problem. This is nonsense. Aside from the military factors (it is probable that Eisenhower's men could never have taken Berlin ahead of the Red Army), these views do not remotely reflect the policies Churchill was advocating. He never thought in terms of denying to the Russians their position in East Europe generally or eastern Germany specifically, a position that had been agreed to much earlier. Once the 1943 cross-Channel attack had been scuttled, there never was the slightest chance that the Russians could be kept out of East Europe. Churchill realized this: His famous agreement with Stalin during their Moscow meetings in the fall of 1944 signified his recognition that Russian domination of East Europe was inevitable.

What Churchill did want from the capture of Berlin was much less grandiose His major concern was prestige. He told Roosevelt that the Russians were going to liberate Vienna. "If they also take Berlin, will not their impression that they have been the overwhelming contributor to our common victory be unduly imprinted in their minds?"

Roosevelt's major concerns, in the weeks before his death on April 12, were to create the United Nations (the San Francisco Conference to draw up the Charter began its sessions shortly thereafter), to insure the participation of the U.S.S.R. in the United Nations, and to maintain cordial relations with Stalin. He refused to take a hard line with Stalin on the Russian occupation of Poland or on Stalin's suspicions about the surrender of the German forces in Italy to the Western Allies. The President was not an experienced diplomat, and right to the end he had no clear goals for the postwar world. His sponsorship of the United Nations indicated that he had adopted Woodrow Wilson's belief in collective security, but the nature of the United Nations Roosevelt wanted, dominated as it was by the great nations on the Security Council, indicated that he retained a belief in spheres of influence for the great powers. So did his frequent remarks about the "Four Policemen" (China, Russia, Britain, and the United States).

But if much of Roosevelt's policy was cloudy, mystifying even his closest advisers, one thing was clear. To the exasperation of some members of the State Department, not to mention the ambassador to Russia, W. Averell Harriman, the President refused to become a staunch anti-Soviet. Harriman, Churchill, and later Truman assumed that Russia would be unreasonable, grasping, probing, power hungry, and impossible to deal with except from a position of great strength and unrelenting firmness. FDR rejected such assumptions. Furthermore, he seems to have felt it was only reasonable for the Russians to be uneasy about the nature of the governments on Russia's western frontier, and therefore was willing to consider Stalin's demands in East Europe. There was also an assumption, shared even by Churchill, that Stalin was stating the obvious when he remarked in early 1945 that "whoever occupies a territory also imposes on it his own social system." Churchill, who had taken the lead in establishing this principle in Italy and Greece, later denounced Stalin for practicing it in East Europe, but the evidence indicates that Roosevelt was realistic enough to accept the quid pro quo.

The nature of the alliance with Russia was generally confusing. After the Nazi invasion the Red Army became heroic, and Stalin appeared as a wise and generous leader in the American press. Whether this had a deep or lasting effect on a people who mistrusted and feared Communism as much as they did Fascism is doubtful. Behind the scenes, meanwhile, and especially in the State Department, anti-Soviet feeling kept bubbling up. George Kennan, though a rather minor functionary in the State Department at the time, best expressed the mood two days after the Nazis invaded Russia in 1941: "We should do nothing at home to make it appear that we are following the course Churchill seems to have entered upon in extending moral support to the Russian cause. It seems to me that to welcome Russia as an associate in the defense of democracy would invite misunderstanding." Kennan felt that throughout Europe "Russia is generally more feared than Germany," and he implied that he agreed with this estimate of the relative dangers of Communism and Fascism.

The sentiment that Kennan expressed in 1941 may have been dominant in the State Department, but the department was not setting policy. Roosevelt extended lend-lease to the Russians and gave moral support to Stalin. Bending to State Department pressure, he did refuse Stalin's request in 1941 for an agreement that would recognize Russian territorial gains under the Nazi-Soviet Pact, remarking that territorial questions could be settled at the end of the war. But beyond that issue Roosevelt concentrated on working together with Stalin against the common enemy. Kennan continued to protest. In 1944, when the Red Army had driven the Germans out of Russia and was preparing for the final offensive, Kennan argued that the time had come for a "full-fledged and realistic political showdown with the Soviet leaders." He wanted to confront them with "the choice between changing their policy completely and agreeing to collaborate in the establishment of truly independent countries in Eastern Europe or of forfeiting Western Allied support and sponsorship for the remaining phases of their war effort."

By this time Kennan was the chief adviser to the American ambassador in Moscow, Harriman, who accepted Kennan's views. Harriman advised FDR to cut back on or even eliminate lend-lease shipments to Russia. Roosevelt refused and the aid continued to flow, providing Russia with essential equipment, especially trucks. The West needed the Red Army at least as badly as the Russians needed lend-lease. Although Kennan had failed to see this, Marshall and Roosevelt were clear enough about who needed whom the most. Their greatest fear was precisely Kennan's greatest hope—that once the Red Army reached Russian borders, it would stop. The Germans could then have turned and marched west, confronting the Western Allies with the bulk of the Wehrmacht. Britain and America had not mobilized nearly enough ground troops to batter their way into Berlin against such opposition.

Further, there was the frightening possibility of new secret weapons. Germany had made rapid strides in military technology during the war, German propaganda continued to urge the people to hold on just a little longer until the new weapons were ready, and FDR knew that the Germans were working on an atomic bomb. The V-weapons,* jet-propelled aircraft, and snorkel submarines were bad enough. To halt lend-lease to the Russians would slow the Red Army advance, giving the Germans more time to perfect their weapons, if it did not cause Stalin to withdraw from the war altogether.

The central dilemma of the war was embodied in these considerations. Until the end almost no one in power wanted Russia to stop its advance, but few Americans or British wanted Russia to dominate East Europe. It had to be one or the other. Roosevelt decided that the greater danger lay in an end to Russian offensives, and he continued to give Stalin aid and encouragement for the Russian drive to the west.

At his own level Eisenhower made his decision about Berlin on military grounds. He thought it was madness to send his forces dashing toward Berlin when there was

---

*The "V" stood for "Vengeance." These were the first guided missiles.

little, if any, chance that they would arrive before the Red Army. He also needed a clearly recognizable demarcation line, so that when his forces met the Russians there would be no unfortunate incidents of the two allies mistakenly shooting at each other. He therefore informed Stalin that he would halt when he reached the Elbe River. Churchill kept pestering him to push on eastward; finally Eisenhower wired the Combined Chiefs of Staff: "I am the first to admit that a war is waged in pursuance of political aims, and if the Combined Chiefs of Staff should decide that the Allied effort to take Berlin outweighs purely military considerations in this theater, I would cheerfully readjust my plans and my thinking so as to carry out such an operation." He was not, in other words, willing to risk the lives of 100,000 or more men for no military gain. The Combined Chiefs made no reply, and for Eisenhower, military considerations remained paramount.

While Eisenhower's forces occupied southern Germany, the Russians battered their way into Berlin, suffering heavy casualties, probably in excess of 100,000. Herbert Feis points out that they gained "the first somber sense of triumph, the first awesome sight of the ruins, the first parades under the pall of smoke." Two months later they gave up to the West over half the city they had captured at such an enormous price. At the cost of not a single life, Great Britain and the United States had their sectors in Berlin, where they remained through the Cold War.

More important, the war ended without any sharp break with the Russians. There had been innumerable strains in the "Strange Alliance," but the United States and Russia were still allies, and in May 1945 the possibility of continued cooperation was, if frail, alive. Much would depend on the attitude of the United States toward Soviet actions in East Europe. It was as certain as the sun's rising that Stalin would insist on Communist dictatorships controlled by Moscow. The economic and political leaders of the old regimes would be thrown out, along with religious leaders and editors. With them would go some of the most cherished concepts in the West—freedom of speech, free elections, freedom of religion, and free enterprise. The men who ran the American government could not look with any approval on the suppression of precisely those liberties they had fought Hitler to uphold. President Harry S Truman (FDR had died in April 1945), his advisers, and the American people would never be able to accept the forced communization of Eastern Europe.

But the experience of World War II indicated that the United States still had alternatives, that hostility was not the only possible reaction to Stalin's probable moves. The United States had demonstrated an ability to make realistic, pragmatic responses to developing situations. America had aided Tito and supported the French Resistance, had refused to get tough with the Russians, had made major decisions solely for the purpose of bringing about the fall of Nazi Germany.

In the spring of 1945 America had enormously more power, both absolutely and in relation to the rest of the world, than she had possessed in 1941. To a lesser degree, that had also been the situation in 1918, but after World War I America had disarmed and for the most part refused to intervene in affairs outside the North American continent. She could do so again, and indeed Roosevelt had privately confessed to Churchill that he doubted if he could keep American troops in Europe for more than a year or so after the conclusion of hostilities.

America was the victor. Her decisions would go far toward shaping the postwar world. In May 1945 she did not have a firm idea of what those decisions would be. It was still possible for the United States to travel down any one of several roads.

3

The War in Asia

When the first atomic bomb went off, at Alamogordo, New Mexico, on July 16, 1945, the temperature at Ground Zero was 100 million degrees Fahrenheit, three times hotter than the interior of the sun and ten thousand times the heat on its surface. All life, plant and animal, within a mile radius of Ground Zero simply vanished. General Leslie Groves, director of the Manhattan Project, turned to his deputy and said, "The war's over. One or two of these things and Japan will be finished."

GORDON THOMAS and MAX MORGAN-WITTS, *Enola Gay*

One of the chief facts about the war in the Pacific was that when the shooting stopped the Americans did not have troops occupying the major nations of mainland Asia—Indochina, Korea, Burma, India, or China.

America failed to get onto mainland Asia because she did not have enough manpower to carry on a large-scale land war in both Europe and Asia. There were other military limitations. It was approximately twice as far from the United States to Asia as it was to Europe, which meant that it took two ships going from the United States to Asia to do as much as one to Europe, and until the very last months of the war merchant shipping was in short supply. The United States devoted nearly 40 percent of its total effort in World War II to the Pacific Theater, but much of that effort was eaten up in shipping, and the amount of force the Americans could bring to bear was much smaller in Asia than in Europe. As a result, the strategy in the Pacific was to avoid Japanese strong points and to initiate operations that would conserve men and materiel.

America pursued a peripheral strategy in the Pacific, never coming to grips with the main forces of the Japanese Army. There was a political price. In Europe the process of closing in on the Germans carried with it the dividends of putting American troops in Antwerp, Paris, and Rome. In Asia the process of closing in on the Japanese only gave the United States control of relatively unimportant islands.

American military policy in the Pacific was geared only in a negative way to the nation's foreign-policy aims. The military effort was dedicated to the destruction of Japan. That was a goal of the first magnitude, to be sure, but just stopping the Japanese was not enough. It became increasingly clear as the war went on that it would be difficult, perhaps impossible, to restore the old order in Asia. Nor did Roosevelt want to return to business as usual, for he was a sincere opponent of old-style colonialism and wanted the British out of India, the Dutch out of the N.E.I., the Americans out of the Philippines, and the French out of Indochina.*

For the Americans the question was what form independence would take, and here, as in Europe, power would reside with the man on the spot with a gun in his hand. Except in Japan, the Philippines, and the N.E.I., that man would not be an American. This fact opened the possibility that Communists would replace the old colonial rulers and that they might shut the Americans out of Asia just as thoroughly as had the Japanese. The challenge for American policy-makers was how to simultaneously drive out the Japanese, prevent the resurgence of European colonialism, and foster the growth of democratic, capitalist local governments, all without actually making the effort necessary to put the man with a gun on the spot. In China, Indochina, and North Korea, it proved to be impossible.

*The United States had long since pledged itself to give independence to the Philippines on July 4, 1946, a pledge that it kept.

In Asia, American priorities combined with military necessities to shape events. The first priority, as in Europe, was the defeat of the enemy. Next came the elevation of China under Chiang Kai-shek and the Kuomintang Party to great power status, which required establishing Chiang's control in China, a control that was contested by the Communists under Mao Tse-tung and by the Japanese, who held most of the China coast. Chiang was corrupt, inefficient, and dictatorial, but he was also friendly to the West. No matter how badly the Americans wanted Chiang to rule China, however, there was little they could do to support him without troops on the scene, and the military realities precluded sending large numbers of American troops to China.

America's Asian policy grew out of military necessity, personality conflict, and political motivation. After retreating from the Philippines in early 1942, the Americans established a base of operations in Australia. They already had one in the Central Pacific on Hawaii. Top Army and Navy officials did not get on well with one another. The result was a division of the area into two theaters of war, the Southwest Pacific and the Central Pacific; the Army under General Douglas MacArthur was responsible for the Southwest Pacific, and the Navy under Admiral Chester Nimitz was in charge in the Central Pacific. MacArthur's base was Australia; his strategy was to move northward through the N.E.I., the Philippines, and Formosa to get at Japan. Nimitz, in Hawaii, wanted to advance westward through the Central Pacific. In the end, both approaches were used.

When MacArthur reached Australia after his flight from Bataan (in February 1942), he announced, "I shall return" to the Philippines.* Senior officers in the Navy

---

*The War Department liked the phrase but thought the statement should read, "We shall return," since presumably MacArthur would need help. MacArthur refused to change it, and "I shall return" it remained.

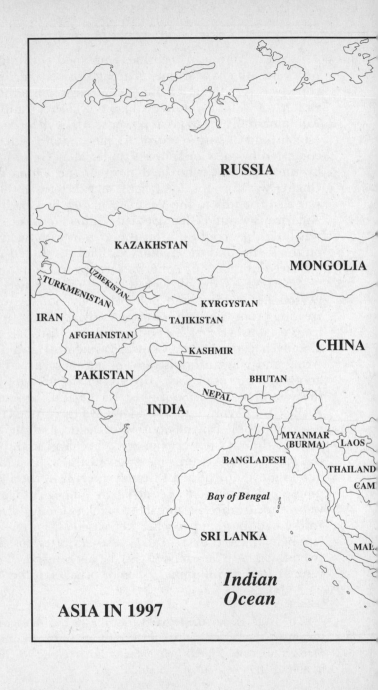

RUSSIA

KAZAKHSTAN

MONGOLIA

UZBEKISTAN

TURKMENISTAN

KYRGYSTAN

IRAN

TAJIKISTAN

AFGHANISTAN

CHINA

KASHMIR

PAKISTAN

BHUTAN

NEPAL

INDIA

MYANMAR
(BURMA)

LAOS

THAILAND

BANGLADESH

CAM

Bay of Bengal

MAL

SRI LANKA

Indian
Ocean

ASIA IN 1997

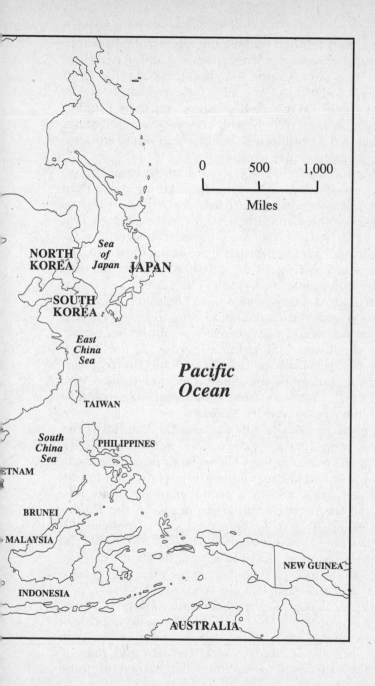

NORTH KOREA

Sea of Japan

JAPAN

SOUTH KOREA

East China Sea

Pacific Ocean

TAIWAN

South China Sea

ETNAM

PHILIPPINES

BRUNEI

MALAYSIA

NEW GUINEA

INDONESIA

AUSTRALIA

0   500   1,000

Miles

objected; they felt that making the effort to get back into the Philippines was not worth the men and materiel required. The Navy wanted to bypass the Philippines and go straight to Formosa or concentrate exclusively on the Central Pacific. MacArthur's critics, and their number was large, believed that the only reason the United States returned to the Philippines (in late 1944) was to enhance MacArthur's personal prestige.

MacArthur's egotism was great, but his desire to go back to the Philippines involved something more than personal satisfaction. MacArthur thought it would be madness for the United States ever to be involved in a land war in Asia, a military judgment that only reinforced his parallel belief that it was imperative for the United States to control the off-shore islands, particularly the Philippines and Japan. The general knew that if the United States bypassed the Philippines, there was a danger that the Hukbalahap, a Communist-led guerilla organization, would take power. It might be impossible to root them out. MacArthur's invasion of the Philippines solved this problem, and in 1946 the United States turned the destiny of the Philippines over to men who were friendly to America and allowed her to keep American military bases and investments.

In China, unlike the Philippines, the Americans did not have troops on the spot and could not control events. The United States hoped Chiang's Kuomintang Party would bring China into the modern world community both as a market and as a producer of raw materials. Americans realized that to accomplish this the Kuomintang would have to be reformed and its policies liberalized. They encouraged Chiang to root out the rampant corruption, make an accommodation with Mao and the Communists, introduce some meaningful land reform, and modernize along Western lines.

The tactical mistakes made in attempting to implement this program were manifold, but more important was the strategic error. The program rested on the twin assumptions that Chiang wanted reform and that he could put it through, assumptions that turned out to be totally unwarranted. But most Americans regarded the Chinese Communists with horror, and there seemed to be no middle ground between Mao and Chiang. Events therefore ground on with what appeared to be a tragic inevitability. America sent huge loans to China, often in the form of direct cash, but with a foreboding of failure since they were really bribes to Chiang and his chief supporters, who threatened to quit the war against Japan otherwise. The possibility that the Chinese might surrender frightened Washington sufficiently to keep the money flowing.

Throughout the war the situation within the Kuomintang's armies was desperate. Senior officers lived in luxury while the enlisted men suffered from body-wracking diseases, seldom ate, were usually shoeless, and had insufficient equipment (one in three had a rifle, usually without ammunition). American officials wanted improvement, for it was imperative that China's vast manpower resources be used against Japan.

There was, in addition, the problem of the Chinese Communists. Chiang was using his only respectable troops against Mao, who in turn deployed a force of up to 2 million men. Full-scale civil war threatened, a war that would be dangerous to the Americans on two counts: It would reduce the potential forces that could be thrown against Japan, and it might lead to Chiang's overthrow and Mao's victory. The Americans therefore tried to force Chiang to bring the Communists into the government and to persuade Mao to cooperate with Chiang. Neither of the Chinese groups, however, would make any but the most impossible demands of the other, and nothing was accomplished.

During the last stages of the war, Chiang was able to obtain Russian promises, honored for the most part, not to support the Chinese Communists and to urge Mao to unite with the Kuomintang. In return, Chiang leased Port Arthur to the Russians and made Dairen a free port, while recognizing Soviet control of Outer Mongolia. Stalin regarded Mao as an adventurer whose wild schemes would anger the West and thus endanger Russian gains in the Far East. Mao regarded Stalin as a backstabber.

For two years, meanwhile, the hopeless American policy of trying to bring Mao and Chiang together continued. After the war, when Truman sent Marshall to China in another attempt to bring the two Chinese leaders together, Secretary of War Stimson warned Marshall: "Remember that the Generalissimo [Chiang] has never honestly backed a thorough union with the Chinese Communists. He could not, for his administration is a mere surface veneer (more or less rotten) over a mass of the Chinese people beneath him." Despite this realism, and despite the proclaimed neutrality of the Marshall mission, America continued to give material support to Chiang. It was never enough, primarily because nothing short of a total American occupation of China would have been sufficient to prevent Mao's eventual victory. Such an occupation would have required millions of American soldiers, far more than the nation was willing to send even to Europe, and there never was the slightest possibility that either the American people or government were willing to make the sacrifice required to save the Kuomintang.

Stalin's willingness to cooperate in Asia with the Americans extended beyond China. Roosevelt first met with Stalin in late 1943 in Teheran, Iran. The American President's dislike of de Gaulle reinforced his general opposition to European colonialism and led to his proposal for Indochina. Roosevelt suggested that Laos, Cambodia, and Vietnam be placed under a four-power trusteeship after the war (the powers being China, the United States, Russia, and Britain). Stalin immediately endorsed the proposal, adding that Indochinese independence might follow in two or three decades. Only the British, fearful for their own empire, objected to thus snatching away a colony from France.

The situation within Vietnam did not lend itself to an easy solution. The Japanese had allowed the French to maintain civil control of Indochina until March 1945, when they gave limited encouragement to Vietnamese nationalism by replacing the French with a royal puppet government under the Bao Dai. The Viet Minh then went into active resistance. Their leader, Ho Chi Minh, told Washington that he wanted independence within five to ten years, land reform, a democracy based on universal suffrage, and national purchase of French holdings. He had worked closely with OSS agents during the war (primarily rescuing downed American pilots) and had copied the Vietnamese Declaration of Independence from the American document. After the war this availed Ho nothing, for the American position toward French colonialism changed. Whatever Roosevelt's personal feelings toward de Gaulle, good relations with France would turn in large part on the American attitude toward Indochina.

There was, in addition, the general American fear of Communism in Asia, of which Ho was obviously a part and potentially a leader. The Americans therefore agreed, in August 1945, that in Indochina the British would accept the Japanese surrender south of the sixteenth parallel, while Chiang's troops would do so to the north. The British held the southern position until de Gaulle could send troops to Saigon, while Chiang's troops looted with abandon until the French returned to Hanoi. America had taken its hard line with Japan in 1941 in large part because of the Japanese occupation of Indochina, and it was at least consistent that at the end of the war she would move again to prevent Southeast Asia from falling into unfriendly hands, distasteful as French colonial rule might be.

Many American decisions in World War II—such as allowing the French to reoccupy Indochina—were made quickly and without the benefit of deep analysis because they concerned issues with a relatively low priority. In some cases these decisions had serious repercussions, as in Vietnam and the agreement to divide Korea. The Russians were to occupy Korea north of the thirty-eighth

parallel and the Americans the area south of that line.
Both agreed that this was merely a matter of conven-
ience—that the Japanese colony eventually would be reunited and given its independence—and both seem to
have meant it at the time, although neither gave Korea
a great deal of thought.

The most important American decision of the war,
however—to build and then use an atomic bomb—was
thoroughly examined and discussed in the highest levels
of the government. The Manhattan Project, the best-
kept secret of the war, began in 1939, with the sole purpose of harnessing the energy of the atom to produce
a bomb that could be carried by aircraft, and to succeed
before the Germans could. J. Robert Oppenheimer, one
of the eminent scientists on the project, later recalled,
"We always assumed if they were needed they would be
used." The tendency was to regard the bomb as simply
another military weapon.

By mid-1945 the military situation dominated thinking about the bomb, because although Japan had clearly
lost the war, she was far from crushed. She had lost most
of her Pacific empire and fleet, to be sure, but she still
retained control of much of China, most of Southeast
Asia, and all of Korea and Manchuria. Her army was
more or less intact, and her air force—based on the
kamikazes—was a major threat. Japan had an army estimated at up to two million men in Manchuria, with
some 5,350 kamikaze planes ready for use with 7,000
more in storage. There were also thousands of kamikaze
PT boats and more than enough young volunteers to
steer the planes and boats. An American invasion of the
home islands would be a bloody affair. Stimson wished
to avoid it, not only becuse he feared the casualties but
also because he did not wish to inaugurate a race war
in the Pacific, where the white man was so badly outnumbered.

A key factor was the Red Army. If Stalin would declare
war, Japan might quit without a last-ditch fight. Contem-
plating the possibility on June 18, 1945, General Mar-

shall noted, "The impact of Russian entry on the already hopeless Japanese may well be the decisive action levering them into capitulation." The U.S. Navy thought the Japanese could be starved into submission through a blockade, and the Army Air Force argued that even without the atomic bomb the enemy could be forced through bombing to surrender (the recently developed napalm was being used in raids on Tokyo with fearful effectiveness), but Truman and Marshall could not accept these optimistic forecasts. If the United States wanted an unconditional surrender, it must first destroy the Japanese Army. Since in the early summer of 1945 the atomic bomb had not yet been tested, it appeared that the only way to destroy the Japanese Army was to fight it, and in Marshall's view it was preferable to have the Red Army do it than the American Army.

There was another alternative. However strong the Japanese Army, whatever cost the enemy could force the United States to pay to overrun the home islands, Japan was a defeated nation and her leaders knew it. They could delay, but not prevent, the final defeat. Japan was fighting on to avoid the humiliation of unconditional surrender. She wanted some explicit conditions before her capitulation. A few Japanese leaders dreamed of holding onto conquered territory on the mainland, but most were realistic enough to know that Japan would lose control of all but her home islands. What they did want was some guarantee of eventual self-rule, and more immediately a guarantee that the Emperor would remain sacrosanct, both physically and in his official position (the American press was carrying demands by some politicians that the Emperor be tried as a war criminal and punished, a view that had strong public support).

American leaders knew that Japanese moderates were trying to find a way out with honor. They had also agreed among themselves that the Emperor had to stay, since his elimination would bring on social chaos in Japan. For reasons of domestic morale and politics, however, the ericans decided not to inform the Japanese of their intentions about the Emperor.

At the February 1945 meetings with the Soviets at Yalta, the Americans pressed Stalin to promise to enter the Pacific war and offered to force Chiang to make concessions to the Russians on the Sino-Soviet border in return. Stalin agreed to come in three months after the conclusion of hostilities in Europe—he said he would need that much time to shift troops from Germany to Manchuria. When in July the Big Three met again at Potsdam, outside Berlin, the Americans remained as anxious as ever to have the Red Army in the Pacific.

Then came the successful test of the first atomic bomb. It inaugurated a new era in the world's history and in the tools of American foreign policy. No longer—or so it seemed—would the United States have to rely on mass armies, either those of its allies or its own. The atomic bomb had the great advantage of being cheaper than mass armies—and much quicker. The Americans immediately began to use the bomb as an instrument of diplomacy. As Churchill summed up the American attitude on July 23, "It was now no longer necessary for the Russians to come into the Japanese war; the new explosive alone was sufficient to settle the matter." Later the same day, reporting on a conversation with Secretary of State James Byrnes, Churchill declared, "It is quite clear that the United States do not at the present time desire Russian participation in the war against Japan." And that evening Stimson recorded that even Marshall, who had pushed hardest for Russian entry, "felt as I felt sure he would, that now with our new weapon we would not need the assistance of the Russians to conquer Japan."

At Potsdam, Truman casually informed Stalin that the United States had a "new weapon" and was pleased when the Soviet leader did not press him for details.* The Big

---

*Stalin already knew, through Communist spies in the Manhattan Project.

Three then agreed to retain the Emperor after Japanese surrender but refused to let the Japanese know this. Instead, they issued the Potsdam Declaration, calling again for unconditional surrender on pain of great destruction. The Japanese rejected the demand, as it contained no guarantee on the Emperor, and Truman gave the order to drop the bomb.

What was the great hurry? This question has bothered nearly everyone who has examined the controversy raging around the decision to use the bomb. The importance of the question stems from three related factors: (1) the United States had no major operations planned before November 1, 1945, so there was time to wait and see what effect the anticipated Russian declaration of war would have on the Japanese, or to see if the Japanese peace feelers were serious; (2) the bomb was not planned for use against a military target, so it would not change the military situation; and (3) the Americans expected the Russians to enter the war on or about August 8, but they dropped the bomb on August 6. When the Japanese did not surrender immediately, they dropped a second bomb on August 9. The British physicist P. M. S. Blackett, and later others, charged that the sequence of events demonstrated that the use of the bomb was "the first major operation of the cold diplomatic war with Russia." Its primary purpose was to keep Russia out of the Far Eastern postwar settlement rather than to save American lives.

A parallel interpretation claims that the American intention was to impress the Russians with the power of the bomb and to make it clear to them that the United States would not hesitate to use it. America had already deployed the bulk of her troops out of Western Europe, as had the British, so that by August of 1945 the Red Army was the most powerful force in all Europe. To those concerned about a possible Russian advance across the Elbe River, the bomb seemed a perfect deterrent.

These interpretations are not necessarily wrong; they are just too limited. They tend to ignore or underestimate Japan's remaining power of resistance, especially the terrifying kamikazes.

Nearly every individual who participated in the decision to use the bomb had his own motive. Some were concerned with the kamikazes, others wanted to punish the Japanese for Pearl Harbor, while there were those who said that the actual use of the bomb was the only way to justify to Congress and the people the expenditure of $2 billion to produce it. Life came cheap in the world of 1945. The Anglo-Americans at Dresden had killed tens of thousands of women and children in air raids that had no discernible military purpose. To kill a few more "Japs" seemed natural enough, and the racial factor in the decision cannot be ignored.

But the simplest explanation is perhaps the most convincing. The bomb was there. Japan was not surrendering. Few in the government thought seriously about not using it. To drop it as soon as it was ready seemed natural, the obvious thing to do. As Truman later put it, "The final decision of where and when to use the atomic bomb was up to me. Let there be no mistake about it. I regarded the bomb as a military weapon and never had any doubt that it should be used."

Unfortunately, the bomb dropped on Hiroshima did not bring an immediate Japanese response. The Russians, meanwhile, declared war on August 8 and the Red Army moved forward in Manchuria and southern Sakhalin. The Japanese Manchurian Army surrendered. In order to prod the Japanese, on August 9 the United States dropped a second bomb, on Nagasaki, which ensured that the Japanese government would surrender to the Americans. Even after the second bomb, however, the Japanese insisted on a guarantee about Emperor Hirohito's safety. Truman decided he would have to give it, the United States made the required promise, and Japan finally surrendered.

Truman's use of the bomb has been one of the most criticized decisions of the war and one of the most highly praised. Two factors, probably unanticipated and generally unnoted in the debate over the use of the bomb, are the effect it had on the Japanese military and on the American public. Japanese officers high and low had been ready to fight to the death because surrender was dishonorable. But the bomb gave them an excuse that allowed surrender: How could they fight against such a weapon? On the other side, the vehement demands of the American public for retribution—most often expressed in the call for the trial of Japanese leaders, especially Emperor Hirohito, as war criminals—subsided immediately after the news of the bombings had been broadcast. Americans felt, in effect, "That's enough, they've suffered enough." Japanese submissiveness in the face of overwhelming power combined with the American conviction that Pearl Harbor had finally been avenged made possible the excellent relations between Japanese and Americans that began immediately after the war.

American troops occupied Japan, excluding the Russians, not to mention the Australians and the British. Even though MacArthur, who headed the occupation, was supposed to be a supreme Allied commander responsible to all the governments that had been at war with Japan, in fact he took his orders only from the United States government. The conclusion of the war therefore found the United States either occupying, controlling, or exerting strong influence in four of the five major industrial areas of the world—Western Europe, Great Britain, Japan, and the United States itself. Only the Soviet Union operated outside the American orbit.

It was an ironic conclusion. Of the Big Three powers, the United States had made relatively the fewest sacrifices but had gained by far the most. Roosevelt's policy of avoiding direct confrontation with the armies of the Axis had saved thousands of lives, while his insistence on maintaining the civilian economy at relatively high levels had strengthened the domestic economy. The United States was the only nation in the world with capital resources available to solve the problems of postwar reconstruction. She could use this capital to dictate the form of reconstruction and to extend the areas of her own influence. America had, in addition, the atomic bomb. In 1945 it seemed the ultimate weapon, and American politicians, ignoring the scientists' warnings that others would soon make their own bombs, believed that they had a secret that would ensure American military dominance for decades.

There were problems. One existed on mainland Asia. Except in South Korea, the United States had no significant numbers of troops on the mainland. Whatever influence she wished to exert could be effected only through the French, British, Dutch, and Chinese Nationalists, all of whom were intensely unpopular with the great masses of Asians. The Japanese had shattered the image of the white man in the Orient. Asians had come to believe that they could control their own lives and resources. They wanted the white man out—out of Indochina, out of India, out of Malaya, out of the N.E.I., out of the Philippines. American foreign policy would either have to adjust to this historic development or her influence would wane.

America's chief assets were her military and economic strength, but she had another asset to call upon, one that was less tangible but potentially more valuable. In September 1945 America's prestige, like its relative power in the world, had never been higher. The United States had provided the tools and the men to save Europe and Russia from Hitler and his Nazis. The United States had driven the Italians out of their African colonies and thrown the Japanese out of China, Indochina, the N.E.I., the Philippines, Burma, and Korea. America had asked nothing for itself in return. After World War I, the Allies had tried to punish Germany with the various punitive clauses in the Versailles Treaty. As a result they got Hitler. After World War II, the U.S. followed a policy of magnanimity toward the losers. In occupied Germany and Japan, the U.S. taught the ways of democracy. Ho Chi Minh hailed the Americans as the true friends of the oppressed of the earth. So did such dissimilar men as de Gaulle, Churchill, and on one occasion even Stalin himself. In a world full of hatred, death, destruction, deception, and double-dealing, the United States at the end of World War II was almost universally regarded as the disinterested champion of justice, freedom, and democracy. American prestige would never be as high again.

4

The Beginnings of the Cold War

> While the British and Americans held firmly... the
> whole position in Africa and the Mediterranean ... and
> the whole of Western Germany... they undertook by
> negotiation and diplomatic pressure to reduce Russia's
> position in Eastern Europe—which the Soviet Union had
> won because the Red Army had defeated two thirds of
> the German Army.
>
> WALTER LIPPMANN

There is no satisfactory date to mark the beginning of
the Cold War, but the issue that gave it life and shaped
its early course was East Europe. For centuries East and
West have struggled with each other for control of the
huge area running from the Baltic to the Balkans, an
area rich in human and industrial resources and strategically vital to both sides, either to Russia as a buffer
against the West, or to Germany and France as the gate-
way for an invasion of Russia. Neither the West nor the
East has been willing to allow East Europe to be strong,
independent, or neutral. Russia and the West have each
wanted the area to be aligned with them. The United
States participated in this process in 1919, when President Woodrow Wilson took the lead in breaking up the
Austro-Hungarian Empire and establishing independent Western-oriented governments designed, in part,
to hold the Soviet Union in check. The attempt ultimately failed because of the inability of the capitalist
states to stick together, a failure helped along by American refusal in the thirties to participate in European
politics.

A climax came at the 1939 Munich conference. For

three years Stalin had sought to form an alliance with Britain and France, but the democracies would do anything to avoid getting into bed with the Soviets, with the result that they wound up sleeping with the Nazis instead. Stalin, no more ready than the West to take on Hitler alone, in 1939 signed the Nazi-Soviet Pact, which provided for a division of East Europe between Germany and Russia. They soon began fighting over the spoils, however, and in 1941 Hitler took all of East Europe, then drove deep into Soviet territory. The British and French, meanwhile, had tried to redeem their abandonment of East Europe by declaring war when Hitler invaded Poland, but the aid they gave to the defense of Poland was useless. In the conflict that followed, the West made no significant contribution to the liberation of East Europe, and when the end came the Red Army was in sole possession of the area east of a line drawn from Stettin on the Baltic to Trieste on the Adriatic.

The Soviet Union occupied East Europe. This crucial result of World War II destroyed the Grand Alliance and gave birth to the Cold War.

America was unwilling to accept Russian domination of East Europe. Nearly every important American leader acknowledged that East Europe could no longer maintain an anti-Soviet position, but at the same time they all wished to promote democracy, freedom of religion and speech, and free enterprise. As Secretary of State James Byrnes put it, "Our objective is a government [in Poland] both friendly to the Soviet Union and representative of all the democratic elements of the country."

It was an impossible program. Given the traditions, prejudices, and social structures of East Europe, any freely elected government would certainly be anti-Russian. It may be that FDR recognized this fact, but was unwilling to explain it to the American people. When he reported on the Yalta Conference in February 1945, he emphasized Stalin's agreement to hold free elections, which fed soaring American expectations about the shape of postwar East Europe. Poland, Bulgaria, Rumania, and the rest of the region would become, it was hoped, democratic capitalist states closely tied to the West. There never was the slightest possibility that this would happen, but when it failed to occur, millions of Americans were outraged. They demanded liberation and rollback, and hurled insults at the Russians, while professional anti-Communists searched for the betrayers of East Europe and found them in the highest circles of American government, including, in the minds of some, President Roosevelt himself.

The struggle centered on Poland. There were two separate but related questions: Who would rule in Poland? What would the Polish boundary be? The British had tried to answer the first question by sponsoring a government-in-exile in London. The Americans had answered the second in early 1942 by refusing to discuss, as Stalin wished to do, the boundary questions in East Europe. The United States insisted that such discussions had to be postponed until Hitler was crushed, partly because FDR did not want to enter into any secret agreements that could later be denounced, but mainly because Stalin was demanding Russia's 1941 frontiers, which had extended Soviet influence into East Europe as a result of the Nazi-Soviet Pact.

Given the general desire at Yalta to hold the Grand Alliance together, based on mutual need, the Big Three tried to find a face-saving formula. The Russians had created an alternative to the London-based Polish government-in-exile, the so-called Lublin government, which was a Soviet puppet. In January 1945, Stalin had recognized the Lublin Poles as the sole government of Poland. At Yalta a month later, Churchill and Roosevelt tried to retrieve the situation by insisting on free elections and a broadly based Polish government that would include major figures from the London government. They believed that they had achieved a miracle when Stalin agreed to "free and unfettered elections as soon as possible on the basis of universal suffrage and secret ballot," and also to "reorganize" the Polish government by bringing in Poles from London. Had these promises been kept, democratic forces in Poland probably would have won power, thereby giving the West the best possible result. Stalin, however, had no intention of giving up Poland, and he never accepted the Western interpretation of the Yalta agreements—that they meant what they said.

Both sides wanted a friendly government in Poland for solid strategic reasons. As Stalin put it at Yalta, "For the Russian people, the question of Poland is not only a question of honor but also a question of security. Throughout history, Poland has been the corridor through which the enemy has passed into Russia. Twice in the last thirty years our enemies, the Germans, have passed through this corridor. . . . Poland is not only a question of honor but of life and death for the Soviet Union." The West saw Poland in reverse, as the outpost of European civilization holding back the hordes of Asians ready to overrun the Continent. This great fear, a constant in European history, was heightened in 1945 because of the vacuum in Germany and because of the Red Army, by then incomparably the strongest power in all Europe. If the Red Army remained intact, if it occupied Poland and East Germany, if the United States demobilized, and if Poland fell into Communist hands— all of which seemed probable in February 1945—then there would be nothing to prevent the Russians from overrunning all Europe.

Because Stalin's concerns were less for the Russo-Polish boundary than for the Polish-German boundary and the nature of the Polish government, he agreed to relatively limited Russian gains at Poland's expense, while insisting that Poland be compensated by taking huge hunks of German territory. He intended to move Poland's western borders all the way to the Oder-Neisse line, taking not only East Prussia and all of Silesia but also Pomerania, back to and including Stettin. From 6 to 9 million Germans would have to be evicted. The Anglo-Americans were alarmed, but there was little they could do about it. Considering German treatment of the Poles, it was difficult to argue that Stalin's proposal was anything less than fair, and in any case what mattered was not so much the frontiers of Poland as who would rule in Poland. By leaving the boundary question in abeyance and emphasizing Stalin's promise to hold free elections, Roosevelt came away from Yalta with a feeling of triumph.

Stalin quickly began to shatter the American illusion. He refused to reorganize the Polish government in any significant way, suppressed freedom of speech, assembly, religion, and the press in Poland, and made no move to hold the promised free elections. To a greater or lesser extent, the Soviets followed this pattern in the rest of East Europe, making it perfectly clear that now that they held the region they would not give it up. They shut the West out completely. By any standard the Soviet actions were high-handed, their suppressions brutal.

The West was shocked and felt betrayed. Stalin either failed to realize this or felt he had no choice. Time and again—at Yalta and later—Stalin emphasized Russia's security problem, her need to protect herself from Germany and the West by controlling the nations on her border, but increasingly Americans dismissed his statements as lies and denounced him as a dictator whose aim was world conquest. Millions of American voters of East European origin, aided by the Catholic Church and military men who were worried about the new strategic balance in Europe, decided that standing up to Stalin was as important as standing up to Hitler.

One of the first, and surely the most important, of those to feel these impulses was President Truman. His inclination was to take a hard line with the Russians, an attitude that was supported by senior American officials stationed in Moscow. A week and a day after Truman assumed office, on April 20, 1945, he met with Ambassador Harriman to discuss America's relations with the Soviet Union, which by then were at a critical stage, with the war coming to an end and new policies required.

Harriman had just come from Moscow, where his chief intellectual adviser was George Kennan, one of the leading anti-Soviets in the Foreign Service. Kennan was opposed to the denazification policy the Americans intended to apply to Germany because he felt the Germans would soon be joining the United States in opposition to Russia. But Kennan stopped short of a call to arms. He believed the Russians would never be able to maintain their hegemony over East Europe, that United States-Russian postwar collaboration was unnecessary, that what was needed was just a clear recognition of each side's sphere of influence, that Stalin had no intention of marching farther west, and most of all that "it was idle for us to hope that we could have any influence on the course of events in the area to which Russian hegemony had already been effectively extended." When Harry Hopkins, Roosevelt's trusted adviser, asked Kennan what the United States should do about the Russian domination of Poland, Kennan merely remarked that "we should accept no share of the responsibility." "Then you think it's just sin," Hopkins rejoined, "and we should be agin it."

"That's just about right," Kennan replied.

Such a do-nothing policy could have been adopted; the indications were that this was the line FDR intended to follow. The President felt that postwar collaboration could be achieved through the United Nations. To get Stalin's cooperation, Roosevelt was willing to overlook much, or, like Kennan, to adopt a realistic attitude toward developments in Poland.

Harriman, however, rejected the do-nothing policy. According to Truman, at their April 20 meeting Harriman "said that certain elements around Stalin misinterpreted our generosity and our desire to cooperate as an indication of softness, so that the Soviet government could do as it pleased without risking challenge from the United States." But he emphasized that the Soviets would need American economic aid to reconstruct their country, so "we could stand firm on important issues without running serious risks." Truman stopped Harriman to inform him that he was "not afraid of the Russians," and that he "intended to be firm," for "the Russians needed us more than we needed them." Truman's statement is a key to much that followed. American postwar policy was based, in part, on the belief that no matter what the United States did or said, the Russians could not protest because they had to have American money.

Harriman then warned that the West was faced with a "barbarian invasion of Europe." After continuing in this vein for some time, he finally added that, in international negotations, "there is give-and-take, and both sides make concessions." Truman argued for the lion's share. He would not, he said, "expect 100 percent of what we proposed," but he did feel that "we should be able to get 85 percent."

As a first practical step to secure 85 percent, Truman promised to tell Soviet Foreign Minister Molotov, who would soon be in Washington, that the Soviets had to immediately hold free elections in Poland. Truman added that he intended to put it to Molotov "in words of one syllable." At the conclusion of the meeting Harriman confessed that he had rushed to Washington because he was afraid that Truman did not understand the true nature of the Soviet problem. "I am greatly relieved," Harriman said, "to discover . . . we see eye-to-eye on the situation."

Two days later Truman met with Molotov. For the most part it was a diplomatic function and the two men were cordial. Truman did point out that he wanted free elections in Poland "because of the effect on American public opinion." Molotov said he understood that point, but added that Truman should understand that Poland was "even more important for the Soviet Union," since Poland was far from America but bordered on Russia. Truman brushed that aside and insisted that Molotov recognize that America was making Poland a test case, "the symbol of the future development of our international relations."

The next afternoon, April 23, 1945, Truman held his first major foreign-policy conference. Secretary of State Edward Stettinius, Secretary of War Stimson, Secretary of the Navy James Forrestal, Admirals William Leahy and Ernest King, General Marshall, Ambassador Harriman, and others attended. The subject was Poland. Truman set the tone by declaring that it was obvious "that our agreements with the Soviet Union had so far been a one-way street and that this could not continue." He then asked each man present to state his views.

Stimson began by saying that unless the United States fully understood "how seriously the Russians took this Polish question we might be heading into very dangerous waters . . ." Forrestal took the opposite view; he said it was his profound conviction that "if the Russians were to be rigid in their attitude we had better have a showdown with them now rather than later." Harriman, too, thought the United States should be firm on Poland. Stimson thought "the Russians perhaps were being more realistic than we were in regard to their own security," and Leahy added that he never expected the Soviets to sponsor free elections in Poland. General Marshall, who favored a cautious policy with regard to Poland, wanted to avoid a break with the Soviets, since it was imperative to get their help in the Pacific war.

Truman, who was to meet with Molotov at 5:30 P.M., still could go either way. His senior advisers were split. He could acquiesce in Soviet actions in Poland, or he could continue to demand 85 percent.

Truman decided upon the latter course. When Molotov arrived the President shouted at him in the language of a Missouri mule driver. The interpreter said "he had never heard a top official get such a scolding." At the end Truman told Molotov that "there was only one thing to do": Stalin had to reorganize the Polish government by bringing in elements from the London Poles, and he had to hold elections. Molotov finally remarked, "I have never been talked to like that in my life." Truman replied, "Carry out your agreements and you won't get talked to like that."

The Russians were puzzled as well as upset, as Stalin indicated on April 24 in a letter to Churchill and Truman. "Poland borders on the Soviet Union which cannot be said about Great Britain or the U.S.A.," he began. Turning to complaints about Soviet actions in Poland, he remarked, "I do not know whether a genuinely representative Government has been established in Greece, or whether the Belgium Government is a genuinely democratic one. The Soviet Union was not consulted when those Governments were being formed, nor did it claim the right to interfere in those matters, because it realizes how important Belgium and Greece are to the security of Great Britain." He said he could not understand why in the West "no attempt is made to consider the interests of the Soviet Union in terms of security as well."

Truman's attitude toward the Polish issue was a compound of many elements. In terms of domestic politics, there were millions of Americans of East European parentage who were enraged by Soviet actions, and Truman had to take their views into account. Churchill was bombarding the President with hard-line telegrams, and Truman had great respect for the Prime Minister. Harriman, the man on the spot in Moscow, had persuaded Truman that no matter how tough the United States got, the Russians would have to yield, for without American aid they could never reconstruct. Truman had recently been briefed on the Manhattan Project, where the atomic bomb was nearing completion, which added to his sense of power. Certainly ideology cannot be ignored. Men like Truman, Harriman, and Kennan were appalled by Russian brutality and Communist denial of the basic Western freedoms.

Truman, Harriman, and others viewed the United States as the chief defender of Western civilization. There were racist undertones to the policy, because insofar as the term Western civilization applied to the colored peoples of the world it meant white man's rule. Western Europe's day was over or ending, and the only white men left to take over in Southeast Asia and the Pacific as well as to hold the line in East Europe were the Americans. But again, most of all, Americans of all classes and shades of opinion were outraged by the Russian actions in East Europe.

Of all the ingredients in the policy mix—such as anti-Communism, the equating of Stalin with Hitler, economic motives, and concerns over military security and democracy—the element that gave body to it all was a sense of awesome power. By every index available, save that of men in arms, the United States was the strongest nation in the world. Many Americans, including leading figures in the government, believed that they could use their power to order the world in the direction of democratic capitalism on the American model.

But it could not be, for a reason that most Americans did not like to think about, seldom discussed, and frequently ignored. This was the simple fact that however great America's military and productive power was, it had limits. Six percent of the world's people could not run the lives of the remaining 94 percent. In practice this led to restraints on what America tried to do—for example, America's disapproval of Stalin's actions in East Europe was always verbal, and no troops ever set forth on a crusade to liberate Poland. But caution in action led to a general frustration, felt not only by millions of ordinary Americans but by the President himself. Truman had unprecedented power at his fingertips and a program for the world that he believed was self-evidently good. Yet he could not block Soviet expansion.

American influence would never be as great as American power. Over the next two decades American leaders and the American people were forced to learn that bitter lesson. American power was vaster than anyone else's, but in many cases it was not usable power and thus could not be translated into diplomatic victory. Vietnam would be the ultimate proof of America's inability to force others to do as she wished, but the process began much earlier, in 1945, with Truman's attempt to shape the course of events in East Europe.

Truman rejected the do-nothing advice of Stimson, Kennan, Leahy, and Marshall at the April 23, 1945, policy conference. Instead, he adopted the get-tough policy of Harriman and Forrestal, primarily because he accepted their view that the Soviet Union was a barbaric nation bent on world conquest. But although he insisted on making an issue out of Poland, he never felt that

Poland was important enough to risk World War III. Truman did not threaten to use force to impose his views. In part, this was because he still thought he could make Stalin behave by applying economic pressure. The world was weary of war, the American people were demanding demobilization, and the Red Army in Europe was too powerful for Truman even to consider war. He was, therefore, following a policy that was doomed to failure because he would be satisfied with nothing less than 85 percent—but could not go to war for it. Given Truman's view of the Soviet Union and his desire to spread American ideals and influence around the globe, he felt he could demand no less. But Stalin would not retreat and the Grand Alliance broke up. Resources that might have been used to reconstruct a war-torn world went instead into new armaments.

On May 8, 1945, Truman suddenly revealed the main outline of America's plan to use economic pressure to force compliance with its demands. On V-E Day he signed an executive order that terminated lend-lease shipments to America's allies and he placed an embargo on all shipments to Russia and other European countries. Some ships headed for Russia were turned around and brought back to port for unloading. There had been no warning to either Russia or Britain, the two principal recipients, and both countries had been planning their reconstruction on the basis of a continuation of lend-lease. In a grand understatement, Secretary of State Stettinius, then in San Francisco for the U.N. organizational meeting, said the order was "particularly untimely and did not help Soviet-American relations." Stalin was irate, and Truman sent Harry Hopkins to Moscow to pacify him. It was Hopkins's job to explain to Stalin that the whole thing was a terrible mistake. Truman countermanded his lend-lease order and the flow of supplies resumed.

Stalin accepted the explanation, but as Stettinius's remark indicated, the mistake was not one of policy but one of timing. The United States had no intention of continuing to send supplies to either Russia or Britain once she no longer needed their help in the Pacific war. What Stettinius found "incredible" was not the termination of lend-lease but that America had revealed the policy change before the Soviets declared war on Japan.

In the end the policy of applying economic pressure, pursued so actively, failed. In January 1945, Stalin had asked for a $6 billion loan. The State Department refused to discuss the request unless, as Harriman put it, Stalin became more receptive to American demands in Europe. Aid should go to the Soviets, Harriman said, only if they agreed to "work cooperatively with us on international problems in accordance with our standards. . . ." Later in 1945, the Soviets asked for a $1 billion loan. The United States government "lost" the request. When it was finally "found," months later, the State Department offered to discuss the loan if the Soviets would pledge "non-discrimination in international commerce," allowing American investment and goods into the Russian sphere of influence. Stalin rejected the offer. Instead the Soviets announced a new five-year plan to rebuild heavy industry and to ensure "the technical and economic independence of the Soviet Union." The Russians would rebuild through forced savings at home, at the expense of their own citizens, and by taking whatever they could move out of the areas in East Europe they occupied.

In his discussions with Stalin on Poland, Hopkins could not influence the Soviet dictator. The United States had to recognize the Russian puppet government or break relations, so in June Truman accepted the inevitable and the United States established relations with the Communist government of Poland. America continued to try to force Poland to accept, as the State Department put it, "a policy of equal opportunity for us in trade, investments and access to sources of information," but there was never any chance that the policy would succeed. America had suffered what many considered to be a major defeat, which caused much resentment and was not forgotten.

Hopkins's other major task was to ensure Soviet entry

into the Pacific war. On May 28 he jubilantly cabled Truman, "The Soviet Army will be properly deployed on the Manchurian position by August 8th." There was, naturally, a price. Stalin expected Truman to see to it that Chiang would keep the promises Roosevelt had made at Yalta; in return Stalin would support Chiang's leadership in China. President Truman had no objections. Hopkins also said Stalin expected to share in the occupation of Japan and he wanted an agreement with the Anglo-Americans to establish zones of occupation in Japan, a demand to which Truman did not reply. Such an agreement could, however, be worked out at Potsdam, where the Big Three had arranged to meet in July 1945.

At Potsdam, Truman said, his "immediate purpose was to get the Russians into the war against Japan as soon as possible," for he realized that "Russia's entry into the war would mean the saving of hundreds of thousands of American casualties." American lives could be saved, however, only by substituting for them Russian lives, which Stalin was not going to sacrifice for nothing. Truman recognized this, which indicated that he was willing to make concessions in return for the Soviet aid, an attitude reinforced by his second objective at Potsdam, "to come out with a working relationship" with the Russians "to prevent another world catastrophe."

As soon as the meeting began, however, irreconcilable differences emerged. Truman proposed as an agenda item an agreement reorganizing the governments of Rumania and Bulgaria with a view to early free elections. Stalin instead proposed to discuss the questions of German reparations, trusteeships for Russia (among other things, he wanted a share of the Italian colonies in Africa), an end to the Franco regime in Spain, and a settlement of Poland's western frontier on the Oder-Neisse line, with a liquidation of the London government-in-exile. Arguments went on and on, with some minor agreements reached, but nothing important could be settled.

Sniping and jabbing were the hallmarks of Potsdam. The Russians had given the Poles administrative control of eastern Germany. Truman and Churchill protested that Polish control meant the forced evacuation or death of millions of Germans, as well as a unilateral decision by Russia to bring another occupying power into Germany. Stalin shrugged off their criticism, saying that all the Germans had already left the territory and that the frontier had been determined at Yalta, neither of which was true. The Soviets wanted to participate with Turkey in the control of the Black Sea straits. Truman proposed an international guarantee that the straits would be open to all nations at all times, as a substitute for fortification or Russian participation in the control of the straits. Molotov asked if the Suez Canal were to be operated under such a principle. Churchill said the question of Suez had not been raised. Molotov retorted, "I'm raising it." Churchill explained that the British had operated Suez for some seventy years without complaints. Molotov replied that there had been many complaints: "You should ask Egypt."

The major issue at Potsdam was Germany. At Yalta the Big Three had agreed to divide Germany into four zones (one to the French), with each area governed by the local military commander. Together, the generals formed the Allied Control Council (ACC), which would lay down rules for reuniting Germany. The ACC would be governed by a rule of unanimity, a rule that proved disastrous for reunification, since the Anglo-Americans wanted one outcome, the French and Russians another. England and the United States aimed to create a politically whole Germany that would have self-sufficient industry; the other two occupying powers wanted to keep Germany divided and weak. No reconciliation of such divergent views was possible and at Potsdam none was really attempted. The Americans did agree that German industry should not exceed a certain level, but within less than a year they violated the agreement.

Potsdam did try to deal with the problem of German reparations. Since the United States had already indicated that it would not continue lend-lease after the war or extend a loan to the Soviet Union, for Stalin the question of German reparations was crucial. Geography was against him, however, because the prime industrial area of Germany, the Ruhr, was in the British zone. His advantage was that the Ruhr could not feed itself and he controlled the major agricultural regions of Germany. In the end a deal was made: The West recognized the Oder-Neisse line as Germany's eastern border, and Stalin accepted 25 percent of German capital equipment from the Western zones as his share of reparations. Fifteen percent of this figure was to be in exchange for food from eastern Germany. Stalin also got carte blanche on reparations from the Russian zone, which he quickly stripped.

Perhaps more important than the agreements and arguments at Potsdam was the attitude Truman took back to the White House. At Potsdam, he learned that the only thing the Russians understood was force. He decided he would no longer "take chances in a joint setup with the Russians," since they were impossible to get along with. The immediate result of this decision was Truman's determination "that I would not allow the Russians any part in the control of Japan. . . . As I reflected on the situation during my trip home, I made up my mind that General MacArthur would be given complete command and control after victory in Japan.*

The successful test of the atomic bomb, which took place while the President was at Potsdam, encouraged him to take a harder line. The notion was widespread in high American government circles that American possession of the atomic bomb would, in Stimson's words, result in "less barbarous relations with the Russians," or, as Byrnes put it in June 1945, the bomb "would make Russia more manageable in Europe."

The bomb, coupled with the financial position the United States enjoyed, gave Truman and his chief ad-

*This was a momentous decision. Earlier plans had called for a joint occupation by U.S., British, Nationalist Chinese, and Red Army troops.

visers a feeling of awesome power. From Potsdam on, the bomb was the constant factor in the American approach to the Soviet Union. The new policy was aptly described by Stimson as wearing "this weapon rather ostentatiously on our hip," which he himself later came to admit had fed "their suspicions and their distrust of our purposes and motives. . . ."

The bomb appeared to be a godsend to the Americans. They could impose their will on any recalcitrant nation merely by threatening to use it. Stopping aggression would be simplicity itself—just drop the bomb. America could retain a powerful position in Europe without having to maintain a mass army there. One of the great fears in American military circles was that, having smashed Germany, the West now had to confront the Red Army, and the only nation capable of doing so was the United States. But in the United States domestic political realities precluded the maintenance of a large, conscripted, standing army in postwar Europe. The Republican Party, soon to take control of Congress, meanwhile had made it clear that taxes had to be cut and the budget balanced. The Administration would have neither the men nor the money to engage actively in war.

The bomb seemed to solve all these problems. America could fight a cold war without demanding any sacrifices of her citizens. America's leaders hoped that through a judicious use of financial credit and the veiled threat of the bomb the United States could shape the postwar world. In the fall of 1945, Truman met with de Gaulle, who was worried about the intentions of General Lucius Clay, head of the American occupation zone in Germany, to reunify Germany and to raise its levels of production. De Gaulle was also concerned about the Red Army in Central Europe. Truman offhandedly remarked that there was nothing to fear. If any nation did become aggressive, he explained, the United States would use the atomic bomb to stop it.

The strategy would later be called massive retaliation. The trouble with it was that even as early as 1945 it bore little relation to reality. The atomic bombs of the 1945–

49 period were not powerful enough to deter the Russians, nor did America have enough of them to institute a true massive retaliation program. These truths were only gradually realized by the politicians, but they colored the military situation from the beginning. Even had the U.S. Air Force been able to deliver all the bombs available in 1947 or 1948, they were hardly sufficient to destroy the Soviet Union.

Should the Russians realize the West's worst fears and march across the Elbe, the most that bombs could achieve would be retaliation on principal Russian population centers, which would kill tens of thousands but which would not hamstring the Russian war machine. Stalin could match American destruction of Moscow with Soviet occupation of Western Europe.

There was a psychological as well as a military problem involved in massive retaliation. Whatever the limitations on the bomb, the world regarded it as the ultimate weapon, an attitude the American press and politicians encouraged. In the end this backfired, since it meant the bomb could only be used in the most extreme situation imaginable. It was easier for the United States to threaten to use the bomb to punish aggression than to find an aggression serious enough to justify its use. When in 1948 the Communists took over Czechoslovakia, for example, no responsible American official thought the outrage serious enough to start dropping bombs on Moscow, but because the United States had put its faith in the bomb there were no other tools available to stop the aggressor. The United States, therefore, could do nothing. This helplessness had been clear, in fact, as early as 1945.

American possession of the bomb had no noticeable effect on Stalin's policy in East Europe. He and Molotov continued to do as they pleased, refusing to hold elections or to allow Western observers to travel freely in East Europe. At foreign ministers' meetings, the Russians continued to insist that the West had to recognize the puppet governments in East Europe before peace treaties could be written. Byrnes's hope that the bomb would "make Russia more manageable" proved abortive, and by the summer of 1946 both sides had accepted the fact of a divided Europe.

Russian mistrust of the West, along with Stalin's determination to maintain an iron grip on his satellites, had grown so great that Molotov refused to consider seriously Secretary of State Byrnes's proposal that the Big Four powers sign a treaty unifying Germany and guaranteeing German demilitarization, an offer sincerely made and one that represented the best hope of solving the German problem. Instead, the Soviets stopped removing machinery from East Germany and began instead to utilize the skilled German manpower to produce finished goods in their zone, goods they then shipped to the Soviet Union. On May 3, 1946, meanwhile, General Clay unilaterally informed the Russians that they could expect no more reparations from the Western zones. Later that year at Stuttgart, Secretary Byrnes gave a highly publicized speech in which he announced that Germany must develop exports in order to become self-sustaining. Byrnes said the Germans should be given primary responsibility for running their domestic affairs and allowed to increase their industrial productivity (policies Clay had already been putting into practice), and emphasized that the American presence in Central Europe would not be withdrawn.

Solutions acceptable to both East and West were hard to find in 1946. This impasse applied especially to the atomic bomb. Whatever the limitations on the size and number of nuclear weapons in the first half decade of the atomic age, it was obvious that the growth potential was almost unlimited. Control of the bomb was crucial to the future welfare of the world. How to get the weapon under control was not so clear. On the one hand, the United States had a monopoly, something no nation would ever give up lightly. On the other hand, all the atomic scientists agreed that it was only a question of time before the Soviets developed the bomb. If the Russians got atomic weapons on their own, and if they continued to be treated as just another military weapon to be used by sovereign nations as they saw fit, the world would live in continual terror.

What made a solution especially difficult was the postwar atmosphere in which America and Russia made their proposals for atomic control. There were almost daily crises in Germany among the occupying powers. Tension dominated the Middle East, reaching its peak in Iran and Turkey. According to the terms of a 1942 occupation treaty, the Russians were required to withdraw their forces from Iran six months after the end of the war. They refused to do so because Stalin wanted oil concessions from the Iranian government. To apply pressure, the Russians supported a revolt in northern Iran. As the crisis moved forward, Byrnes sent a strong note (March 6, 1946) to Moscow demanding immediate Russian withdrawal. Three weeks later Iran and the U.S.S.R. announced that the Soviet occupation troops would be pulled out of northern Iran and that a joint Iranian-Soviet oil company would be formed by treaty, subject to ratification by the Persian Parliament. On May 6 the Russians withdrew; early in 1947 the Parliament rejected the oil company treaty.

The reaction to this major Soviet diplomatic defeat illustrated how far apart the former allies had drifted. To the Russians it seemed only fair that they be allowed to participate in the exploitation of Iranian oil. To be forced out showed that the West was up to its old tricks of encircling the Soviet Union and doing everything it could to keep it weak. To the Americans the crisis proved once again that the Soviets were bent on world conquest.

Churchill interpreted these and other events for the benefit of the American public on March 5, 1946, in a speech at Fulton, Missouri, with Truman on the platform beside him. Churchill declared that "from Stettin in the Baltic to Trieste in the Adriatic, an iron curtain has descended across the Continent." He wanted to lift that curtain, to liberate East Europe, and to hold the Russians back elsewhere, as in Iran and Turkey. He suggested that a fraternal association of the English-speaking peoples, operating outside the United Nations, should do it. The tool would be the atomic bomb, which Churchill said, "God has willed" to the United States alone.

Churchill's speech did not help American efforts, then being undertaken, to find an acceptable solution to international control of the bomb. Stalin reacted with the full fury of a wounded animal at bay. He compared Churchill and his "friends" in America to Hitler, charging that like Hitler they held a racial theory that proposed world rule for the English-speaking peoples. Stalin said Churchill's speech was "a call to war with the Soviet Union." He reminded the West that twice in the recent past Germany had attacked Russia through East European countries that had "governments inimical to the Soviet Union." Within three weeks of Churchill's iron curtain speech, the Soviets rejected membership in the World Bank and in the International Monetary Fund, announced the start of a new five-year plan designed to make Russia self-sufficient in the event of another war, built up the pressure on Iran, and mounted an intense ideological effort to eliminate all Western influences within the Soviet Union.

But Stalin was no more ready for war than Truman, as events in Turkey showed. The issue there was control of the Dardanelles. In August 1946, Stalin demanded of the Turks equal partnership in running the straits. This participation was an ancient Russian dream. But Under Secretary of State Dean Acheson interpreted the demand as a Soviet attempt to dominate Turkey, threaten Greece, and intimidate the remainder of the Middle East. He advised a showdown. Truman agreed: "We might as well find out whether the Russians were bent on world conquest now as in five years or ten years." The United States told the Turks to stand firm. To back them up, Truman sent the most modern American aircraft carrier through the straits. The Soviets backed down.

In this atmosphere of threat and counterthreat, bluff and counterbluff, achieving workable international control of atomic weapons was almost hopeless. Still, the Americans tried. On March 16, 1946, the United States released a plan, the Acheson-Lilienthal proposal, which called for international control to be reached through a series of stages. The proposal was an honest attempt to avoid the horrors of a world in which Russia and the United States rattled nuclear-tipped sabers at each other. It did not, however, satisfy the Soviets, for during the transitional stages the Acheson-Lilienthal proposal reserved to the United States full control of its own bombs. "Should there be a breakdown in the plan at any time during the transition," Acheson declared, "we shall be in a favorable position with regard to atomic weapons." The Soviets, meanwhile, would not be allowed to develop their own bomb.

Given the tension in Soviet-American relations, it was unthinkable that the United States could go further in sharing the bomb; it was equally unthinkable that the Russians could accept. The Soviet counterproposal called for an end to the production and use of atomic weapons and insisted on the destruction within three months of all existing stocks of atomic bombs. Only then would they discuss international control.

No way could be found out of the impasse. In April 1946, Truman appointed Bernard Baruch, financier and adviser to presidents, as the American delegate to the U.N. Atomic Energy Commission. Baruch thought the Acheson-Lilienthal proposal had gone much too far because it contained no reference to Russia's veto power. Baruch wanted majority rule at all stages, which meant that the Soviets could not veto the use of the bomb against themselves if violations were discovered, nor could they prevent inspection teams roaming at will through their country. It could hardly have been expected that they would accept Baruch's proposal.

Baruch, however, insisted upon the elimination of the veto. He was backed by Army Chief of Staff Eisenhower, who advised him that only through effective international control of atomic energy could there be any hope of preventing atomic war, but who also insisted that national security required that methods of such control be tested and proven before the United States gave up its monopoly. "If we enter too hurriedly into an international agreement to abolish all atomic weapons," Eisenhower pointed out, "we may find ourselves in the position of having no restraining means in the world capable of effective action if a great power violates the agreement." He warned that the Russians might deliberately avoid the use of atomic weapons and undertake aggression with other—but equally decisive—weapons.

This was the central dilemma for the United States in its efforts to get some international control of atomic energy before it was too late, an issue more important by far than the veto or inspection. The question Eisenhower raised was straightforward enough: If the United States gave up the atomic bomb, how could it stop the Red Army? The only alternatives to American possession of the bomb were to build up a mass army or get the Russians to demobilize, and in 1946 there was little chance of doing either one. Both sides made various concessions, but neither would back down on the crucial points. America insisted on retaining the bomb until it was satisfied with the effectiveness of international control, and the Russians would not give up the veto.

The only hope of eliminating the bomb, which in the political atmosphere of 1946 was never very great, was gone. America would not give up its monopoly as long as the Red Army was intact and the Russians would never demobilize as long as the Americans had the bomb. In a relatively short period of time the Russians would have their own bomb; eventually the United States would be maintaining a large standing army. An arms race unprecedented in the world's history would be under way. This would force a qualitative change in American foreign policy and in international relations generally. Every crisis would strike terror into the hearts of people everywhere. There would be no security, no defense. Much of American foreign policy after Baruch's proposal has been a search for a viable method of using the bomb to achieve overseas goals. The bomb had already failed America once, in East Europe, where the Soviets refused to behave. How effectively it could be used elsewhere remained to be seen. Russian probes toward Iran and Turkey had been met and stopped. By the end of 1946 spheres of influence in Europe were clearly drawn, but elsewhere what belonged to whom was uncertain. Perhaps, as with Iran and Turkey, there would have to be a confrontation at each point around the world until the line was drawn and accepted everywhere. The Cold War would meanwhile continue to be fought under the shadow of the mushroom-shaped cloud.

5

The Truman Doctrine and the Marshall Plan

At the present moment in world history nearly every nation must choose between alternative ways of life. . . . One way of life is based upon the will of the majority, and is distinguished by free institutions, representative government, free elections, guarantees of individual liberty, freedom of speech and religion, and freedom from political oppression. The second way of life is based upon the will of a minority forcibly imposed upon the majority. It relies upon terror and oppression, a controlled press and radio, fixed elections, and the suppression of personal freedoms. I believe that it must be the policy of the United States to support free peoples who are resisting attempted subjugation by armed minorities or by outside pressures.

HARRY S TRUMAN
March 12, 1947

There are limits to the extent that even the most powerful nation can project its influence beyond its borders. In a democracy one of the most important limitations is the mood on the domestic scene, which involves both a general perception of a need to exert influence and a willingness to make the sacrifices required to generate usable military power. In the United States at the beginning of 1947, neither was present. If there was no retreat to isolation as in 1919, there was a popular feeling that America could handle her foreign problems through possession of the atomic bomb. In November 1946 the Republicans had won control of Congress by emphasizing a modified version of Warren Harding's return to normalcy—demobilization, business as usual, a cutback in the role and spending of the government, and lower taxes. These domestic facts severely restricted the Truman administration's ability to carry on the Cold War.

By the beginning of 1947 the United States had almost completed the most rapid demobilization in the history of the world. The Army had been cut from 8 million to 1 million men; the Navy from 3.5 million to less than 1 million; the Air Force from over 200 to less than 50 effective combat groups. As General Marshall later recalled, "I remember, when I was Secretary of State I was being pressed constantly, particularly when in Moscow [March, 1947], by radio message after radio message to give the Russians hell. . . . When I got back, I was getting the same appeal in relation to the Far East and China. At that time, my facilities for giving them hell—and I am a soldier and know something about the ability to give hell—was 1⅓ divisions over the entire United States. That is quite a proposition when you deal with somebody with over 260 and you have 1⅓."

Foreign policy and military policy were moving in opposite directions. Truman and his advisers wanted to meet the Communist challenge wherever it appeared, but except for the atomic bomb they had nothing with which to meet it. Stimson and Forrestal, among others, urged Truman to stop the demobilization process by dramatically warning the nation about the scope of the Soviet threat. In January 1946 Secretary of the Navy Forrestal advised the President to call in "the heads of the important news services and the leading newspapers . . . and state to them the seriousness of the present situation and the need for making the country aware of its implications abroad." Throughout 1946 he pressed Truman, but the results were meager, for Truman wanted a balanced budget and was enough of a politician to realize that the public would not support higher taxes for a larger military establishment.

Simultaneously, with the decrease in military force there was an increasing fear in Washington of the scope and nature of the Soviet threat. In a speech at the National War College in mid-1947, William C. Bullitt of the

State Department summed up the attitudes then dominant in Washington. "The Soviet Union's assault upon the West is at about the stage of Hitler's maneuvering into Czechoslovakia," he asserted, which immediately linked Stalin with Hitler. "The final aim of Russia is world conquest," which outlined the scope of the problem. The Soviet method, however, differed from Hitler's and was potentially more dangerous. Because of the American atomic monopoly, the Russians would not inaugurate large-scale war but would rather avoid armed conflict while advancing their aims through internal subversion.

Since the challenge was worldwide, it had to be met everywhere, at once. As one step Bullitt advocated a "European Federation of Democratic States" in order to "face up to Russia." He was thinking primarily in terms of a military organization, under American leadership, supplied with American arms. Meeting the Russian threat by arming Europeans was in practice a continuation of the wartime policy of lend-lease. Another part of the response was to provide economic and technical aid to threatened nations. There was general agreement in the American government that Communism thrived on chaos and poverty; the way to respond to it was to promote stability and prosperity through economic aid.

At the end of 1946 most discussion of the optimum American response to the Soviet challenge revolved around three possibilities: build up America's own military resources; send military aid to threatened nations; give economic and technical assistance to needy peoples. These proposals were not mutually exclusive, and most officials wanted a combination of the three, with an emphasis on one. All rested on Bullitt's assumptions about the nature of the threat, and all would cost money.

The Republican Congress controlled the money and it saw no pressing reason to spend it on any of those courses. Neither did a majority of the American people. In January 1947 there was a popular feeling that postwar tensions with the Russians were easing, based primarily

on the completion of peace treaties signed by the Big
Three with the Eastern European countries that had
fought alongside Hitler. These treaties constituted a
practical recognition by the United States of the Soviet
sphere of influence in East Europe, for they were signed
with Communist satellite governments. Robert Taft, a
prominent Republican in the Senate and leader of the
drive for economy in government, expressed the current
mood when he objected to any attempt by the Administration to divide the world into Communist and anti-
Communist zones, for "I do not want war with Russia."
The Democrats accused Taft—and other Republicans
who resisted joining a crusade against Communism—of
isolationism, but despite the negative connotations of the
label there was no denying that a majority of the American people did not want to embark on a crusade.

To obtain the economic and military resources to carry
out an aggressive foreign policy, Truman had to convince
Americans of the reality and magnitude of the Soviet
threat. To do that, he needed a dramatic issue. Greece
stood near the top of the list of potential trouble spots.
Great Britain had been supporting the Royalist government there, but a severe storm in January 1947 had
raised havoc with an already weak British economy and
underscored the impossibility of Britain's continuing to
play a leading world role. As early as September 1946,
the American government had quietly prepared programs for military aid for Greece. In January 1947, the
State Department began intensified planning to provide
military aid. The United States was prepared to move
into Greece whenever the British pulled out.

In January 1947, Secretary of State Byrnes resigned;
his successor was General Marshall. Marshall's first task
was to prepare for a meeting of the Council of Foreign
Ministers in Moscow to begin on March 10, and he was
spending most of his time on the German problem, the
main issue on the agenda of the Moscow conference.

While Marshall prepared for Moscow, events in
Greece rushed forward. In January 1947, Truman sent
the Greek government an offer to provide advisers and

funds for a program of economic stabilization. The Greek government had already complained in the United Nations that the insurgents were receiving outside assistance, and a U.N. mission had gone to Greece to investigate. Truman had sent his own agent to make a report. The damaged British economy, meanwhile, made it increasingly doubtful that Britain could maintain its 40,000 troops in Greece. On February 3, the American ambassador in Athens reported a rumor that the British would be pulling out soon. On February 18, Truman's personal representative in Greece cabled that everything pointed to an impending move by the Communists to seize the country, and two days later the American Embassy in London reported that the British Treasury could give no further aid to Greece. The stage was set.

On February 21, 1947, the British ambassador to the United States informed the State Department that London would no longer provide aid to Greece or Turkey. Britain would pull out by the end of March. To Secretary Marshall this "was tantamount to British abdication from the Middle East with obvious implications as to their successor." Within five days the State Department had consulted with the War Department, held meetings of its own, and was ready to move. Under Secretary Dean Acheson took the lead, as Marshall was busy preparing for the Moscow conference. On February 26 Truman, Marshall, and Acheson met to discuss the result of the studies of the experts.

Acheson made the presentation. He emphasized that if Greece were lost, Turkey would be untenable. Russia would move in and take control of the Dardanelles, with the "clearest implications" for the Middle East. Morale would sink in Italy, Germany, and France. Acheson was describing what would later be called the domino theory, which held that if one nation fell to the Communists, its neighbors would surely follow. In this case, Acheson said one rotten apple would infect the whole barrel. Put in those terms, the Administration had no choice but to act vigorously and quickly. Truman felt, he later told his

Cabinet, that "he was faced with a decision more serious than had ever confronted any President," which took in quite a lot of ground and was in any case overly dramatic in its implications, for it implied that he was tossing in bed at night trying to decide what to do. Actually, he had long since made the decision and the real task was to sell the program to Congress.

On February 27, Truman called in the congressional leaders. He concentrated on Senator Arthur Vandenberg, a Republican "isolationist turned internationalist" who, as chairman of the Senate Foreign Relations Committee, was one of architects of the bipartisan foreign policy. Truman described the Greek situation in dark terms, then said he wanted to ask Congress for $250 million for Greece and $150 million for Turkey. Most, if not all, of what he said was news to the Congressmen, but the way in which he outlined the issues, coupled with Vandenberg's support for the policy, won them over.

During the following weeks, the State, Navy, and War departments worked out the details of the aid program while Vandenberg and the other congressional leaders built support in Congress for the new policy. Not until March 7 did Truman go before his Cabinet to explain developments; there, perhaps unexpectedly, he found some opposition. Although Forrestal wanted a full mobilization for the struggle with the Russians, others were not so convinced. The Secretary of Labor objected to pulling British chestnuts out of the fire. Someone wondered if it was good policy to support the corrupt, inefficient, right-wing Greek government. Most of all, however, the Cabinet was concerned about the way the public would receive such a sharp break with America's historic foreign policy, especially as it promised to be so expensive. As Truman laconically put it in his *Memoirs*, "There was considerable discussion on the best method to apprise the American people of the issues involved."

The State Department, meanwhile, was preparing a message for Truman to deliver to the Congress and the nation. He was unhappy with the early drafts, for "I wanted no hedging in this speech. This was America's answer to the surge of expansion of Communist tyranny. It had to be clear and free of hesitation or double talk." Truman told Acheson to have the speech toughened, simplified, and expanded to cover more than just Greece and Turkey. Truman's strategy was to explain aid to Greece not in terms of supporting monarchy but rather as part of a worldwide program for freedom.

George Kennan saw one of the revised drafts. Kennan had risen in prestige and power in the State Department since the end of the war and Marshall had just named him head of a new Policy Planning Staff. His rise was due in part to a seven-thousand-word telegram which he sent from Moscow, warning of the Soviet Union's postwar intentions. The warning was well received. Truman read it, and Forrestal had it reproduced and made it required reading for thousands of senior officers. Kennan's analysis provided the intellectual justification for a policy of containment, and Kennan was widely understood in Washington to be the father of that policy.

Despite all this, Kennan was upset when he read the speech Truman was to deliver to the Congress. First, he saw no need for any military aid to Turkey, where no military threat existed. So too in Greece—Kennan was all for helping the Greek government but thought it should be done through political and economic aid. In his view the Soviet threat was primarily political. Kennan was also upset at the way in which Truman had seized the opportunity to declare a worldwide, open-ended doctrine, when what was called for was a simple declaration of aid to a single nation. Truman was preparing to use terms, Kennan later remarked, "more grandiose and more sweeping than anything that I, at least, had ever envisaged." Kennan protested, but to no avail. He was told that it was too late to change the speech.

The point Kennan had missed was the need to rally the public in support of a policy that broke sharply with America's past. Kennan was not a politician—in fact, he had hardly been in the United States through most of his adult life—while Truman was *the* expert on domestic

politics. Like the President, Kennan wanted to stop the
Communists, but he wanted to do so in a realistic way,
at little cost, and with minimal commitments. Truman
realized that he could never get the economy-minded
Republicans—and the public that stood behind them—
to shell out tax dollars to support the King of Greece.
Truman had to describe the Greek situation in universal terms, good versus evil, to get support for
containment.

At 1:00 P.M. on March 12, 1947, Truman stepped to
the rostrum in the hall of the House of Representatives
to address a joint session of the Congress. The speech
was also carried on nationwide radio. Truman asked for
immediate aid for Greece and Turkey, then explained
his reasoning: "I believe that it must be the policy of the
United States to support free peoples who are resisting
attempted subjugation by armed minorities or by outside
pressures."

The statement was all-encompassing. In a single sentence Truman had defined American policy for the next
generation and beyond. Whenever and wherever an anti-
Communist government was threatened, by indigenous
insurgents, foreign invasion, or even diplomatic pressure
(as with Turkey), the United States would supply political, economic, and, most of all, military aid. The Truman Doctrine came close to shutting the door against
any revolution, since the terms "free peoples" and "anti-
Communist" were thought to be synonymous. All the
Greek government, or any dictatorship, had to do to get
American aid was to claim that its opponents were
Communist.

It has often been noted that Americans expect their
wars to be grand heroic crusades on a worldwide scale,
a struggle between light and darkness with the fate of
the world hanging on the outcome. The Truman Doctrine met that requirement. At one of the meetings between the President and the congressional leaders,
Vandenberg had warned Truman that if he wanted the
public to support containment, he would have to "scare
hell out of the American people." Truman did. He

painted in dark hues the "totalitarian regimes" that threatened to snuff out freedom everywhere. The time had come, he said, when "nearly every nation must choose between alternative ways of life." Truman had struck a responsive chord with the majority of his countrymen. As they had done on December 7, 1941, so again on March 12, 1947, the American people rallied behind their leader in a cause that transcended national, economic, social, and military interests: the cause of freedom itself.

On May 15, 1947, Congress appropriated $400 million for Greece and Turkey. By later standards the sum was small, but nevertheless America had taken an immense stride. For the first time in its history, the United States had chosen to intervene during a period of general peace in the affairs of peoples outside North and South America. The symbolic act could not have been more significant. The commitment had been made. It would take years to persuade Congress and the public to provide all the enormous funds needed for the new policy, but having accepted the premises of the Truman Doctrine, there would be no turning back.

Simultaneously with the announcement of the Truman Doctrine, the Moscow Council of Foreign Ministers failed. Positions on Germany had hardened. Neither the Americans nor the Soviets had any intentions of working toward a peace treaty with Germany and German reunification, except on their own terms, which they knew in advance were unacceptable to the other side. All anyone could do at Moscow was issue propaganda.

The immediate situation in Europe was acute. When Marshall returned from Moscow, he reported that "the patient [Europe] is sinking while the doctors deliberate." "Agreement was impossible" at Moscow, Marshall reported in a radio talk to the nation on April 28, because the Soviet proposals "would have established in Germany a centralized government adapted to the seizure of absolute control." As General Clay later put it, "The principal result was to convince the three foreign ministers

representing the Western Powers of the intransigence of
the Soviet position." This, in turn, "led them to work
more closely together in the future," which meant it
speeded the process of unifying the Western zones and
bringing western Germany into the budding alliance
against the Soviets.

While in Europe, Marshall had been shaken by the
seriousness and urgency of the plight of Western Europe, where economic recovery from the ravages of war
had been slow. Total economic disintegration appeared
to be imminent. The Secretary of State's discussion with
the Russians, according to Kennan, "had compelled him
to recognize, however reluctantly, that the idea of approaching the solution to Europe's problems in collaboration with the Russians was a pipe dream." Stalin,
Marshall had concluded, wanted the European economy
to come crashing down.

The Truman Doctrine had cleared the way for a massive American aid program to Europe. Marshall ordered
Kennan and the Policy Planning Staff to draw one up.
Round-the-clock meetings began. The general aim was
to revive the economy of Western Europe, which was
imperative for both economic and military reasons. As
Acheson explained, American exports were running at
$16 billion a year, imports at less than $8 billion. Most
of the exports went to Europe. If the Europeans were
to pay for them, they had to have dollars, which they
could only get by producing goods America could im-
port. Otherwise, America's export market would dry up.
Militarily, only with a healthy economy could Europe
support the troops necessary to stop the Red Army.

The key was Germany. To get European production
rolling again, Germany's coal mines and steel mills had
to be worked at maximum capacity. Kennan emphasized
this point, saying, "It is imperatively urgent today that
the improvement of economic conditions and the revival
of productive capacity in the west of Germany be made
the primary object of our policy . . . and be given top
priority." It would have been absurd to expect the Russians to cooperate in the revival of Germany without

themselves controlling the Ruhr, and indeed Kennan had no such expectations. The problem was that if the United States went ahead on its German program, the division of Europe would be complete, and responsibility for the split would rest with the United States.

There would be no progress in Europe without including Germany, and there could be no improvement in Germany without antagonizing the Russians. What to do about the Soviets thus became a prime consideration. Kennan insisted that the United States should "play it straight" by inviting the Russians to participate in any Europe-wide recovery program. "We would not ourselves draw a line of division through Europe." He recognized the dangers. "What if," he himself asked, "the Russians spiked it" by accepting the invitation and "trying to link it to Russian participation in the administration of the Ruhr?" Kennan's answer was straightforward: "In that case I think we can only say 'no' to the whole business as pleasantly and firmly as we know how. . . ."

Even in making an offer to the Russians, Kennan wanted strict controls. He insisted that the Russians would have to open their economic records for American scrutiny, and he wanted the East European economy integrated into that of Western Europe. Despite Marshall's famous sentence stating that the policy was "directed not against any country or doctrine but against hunger, poverty, desperation and chaos," in fact Kennan and the State Department did not want Soviet participation and did all they could to prevent it while making it appear that a genuine offer was being made.

Kennan applied the same formula in a more general way to the Soviet satellites. Insofar as they were free to accept the American offer and integrate their economies into those of the West, Kennan was willing to offer them aid. He insisted, however, that it be done in such a way that they would "either exclude themselves by unwillingness to accept the proposed conditions or agree to abandon the exclusive orientation of their economies."

A final aim of Kennan's Policy Planning Staff was "to

correct what seemed to us to be the two main mis-
impressions that had been created in connection with
the Truman Doctrine." These were the notions that
America's foreign policy was a defensive reaction to
Communist pressure, and that the doctrine was a blank
check to give aid to any area of the world threatened by
the Communists. Truman was more nearly correct, however, in stating that his doctrine and the Marshall Plan
"are two halves of the same walnut." The emphasis in
Greece and Turkey was military, while initially in West
Europe it was economic, but both were designed to contain the Soviets.

On June 5, 1947, speaking at Harvard University,
Marshall announced the new policies. The general proposals, like the man himself, were high-minded. He recognized the Continent-wide nature of the problem.
Marshall recalled the disruption of Europe's economy
because of the war and the destructive rule of the Nazis.
Europe could not feed itself, so it was using up scarce
foreign credits to buy food. If the United States did not
provide help, "economic, social and political deteriora-
tion of a very grave character" would result, with serious
consequences for the American economy. The assistance
should not be piecemeal but "should provide a cure
rather than a mere palliative." He asked the European
nations to gather themselves together, draw up a plan,
and submit it to the United States.

The reaction in Western Europe was enthusiastic.
Even traditional fears of Germany quieted. Although
Marshall had made it clear that "the restoration of Eu-
rope involves the restoration of Germany," the French
were anxious to go ahead, for the Marshall Plan tied
Germany to Western Europe generally and offered vast
sums to everyone. French Foreign Minister Georges Bi-
dault began meetings in Paris. He neglected to invite the
Russians to participate, but pressure from the powerful
French Communist Party made him change his mind.
On June 26, Molotov arrived in Paris with eighty-nine
economic experts and clerks, which indicated that the
Russians were seriously considering the proposal, as

indeed they had to. As the American ambassador to Moscow, General Walter B. Smith, said, "They were confronted with two unpalatable alternatives." They were afraid of a Western bloc and realized that "to refrain from participation in the Paris Conference would be tantamount to forcing the formation of such a bloc." On the other hand, if they joined up, "they would create the possibility of a certain amount of economic penetration by the western democracies among the satellite states."

Molotov spent three days at the conference, most of it on the telephone talking to Stalin in Moscow. He finally proposed that each nation establish its own recovery program. The French and British refused. They insisted on following the American line of making the program Europewide. Molotov angrily walked out, warning that a revived Germany would dominate Western Europe, and that the plan would divide "Europe into two groups of states." He returned to Moscow, where within a week the Soviets announced a "Molotov Plan" for their satellites. The Poles and Czechs, who had wanted to participate in Paris, had to inform the West that they could not join the Marshall Plan because "it might be construed as an action against the Soviet Union."

All that remained was for the Western Europeans to work out the details of a plan and for the American Congress to accept it. At the end of August, the sixteen Western European nations represented at Paris presented a plan calling for $28 billion over a four-year period. After thorough examination the Truman administration accepted the program and Truman presented it to Congress on December 19, although he reduced the proposed amount to $17 billion.

Despite the reductions, the plan faced a hostile Congress, and 1948 was a presidential election year. Some Republicans did not want to give Truman a major diplomatic triumph or throw American dollars away. They called the plan a "bold Socialist blue-print," and a plain waste of American money. But Vandenberg ardently championed the bill. In presenting it to the Senate, he called it a "calculated risk" to "help stop World War III before it starts." The area covered by the plan, he declared, contained "270,000,000 people of the stock which has largely made America. . . . This vast friendly segment of the earth must not collapse. The iron curtain must not come to the rims of the Atlantic either by aggression or by default." Administration witnesses before congressional committees considering the plan underscored Vandenberg's emphasis on containment. They pointed out that a rejuvenated Europe could produce strategic goods that the United States could buy and stockpile, preserve Western control over Middle Eastern oil supplies, and free Europeans from economic problems so they could help the United States militarily.

Indeed, as Walter LaFeber has pointed out, the plan offered all things to all people. Those who feared a slump in exports and a resulting depression within the United States could envision a continued vigorous export trade; those who thought Communist expansion would result from economic chaos saw salvation in an integrated, healthy European economy; those who thought the real threat was the Red Army were delighted by the prospect of reviving Germany and then rebuilding the German army. For the humanitarian the plan offered long-term aid to war-torn Europe.

Still the plan met intense opposition. Senator Taft proclaimed that American money should not be poured into a "European TVA." Like many of his Republican colleagues, he was deeply disturbed at European steps toward socialism, and he feared that the Europeans might use Marshall Plan money to nationalize basic industries, including American-owned plants. The Republican-dominated Congress would not budge. Committee meetings ground on, with no results.

All in all, 1947 had been a frustrating year for the new foreign policy. In Greece guerrilla warfare raged on despite increased American military assistance to the government. The Chinese Communists continued to push Chiang back. Russia retained her grip on East Europe; indeed, she strengthened it, for immediately after Molotov left the Paris Conference he announced the formation of the Communist Information Bureau (Cominform), a replacement for the old Communist International, abolished during World War II. In Hungary the Soviets purged left-wing anti-Communist political leaders, rigged the elections on August 31, 1947, and destroyed all anti-Communist opposition. Truman had been forced by the Republicans and the public generally to call off the peacetime drafting of young men into the armed services and demobilization continued, which left the Administration with inadequate tools to pursue the policy of containment.

Truman was unable to achieve unification of the armed forces, a proposal designed to make them more efficient and cheaper. In July 1947, Congress passed the National Security Act, which provided for a single Department of Defense to replace the three independently run services, gave statutory status to the Joint Chiefs of Staff, established a National Security Council to advise the President, and created a Central Intelligence Agency to gather information and to correlate and evaluate intelligence activities around the world. Truman appointed the leading anti-Communist in his Cabinet, Forrestal, as the first Secretary of Defense, but the act as a whole fell far short of what he, Marshall, and Army Chief of Staff Eisenhower had wanted. They had envisioned the creation of a single armed force, small but efficient, that could move quickly to trouble spots or be expanded rapidly through the draft. Instead they got a loosely federated system with an independent Air Force, and no draft.

The Air Force doctrine was to punish misbehavior through strategic bombing, including the atomic bomb, which made the new service popular with Congress, since massive retaliation seemed a cheap way of providing for national defense. Taft and some other Senators indicated that they were nearly ready to abolish the Army and Navy and concentrate funds on the Air Force. This doctrine, however, did not fit in at all with containment; mass bombardment from the air clearly was not an effective answer to the problems raised in Greece or Hungary or even China. It did appear to be a good way to protect the United States from any mass assault, which indicated that its proponents were retreating to isolation and had not fully accepted the doctrine of containment, with its implication of an active military policy around the world.

The alternative to an American armed force that could stand up to the Communists was one manned by Europeans, but this too had so far failed. The Greek government and army showed scarcely any improvement. In Western Europe, proposing the Marshall Plan had helped to draw a line across the Continent, but the unwillingness of Congress to appropriate money had left the area much too weak to support any sizable armed forces. The last, faint hope of redeeming Eastern Europe through the economic policies of the Marshall Plan had gone aglimmering when Molotov walked out of the Paris Conference. Indeed, the Molotov Plan and the Cominform had made the situation worse.

The Marshall Plan had now become the keystone to containment, and on January 2, 1948, Truman tried to get some action from Congress by dropping the $17 billion request and asking instead for $6.8 billion to cover the first fifteen months of the plan's operation. He got no immediate response.

Then came the Communist coup in Czechoslovakia.

Soviet and American troops had jointly occupied Czechoslovakia after the war. Both sides pulled out on December 1, 1945, although the Soviets kept a number of divisions on Czechoslovakia's borders. Czechoslovakia was, in addition, caught between Poland and eastern Germany on the north and Hungary on the south, which made Soviet influence there pervasive.

In May 1946, Czechoslovakia held her first postwar elections. The Communists won 38 percent of the vote and Klement Gottwald, who had spent World War II in

Moscow, became the Prime Minister. Neither the President, Eduard Benes, nor the foreign minister, Jan Masaryk, were Communist, and both were greatly admired in the West. They tried to maintain a balance between East and West, but in February 1948, Gottwald refused to cooperate with Benes on a plan to reorganize the police and the Cabinet broke up. Gottwald issued an ultimatum for a new government under his power and a Soviet mission flew to Prague to demand Benes's surrender. On February 25, 1948, Benes capitulated and the Communists assumed control. Two weeks later they assassinated Masaryk.

The Czechoslovakian coup did two things absolutely necessary for the adoption of the containment policy. First, as Truman noted, it "sent a shock throughout the civilized world." Americans had regarded Czechoslovakia as a model democracy. Nearly everyone remembered, and discussed, Hitler and Munich. It seemed the same play was about to be performed, ten years later, with new actors. Second, the coup dramatically illustrated the limitations of current American policy, for not only could the United States do nothing to help save Czechoslovakia, it was doing nothing to prevent similar occurrences in the remainder of Europe.

Events now began to rush forward. On March 5, 1948, Clay sent a telegram from Germany. Although "I have felt and held that war was unlikely for at least ten years," the general began, "within the last few weeks, I have felt a subtle change in the Soviet attitude which . . . gives me a feeling that it may come with dramatic suddenness." The Soviet officials in Germany had adopted a new attitude, "faintly contemptuous, slightly arrogant, and certainly assured." On March 11, Marshall described the situation as "very, very serious." Three days later the Senate endorsed the Marshall Plan by a vote of sixty-nine to seventeen.

In Washington, London, and Paris, there was a real war scare. In Europe, France, Britain, and the Benelux countries held a series of meetings in Brussels and on

March 16, 1948, signed the Brussels Treaty, pledging mutual defense arrangements. In the United States, Averell Harriman warned: "There are aggressive forces in the world coming from the Soviet Union which are just as destructive in their effect on the world and our own way of life as Hitler was, and I think are a greater menace than Hitler was."

On March 17, Truman, noting "the grave events in Europe . . . moving so swiftly," canceled an engagement in New York and instead went before Congress. The President declared that the Soviet Union was the "one nation" that was blocking all efforts toward peace. America must, he said, meet "this growing menace . . . to the very survival of freedom." He welcomed the Brussels Treaty and promised to extend American aid to the signatories "to help them to protect themselves."

Truman asked for an immediate favorable vote in the House on the Marshall Plan, but that was only a beginning. He also wanted a resumption of selective service. Even after the Czech coup, however, Congress was not willing to respond wholeheartedly to a call to arms. The House gave Truman the Marshall Plan on March 31 (although it appropriated $4 billion, not the $6.8 billion Truman had requested), but it refused to resume the draft.

The Czech coup had another immediate result with immense long-range consequences. At the end of the war, Truman had abolished the OSS, on the grounds that a Gestapo-like organization was incompatible with American traditions and values. In 1947, Truman had agreed to the creation of the Central Intelligence Agency (CIA) as part of the National Defense Act of that year, but the CIA was not given authority to carry out covert operations abroad. It was restricted to gathering and analyzing intelligence. After the Czech coup, Forrestal set about raising money from his Wall Street friends to create a private clandestine organization to carry out covert actions abroad. Allen Dulles, deputy director of the new CIA, insisted that his organization had to have exclusive control of any such activities. In June 1948, the Truman administration authorized the CIA to engage in a broad range of covert operations directed against the Soviet Union and Communists elsewhere, including political and economic warfare and paramilitary activities.

The immediate fear was the upcoming election in Italy. The Communist Party was strong there, and thanks to the Russians it had plenty of money to spend in the campaign. The CIA countered by placing a few million dollars in the hands of the anti-Communist Christian Democrats, who ended up winning the election. This result, quite naturally, delighted the CIA and impressed the Administration. To have kept Italy out of Communist hands for a relatively minuscule amount of money was a great bargain.

The CIA was off and running, to the eventual dismay of the two men most responsible for giving it a covert mission, Kennan and Truman. Kennan had thought that the CIA might intervene in an occasional European election; in 1975 he confessed to a congressional committee, "It did not work out at all the way I had conceived it." And in 1963, Truman himself had said, "I never had any thought that when I set up the CIA that it would be injected into peacetime cloak-and-dagger operations." Truman's lament was disingenuous, however. He wanted to contain the Communists, and like his successors, he found it convenient to turn the unsavory aspects of the job over to the CIA and then not ask embarrassing questions.

Congressional action on the draft, meanwhile, had indicated that the politicians would not use American boys to contain the Russians. The implementation of the policy of containment was still in debate. One of the Administration's promises about the Marshall Plan, however, had been that it would strengthen Europe's economy to the point where the Europeans could man their own barricades. With invaluable assistance from Soviet actions in Czechoslovakia, the Administra-

tion had gotten agreement on a policy. The Truman
Doctrine and the Marshall Plan had set forth some of
the details of containment in Europe. The rest could
now be worked out. Events in Berlin would help speed
the process.

6

Containment Tested

We are going to stay, period.

HARRY S TRUMAN

In July 1947, when George Kennan's influence within the government was at its peak, he published an article in the journal *Foreign Affairs* entitled "The Sources of Soviet Conduct" and signed only "By X." Its author was soon widely known; its reception nothing short of spectacular. It quickly became the quasi-official statement of American foreign policy.

Kennan argued that the Soviets were motivated by two beliefs: (1) the innate antagonism between capitalism and socialism; and (2) the infallibility of the Kremlin. Their goal was world conquest, but because of the Soviet theory of the inevitability of the eventual fall of capitalism they were in no hurry and had no timetable. The Kremlin's "political action is a fluid stream which moves constantly, wherever it is permitted to move, toward a given goal. Its main concern is to make sure that it has filled every nook and cranny available to it in the basin of world power."

Kennan was an intellectual and he filled the X article with qualifications, although he would later lament that he had not qualified sufficiently and that therefore his article had been misread. He did not believe the Russians posed any serious military threat nor that they wanted war. The challenge Kennan saw was a political and economic one, which should be met on those grounds by "long-term, patient but firm and vigilant containment."

The sentence in Mr. X's article that was most frequently quoted, however, and the one that became the touchstone of American policy, declared that what was needed was "the adroit and vigilant application of counterforce at a series of constantly shifting geographical and political points, corresponding to the shifts and maneuvers of Soviet policy." This implied that crisis would follow crisis around the world, as the Soviet-masterminded conspiracy used its agents to accelerate the flow of Communist power into "every nook and cranny." It also implied that the threat was military, which made it the responsibility of the United States to meet and throw it back wherever it appeared. Containment meant building up the military strength of America and her allies, and a willingness to stand up to the Russians wherever they applied pressure.

The first test came in Berlin, where in June 1948 the Western powers indicated that they intended to go ahead with the formation of a West German government. Simultaneously, the American Joint Chiefs proposed a military alliance with the Brussels powers. They urged the establishment of a central military command for the new organization with an American supreme commander. At the time there were twelve ill-equipped and poorly trained divisions in all Western Europe. The Joint Chiefs wanted eighty-five divisions, which could be had only through extensive rearmament of Western Europe. Unspoken but implicitly understood by everyone involved in the discussions was the fact that the only way to get the required number of men in arms was to use German troops. Because of British, Benelux, and especially French fears, however, this could not be broached at once. The first step was to form a Western Union without Germany but at the same time continue efforts toward West German independence.

Even in the United States, acceptance of the program would not be easy. There were three major objections: the cost; the abandonment of America's historic position of no entangling alliances; and doubts about the wisdom of rearming the Germans. Truman would need all the help he could get. Senator Vandenberg responded handsomely. In early June 1948, he introduced a resolution in the Senate that encouraged "the progressive development of regional and other collective arrangements" for defense and promised to promote the "association of the United States" with such organizations. Vandenberg explicitly repudiated the idea that the United States should help the Europeans in building up a sizable force-in-being. On June 11, the Vandenberg Resolution passed the Senate by a vote of sixty-four to four.

At the beginning of the summer of 1948, the Soviets were thus faced with a series of what they considered threatening developments. The Marshall Plan was beginning to draw the Western European nations closer together. France, Britain, and the Benelux nations had signed a military pact that the United States had officially welcomed and had indicated it intended to join. Americans were already beginning to talk of bringing others into the proposed organization, among them Canada, Portugal, Denmark, Iceland, Norway, and Italy. Since these countries could contribute little to ground defense, the Soviets judged that the Americans wanted them included in order to use their territory for air and sea bases. Equally ominous was the Western determination to give independence to West Germany. In the long run this could only mean that the West intended to merge West Germany into the proposed anti-Soviet military alliance.

Adding to Stalin's difficulties, Marshal Tito in Yugoslavia struck out on an independent course. Truman extended American economic aid to Tito, thus widening the split in the supposedly monolithic Communist bloc. Stalin tried to topple Tito, failed, and in despair expelled Yugoslavia from the Cominform. The example Tito had set, however, could not be so easily dismissed.

Soviet foreign policy, based on an occupied and divided Germany, a weakened Western Europe, and tight control of East Europe, faced total collapse. Whether Stalin had expansive plans is unclear and at least doubtful, but what had happened threatened the security of the Soviet Union itself. The victor in the war was being hemmed in by the West, with the vanquished playing a key role in the new coalition. Worst of all was the Western listening post and outpost in the heart of the Soviet security belt, the Western sector in Berlin.

Stalin responded to these challenges by arguing that since the West had abandoned the idea of German reunification, there was no longer any point to maintaining Berlin as the future capital of all Germany. The Western powers, through the logic of their own acts, ought to retire to their own zones. The Russians clamped down a total blockade on all ground and water traffic to Berlin. The British joined the Americans in a counterblockade on the movement of goods from the east into western Germany.

In the West there was sentiment to abandon Berlin. For many, it seemed foolish to risk World War III for the sake of the ex-Nazis, especially since there was some force to Stalin's argument that if the West was going to create a West Germany nation it had no business staying in eastern Germany. Clay and Truman quickly scotched such talk. As Clay told the War Department, "We have lost Czechoslovakia. Norway is threatened. We retreat from Berlin. When Berlin falls, western Germany will be next." Then all Europe would go Communist. The Americans felt they could not give an inch. Marshall declared, "We had the alternative of following a firm policy in Berlin or accepting the consequences of failure of the rest of our European policy," a statement that described equally well Stalin's feelings. Truman provided the last word in a succinct, simple declaration: "We are going to stay, period."

Clay wanted to shoot his way through the Russian blockade. He thought the United States might just as well find out immediately whether the Russians wanted war or not. Given the ten-to-one disparity of ground strength in Europe, Army Chief of Staff Omar Bradley was able to convince Truman that there must be a better way. It was found with air transport, which soon began flying round-the-clock missions into Berlin, supplying up to 13,000 tons of goods per day. In an amazing performance, American fliers undertook to supply a great city completely from the air, and somehow managed to do it. The Berlin airlift caught the imagination of the world.

The war scare continued. On July 15 the National Security Council decided to send two groups of B-29s to Britain; B-29s were known around the world as the bombers that carried atomic weapons. In his diary Forrestal noted the rationale: (1) it would show the American public "how seriously the government . . . views the current sequence of events"; (2) it would give the air force experience and "would accustom the British" to the presence of the U.S. Air Force; and (3) "we have the opportunity *now* of sending these planes, and once sent they would become somewhat of an accepted fixture," whereas if America waited, the British might change their minds about the wisdom of having American bombers carrying atomic bombs on their soil.

The principle of American forward air bases in Europe had been established; it was obvious that if they were to be effective they would have to be scattered and that there would have to be more of them. Meanwhile, the need for a closer military connection with Western Europe had been emphasized. The draft was reintroduced and the army began to build up. To Kennan's great discomfort, the economic orientation of the Marshall Plan had been nearly forgotten, as containment took on a military look.

There was one part of the world in which the United States and the Soviet Union were operating in cooperation, not confrontation. It was the Middle East. There, the superpowers made the Arabs pay a part of the price for the German death camps. Like so many of the problems of the modern world, Hitler created this one. Zionism, a movement born in Russia, advocated that Jews return to their homeland in Palestine after two thousand years of wandering, in order to establish their own nation. Zionism became a driving force among world Jewry only in response to the Nazi Final Solution. Most of those European Jews who survived the Holocaust had no desire to return to the old country; they wanted to go to Palestine, where a sizable Jewish population had already been built up in the first forty years of the century. Britain had a mandate to govern Palestine. Anxious to placate the Arabs, because of their large oil interests, the British tried to prevent further Jewish immigration into Palestine, while the Jews tried to drive the British out through terroristic tactics, of which the blowing up of a wing of the King David Hotel in Jerusalem (a feat engineered by Menachem Begin, later to become Israeli Prime Minister) was the most famous. Exhausted, the British turned the problem over to the United Nations, where the Soviets and Americans banded together to force a solution on the Arabs. That solution was the partition of Palestine to create a Jewish state along the Mediterranean coast, with almost indefensible borders. On May 14, 1948, Israel proclaimed its independence. The United States was the first country to recognize the new state, Russia a close second. Israel looked to Russia, not to the United States, for the arms she needed to defend herself.

The Arabs invaded, and in the first few weeks the Israelis retreated before the combined might of the Egyptian, Jordanian, Lebanese, Syrian, and Iraqi armies. The Israelis asked the United Nations for help, and once again the United States and the Soviet Union worked together to bring about a four-week truce. During this time, the Israelis procured quantities of heavy arms from Communist Czechoslovakia. When the shooting started again, it was the Israelis who drove their enemies from the field. The United States forced a cease-fire resolution through the United Nations, but it was generally ignored and Israel continued to conquer Arab territory, including western Galilee and parts of the Negev Desert. The Egyptians, their best army surrounded, sued for peace. In what would become a familiar role, American statesman Dr. Ralph Bunche stepped forward in January 1949 to arrange the disengagement of forces. After tortuous negotiations, Bunche arranged for armistice agreements among all the parties.

Israel was born, thanks in part to Russian military support and American negotiating skill. Her boundaries already exceeded those assigned her by the U.N. partition, and included thousands of unhappy Palestinian Arabs. There were, in addition, other Palestinians who had fled or who had been forced out by the fighting, thus beginning the problem of the Palestinian refugee. Another pattern in American relations with Israel began at this time, as President Truman put exceedingly strong pressure on Prime Minister David Ben-Gurion for concessions on both the refugee and boundary issues, only to meet with an indignantly negative response, backed by the veiled threat that the American Jewish community would turn against Truman if he persisted.

Truman, triumphant after his reelection (foreign policy had not been an issue between the major parties in the 1948 campaign), pledged in his Inaugural Address to aid those European nations willing to defend themselves. His Secretary of State, Dean Acheson, pushed forward a treaty with the Europeans. On April 4, 1949, the North Atlantic Treaty was signed in Washington. Britain, France, Belgium, the Netherlands, Italy, Portugal, Denmark, Iceland, Norway, Canada, and the United States pledged themselves to mutual assistance in case of aggression against any of the signatories.

The North American Treaty Organization (NATO) signified the beginning of a new era. In the nineteenth century, America had broken the bonds of a colonial, extractive economy and become a great industrial power, thanks in large part to private European loans. In the first forty-five years of the twentieth century, the United States had gradually achieved a position of equality with Europe. The Marshall Plan, followed by NATO, began in earnest an era of American military, political, and economic dominance over Europe.

In the spring of 1949, Truman enjoyed success after success. The creation of Israel and NATO was followed by a victory in Berlin, where on May 12 the Russians lifted the blockade. They had decided—as Clay had felt they would—that the counterblockade was hurting them more than they were injuring the West, and they realized there was no longer any hope of stopping the movement toward a West German government (the Bonn Republic came into being on May 23, 1949).

It had been a good spring for the President, but trouble lay ahead. The end of the war scare, combined with the fear that NATO was going to cost a good deal of money, began to put an end to bipartisanship in foreign policy. The old issues, buried since Truman's dramatic speech on Greece, reemerged. Should the United States be a world policeman? How much should it pay to play such a role? And, at bottom, what was the nature and extent of the Soviet threat and how should it be met? Thoughtful Republicans, led by Senator Taft, began to question the wisdom of provoking the Soviets thousands of miles from America's shores. In the committee meetings to consider ratification of the NATO Treaty, Congressmen began to ask embarrassing questions about the purpose of NATO.

Senator Henry Cabot Lodge wanted to know if NATO was the beginning of a series of regional organizations designed to hem in the Russians. Acheson reassured him by stressing that no one in the Administration contemplated following NATO with "a Mediterranean pact, and then a Pacific pact, and so forth." Other Senators wondered why the United States did not rely upon the United Nations. One reason was the Russian veto; another was that the Europeans required some sort of special guarantee. Acheson explained that "unity in Europe requires the continuing association and support of the United States. Without it free Europe would split apart."

All these arguments had appeal, but serious questions remained. Could not as much be accomplished through the Marshall Plan? Why permanently split Europe, thereby abandoning any hope of freeing East Europe in the immediate future? What was the substance of the military guarantees that Americans were making or supporting?

The last question was crucial. The West already had

adequate power with the atomic bomb. NATO, as it stood, added nothing to this power. The ground figures remained the same, with the Russians enjoying a ten-to-one advantage. Did the Secretary of State plan to send "substantial" numbers of American troops to Europe? Acheson responded, "The answer to that question, Senator, is a clear and absolute 'No.' " Did he plan to put Germans back in uniform? "We are very clear," Acheson replied, "that the disarmament and demilitarization of Germany must be complete and absolute."

This deepened the mystery rather than clarifying it. What would NATO do? The problem, as French Premier Henri Queuille put it in a much-quoted statement, was easily described: "We know that once Western Europe was occupied, America would again come to our aid and eventually we would again be liberated. But the process would be terrible. The next time you probably would be liberating a corpse." The solution was not so easily seen. In the absence of an imminent attack, neither the Europeans nor the Americans were remotely prepared to undertake the rearmament effort on the required scale to match the Red Army. The Europeans were unwilling to jeopardize their economic revival by building new standing armies.

Each side was trying to carry water on both shoulders. In order to persuade their peoples of the necessity of accepting a provocative alliance, the NATO governments had to insist that the alliance could defend them from invasion. But the governments also had to simultaneously insist that no intolerable sacrifices would be required. As Robert Osgood noted, "These two assurances could only be fulfilled, if at all, by the participation of West Germany in the alliance, but for political reasons this measure was no more acceptable to the European countries than a massive rearmament effort."

The Truman Administration continued to insist that it had no intention of encouraging a German buildup. Nor, the Senators were assured, would NATO lead to an arms race or require the Americans to provide military material to the Europeans. Taft was still opposed to the treaty but was persuaded to vote for it after the Senate specifically repudiated any obligation either to build up the armed forces of the eleven allies or to extend to them continued economic aid for the twenty-year period covered by the treaty. The Senate then ratified the NATO pact by a vote of eighty-four to twelve.

On July 23, 1949, Truman signed the North Atlantic Treaty. It marked the high point of bipartisanship and of containment in Europe. It also completed one phase of the revolution in American foreign policy. For the first time America had entered an entangling alliance in peacetime. American security thereafter could be immediately and drastically affected by changes in the overseas balance of power over which the United States could not exercise much effective control. It meant that the United States was guaranteeing the maintenance of foreign social structures and governments for the next twenty years. It committed the United States to close peacetime military collaboration with the armed services of foreign nations. It signified the extent both of America's break with her past and of her determination to halt Communist expansion.

The presence of Italy (and later Greece and Turkey) among the members of the alliance made a misnomer of the words "North Atlantic" in the title; Portugal's presence weakened the assertion that it was an alliance in defense of democracy. Even weaker was the claim that NATO represented a pact between equals, for the United States had no intention of sharing the control of its atomic weapons with its NATO partners, and the bomb was the only weapon that gave NATO's military posture validity. Acheson's denials to the contrary notwithstanding, the treaty paved the way for German rearmament. It also underscored the European orientation of Truman's foreign policy, an orientation for which he would soon have to pay a price.

First, however, it was the Senate's turn to pay. On the very day that the President signed the NATO Treaty, he presented the bill to Congress. All the assurances that the treaty would not inaugurate an arms race or cost the

United States anything were brushed aside. Truman sent to Congress a Mutual Defense Assistance Bill asking for $1.5 billion for European military aid. The President described the object in modest terms: "The military assistance which we propose for these countries will be limited to that which is necessary to help them create mobile defensive forces"; in other words, to equip and bring up to strength Europe's twelve or so divisions.

There was immediate opposition. Such a limited program would hardly give a "tangible assurance" to the peoples of Western Europe that they would be protected from the Red Army. The Military Assistance Program of 1949 was, obviously, only a small down payment on a large long-term investment. Senator Taft and other skeptics said this would never do, for the military assistance would be large enough only to provoke the Russians and precipitate an arms race without being adequate to halt the Red Army. Taft charged that the Administration was committing the United States to a futile, obsolete, and bankrupt strategy of defending Europe by large-scale land warfare. He much preferred a unilateral American defense of Europe through building up the American air force and stepping up the production of atomic bombs.

This got to the heart of the matter, for in point of fact the meaning of NATO was that the United States promised to use the bomb to deter a Russian attack. The only alternative was to build up Western ground strength to match the Red Army, a politically impossible task.

The United States's promise to use the bomb to deter Russian aggression made sense only if the Americans had bases in Europe from which to deliver the bombs and if the Americans retained their nuclear monopoly. The great need was bases for American bombers, which was the first and most important accomplishment of NATO. This, however, could have been accomplished through bilateral agreements and did not require a multinational treaty; it also did not require military aid to the NATO countries. Opposition to Truman's Military Assistance Program continued.

Then, on September 22, 1949, the President announced that the Soviets had exploded an atomic bomb. "This is now a different world," Vandenberg painfully recorded. It was indeed. The urge to do something, anything, was irrepressible. Six days later Congress sent the NATO appropriations to the President for his approval. Truman ordered the development of the hydrogen bomb accelerated. Nothing, however, could change the fact that America's promise to defend Europe with the bomb had been dissipated almost before it had been given. If the Russians could make the bomb, they surely could develop the means to deliver it, first to Western European targets and then to the United States itself. The Soviets now had two trumps, the bomb and the Red Army, to the West's one.

German remilitarization and Western Europe rearmament was the obvious way to counter the Red Army threat. The Americans could pay the bill, in an updated version of lend-lease. But the Europeans were suspicious, and France especially so. Europeans could see little point in accepting American arms if it also meant accepting American orders, the central problem in NATO both then and later. A strategy that used American equipment and European lives to counter the Red Army had little appeal to the Europeans, especially since only the Americans could decide when or where to use the troops, only the Americans could pull the nuclear trigger, and the battlefield where Russia and America would fight it out was Europe.

If the Europeans would not rearm, the Americans would have to do so themselves. Here the problem, as Samuel Huntington stated it, was "Could a democracy arm to deter or could it only arm to respond?" An election year was coming up. The House was changing Truman's tax-revision bill into a tax-reduction bill. The Soviet threat was largely theoretical—the Red Army had not marched beyond the position it held in May of 1945, not even into Czechoslovakia. How much support, if any beyond what they were already paying, would the American people give to a policy of deterrence designed to forestall a threat that could only with difficulty be seen to endanger American security? Billions of dollars would be needed. Even if the taxpayers agreed to pay the bill, could the economy afford it? These were serious questions, but so were the ones on the other side. Could America afford not to rearm? Would not the failure to do so automatically abandon Western Europe to the Communists? It seemed to many in the government that it would.

In Asia the problem had reached crisis proportions. Mao's troops were on the verge of driving Chiang off the mainland. American support for Chiang had been limited and halting, partly because of the Europe-first orientation of the Truman administration, mainly because of the budget ceilings within which the Congress forced the government to operate. Millions of Americans believed that more aid would have saved Chiang. A great nation had been "lost" to Communism because Congress was stingy.

This widespread attitude underscored one of the basic assumptions of American foreign policy during the Cold War. Americans high and low implicitly assumed that with good policies and enough will, the United States could control events anywhere. If things did go wrong, if Poland or China did fall to the enemy, it could only have happened because of mistakes, not because there were areas of the world in which what America did or wanted made little difference. The assumption that in the end every situation was controllable and could be made to come out as the United States wished—what Senator William Fulbright later called "the arrogance of power"—colored almost all foreign-policy decisions in the early Cold War. It also prepared the way for the right-wing charge that the Truman administration was shot through with traitors, for there could be no other explanation for American failures.

The roots of the assumption were deep and complex. The American belief that the United States was different from and better than other countries was part of it. American success in 1917-18 and 1941-45 contributed to the conceit that the United States could order the world. So did the feeling of power that came with a monopoly of the atomic bomb, American productivity, and the American military position at the conclusion of World War II. There were racial connotations to the idea. Although most Americans were too sophisticated to talk about the "white man's burden" and the "little brown brothers," they still believed in white superiority.

Given all the power America had at her disposal, given American goodwill, and given the eagerness of peoples everywhere to follow the American example, how had it happened that East Europe and China fell to the Communists? The junior Senator from Wisconsin, Joseph R. McCarthy, had one answer. On February 9, 1950, in a speech at Wheeling, West Virginia, he declared, "I have in my hand 57 cases of individuals [in the State Department] who would appear to be either card-carrying members or certainly loyal to the Communist Party, but who nevertheless are helping to shape our foreign policy." A few days later the figure had gone up to 205 Communists in the department; at another time the figure was 81. The charge, however, was consistent—America had been betrayed.

McCarthy's charges came less than eight weeks after Chiang fled to Formosa, five days before the Soviet Union and Communist China signed a thirty-year mutual-aid treaty, and three weeks before Klaus Fuchs was found guilty of giving atomic secrets to agents of the Soviet Union. The last was, perhaps, the most important cause of the spectacular popularity of McCarthy and of the forces he represented, for it seemed to be the only explanation of how the backward Russians matched America's achievements in atomic development so quickly. McCarthyism swept the country. The Republicans suddenly had an issue that could bring them, after twenty years ("twenty years of treason," according to McCarthy), back to power.

McCarthy never had a majority of the public behind him, but he nevertheless enjoyed broad support, and the threat he represented was real. The Federal government, to fight back, strengthened and extended its loyalty investigations. At times it seemed that everyone in America was checking on everyone else for possible Communist leanings. Millions of Americans agreed with McCarthy's basic premise—America had failed in the Cold War not because of inherent limitations on her power, nor because of her refusal to rearm, but because of internal treason. Even those public figures who did speak out against McCarthy—and their numbers were few—objected to his methods, not his assumptions. The opponents also wanted to ferret out the guilty, but they insisted that the rights of the innocent should be protected.

There was an *Alice in Wonderland* quality to the entire uproar. Truman administration officials, up to and including Acheson, had to defend themselves from charges that began with their being soft on Communism and escalated to treason. The Democrats were bewildered and angry. With some justice, they wondered what more they could have done to stand up to the Russians, especially in view of the funds available, funds drastically limited by the very Republicans who now demanded blood for the State Department's shortcomings. Chickens had come home to roost. From the time Truman had "scared hell out of the American people" in March of 1947 to the explosion of the Russian bomb and the loss of China in 1949, Democratic officials in the State Department had been stressing the worldwide threat of Communism along with the danger of internal subversion in foreign governments. McCarthy and his adherents followed the same path, only they went farther along it.

There was in McCarthyism an appeal to the inland prejudice against the eastern-seaboard establishment and the things it stood for in the popular mind—the New Deal, among others. Anti-intellectualism was always prominent in the movement. McCarthy drew strong support from those Asia-firsters who had been opposed to the trend of American foreign policy, with its European orientation, at least since the early days of World War

II. Americans of East European origin were among the first to flock to McCarthy's standard; much of the Catholic Church in America came with them. Above all, McCarthy provided a simple answer to those who were frustrated as America seemed to suffer defeat after defeat in the Cold War.

One of the appeals of the McCarthy explanation of the world situation was that it would not cost much to set things right. All that was required was to eliminate the Communists in the State Department. Few of McCarthy's supporters, and none of those like Senator Taft who tolerated him, were ready to go to war with Russia to liberate the satellites or to send millions of American troops to China to restore Chiang. They did want to root out those who had sold out America at Yalta, Potsdam, and in China; then, with honest patriots in the State Department, world events would develop in accordance with American wishes.

The Administration could not accept such a limited program for the Cold War, but it too wanted the same results. It was difficult, however, to develop a comprehensive program in this atmosphere of fear, even hysteria. Nevertheless, something had to be done. China had been lost. Russia did have the bomb. The Europeans were not willing to assume the burden of rearmament. The McCarthy assault was there. The United States had practically no usable ground power. And the President, primarily for domestic political purposes, was still trying to cut the budget. His new Secretary of Defense, Louis Johnson, had set out to "cut the fat" from the Defense Department. He began by canceling the Navy's supercarrier. Truman set a limit of $13 billion for defense in the upcoming budget, by no stretch of the imagination enough to support a get-tough-with-the-Russians stance. American foreign policy had arrived at a crossroads.

On January 30, 1950, President Truman had authorized the State and Defense departments "to make an over all review and re-assessment of American foreign and defense policy in the light of the loss of China, the Soviet mastery of atomic energy and the prospect of the fusion bomb." Through February, March, and early April, as events whirled around it, a State-Defense committee met. By April 12 it had a report ready, which Truman sent to the National Security Council. It came back as an NSC policy paper, number 68; it was, as Walter LeFeber says, "one of the key historical documents of the Cold War." NSC 68, Senator Henry Jackson declared, was "the first comprehensive statement of a national strategy."

As one of the principal authors stated, NSC 68 advocated "an immediate and large-scale build-up in our military and general strength and that of our allies with the intention of righting the power balance and in the hope that through means other than all-out war we could induce a change in the nature of the Soviet system." How the change was to be brought about was unclear, except that it would not be through war. NSC 68 postulated that while the West waited for the Soviets to mellow, the United States should rearm and thereby prevent any Russian expansion. The program did not look to the liberation of China or of Eastern Europe, but it did call on the United States to assume unilaterally the defense of the non-Communist world.

NSC 68 represented the practical extension of the Truman Doctrine, which had been worldwide in its implications but limited to Europe in its application. The document provided the justification for America's assuming the role of world policeman and came close to saying that all change was directed by the Communists and should therefore be resisted. NSC 68 also assumed that if America were willing to try, it could stop change. This was satisfying to the McCarthyites, but the willingness to abandon East Europe, China, and Russia to Communism was not. The McCarthyites, however, had no very clear idea on how to liberate the enslaved peoples either.

NSC 68 was realistic in assessing what it would cost America to become the world policeman. State Department officials estimated that defense expenditures of $35 billion a year would be required to implement the program of rearming America and NATO. Eventually, more could be spent, for NSC 68 declared that the United States was so rich it could use 20 percent of its gross national product for arms without suffering national bankruptcy. In 1950 this would have been $50 billion.

That was a great deal of money, even for Americans. It was necessary, however, because the danger was so great. The document foresaw "an indefinite period of tension and danger" and warned that by 1954 the Soviet Union would have the nuclear capability to destroy the United States. America had to undertake "a bold and massive program" of rebuilding the West until it far surpassed the Soviet bloc; only thus could it stand at the "political and material center with other free nations in variable orbits around it." The United States could no longer ask, "How much security can we afford?" nor could it attempt to "distinguish between national and global security."

Truman recognized, as he later wrote, that NSC 68 "meant a great military effort in time of peace. It meant doubling or tripling the budget, increasing taxes heavily, and imposing various kinds of economic controls. It meant a great change in our normal peacetime way of doing things." He refused to allow publication of NSC 68 and indicated that he would do nothing about revising the budget until after the congressional elections. He realized that without a major crisis there was little chance of selling the program to the Congress or the public. He himself had only two and a half years to serve, while NSC 68 contemplated a long-term program. If the Republicans entered the White House, the chances were that their main concern would be to lower the budget, in which case the nation would have to wait for the return of the Democrats to really get NSC 68 rolling. Thus, when Truman received NSC 68 in its final form in early June 1950, he made no commitment. What he would have done with it had not other events intruded is problematical.

While Truman was studying the paper, he may have noted a sentence that declared it should be American policy to meet "each fresh challenge promptly and unequivocally." If so, he was about to have an opportunity to put it into practice. The crisis that would allow him to implement NSC 68 was at hand.

[An all-out war with China] would be the wrong war at the wrong time in the wrong place against the wrong enemy.

GENERAL OMAR BRADLEY

Truman had pried the money for containment in Europe from a reluctant Congress only with the help of the crises in Greece and Czechoslovakia. In June 1950 he badly needed another crisis, one that would allow him to prove to the American people that he and the Democratic Party were not soft on Communism, to extend containment to Asia, to shore up Chiang's position on Formosa, to retain American bases in Japan, and most of all to rearm America and NATO. The whole package envisioned in NSC 68, in short, could be wrapped up and tied with a ribbon by an Asian crisis.

The possibilities were there. In China, Mao's armies were being deployed for an assault on Formosa, where the remnants of Chiang's forces had retreated. The United States had stopped all aid to Chiang, thereby arousing the fury of the Republicans. Truman was under intense pressure to resume the shipment of supplies to the Nationalist Chinese. Former President Herbert Hoover joined with Senator Taft in demanding that the U.S. Pacific Fleet be used to prevent an invasion of Formosa.

In Japan, the United States was preparing to write a unilateral peace treaty with that country, complete with agreements that would give the United States military bases in Japan on a long-term basis. But in early 1950 the Japanese Communist Party staged a series of violent demonstrations against American military personnel in

Tokyo. Even moderate Japanese politicians were wary of granting base rights to the American forces. The U.S. Air Force was confronted with the possibility of losing its closest airfields to the eastern Soviet Union.

In Korea all was tension. Postwar Soviet-American efforts to unify the country, where American troops had occupied the area south of the thirty-eighth parallel and Russia the area to the north, had achieved nothing. In 1947 the United States had submitted the Korean question to the U.N. General Assembly for disposition. Russia refused to go along. Elections were held anyway in South Korea in May 1948 under U.N. supervision. Syngman Rhee became President of the Republic of Korea. The Russians set up a Communist puppet government in North Korea. Both the United States and the Soviets withdrew their occupation troops; both continued to give military aid to their respective sides, although the Russians did so on a larger scale.

Rhee was a rigid right-wing leader and thus something of an embarrassment to the United States. In April 1950, Acheson told Rhee flatly that he had to hold elections. Rhee agreed, but his own party collected only 48 seats in the Assembly, with 120 going to other parties, mostly on the left. The new Assembly immediately began to press for unification, even if on North Korean terms. Rhee was on the verge of losing control of his government.

Rhee's position was also tenuous because he was losing American backing, despite having held free elections. On May 2, 1950, Senator Tom Connally, Chairman of the Senate Foreign Relations Committee, said he was afraid that South Korea would have to be abandoned. He thought the Communists were going to overrun Korea when they got ready, just as they "probably will overrun Formosa." Connally said that he did not think Korea was "very greatly important. It has been testified before us that Japan, Okinawa, and the Philippines make the chain of defense which is absolutely necessary." His statement was widely reported in the United States and Japan, causing consternation in both MacArthur's headquarters in Tokyo and in Rhee's capital, Seoul. Connally's position was consistent with the entire policy of the Truman administration to date,* but it ran counter to the thoughts just then being set down in NSC 68, and with the concurrent rise of McCarthyism, the abandonment of Rhee and Chiang was rapidly becoming a political liability of the first magnitude.

By June 1950 a series of desperate needs had come together. Truman had to have a crisis to sell the NSC 68 program; Chiang could not hold on to Formosa nor Rhee in South Korea without an American commitment; the U.S Air Force and Navy needed a justification to retain their bases in Japan; the Democrats had to prove to the McCarthyites that they could stand up to the Communists in Asia as well as in Europe. The needs were met on June 25, 1950, when North Korean troops crossed the thirty-eighth parallel in force.

Within hours of the attack, Truman moved boldly. He began with a massive diplomatic counterattack. In the Security Council the United States pushed through a resolution branding the North Koreans as aggressors, demanding a cessation of hostilities, and requesting a withdrawal behind the thirty-eighth parallel. The resolution's sweeping nature gave the United States the advantage of United Nations approval and support for military action in Korea. This was the first time ever that an international organization had actually taken concrete steps to halt and punish aggression (Russia failed to veto the resolution because she was boycotting the United Nations at the time because it refused to give Chiang's seat on the Security Council to Mao), and it lifted spirits throughout the country. Despite the U.N. involvement, however, the overwhelming bulk of equipment used in Korea and the overwhelming number of non-Korean fighting men came from the United States.

They came almost immediately. On June 26, the day

*Secretary of State Acheson had made identical remarks in February 1950.

after the assault, in a statement released at noon from
the White House, the President formally extended the
Truman Doctrine to the Pacific by pledging the United
States to military intervention against any further expansion of Communist rule in Asia. He announced that
he was extending military aid to the French, who were
fighting Ho Chi Minh and the Viet Minh in Indochina,
and to the Philippines, where the Huks continued to
challenge the government. Truman also ordered the Seventh Fleet to "prevent any attack on Formosa," declaring
that the determination of Formosa's future status "must
await the restoration of security in the Pacific, a peace
settlement with Japan, or consideration by the United
Nations." America had thus become involved in the
Chinese civil war, the Philippines' insurrection, and the
war of national liberation in Indochina, in one day.

Simultaneously the United States entered the Korean
War. Truman announced that he had "ordered United
States air and sea forces to give the Korean Government
troops cover and support." His Air Force advisers had
convinced him that America's bombers would be able to
stop the aggression in Korea by destroying the Communist supply lines. Truman believed that it was possible
to defeat the North Koreans without any commitment
of American ground troops, just as he evidently expected that the French could defeat Ho Chi Minh without having to use American soldiers.

Truman tried to limit the sweeping nature of his actions by carefully refraining from linking the Russians
to the Korean attack. On the day of his White House
announcement Truman sent a note to Moscow assuring
Stalin that American objectives were limited and expressing the hope that the Soviets would help in restoring the status quo ante bellum. This implied that all the
United States wished to do was to contain, not conquer,
North Korea.

The underlying assumption of Truman's approach to
the war was that Communist aggression in Asia could be
stopped at a fairly low cost in lives. American money and
equipment would do the job in Indochina and the Phil-

ippines; the American navy would save Chiang; American bombers would force the North Koreans to pull back. Much of this was wishful thinking. It was partly based on the American Air Force's strategic doctrine and its misreading of the lessons of air power in World War II, partly on the racist attitude that Asians could not stand up to Western guns, and partly on the widespread notion that Communist governments had no genuine support. Lacking popularity, the Communists would be afraid to commit their troops to battle, and if they did, the troops would not fight.

That last point was a big mistake. The North Korean Army drove the South Korean Army down the peninsula in a headlong retreat. American bombing missions hardly slowed the aggressors. The South Koreans fell back in such a panic that two days after Truman sent in the Air Force he was faced with another major decision: He would either have to send in American troops to save the position, which meant accepting a much higher cost for the war, or else face the loss of all Korea, at a time when the Republicans were screaming, "Who lost China?"

On June 30, Truman ordered United States troops stationed in Japan to proceed to Korea. America was now at war on the mainland. The President promised that more troops would soon be on their way from the United States. In an attempt to keep the war and its cost limited, he emphasized that the United States aimed only "to restore peace and . . . the border." At the United Nations, the Americans announced that their purpose was the simple one of restoring the thirty-eighth parallel as the dividing line. The policy, in other words, was containment, not rollback.

It had been arrived at unilaterally, for Truman had not consulted his European or Asian allies, not to mention Congress, before acting. Once again, as in FDR's war in the Atlantic in the summer of 1941, the United States found itself at war without the Constitutionally required congressional declaration.

In Korea, American reinforcements arrived just in

time, and together with the South Koreans they held on the Pusan bridgehead through June and July. By the beginning of August, it was clear that MacArthur would not be forced out of Korea and that when MacArthur's troops broke out of the perimeter they would be able to destroy the North Korean Army.

In Washington there was a surge of optimism. Perhaps it was possible to do more than contain the Communists. MacArthur wanted to reunify Korea, an idea that found great favor in the White House. It would mean rollback, not containment, and thus represented a major policy change, but the opportunity was too tempting to pass up. On September 1, Truman announced that the Koreans had a right to be "free, independent, and united." Pyongyang, the Americans boasted, would be "the first Iron Curtain capital" to be liberated. This seemed to imply that others would follow.

The risks were obvious. Truman moved to minimize them by building up American military strength. Congress had voted all the funds he had requested for defense since June; on September 9, he announced that the rapid increase in the Army would continue and that he was sending "substantial" numbers of new troops to Europe. Simultaneously, Acheson met with the British and French foreign ministers at the Waldorf Astoria Hotel in New York City. On September 12, he dropped— as one official called it—"the bomb at the Waldorf." The United States proposed the creation of ten German divisions. French and British protests were loud and numerous, but Acheson insisted. To make German rearmament on such a scale palatable to the Europeans, the United States sent four divisions to Europe, and three months later Truman appointed Eisenhower, who was extremely popular and trusted in Europe, as the supreme commander of an integrated NATO force.

On September 15, MacArthur successfully outflanked the North Koreans with an amphibious landing at Inchon, far up the Korean peninsula. In a little more than a week, MacArthur's troops were in the capital, Seoul, and they had cut off the North Korean forces around

Pusan. On September 27, the Joint Chiefs ordered MacArthur to destroy the enemy army and authorized him to conduct military operations north of the thirty-eighth parallel. On October 7, American troops crossed the parallel. The same day the United Nations approved (forty-seven to five) an American resolution endorsing the action.

MacArthur's broad authority to invade North Korea, it is important to note, came after full discussion and consideration at the highest levels of the American government. Truman, with the full concurrence of the State and Defense departments and the Joint Chiefs, made the decision to liberate North Korea and accept the risks involved, changing the political objective of the war from containment to liberation.

The Chinese issued a series of warnings, culminating with a statement to India for transmission to the United States, that China would not "sit back with folded hands and let the Americans come to the border." When even this was ignored, the Chinese publicly stated on October 10 that if the Americans continued north, they would enter the conflict. The Russians were more cautious, but when on October 9 some American jet aircraft strafed a Soviet airfield only a few miles from Vladivostok, they sent a strong protest to Washington. Truman immediately decided to fly to the Pacific to see MacArthur and make sure he restrained the Air Force. Fighting Chinese forces in Korea was one thing, war with Russia another. The Americans were willing to try to liberate Pyongyang, but they were not ready to liberate Moscow.

The Truman-MacArthur meeting at Wake Island in October accomplished its main purpose, for the Air Force thereafter confined its activities to the Korean peninsula. More important was what it revealed. Commentators have concentrated almost exclusively on MacArthur's statement that the Chinese would not dare enter the war. On this point, everybody—not just MacArthur—was wrong. Other differences between Truman and MacArthur were more those of method than of goals. MacArthur was excessively dramatic in the way he put things and he had a millennial quality about him, but like Truman his immediate aim was to liberate North Korea. At various times he indicated that he also wanted to help Chiang back on to the mainland, a long-range goal that Truman had not accepted as realistic, but for the immediate future the general and the President were together. They differed on means: MacArthur was not at all sure he could unify Korea without striking at the Chinese bases across the Yalu. Truman, more concerned about Europe and the dangers there, especially since neither the German nor the American rearmament programs were yet well under way, insisted on keeping limits on the area of military operations.

MacArthur advanced into North Korea on two widely separated routes, with his middle wide open. The Chinese poured thousands of "volunteers" into the gap and soon sent MacArthur's men reeling. In two weeks the Chinese cleared much of North Korea, isolated MacArthur's units into three bridgeheads, and completely reversed the military situation.

The Americans, who had walked into the disaster together, split badly on the question of how to get out. MacArthur said he now faced "an entirely new war" and indicated that the only solution was to strike at China itself. But war against China might well mean war against Russia, which Truman was not prepared to accept. Instead, the administration decided to return to the pre-Inchon policy of restoring the status quo ante bellum in Korea while building NATO strength in Europe. All talk of liberating iron curtain capitals disappeared. Never again would the United States attempt by force of arms to free a Communist state.

A lesson had been learned, but not fully accepted immediately, and it was enormously frustrating. Just how frustrating became clear on November 30, when at a press conference Truman called for a worldwide mobilization against Communism and, in response to a question, declared that if military action against China was authorized by the United Nations, MacArthur might be empowered to use the atomic bomb at his discretion.

Truman casually added that there had always been active consideration of the bomb's use, for after all it was one of America's military weapons.

Much alarmed, British Prime Minister Attlee flew to Washington, fearful that Truman really would use the bomb for the third time in five years against an Asian people. Attlee, in a series of meetings, hammered away at the Americans. There was much talk in Washington (and Tokyo) of pulling out of Korea altogether. Attlee thought that if this were done the humiliation of defeat would lead the Americans to an all-out war with China. He suspected that such a development was exactly what MacArthur had in mind. Truman, Acheson, Bradley, and the newly appointed Secretary of Defense, General Marshall, all assured Attlee that every effort would be made to stay in Korea and then promised that as long as MacArthur held on there would be no atomic bombs dropped.

With Attlee's departure, Truman and Acheson quickened the pace of their policy. They accomplished so much that by the end of January 1951 only the most extreme McCarthyite could complain that they were ignoring the Communist threat. Truman put the nation on a Cold War footing. He got emergency powers from Congress to expedite war mobilization, reintroduced selective service, submitted a $50 billion defense budget that followed the guidelines of NSC 68, sent two more divisions (a total of six) to Europe, doubled the number of air groups to ninety-five, obtained new bases in Morocco, Libya, and Saudi Arabia, increased the Army by 50 percent to 3.5 million men, pushed forward the Japanese peace treaty, stepped up aid to the French in Vietnam, initiated the process of adding Greece and Turkey to NATO, and began discussions with Franco that led to American aid to Fascist Spain in return for military bases there.

Truman's accomplishments were breathtaking. He had given the United States a thermonuclear bomb (March 1951) and rearmed Germany. He pushed through a peace treaty with Japan (signed in September

1951) that excluded the Russians and gave the Americans military bases, allowed for Japanese rearmament and unlimited industrialization, and encouraged a Japanese boom by dismissing British, Australian, Chinese, and other demands for reparations. Truman extended American bases around the world, hemming in both Russia and China. He had learned, in November of 1950, not to push beyond the iron and bamboo curtains, but he had made sure that if any Communist showed his head on the free side of the line, someone—usually an American—would be there to shoot him.

There had to be a price. It was best summed up by Walter Millis, himself a Cold Warrior and a great admirer of Forrestal. The Truman administration, Millis wrote, left behind it "an enormously expanded military establishment, beyond anything we had ever contemplated in time of peace. . . . It evoked a huge and apparently permanent armament industry, now wholly dependent . . . on government contracts. The Department of Defense had become without question the biggest industrial management operation in the world; the great private operations, like General Motors, du Pont, the leading airplane manufacturers had assumed positions of monopoly power. . . ." The Administration produced thermonuclear supergiant weapons, families of lesser atomic bombs, guided missiles, the B-52 jet bomber, new supercarriers and tanks and other heavy weapons. It had increased the risk of war while making war immeasurably more dangerous.

Truman gave America power and a policy, but it seemed to many that with all the power he had generated, and the justification he had given for the policy, the policy itself was much too modest. Containment had never been very satisfying emotionally, built as it was on the constant reiteration of the Communist threat and the line that divided the world into areas that were free and those that were enslaved. Millions of Americans wanted to accept their Christian obligation and free the slaves. Other millions wanted to destroy, not just contain, the Communist threat, on the grounds that if it were allowed to exist, the Cold War would go on forever, at a constantly increased cost. There were those who felt that the only justification for a garrison state was the old one of putting it on a temporary basis, which was to say, to fight a war to destroy the threat.

This criticism of the Truman-Acheson foreign policy, which centered around the towering figure of Mac-Arthur, turned Attlee's criticism on its head. The Prime Minister had warned the Americans that they could not do it all alone, not forever anyway. He said they would either have to fight all out in Asia or negotiate, and he urged them to negotiate. MacArthur wanted to fight all out. American liberals derided MacArthur and his followers for the simplicity of their views, but there was no denying MacArthur's appeal or the frustration built into the containment program, an appeal and a frustration based on Truman's and Acheson's own descriptions of the world scene.

If America made permanent Cold War its policy, with a commitment to continuous military superiority to back an attitude of unrelenting hostility toward China and Russia, without ever doing anything to destroy the Communist nations, it would be accepting permanent tension, permanent risk, and a permanent postponement of the social and economic promises of the New Deal.

The difference in outlook soon erupted into one of the great emotional events of American history. In January and February 1951, MacArthur resumed the offensive and drove the Chinese and North Koreans back. By March he was again at the thirty-eighth parallel. The Administration was now ready to negotiate. MacArthur sabotaged the efforts to obtain a ceasefire by crossing the parallel and by demanding an unconditional surrender from the Chinese. Truman was furious. He decided to remove the general at the first opportunity.

It came shortly. On April 5, Representative Joseph W. Martin, Jr., a Republican, read to the House a letter from MacArthur calling for a new foreign policy. The general wanted to reunify Korea, unleash Chiang for an attack on the mainland, and fight Communism in Asia rather than in Europe. "Here in Asia," he said, "is where the Communist conspirators have elected to make their play for global conquest. Here we fight Europe's war with arms while the diplomats there still fight it with words."

Aside from the problem of a soldier challenging presidential supremacy by trying to set foreign policy, the debate centered on the doctrine of containment. Initially MacArthur had a large majority of the people with him. After Truman had relieved him of his command, MacArthur returned to the United States to receive a welcome that would have made Caesar envious. Public opinion polls showed that three out of every four Americans disapproved of the way Truman was conducting the war.

The American people seemed to be rejecting containment, and Truman had rejected victory; that left only Attlee's alternative of peace. Even Attlee, however, had wanted peace only in Asia, and as Truman pointed out to him time and again, Congress would not accept a policy of intervention in Europe and isolation in Asia. As it was, Truman was in trouble because he spent most of the money Congress voted for defense on NATO at a time when most Americans wanted the effort to go into Korea. If the Korean War came to a sudden end, so would NSC 68 and the entire program that went with it.

The pressure from the United Nations and the NATO allies to negotiate could not be totally ignored, however, and on July 10, 1951, peace talks—without a ceasefire—began. They broke down on July 12. For the remainder of the year they were on again, off again. The front lines began to stabilize around the thirty-eighth parallel while American casualties dropped to an "acceptable" weekly total. The war—and rearmament—continued.

Truman had won. Administration witnesses at the MacArthur hearings in the Senate (held to examine foreign policy and MacArthur's dismissal) argued convincingly that America could neither destroy Russia or China nor allow them to expand. Public opinion swung back to Truman. America remained committed to contain-

⸺ht and permanent Cold War. MacArthur's alternative of victory, like Attlee's of peace in Asia, had been rejected. America girded for the long haul.

→The Cold War would be fought Truman's way. There would be clashes on the periphery but none between the major powers. America would extend her positions of strength around the Communist empire. The military-industrial complex in the United States would become a major social and economic force. The United States would make no settlement or compromise with Russia or China. America would build up the mightiest armed force the world had ever known and, if necessary, defend the barricades of freedom alone.

When Truman became President, he led a nation anxious to return to traditional civil-military relations and the historic American foreign policy of noninvolvement. When he left the White House, his legacy was an American presence on every continent of the world and an enormously expanded armament industry. He had turned America decisively away from the policy of the 1930s of unilateral disarmament and neutrality to an arms build-up and collective security. He had established the policy of containment of America's enemies rather than their destruction. The measure of his triumph was that all his successors stayed with his policies.

[8]

Eisenhower, Dulles, and the Irreconcilable Conflict

It is now clear that we are facing an implacable enemy whose avowed objective is world domination by whatever means and at whatever cost. There are no rules in such a game. Hitherto acceptable norms of human conduct do not apply. We must develop effective espionage and counterespionage services and must learn to subvert, sabotage and destroy our enemies by more clever, more sophisticated, and more effective methods than those used against us.

The Doolittle Committee,
charged by President Eisenhower
in 1955 to investigate and
report to him on activities
of the CIA

"We can never rest," General Eisenhower declared during his 1952 campaign for the presidency, "until the enslaved nations of the world have in the fullness of freedom the right to choose their own path, for then, and then only, can we say that there is a possible way of living peacefully and permanently with Communism in the world." Like most campaign statements, Eisenhower's bowed to both sides of the political spectrum. For the bold he indicated a policy of liberation, while the cautious could take comfort in his willingness to someday live peacefully with the Communists.

The emphasis was on liberation. John Foster Dulles, the Republican expert on foreign policy, author of the Japanese peace treaty, and soon to be Secretary of State, was more explicit than Eisenhower. Containment, he charged, was a treadmill policy "which, at best might perhaps keep us in the same place until we drop exhausted." It cost far too much in taxes and was "not designed to win victory conclusively." One plank in the Republican platform damned containment as "negative, futile and immoral," for it abandoned "countless human beings to a despotism and Godless terrorism." It hinted that the Republicans, once in power, would roll back the atheistic tide. Rollback would come not only in East Europe but also in Asia. The platform denounced the "Asia-last" policy of the Democrats and said, "We have no intention to sacrifice the East to gain time for the West."

The Eisenhower landslide in the 1952 election was a compound of many factors, the chief being the general's enormous personal popularity. Corruption in the Truman administration and the McCarthy charges of Communist infiltration into the government also helped ("There are no Communists in the Republican Party," one platform plank piously declared). So did Eisenhower's promise to go to Korea and end the war there. But one of the major appeals of the Eisenhower-Dulles team was its rejection of containment. The Republican pledge to do something about Communist enslavement—it was never clear exactly what—brought millions of former Democratic voters into the Republican fold, especially those of East European descent. Eisenhower reaped where McCarthy sowed. Far from rejecting internationalism and retreating to isolationism, the Republicans were proposing to go beyond containment. They would be more internationalist than Truman.

Republican promises to liberate the enslaved, like nineteenth-century abolitionist programs to free the Negro slaves, logically led to only one policy. Since the slaveholders would not voluntarily let the oppressed go, and since the slaves were too tightly controlled to stage their own revolution, those who wished to see the slaves freed would have to fight to free them. In the second half of the twentieth century, however, war was a much different proposition than it had been a hundred years earlier.

Freeing the slaves would lead to the destruction of much of the world; most of the slaves themselves would die in the process.

There was another major constraint on action. The Republicans were wedded to conservative fiscal views that stressed the importance of balancing the budget and cutting taxes. All of Eisenhower's leading Cabinet figures, save Dulles, were businessmen who believed that an unbalanced federal budget was immoral. Government expenditures could be reduced significantly, however, only by cutting the Defense Department budget, which the Republicans proceeded to do. The cuts made liberation even more difficult.

In Korea, in July 1953, Eisenhower accepted an armistice that restored the status quo ante bellum. General MacArthur, President Rhee, and many Republicans were furious. They wanted to fight on until North Korea was liberated, a policy they thought Eisenhower had endorsed in his "We shall never rest" statement. But Eisenhower, after considering and rejecting the use of atomic weapons, decided that the price of victory was too high, and instead made peace.

In practice, therefore, Eisenhower and Dulles continued the policy of containment. There was no basic difference between their foreign policy and that of Truman and Acheson. Their campaign statements frequently haunted them, but they avoided embarrassment over their lack of action through their rhetoric. "We can never rest," Eisenhower had said, but rest they did, except in their speeches, which expressed perfectly the assumptions and desires of millions of Americans.

Better than anyone else, Dulles described the American view of Communism. A devout Christian and highly successful corporate lawyer, Dulles's unshakeable beliefs were based on American ideas. They differed hardly at all from those of Truman, Acheson, Main Street in Iowa City, or Madison Avenue in New York City. All the world wanted to be like America; the common people everywhere looked to America for leadership; Communism was unmitigated evil imposed by a conspiracy on helpless people, whether it came from the outside as in East Europe or from within as in Asia; there could be no permanent reconciliation with Communism because "this is an irreconcilable conflict."

Dulles's speeches helped hide the fact that the Republicans did nothing about their promise to liberate the enslaved, but perhaps more important to their popularity was their unwillingness to risk American lives, for here too they were expressing the deepest sentiments of their countrymen. On occasion the Republicans rattled the saber and always they filled the air with denunciations of the Communists, but they also shut down the Korean War, cut corporate taxes, and reduced the size of the armed forces. Despite intense pressure and great temptation, they entered no wars. They were willing to supply material, on a limited scale, to others so that they could fight the enemy, but they would not commit American boys to the struggle. Like Truman they did their best to contain Communism; unlike him they did not use American troops to do so. They were unwilling to make peace but they would not go to war. Their speeches provided emotional satisfaction but their actions failed to liberate a single slave.

When General Marshall was Secretary of State, he had complained that he had no muscle to back up his foreign policy. Truman agreed and did all he could to increase the armed forces. Dulles did not make such complaints. He worked with what was available—which was, to be sure, far more than Marshall had at hand in 1948—for he shared the Republican commitment to fiscal soundness.

The extent of the commitment was best seen in the New Look, a term Eisenhower coined to describe his military policy. It combined domestic, military, and foreign considerations. The New Look rejected the premise of NSC 68 that the United States could spend up to 20 percent of its GNP on arms; it rejected deficit financing; it supported a policy of containment. It came into effect at a time of lessening tension. The Korean War had ended and Stalin had died in March 1953. The world seemed less dangerous. The New Look was based in large part on the success of the NSC 68 program, for the first two years of the New Look were the high-water mark of relative American military strength in the Cold War. As Samuel Huntington has noted, "The basic military fact of the New Look was the overwhelming American superiority in nuclear weapons and the means of delivering them." Between 1953 and 1955, the United States could have effectively destroyed the Soviet Union with little likelihood of serious reprisal. The fact that America did not do so indicated the basic restraint of the Eisenhower administration, as opposed to its verbiage.

The New Look became fixed policy during a period of lessened tensions and American military superiority, but it did not depend on either for its continuation. In its eight years of power, the Eisenhower administration went through a series of war scares and it witnessed the development of Soviet long-range bombers, ballistic missiles, and nuclear weapons. Throughout, however, Ike held to the New Look. His Defense Department expenditures remained in the $35-to-$40-billion range.

The key to the New Look was the American ability to build and deliver nuclear weapons. Put more bluntly, Eisenhower's military policy rested on America's capacity to destroy the Soviet Union. Soviet strides in military technology gave them the ability to retaliate but not to defend Russia, which was the major reason Eisenhower could accept sufficiency. The United States did not have to be superior to the Soviet Union to demolish it.

To give up superiority was not easy, however, and it rankled many Americans, especially in the military. Eisenhower had his greatest difficulties with the Army, for it suffered most from his refusal to increase the Defense Department budget. Three Army Chiefs of Staff resigned in protest, and one of them, Maxwell Taylor, later became the chief adviser on military affairs to Ike's successor. The Army wanted enough flexibility to be able to meet the Communist threat at any level. The trouble with Eisenhower's New Look, the Army chiefs argued, was that it locked the United States into an all-or-nothing response. Wherever and whenever conflict broke out, the chiefs wanted to be capable of moving in. To do so, they needed a large standing army, with specialized divisions, elite groups, a wide variety of weapons, and an enormous transportation capacity.

Eisenhower insisted that the cost of being able to intervene anywhere, immediately, was unbearable. "Let us not forget," the President wrote a friend in August 1956, "that the Armed Services are to defend a 'way of life,' not merely land, property or lives." He wanted to make the chiefs accept the need for a "balance between minimum requirements in the costly implements of war and the health of our economy. . . ." As he told the American Society of Newspaper Editors on April 16, 1953: "Every gun that is made, every warship launched, every rocket fired signifies, in the final sense, a theft from those who hunger and are not fed, those who are cold and are not clothed."

The New Look meant that Eisenhower had abandoned his former advocacy of universal military training, with its assumption that the next war would resemble World War II. More fundamentally, he had abandoned the idea of America fighting any more Korean wars. Eisenhower's policy emphasized both the importance of tactical nuclear weapons and the role of strategic airpower as a deterrent to aggression. He used technology to mediate between conflicting political goals. Big bombers carrying nuclear weapons were the means through which he reconciled lower military expenditures with a foreign policy of containment.

Under Eisenhower, the United States developed smaller atomic weapons that could be used tactically on the battlefield. Dulles then attempted to convince the world that the United States would not hesitate to use them. The fact that the NATO forces were so small made the threat persuasive, for there was no other way to stop the Red Army in Europe. Both Dulles and Eisenhower made this explicit. If the United States were engaged in a major military confrontation, Dulles said, "Those weapons would come into use because, as I say, they are becoming more and more conventional and replacing what used to be called conventional weapons." Eisenhower declared, "Where these things are used on strictly military targets . . . I see no reason why they shouldn't be used just exactly as you would use a bullet or anything else."

Dulles called the policy massive retaliation. In a speech in January 1954, he quoted Lenin and Stalin to show that the Soviets planned to overextend the Free World and then destroy it with one blow. Dulles held that the United States should counter that strategy by maintaining a great strategic reserve in the United States. The Eisenhower administration had made a decision to "depend primarily upon a great capacity to retaliate, instantly, by means and at places of our own choosing."

Dulles used massive retaliation as the chief instrument of containment. He called his overall method brinksmanship, which he explained in an article in *Life* magazine. "You have to take chances for peace, just as you must take chances in war. Some say that we were brought to the verge of war. Of course we were brought to the verge of war. The ability to get to the verge without getting into the war is the necessary art. . . . If you try to run away from it, if you are scared to go to the brink, you are lost. We've had to look it square in the face. . . . We walked to the brink and we looked it in the face. We took strong action."

Dulles implicitly recognized the limitations on brinksmanship. He never tried to use it for liberation and he used it much more sparingly after the Soviets were able to threaten the United States itself with destruction. It was a tactic to support containment at an acceptable cost, within a limited time span under a specific set of military circumstances, not a strategy for protracted conflict.

In the *Life* article, Dulles cited three instances of going to the brink. All were in Asia. The first came in Korea. When Eisenhower took office in January 1953, the truce talks were stalled on the question of prisoner-of-war repatriation. The Chinese wanted all their men held by the U.N. command returned, while the Americans insisted on voluntary repatriation, which meant that thousands of Chinese and North Koreans would remain in South Korea, for they did not want to return to Communism. Truman and Acheson had first raised the issue. They could have had peace early in 1952 had they accepted the usual practice—firmly established in international law—of returning all prisoners, but they decided to offer a haven to those prisoners who wished to defect. The talks—and the war—continued.

Determined to cut losses and get out, Eisenhower warned that unless the war ended quickly the United States might retaliate "under circumstances of our own choosing." On February 2, in his first State of the Union message, the President said there was no longer "any sense or logic" in restraining Chiang, so the U.S. Seventh Fleet would "no longer be employed to shield Communist China." Chiang then began bombing raids against the China coast. Eisenhower's threats to widen the war accomplished his goal—the Chinese agreed to a resumption of armistice talks.

Dulles then hinted to the Chinese that if peace did not come, the United States would bring in atomic weapons. Eleven days later the Chinese agreed to place the question of prisoner repatriation in the hands of international, neutral authorities.

In its first test massive retaliation had won a victory. Ominous portents for the future, however, soon appeared. Dulles's policy was based on a bipolar view of the world. He believed that the United States could make the major decisions for the Free World while Russia would make them for the Communists. He refused to accept, or perhaps even recognize, the diversity of the world, for he thought all important issues were related to the Cold War and was impatient with those who argued that the East-West struggle was irrelevant to many world problems. His negative expression of this belief in bipolarity was his denunciation of neutrality, which he characterized as immoral.

The second application of brinksmanship came in

Vietnam. In December 1952 the lame-duck Truman administration approved $60 million for support of the French effort against Ho Chi Minh's Viet Minh. Truman—and later Eisenhower—labeled Ho a Communist agent of Peking and Moscow, characterizing the war in Vietnam as another example of Communist aggression.

Eisenhower continually urged the French to state unequivocally that they would give complete independence to Vietnam upon the conclusion of hostilities. Eisenhower said he made "every kind of presentation" to the French to "put the war on an international footing," that is, to make it clear that this was a struggle between Communism and freedom, not a revolt against colonialism. If France promised independence, and Ho continued to fight, Eisenhower reasoned that the Viet Minh could no longer pretend to be national liberators but would stand revealed as Communist stooges of Moscow. At that point Britain and the United States could enter the conflict to halt "outside" aggression.

For their part, the French were willing enough to talk about the Communist menace in order to receive American aid, but they had no intention of giving up Vietnam. They knew perfectly well that their enemies were in the interior of Vietnam, not in Peking or Moscow, and they were determined to retain the reality of power. If the Americans wanted to fight Communists, that was fine with the French; their concern was with continuing to control Vietnam.

But the war did not go well for the French. By early 1954, the Viet Minh controlled over half the countryside. The French put their best troops into an isolated garrison north of Hanoi, called Dien Bien Phu, and dared the Viet Minh to come after them. They assumed that in open battle the Asians would crumble. The results, however, went the other way, and by April it was the French garrison at Dien Bien Phu that was in trouble. War weariness in France was by then so great, and the French had attached so much prestige to Dien Bien Phu, that it was clear that the fall of the garrison would mean the end of French rule in Vietnam. Eisenhower and

Dulles saw such an outcome as a victory for Communist aggression and a failure of containment.

On April 3, 1954, Dulles and Admiral Radford met with eight congressional leaders. The Administration wanted support for a congressional resolution authorizing American entry into the war. The Congressmen, including Senator Lyndon B. Johnson of Texas, the Senate majority leader, were aghast. They remembered all too well the difficulties of the Korean War and they were disturbed because Dulles had found no allies to support intervention. Congressional opposition hardened when they discovered that one of the other three Joint Chiefs disagreed with Radford's idea of saving Dien Bien Phu through air strikes.

Eisenhower was as adamant as the congressional leaders about allies. He was anxious to support the French, but only if they promised complete independence and only if Britain joined the United States in intervening. Unless these conditions were met he would not move, but he was worried about what would happen if the French lost. On April 7, he introduced a new political use for an old word when he explained at a press conference that all Southeast Asia was like a row of dominoes. If you knocked over the first one, what would happen to the last one was "the certainty that it would go over very quickly."

To make sure the dominoes stood, Eisenhower sought allies. He wanted "the U.S., France, United Kingdom, Thailand, Australia, and New Zealand, et al., to begin conferring at once on means of successfully stopping the Communist advances in Southeast Asia." He proposed to use the French Army already there, while "additional ground forces should come from Asiatic and European troops." America would supply the material, but not the lives. The policy had little appeal to Britain, Australia, New Zealand, et al., but it was consistent with the approach of both of Eisenhower's predecessors. The trouble was it had no chance of success. The proposed allies figured that if Americans would not fight in Korea, they would not fight in Vietnam. Even when Eisenhower wrote Churchill and compared the threat in Vietnam to the dangers of "Hirohito, Mussolini and Hitler," the British would not budge.

The Vice-President, Richard M. Nixon, then tried another tack. On April 16, he said that "if to avoid further Communist expansion in Asia and Indochina, we must take the risk now by putting our boys in, I think the Executive has to take the politically unpopular decision and do it." The storm that followed this speech was so fierce that the possibility of using "our boys" in Vietnam immediately disappeared. Eisenhower would never have supported it anyway, and his Army Chief of Staff, Matthew Ridgway, was firmly opposed to rushing into another ground war in Asia.

What to do? The question was crucial because a conference on Vietnam was scheduled to begin in Geneva on April 26. Like Truman in Korea, the Eisenhower administration was flatly opposed to a negotiated peace at Geneva that would give Ho Chi Minh any part of Vietnam. The United States was paying 75 percent of the cost of the war, an investment too great simply to abandon. But the French position at Dien Bien Phu was deteriorating rapidly. Air Force Chief of Staff Nathan Twining had a solution. He wanted to drop three small atomic bombs on the Viet Minh around Dien Bien Phu "and clean those Commies out of there and the band could play 'The Marseillaise' and the French would come marching out . . . in fine shape." Eisenhower said he would not use atomic bombs for the second time in a decade against Asians, but he did consider a conventional air strike. Dulles flew to London a week before the Geneva conference to get Churchill's approval. Churchill would not approve, and Eisenhower did not act. Brinksmanship had failed.

On May 7, 1954, Dien Bien Phu fell. Still there was no immediate progress in Geneva and the Americans walked out of the conference. At the insistence of the NATO allies, Eisenhower eventually sent his close friend Walter B. Smith as an observer. Dulles himself refused to return to Geneva, and the negotiations dragged on.

The break came when the French government fell, and in mid-June the Radical-Socialist Pierre Mendès-France assumed the position of foreign minister as well as Premier. On the strength of his pledge to end the war or resign by July 20, he had a vote of confidence of 419 to 47. Mendès-France immediately met Chinese Premier Chou En-lai privately at Bern, which infuriated the Americans, and progress toward peace began. Eisenhower, Dulles, and Smith were bystanders. On July 20-21, 1954, two pacts were signed: the Geneva Accords and the Geneva Armistice Agreement.

The parties agreed to a truce and to a temporary partition of Vietnam at the seventeenth parallel, with the French withdrawing south of that line. Neither the French in the south of Vietnam nor Ho Chi Minh in the north could join a military alliance or allow foreign military bases on their territory. There would be elections, supervised by a joint commission of India, Canada, and Poland, within two years to unify the country. France would stay in the south to carry out the elections. The United States did not sign either of the pacts, nor did any South Vietnamese government. The Americans did promise that they would support "free elections supervised by the United Nations" and would not use force to upset the agreements. Ho Chi Minh had been on the verge of taking all of Vietnam, but he accepted only the northern half because he needed time to repair the war damage and he was confident that when the elections came he would win a smashing victory. After all, he was sure of 100 percent of the vote from the north.

After Geneva the Secretary of State moved in two ways to restore some flexibility to American foreign policy. One of the major problems had been the lack of allies for an intervention. Dulles tried to correct this before the next crisis came by signing up the allies in advance. In September 1954, he persuaded Britain, Australia, New Zealand, France, Thailand, Pakistan, and the Philippines to join the Southeast Asian Treaty Organization (SEATO), in which the parties agreed to consult if any signatory felt threatened. They would act together to meet an aggressor if they could unanimously agree on designating him and if the threatened state agreed to action on its territory. Protection for Cambodia, Laos, and South Vietnam was covered in a separate protocol. Thus did the United States bring South Vietnam into an alliance system. The absence of India, Burma, and Indonesia in SEATO was embarrassing, as was the presence of so many white men. Clearly this was no NATO for Southeast Asia but rather a Western—especially American—effort to regulate the affairs of Asia from the outside. The United States, as Dulles put it, had "declared that an intrusion [in Southeast Asia] would be dangerous to our peace and security," and America would fight to prevent it.

Not, however, with infantry. Dulles assured a suspicious Senate that the New Look policies would continue, that the American response to aggression would be with bombs, not men. This solved one problem but left another. What if the aggression took the form of internal Communist subversion directed and supported from without? In such an event it would be difficult to get the SEATO signatories to agree to act. Dulles was aware of the danger and assured the Cabinet that in such an event the United States was ready to act alone. He took a different tack in the Senate Foreign Relations Committee, where he stated that "if there is a revolutionary movement in Vietnam or in Thailand, we would consult together as to what to do about it . . . but we have no undertaking to put it down, all we have is an undertaking to consult," Reassured, the Senate passed the treaty by a vote of eighty-two to one.

Dulles's other major post-Geneva move was to unilaterally shore up the government of South Vietnam. In so doing, he revealed much about American attitudes toward revolution in the Third World. Dulles grew almost frantic when he thought about the "colored" peoples of the world, for he realized that the struggle for their loyalty was the next battleground of the Cold War, and he knew that American military might was often irrelevant in the struggle. Russia had a tremendous initial advantage, since the Third World did not regard the Russians as white exploiters and colonists. Furthermore, the Russian example of how a nation could build its economy through controlled production and consumption, rather than by waiting for the slow accumulation of capital through the profits of free enterprise, appealed to the emerging nations. Finally, the oppressed peoples of the world were not overthrowing their white masters in order to substitute local rules with the same policies. The revolutionaries were just what they said they were: men determined to change the entire social, political, and economic order.

Given the American habit of defining social change as Communist aggression, given the needs of American business to maintain an extractive economy in the Third World, and given the military desire to retain bases around Russia and China, the United States had to set its face against revolution. "American policy was designed to create maximum change behind the Iron Curtain and to prevent it elsewhere," Norman Graebner has written. "On both counts, this nation placed itself in opposition to the fundamental political and military realities of the age." In 1960 V. K. Krishna Menon of India invited the American delegation to the United Nations to read the Declaration of Independence. "Legitimism cannot be defended," he declared, "and if you object to revolutionary governments, then you simply argue against the whole of progress." But America did object to revolution.

In September 1954, Dulles announced that henceforth American aid would go directly to the South Vietnamese and not through the French. In November, American military advisers began training a South Vietnamese Army. The Americans approved the seizure of power by Ngo Dinh Diem, who drew his support from the landlords and had good relations with the French plantation owners, and Eisenhower pledged American economic aid to Diem. The President tried to require social and economic reforms from Diem, but it was understood that Diem could do almost as he wished as long as he remained firmly anti-Communist.

American aid began to pour into Diem's hands as the United States tried to promote South Vietnam as a model for Third World development. Brinksmanship had failed to prevent the loss of North Vietnam and was of little or no help in dealing with the problems of the underdeveloped nations, so Dulles offered the Diem example as a method of handling what he regarded as the most important problem of the era. Whether it would be a convincing example or not remained to be seen.

If brinksmanship failed to halt or even shape the revolution of rising expectations, it could still be used to protect what was already clearly America's. Dulles faced his third major challenge, and used brinksmanship for the third time, in the Formosa Straits, where he did succeed in achieving his objective.

In January 1953, Eisenhower had "unleashed" Chiang.* The Nationalist Chinese then began a series of bombing raids, in American-built planes, against mainland shipping and ports. The pinprick war was just enough to keep the Chinese enraged without injuring them seriously. In January 1955, the Chinese were ready to strike back. They began by bombing the Tachen Islands, 230 miles north of Formosa and held by a division of Chiang's troops. The Chinese also began to build up strength and mount cannon opposite Quemoy and Matsu, small islands sitting at the mouths of two Chinese harbors and garrisoned by Nationalist divisions. Eisenhower—although not some of his advisers—was willing to write off the Tachens, which were soon evacuated, but he was determined to hold Quemoy and Matsu as he

---

*In fact, Truman had done so two years earlier, but kept it a secret. Eisenhower made it public for domestic political reasons, to appease the right wing of the Republican Party. In any case there was little Chiang could do militarily against the mainland.

believed they were integral to the defense of Formosa
itself. His reasoning, as he explained during a 1958 crisis
over the same issue, was that if Quemoy and Matsu fell,
Formosa would follow, which would "seriously jeopardize the anti-Communist barrier consisting of the insular
and peninsular position in the Western Pacific, e.g.,
Japan, Republic of Korea, Republic of China, Republic
of the Philippines, Thailand and Vietnam." Indonesia,
Malaya, Cambodia, Laos, and Burma "would probably
come fully under Communist influence."

To avoid the "catastrophic consequences" of the loss
of Quemoy and Matsu, on January 24, 1955, Eisenhower
went before Congress to ask for authority to "employ
the armed forces of the United States as [the President]
deems necessary for the specific purpose of protecting
Formosa and the Pescadores against armed attack," the
authority to include protection for "related positions,"
which meant Quemoy and Matsu. Eisenhower feared
that if the Chinese moved and he had to go to Congress
for authority to act, it would be too late, so he asked for
a blank check on which he could draw at will. As the
legal adviser of the Department of State who helped
draft the resolution remarked, it was a "monumental"
step, for "never before in our history had anything been
done like that." Nevertheless, there was hardly a debate.
The House passed the resolution by 409 to 3, while it
went through the Senate by 85 to 3.

A major war scare then ensued. As the Chinese began
to bombard Quemoy and Matsu, the Eisenhower administration seriously considered dropping nuclear weapons
on the mainland. At no other time in the Cold War did
the United States come so close to launching a preventive
war. Had the Chinese actually launched invasions of the
islands, it is probable that the United States would have
done so. In a speech on March 20, Dulles referred to
the Chinese in terms usually reserved for use against
nations at war. The Secretary said the Chinese were "an
acute and imminent threat, . . . dizzy with success." He
compared their "aggressive fanaticism" with Hitler's and
said they were "more dangerous and provocative of war"

than Hitler. To stop them, he threatened to use "new and powerful weapons of precision, which can utterly destroy military targets without endangering unrelated civilian centers," which meant tactical nuclear bombs. Eisenhower backed him up.

On March 25, the Chief of Naval Operations, Admiral R. B. Carney, briefed correspondents at a private dinner. He said the President was considering acting militarily on an all-out basis "to destroy Red China's military potential and thus end its expansionist tendencies." Dulles told the President that before the problem was solved, "I believe there is at least an even chance that the United States will have to go to war." Dulles thought that small atomic air bursts, with minimal civilian casualties, would do the job quickly, and "the revulsion might not be long-lived."

Eisenhower, however, began to doubt that the operation could be limited in time or scope, and he rejected preventive war. He pointed out to reporters that even if successful, such a war would leave China utterly devastated, full of human misery on an unprecedented scale. What, he demanded to know, "would the civilized world do about *that*?" At a press conference on April 28, he said he had a "sixth-sense" feeling that the outlook for peace had brightened, and he revealed that he had been in correspondence with his old wartime friend, Marshal G. K. Zhukov, one of the current Soviet rulers. Chinese pressure on Quemoy and Matsu lessened and the crisis receded. Brinksmanship had held the line.

In the process, however, it had frightened people around the globe, even members of the Eisenhower administration itself, with good reason. The nuclear weapons of 1955 were a thousand times more destructive than the atomic bombs of the forties—one American bomber carried more destructive power than all the explosives set off in all the world's history put together—and everyone was alarmed. The small tactical atomic bombs Dulles was talking about were much larger than those dropped on Japan. Ever since the first American tests of the new fission bomb, Winston Churchill had been urging the United States and the Soviets to meet at a summit to try to resolve their differences. The Americans had consistently rejected his calls for a summit meeting, but by mid-1955, as the Russians began to improve both the size of their bombs and their delivery capabilities, and as the Formosa crisis made the United States face squarely the possibility of a nuclear exchange, Eisenhower and Dulles became more amenable.

Eisenhower's willingness to go to the summit meant the end of any American dreams of winning the Cold War by military means. The Russians had come so far in nuclear development that Eisenhower himself warned the nation that nuclear war would destroy the world. There could be no "possibility of victory or defeat," only different degrees of destruction. As James Reston reported in *The New York Times,* "Perhaps the most important single fact in world politics today is that Mr. Eisenhower has thrown the immense authority of the American Presidency against risking a military solution of the cold war." Since Eisenhower would not lead the nation into a nuclear war, and since he did not have the troops to fight a limited war, nor could he get them from his allies, and since the Republicans were more determined to balance the budget and enjoy the fruits of capitalism than they were to support a war machine, the only alternative left was peace of some kind with the Russians.

Events broke rapidly in the late spring of 1955, helping to drive Eisenhower and the Russians to the summit. On May 9, West Germany became a formal member of NATO. On May 14, the Soviet Union and the Eastern European nations signed the Warsaw Pact, the Communist military counter to NATO. The next day Russia and America finally solved one of the long-standing problems of World War II by signing the Austrian State Treaty, which gave Austria independence, forbade its union with Germany, and made it a permanent neutral. Both sides had been responsible for various delays. The Russians signed because they wanted to ease tensions and advance to the summit, whereas the Americans accepted it as a reasonable solution for the Austrian problem. Dulles was unhappy. As Eisenhower later recalled, "Well, suddenly the thing was signed one day and [Dulles] came in and he grinned rather ruefully and he said, 'Well, I think we've had it.' "

What Dulles feared was misinterpretation. The fear was justified, for columnists and pundits began to advocate a similar solution for Germany. Actually, far from being a step toward German unity and neutrality, the Austrian treaty was a step toward making German division permanent. Russia and America in effect agreed that neither of the Germanies would get Austria.

This in turn illustrated one of the most important results of World War II, the division of Hitler's Reich into three parts. A united Germany, whether Nazi, Communist, or capitalist, is always a threat to peace—or so the Russians and Americans decided. Both retained a formal commitment to the reunification of Germany, but neither wanted it.

On May 19, 1955, in an air show, the Soviets displayed impressive quantities of their latest long-range bombers. A week later the new top Russian leaders, Nikita Khrushchev and Nikolai Bulganin, flew to Yugoslavia, where they apologized for Stalin's treatment of Tito and begged Tito's forgiveness. The Soviets were also initiating an economic assistance program for selected Third World countries. Clearly, Russia had emerged from the confusion that followed Stalin's death and was on the offensive.

Some ground rules for the Cold War, of spirit if not of substance, were needed. America's NATO allies were adamant about this need, insistently so after NATO war games in June of 1955 showed that if conflict started in Europe (and if the war game scenario was accurate), 171 atomic bombs would be dropped on West Europe. For the United States to continue to take a stance of unrestrained hostility toward Russia was intolerable. This deeply felt sentiment in Europe plus Eisenhower's personal dedication to peace were the main factors in making the 1955 summit meeting at Geneva possible.

The Geneva meeting, the first summit since Potsdam ten years earlier, was not the result of any political settlement. Neither side was willing to back down from previous positions. Dulles made this clear when he drew up the American demands on Germany. His first goal was unification "under conditions which will neither 'neutralize' nor 'demilitarize' united Germany, nor subtract it from NATO." There was not the slightest chance that the Russians would accept such a proposal. Neither would they ever agree to the only new American offer, Eisenhower's call for an "open skies" agreement, for to them that was only another heavy-handed American attempt to spy on Russia.* Bulganin, who fronted for Khrushchev at Geneva, was no more ready to deal than were the Americans. His position on Germany was to let things stand as they were.

On July 18, 1955, the summit meeting began. It had been called in response to the arms race, and it was no surprise that there was no progress toward political settlements. What Dulles had feared most, however, did happen—there emerged a "spirit of Geneva." Before the meeting, Dulles had warned Eisenhower to maintain "an austere countenance" when being photographed with Bulganin. He pointed out that any pictures taken of the two leaders smiling "would be distributed throughout the Soviet satellite countries," signifying "that all hope of liberation was lost and that resistance to Communist rule was henceforth hopeless." But the pictures were taken and Eisenhower could not restrain his famous grin, and the photographs were distributed.

Dulles had been unable to prevent this symbolic recognition of the failure of Republican promises for lib-

---

*The Russians were indignant in their rejection on the "open skies" proposal, but actually Eisenhower was just slightly ahead of technology. The United States began spying on the Russians from the skies anyway, with the CIA's U-2 airplane, and within a few years both sides had satellites that were constantly spying on each other.

eration of Communist satellites. Geneva did not mean the end of the Cold War but it did put it on a different basis. The West had admitted that a thermonuclear stalemate had developed, and that the status quo in Europe and China (where tensions quickly eased) had to be substantially accepted.

Dulles was bitter but helpless. He was especially infuriated because the battleground now shifted to the areas of economic and political influence in the Third World, a battleground on which Russia had great advantages. Dulles warned the NATO foreign ministers in December 1955 that the Soviets would thereafter employ "indirect" threats "primarily developed in relation to the Near and Middle East and South Asia." To fight back, Dulles needed two things—money and an American willingness to accept radicalism in the emerging nations. He had neither. Republicans who resented giving money to West Europe through the Marshall Plan were hardly likely to approve significant sums for nonwhite revolutionaries.

Beyond diplomatic pressure and threats of all-out war or nuclear holocaust, the United States during the Eisenhower administration developed another method of achieving its foreign policy objectives, especially in the Third World. As noted earlier, the CIA got its start under Truman, but it really began to operate on a grand scale after 1953, when Allen Dulles, younger brother of the Secretary of State, became the director of Central Intelligence. Allen Dulles, an OSS agent during the war, worked behind the scenes on covert operations to accomplish the same objectives his brother worked on in public—primarily the containment of Communism. An idealist himself, Allen Dulles attracted other idealists into the CIA. According to the Church Committee of the Senate, which in 1976 undertook a thorough investigation of the CIA, "during the 1950s the CIA attracted some of the most able lawyers, academicians, and young, committed activists in the country." The CIA was, indeed, thought to be a "liberal institution . . . that fostered free and independent thinking." To those who joined the CIA it was the "good way" to fight Communism, as opposed to Senator McCarthy's "bad way."

The fifties were the glory years for the CIA. Few questions were asked of it. Congressional watchdog committees specifically told Allen Dulles they did not want to know about clandestine operations. The President and the public took it for granted that the only way to fight the Russians and their KGB (secret police) was to use dirty tricks about which the less that was known, the better. No questions were asked about cost, either, for who could put a value on advance information that, for example, the Russians were massing in East Germany for a strike across the Elbe River? That generation of American leaders had been through Pearl Harbor and was determined never again to be surprised. Consequently, West Berlin was crawling with CIA agents, who had spies located throughout East Europe, reporting on the movements and activities of the Red Army. The agents, however, could not pull off major covert operations behind the iron curtain, such as toppling the government of Poland or East Germany, because the secret police of the satellite governments were too well organized and too active.

In the Third World, however, the application of a little force or a little money could have dramatic results. Allen Dulles's first triumph came in 1953 in Iran. Premier Mohammed Mossadegh had, in the view of the Dulles brothers, drawn too close to the Tudeh, Iran's Communist party, and would have to be overthrown before he made a deal with the Russians. Mossadegh had already nationalized Iran's oil fields, to the consternation of the British, who previously had enjoyed a monopoly on Iranian oil production. Mossadegh was also thought to be a threat to Shah Mohammed Riza Pahlavi's retention of his throne.

Allen Dulles decided to save Iran by sending his best agent, Kim Roosevelt (Theodore Roosevelt's grandson), to Teheran, along with General H. Norman Schwarzkopf (father of General Norman Schwarzkopf, who led the U.S. Army during the Gulf War of 1991), who had organized the Shah's secret police after World War II. (Organizing and equipping the police force and army of small nations was another method of control often used by the United States in the Cold War.) Roosevelt and Schwarzkopf, spending money as if they did not have to account for it—as they did not—organized demonstrations in the streets of Teheran that overthrew Mossadegh, who went to jail, and brought the young Shah back from exile. The new Premier then divided up Iranian oil production to suit the West: The British kept 40 percent; American oil companies got 40 percent; the French got 6 percent; and the Dutch 14 percent. It would be years before the Iranians tried again to take control of their own resources, and then it would be the Shah that the CIA saved who would do the taking. Meanwhile, however, the Communist tide had been stopped.

In the New World, too, the CIA scored a victory. In 1951, Jacob Arbenz Guzman had become President of Guatemala. He worked closely with the Communist Party. Arbenz carried out some land reforms and expropriated 225,000 acres of the United Fruit Company's holdings. That was bad enough; worse was the threat that Communism would spread. Allen Dulles proposed to drive Arbenz from office. After listening to the pros and cons, Eisenhower gave him permission to go ahead. CIA agents in Guatemala selected Colonel Carlos Castillo Armas to lead a coup. He set up his base and received his equipment in Honduras. Eisenhower would not commit the United States to any direct military support of the operation, but he did tell the Dulles brothers, "I'm prepared to take any steps [short of sending in troops] that are necessary to see that it succeeds."

When the invasion bogged down, Eisenhower allowed Allen Dulles to send Castillo Armas a few old World War II bombers. These planes then carried out a bombing mission over Guatemala City. Arbenz lost his nerve, resigned, fled, and Guatemala was "saved." To the CIA's critics, it had been saved for United Fruit; to its defenders, the CIA had acted decisively to prevent Communism from getting a foothold in the New World.

Driving Latin American Communists from power was much easier than driving the Russians out of East Europe. Secretary of State Dulles had promised liberation and had failed. Neither brinksmanship nor moral persuasion had freed a single slave or prevented North Vietnam from going Communist.

On Christmas Day 1955 the White House sent its usual message to the peoples of Eastern Europe "to recognize the trials under which you are suffering" and to "share your faith that right in the end will bring you again among the free nations of the world." When Khrushchev complained that this "crude interference" was not in accord with the spirit of Geneva, the White House pointed out that the goal of liberation was permanent. The statement said, "The peaceful liberation of the captive peoples is, and, until success is achieved, will continue to be a major goal of United States foreign policy."

A presidential election year had just begun. As in 1952, captive nations' pronouncements made good campaign material. Unfortunately, some of the captive people did not know how to distinguish between campaign bombast and actual policy. They were about to demand payment on American liberation promises.

9

From Hungary and Suez to Cuba

> In the councils of government, we must guard against
> the acquisition of unwarranted influence, whether sought
> or unsought, by the military-industrial complex.
>
> DWIGHT D. EISENHOWER,
> Farewell Address

The overwhelming first impression of American foreign
policy from 1956 to 1961 was one of unrelieved failure.
America's inability to do anything at all to aid Hungary's
rebels made a mockery of the Republican calls for liberation. Eisenhower and Dulles were unable to contain
the Russians, who succeeded in their centuries-old
dream of establishing themselves in the Mediterranean
and the Middle East. Spectacular Soviet successes in
rocketry, beginning with Sputnik, sent the United States
into a deep emotional depression. Russia seemed to have
won the arms race, and in 1959 it was Khrushchev who
played at brinksmanship from a position of strength.
After the Suez crisis, the French, British, and Americans
could never fully trust each other. In Southeast Asia,
Communist guerrillas in South Vietnam and Laos
threatened to upset the delicate balance there in favor
of the Communists. In Latin America, the Eisenhower
administration was helpless in the face of a revolution
in Cuba, which soon allowed the Russians to extend their
influence to within ninety miles of the United States.

Surface appearances, however, reveal only surface
truths. Eisenhower's outstanding achievement was to
avoid war. However irresponsible Republican emotional
appeals to the anti-Communist vote may have been, and
despite the Russian shift to the offensive in the Cold

War, Eisenhower refused to engage American troops in armed conflict. He was not immune to intervention, nor to provocative rhetoric, nor to nuclear testing, nor to the arms race (within strict limits), but he did set his face against war. It became the Democrats' turn to complain that the United States was not "going forward," that it was not "doing enough," that America was "losing the Cold War."

But despite the Democrats' complaints, the United States emerged from the Eisenhower years in a strong position. The American gross national product went up—without inflation. The Western European economy continued to boom. NATO was intact. Anglo-American oil interests in the Middle East were secure. The Latin American economy remained under American domination. American military bases in the Pacific were safe. Chiang remained in control of Formosa. And the United States, although Eisenhower was spending only about two thirds the amount that the Democrats wanted him to on defense, was militarily superior to the Soviet Union.

Eisenhower had been unable to contain the Communists, much less liberate East Europe, and he remained wedded to the clichés of the Cold War, but he was a man of moderation and caution with a clear view of what it would cost the United States to resist Communist advances everywhere. He thought the American economy could not pay the price, which was the fundamental distinction between Eisenhower and his Democratic successors.

Eisenhower showed his reluctance to take aggressive action most clearly in response to the events that preceded and accompanied the 1956 presidential campaign. The Democratic nominee, Adlai Stevenson, accused Eisenhower of not doing enough to stop the Communists. Half of Indochina had become a "new Communist satellite," Stevenson declared, and the United States "emerged from the debacle looking like a 'paper tiger'." Stevenson was also upset at what he called NATO's decline, wanted the American armed forces strengthened,

and charged that Eisenhower had rejected "great opportunities to exploit weaknesses in the Communist
ranks." Finally, Stevenson charged that Eisenhower had
allowed the Russians to get ahead in the arms race. There
was, he warned, a "bomber gap."

Eisenhower would not be stampeded, although the
opportunities for action were certainly present. In the
Middle East, ignoring ideology, the Russians were extending their influence. Although Dulles had broken
with Truman's policy of support for Israel and was trying
to improve relations with the Arabs, he was either unable
or unwilling to match Communist aid programs for the
area. In late 1955, he had a "conniption fit" when he
learned that the Egyptians had negotiated an arms deal
with the Czechs. Dulles's initial response was to offer the
Egyptian leader, Colonel Gamal Abdel Nasser, American
aid for the Aswan Dam, a gigantic project designed to
harness the power of the lower Nile. Technical experts
then studied the project and pronounced it feasible. By
February 1956, Nasser was ready to conclude the deal.

Dulles, however, had trouble selling the Aswan Dam
in the United States. Pro-Israeli politicians denounced
the dam. Southern Congressmen wondered why the
United States should build a dam that would allow the
Egyptians to raise more cotton. In the Cabinet, old-
guard Republicans feared the cost of the dam would
unbalance the budget. All the opponents agreed that the
Egyptians could not possibly provide the technicians nor
the industry to use the dam properly. Dulles himself
began to back off when in April 1956 Nasser formed a
military alliance with Saudi Arabia, Syria, and Yemen
and refused to repudiate the Czech arms deal. The Secretary assumed that the Russians could not replace the
Americans as backers of the Aswan Dam, an assumption
based on the curious notion that the Russians did not
have the technological know-how. When Nasser withdrew recognition from Chiang Kai-shek and recognized
Communist China in May, Dulles had had enough. He
decided to withdraw from the Aswan Dam project, but
he did not make the decision public.

Then, on July 19, 1956, at the moment the Egyptian foreign minister was arriving in Washington to discuss the project, Dulles announced that America was withdrawing its support from the Aswan Dam. Nasser's immediate response was to seize the Suez Canal, which restored his lost prestige at a stroke and gave him the $25-million annual profit from the canal operation. Now it was the British and French who were furious. They were dependent on the canal for oil, they were certain that the Arabs did not have the skills to run the canal properly, they feared that Nasser would close it to their ships, and their self-esteem had suffered a serious blow. Long, complicated negotiations ensued. They got nowhere. Dulles's main concern was to protect American oil interests in the Middle East, whereas the British and French could be satisfied by nothing less than complete control of the canal. Dulles, fearing Arab reaction, was unwilling to restore the colonial powers and was in any event strongly opposed to old-style European colonialism.

It was indeed a mess. In a later investigation Senator Fulbright charged that the Aswan Dam project was sound, that its repudiation was a personal decision by Dulles, that Dulles misjudged both Nasser's attitude toward the Soviet Union and the importance of the dam to Egypt, that he confused Egyptian nationalism and neutralism with Communism, and that he never made any serious effort to persuade the congressional opponents of the project. Dulles had damaged the American position in France, Britain, and NATO, lost a chance to tie Nasser to the West, allowed the Soviet Union to begin preparation for a naval base in the Mediterranean, alienated Israel and her supporters, and failed to gain any more Arab adherents.

The anger of the critics was justified, but it did not take everything into account. The Middle East contained 64 percent of the world's then-known oil reserves. The leading producers were Kuwait, Saudi Arabia, and Iraq. During and after World War II, American oil companies, aided by the United States government, had forced concessions from both the British and the Arabs and now had a major interest in the Middle Eastern oil. Despite Dulles's bumbling, these interests were secure.

The Suez Canal remained necessary to move the oil. Dulles began a complex series of negotiations designed to help Nasser run the canal without the British or French. The Europeans thereupon decided to take matters into their own hands. In conjunction with Israel, the British and French began plans for an invasion of Egypt. They did not inform the United States.

Another development, in East Europe, complicated everything. At the twentieth Party Congress in February 1956, Khrushchev shocked the party by denouncing Stalin for his crimes, confessing that there could be several roads to Communism and indicating that Stalinist restrictions would be loosened. Two months later the Russians dissolved the Cominform. The CIA got a copy of Khrushchev's secret speech and distributed copies of it throughout the world. Ferment immediately swept through East Europe. Riots in Poland forced Khrushchev to disband the old Stalinist Politburo in Warsaw and allow Wladyslaw Gomulka, an independent Communist, to take power (October 20, 1956). Poland remained Communist and a member of the Warsaw Pact, but it won substantial independence and set an example for the other satellites.

The excitement spread to Hungary, before the war the most Fascist of the East European states and the one where Stalin's imposition of Communism had been most alien. On October 23, Hungarian students took to the streets to demand that the Stalinist puppets be replaced with Imre Nagy. Workers joined the students and the riot spread. Khrushchev agreed to give power to Nagy, but that was no longer enough. The Hungarians demanded the removal of the Red Army from Hungary and the creation of an anti-Communist political party. By October 28, the Russians had given in and begun to withdraw their tanks from around Budapest.

Liberation was at hand. Eisenhower was careful in his campaign speeches to use only the vaguest of phrases,

although the Voice of America and Radio Free Europe
did encourage the rebels. So did Dulles, who promised
economic aid to those who broke with the Kremlin. At
the decisive moment, however, just as it seemed that the
European balance of power was about to be drastically
altered, the Israeli Army struck Egypt. In a matter of
hours it nearly destroyed Nasser's army and took most
of the Sinai Peninsula. Britain and France then issued
an ultimatum, arranged in advance with the Israelis,
warning the combatants to stay away from the Suez
Canal. When Nasser rejected the note, the Europeans
began bombing Egyptian military targets and prepared
to move troops into Suez, on the pretext of keeping the
Israelis and Arabs apart.

On October 31, the day after the bombing in Egypt
began and less than a week before the U.S. presidential
elections, Nagy announced that Hungary was withdrawing from the Warsaw Pact. The Soviets decided to move.
Russian tanks crushed the Hungarian rebels, who fought
back with Molotov cocktails. Bitter street fighting left
7,000 Russians and 30,000 Hungarians dead. Radio
pleas from Hungary made the tragedy even more painful: "Any news about help? Quickly, quickly, quickly!"
And the last desperate cry, on a teletype message to the
Associated Press: "HELP!—HELP!—HELP!—SOS!—SOS!—
SOS! They just brought us a rumor that the American
troops will be here within one or two hours. . . . We are
well and fighting."

There never would be any American troops. Eisenhower did not even consider giving military support to
the Hungarians, and he would not have done so even
had there been no concurrent Middle Eastern crisis.
Under no conceivable circumstances would he risk
World War III for East Europe. Liberation was a sham;
it had always been a sham. All Hungary did was to expose
it to the world. However deep Eisenhower's hatred of
Communism, his fear of nuclear war was deeper. Even
had this not been so, the armed forces of the United
States were not capable of driving the Red Army out of
Hungary, except through a nuclear holocaust that would

have left all Hungary and most of Europe devastated. The Hungarians, and the other Eastern European peoples, learned that they would have to make the best deal they could with the Soviets. The Russian capture and execution of Nagy made the point brutally clear.

In Egypt, meanwhile, the British and French had bungled. They blew their cover story almost immediately. Their advance was so rapid that they could not pretend that their invasion was one by a disinterested third party designed to keep the Israelis and Egyptians apart. Eisenhower was upset at their use of nineteenth-century colonial tactics; he was livid at their failure to inform him of their intentions. The Americans introduced a resolution in the U.N. General Assembly urging a truce and imposed an oil embargo on Britain and France. Khrushchev, meanwhile, rattled his rockets, warning the British and French on November 5 to withdraw before he destroyed them. Although they were only hours away from taking the Suez Canal, the Anglo-French governments agreed to a ceasefire and pullback.

It had been quite a week for lessons. American politicians learned to stop their irresponsible prattling about liberation. The Russians learned just how strong a force nationalism was in East Europe, while the Israelis saw that they would have to make it on their own in their conflict with the Arabs. United States and United Nations pressure soon forced the Israelis to give up their gains in Sinai. The Egyptians learned to look to the Soviet Union for support—encouraged by Nasser, they believed that the Russian ultimatum, not the United States' U.N. actions and oil embargo, had saved them. The British and French learned that they no longer stood on the center of the world stage—they were second-rate powers incapable of independent action.

Eisenhower wanted to retain good relations with the oil-rich Arab states, especially the Saudis, who were unwilling to fight the Israelis themselves but supported those who did. So Eisenhower stepped forward as the defender of Egypt, but he got precious little thanks for it. Instead, Nasser praised the Russians, who were build-

ing the Aswan High Dam for him and who were so
delighted to have a foot on the ground in the Middle
East that they abandoned their decade-old policy of support for Israel.

As Nasser continued to spread propaganda for Arab
unity and socialism while taking more aid from the Soviet
Union and allowing more Russians into his country, Eisenhower and Dulles feared that the Russians would
move into the Middle East "vacuum" (the phrase always
infuriated the Arabs) and had to be forestalled. Attempted coups and countercoups in Syria, Jordan, and
Iraq by pro- and anti-Nasserites increased American
anxiety. So on January 5, 1957, Eisenhower asked Congress for authority to use American armed forces in the
Middle East "if the President determines the necessity . . . to assist any nation . . . requesting assistance
against armed aggression from any country controlled
by international communism." The next year Eisenhower used the authority granted him in the so-called
Eisenhower Doctrine when on July 15, 1958, he sent the
Marines into Lebanon to support President Camille
Chamoun.

The intervention in Lebanon illustrated Eisenhower's
methods. It was a unilateral action that risked general
war in support of a less than democratic government
threatened by pro-Nasser Arabs. Eisenhower tried to tie
the action into great historic precedents by invoking
Greece and the 1947 Truman Doctrine. He emphasized
the danger by mentioning the Communist takeovers in
Czechoslovakia and China, and he explained that the
United States "had no intention of replacing the United
Nations in its primary responsibility of maintaining international peace and security." The United States had
acted alone merely "because only swift action would
suffice."

The rhetoric was grand, the intervention itself less
sweeping. The Joint Chiefs wanted American troops to
overrun all of Lebanon, but Eisenhower ordered the
men to limit themselves to taking the airfield and the
capital. If the government could not survive even after

American troops had secured the capital, Eisenhower said, "I felt we were backing up a government with so little popular support that we probably should not be there."

The Russians, too, were unwilling to take drastic action. Nasser flew to Moscow to ask for aid; Khrushchev turned him down. The Soviet ruler knew that Eisenhower acted to protect Western oil holdings and he knew how vital those holdings were to the West. As long as Eisenhower was willing to hold down the scope of the intervention, Khrushchev would not interfere.

Khrushchev's caution surprised many observers, since the Russians were generally believed to have achieved military superiority. On October 4, 1957, the Soviet Union successfully launched the world's first man-made satellite, Sputnik. Two months earlier they had fired the world's first intercontinental ballistic missile (ICBM). Americans were frustrated, angry, ashamed, and afraid all at once. As Walter LaFeber puts it, " 'gaps' were suddenly discovered in everything from missile production to the teaching of arithmetic at the preschool level." Eisenhower dispersed Strategic Air Force units and installed medium-range ballistic missiles in Turkey and Italy, but this was hardly enough to assuage the sudden fear. When the Russians began trumpeting about their average increase in their GNP (supposedly nearly twice the American rate), the pressure on Eisenhower to "get the country moving again" became almost irresistible.

Eisenhower refused to panic, even when in late 1957 the newspapers discovered and published the findings and recommendations of a committee headed by H. Rowan Gaither, Jr., of the Ford Foundation, which painted an exceedingly dark picture of the future of American security. The Gaither Report, as Eisenhower typically understated it, included "some sobering observations." It found that the Soviet G.N.P. was increasing at a much faster rate than that of the United States, that the Russians were spending as much on their armed forces and heavy industry as the Americans were, that by 1959 the Soviets might be able to launch an attack against the United States with one hundred ICBMs carrying megaton-sized nuclear warheads, and that if such an attack should come, the civilian population and American bombers would be vulnerable.

The Gaither Report was similar to NSC 68 in its findings, and like NSC 68 it recommended a much-improved defense system. The committee wanted fallout shelters built on a massive scale, an improvement in America's air-defense capability, a vast increase in offensive power, especially missile development, a buildup of conventional forces capable of fighting limited war, and another reorganization of the Pentagon. As a starter the Gaither Report urged an increase in defense spending to $48 billion.

Eisenhower said no. "We could not turn the nation into a garrison state," he explained in his memoirs, adding as an afterthought that the Gaither Report was "useful; it acted as a gadfly. . . ." He kept the Defense budget under $40 billion, quietly rejected the demands for fallout shelters and increased conventional-war capability, and cut one Army division and a number of tactical air wings from active duty. He did speed up the ballistic-missile program, although Congress appropriated more funds than the administration requested for the ICBM and Polaris missile to get those programs into high gear.

Democrats charged that the Republicans were allowing their fiscal views to endanger the national security, but Eisenhower knew what he was doing. The CIA, in one of the great intelligence coups of all time, had in 1956 inaugurated a series of flights over the Soviet Union in specially built high-altitude airplanes called U-2s. The photographs that resulted from the flights revealed, as Eisenhower later put it, "proof that the horrors of the alleged 'bomber gap' and the later 'missile gap' were nothing more than imaginative creations of irresponsibility." The United States still had a substantial lead in strategic weapons.

One of the most important points about the U-2 flights was that Khrushchev knew they were taking place (none of the Russian fighter airplanes could reach the altitude at which the U-2s flew, so they could not knock them down), which meant that Khrushchev knew that Eisenhower knew how false were the Soviet boasts about their strategic superiority. The fact that Eisenhower made no strong statements about Soviet inferiority during the American domestic controversy about the missile gap should have reassured the Soviets and convinced them that Eisenhower really was a man of moderation who was sincerely interested in some sort of *modus vivendi*. The flights, the information they produced, and Eisenhower's rejection of the Gaither Report, all indicated to the Soviets that Eisenhower had accepted the fundamental idea that neither side could win a nuclear war and that both would lose in an arms race.

The events in the year following Sputnik had the effect of establishing ground rules for the Cold War. By staying out of the Lebanon situation the Soviets indicated that they recognized and would not challenge the West's vital interests. By refusing to take the easy way out of the missile gap controversy, Eisenhower indicated that he did not want an arms race and was eager for détente. Through their negative signals both sides showed that they would keep the threshold of conflict high. The years of Eisenhower's second term marked the height of bipolarity, for, as the British, French, Israelis, and Egyptians could testify, what the Big Two wanted they got. Whether they could continue to control their allies, especially France and China,* much less the Third World, was an open question. Indeed, it was not at all clear that Eisenhower and Khrushchev could control the hardliners in their own countries.

A major test soon came in divided Berlin. Eisenhower's desire for détente was based on a continuation of the status quo, which Khrushchev could not accept everywhere and certainly could not accept in Berlin.

---

*Much to the Americans' displeasure, France was pushing forward the development of its own nuclear weapons; China, in August 1958, inaugurated the second Quemoy crisis.

West Berlin was a bone in his throat. Each year 300,000 East Germans defected to the West via Berlin, most of them young, talented, educated, and professional people. Since 1949 East Germany had lost 3 million people through the West Berlin escape hatch. West Berlin also contained the largest combination of espionage agencies ever assembled in one place, 110 miles deep in Communist territory, as well as radio stations that constantly beamed propaganda into East Europe.

Equally important was the West Berlin economic miracle. The Americans had poured $600 billion into the city, which the Bonn government had matched. West Berlin was turning out nearly $2 billion worth of goods per year. It had become the greatest manufacturing city in Germany and its GNP exceeded that of more than half the members of the United Nations. The glittering social, intellectual, and economic life in West Berlin stood in sharp contrast to the drab, depressed life of East Berlin. What made the situation especially intolerable for Khrushchev was the steady flow of American propaganda about Berlin. Americans used the refugees and the economic contrast between the two Berlins as the ultimate proof of the superiority of capitalism over Communism.

The situation had, however, existed for over a decade. Why did Khrushchev decide to move against West Berlin in late 1958, during a period of relative calm in the Cold War? He may have reasoned that since Eisenhower would not build up conventional forces, and since the President would do everything possible to avoid a nuclear exchange, a diplomatic solution was now possible. More immediately, Khrushchev feared the growing rearmament of West Germany. The Americans had sent artillery capable of firing nuclear shells and airplanes that could carry nuclear bombs to West Germany. Konrad Adenauer, the West German leader, was increasing the pace of rearmament. Finally, the Bonn government was on the verge of joining with France, Italy, and the Benelux nations in the Common Market, which would tie West Germany more firmly than ever into the Western bloc.

Khrushchev was under intense pressure to do something about the German situation.

On November 10, 1958, Khrushchev declared that the Soviet Union was ready to turn over control of Berlin to East Germany. When that happened the West would have to negotiate rights of access to West Berlin with the East German government, which none of the Western governments recognized. The West was in Berlin only on the basis of presurrender occupation agreements; if Khrushchev signed a peace treaty with the East Germans, the occupation presumably would have to come to an end. Khrushchev warned that any attack against East Germany would be considered an attack on the Soviet Union. He set a time limit of six months and said that if agreement were not reached by then, the West would have to deal with the East Germans. In later speeches he indicated that the only satisfactory resolution of the Berlin situation was to turn West Berlin into a free city with the British, French, and Americans withdrawing their ten thousand troops. He also wanted the West Berlin economy integrated into that of East Germany and the Soviet Union.

Eisenhower rejected the free-city proposal, but he also refused to increase the armed services dramatically as a prelude to taking a hard line over Berlin. In March 1959, as Khrushchev's deadline approached and Democrats urged him to mobilize, Eisenhower told Congress that he did not need additional money for missiles or conventional-warfare forces to deal with the crisis. At a press conference on March 11, with considerable emotion, he dismissed demands that he refrain from carrying out his plans to further reduce the size of the Army. He wanted to know what in heaven's name the United States would do with more ground forces in Europe. Thumping the table, he declared, "We are certainly not going to fight a ground war in Europe," and he pointed out the elementary truth that a few more men or even a few more divisions in Europe would have little effect on the military balance there. He thought the greatest danger in the Berlin crisis was that the Russians would frighten the United States into an arms race that would bankrupt the country.

Khrushchev, who wanted to reduce his own armed forces and who was no more anxious to exchange nuclear strikes than Eisenhower, began to back down. He denied that he had ever set a time limit, accepted an invitation to visit the United States in September of 1959, and arranged with Eisenhower for a summit meeting in Paris, scheduled for May 1960.

During private talks with Khrushchev at Camp David, Maryland, in the fall of 1959, Eisenhower admitted that the situation in Berlin was abnormal and that some modification would be necessary. Eisenhower was prepared to make concessions in order to normalize the situation. He had managed to avoid a crisis over Berlin by simply denying that a crisis existed, in a sense an awesome display of presidential power—a "crisis" can exist only when the President says it exists.

Eisenhower had opted for peace. Throughout his second term he warned of the danger of turning America into a garrison state. As a professional soldier of the old school, Eisenhower felt his first responsibility was the nation's security, which he realized could never be enhanced by an arms race in the nuclear age. This was Eisenhower's fundamental insight, that the more one spent on atomic weapons, the less secure one became, because as the United States built more weapons, the Russians were sure to follow.

Negotiation with the Russians was a more effective way to enhance the nation's security. Democrats thought the primary reason for Eisenhower's concern was his commitment to a balanced budget, and it was true that he had decided that the cost of the Cold War was more than America would bear, but there was something else. By 1958, Eisenhower realized that he had only two more years on the world stage, that if he were to leave any lasting gift to the world he would have to do it soon. His deepest personal desire was to leave mankind the gift of peace.

Eisenhower and Khrushchev were anxious to solidify

the concept of peaceful coexistence, each for his own reasons, but by 1959 the Cold War had gone on for so long that calling it off was no easy task. Both men had to fend off hard-liners at home, both had troubles with their allies, and both were beset by Third World problems that they could not control. Eisenhower had to deal with the Democrats, who believed government spending on defense would help, not hurt, the economy. The Democrats, led by Senators John F. Kennedy, Lyndon B. Johnson, and Hubert H. Humphrey, were impatient with Eisenhower's conservatism, yearned for a dynamic President, and talked incessantly about America's loss of prestige. They wanted to restore America to world leadership, which in practice meant extending American commitments and increasing American arms. On the other side, Eisenhower was beset by Republicans who wanted to hear more about liberation and getting tough with the Communists, and the President himself had by no means escaped fully from the patterns of thought of the Cold War.

Neither had Khrushchev, who also had hard-liners in Moscow pushing him toward the brink. In addition, Mao had become as much a problem for Khrushchev as Chiang was for Eisenhower. Khrushchev's refusal to support Mao's call for wars of national liberation signified to Mao that the Russians had joined the have powers against the have-nots. There was other evidence, such as Khrushchev's trip to the United States, his willingness to go to the summit again, and the cooling of the Berlin crisis. As the Chinese saw it, the Soviets were selling out both Communism and the Third World. They accused Khrushchev of appeasement. Mao challenged, directly and successfully, Khrushchev's leadership of the Communist world. Indirectly, he challenged bipolarity. The world was simply too large, with too much diversity, to be controlled by the two superpowers, no matter how closely together they marched.

Khrushchev and Eisenhower, in short, had gone too far toward coexistence for the Cold Warriors in their own countries and for their allies. Khrushchev was in the weaker position at home, since Eisenhower was almost immune to criticism, especially on military matters. Khrushchev did not have such prestige, and he found it increasingly difficult to ward off those in the Kremlin who wanted more arms and something done about Berlin. He also had to face the Chinese challenge for Communist leadership.

Khrushchev badly needed a Cold War victory, both for internal political reasons and to compete with China for followers. He may have felt that Eisenhower, who would shortly be leaving office, would be willing to allow him a victory. Whatever his reasoning, Khrushchev announced on May 5, 1960, on the eve of the Paris summit meeting, that a Russian surface-to-air missile (SAM) had knocked down an American U-2 spy plane inside Russia.

The event showed how entrenched Cold War interests could block any move toward peace. Having finally achieved the ability to knock down the U-2s, the Soviets could have waited for the results of the Paris meeting to actually do it. On the other side, the CIA could have suspended the flights in the period preceding the meeting. Or Khrushchev could have kept quiet about the entire affair, hoping that the CIA had learned a lesson and would cease and desist thereafter. Instead, he deliberately embarrassed the President. Khrushchev boasted about the performance of the SAMs but concealed pilot Francis Gary Powers's survival in order to elicit an American explanation that could be demolished by producing Powers. When Eisenhower fell into the trap, Khrushchev crowed over his discomfort and demanded an apology or a repudiation of presidential responsibility. He had misjudged the man. Eisenhower stated instead that the United States had the right to spy on the Soviet Union and he took full personal responsibility for the flight. The summit conference was ruined. The best hope for an agreement on Berlin was gone, although Khrushchev did abandon his effort to change the status quo there. He said he would wait for the new President to take office before he brought it up again. The Paris summit, meanwhile, broke up at the opening meeting when Eisenhower refused to apologize for the U-2 flight.

Khrushchev had improved his position at home, and with the Chinese, but not much. Eisenhower had tried but in the end he was unable to bring the Cold War to a close. Despite the U-2 and the wrecked summit meeting, he had improved Russian-American relations. He had failed to liberate any Communist slaves—indeed, he had been forced to acquiesce in the coming of Communism to Indochina and in the establishment of a Russian base in the Mediterranean—but he had avoided war and kept the arms race at a low level. He had tried, insofar as he was capable, to ease the policy of permanent crisis he had inherited from Truman.

Eisenhower's major weakness was that he was an old man, head of an old party, surrounded by old advisers. He dealt with old problems. His image, deliberately promoted by the Republicans, was that of a kindly grandfather. He could not anticipate new problems nor adjust to the winds of change.

As in Cuba. Three times after 1902 the United States had intervened in Cuba to protect American investments, which by the end of World War II had grown to impressive proportions. Americans owned 80 percent of Cuba's utilities, 40 percent of its sugar, 90 percent of its mining wealth, and occupied the island's key strategic location of Guantanamo Bay. Cuban life was controlled from Washington, for almost the only source of income was sugar, and by manipulating the amount of sugar allowed into the United States, Washington directed the economy.

Fulgencio Batista was the Cuban dictator. He had come to power as a revolutionary but had adjusted to the realities of leading a small nation in which the United States had a large investment. Postponing land reform and other promised improvements, by the 1950s his sole support was the Cuban Army, which was equipped by the United States, and his policies were repressive. In January 1959, after a long struggle, Fidel Castro, who had placed himself at the head of the various anti-Batista guerrilla movements, drove Batista from Havana. At first the general public in the United States welcomed Castro, casting him in a romantic mold and applauding his democratic reforms. Castro helped by putting leading Cuban liberals in important posts on his Cabinet. American supporters of Castro expected him to restore civil liberties, introduce gradual and compensated land reform and look to the United States for leadership.

Within the American government, however, Castro did not receive an enthusiastic welcome. Allen Dulles told Eisenhower that "Communists and other extreme radicals appear to have penetrated the Castro government"; Dulles warned that the Communists would probably participate in the government. The limitations on American policy then became apparent. Someone suggested that the United States help Batista return to power. Eisenhower refused—Batista was too much the dictator. Since Castro was too close to the Communists to deserve American support, the Administration began working on a third alternative. "Our only hope," Eisenhower said, "lay with some kind of non-dictatorial 'third force,' neither Castroite nor Bastistiano."

In Cuba, meanwhile, Castro moved to the left. He began an extensive land-reform program and a nationalization of American-owned property, without compensation. The United States turned down his requests for loans and relations steadily worsened. Cuban liberals began to flee the country; Cuban Communists rose to power under Castro. Khrushchev welcomed Castro as a new force in Latin America, pronounced the Monroe Doctrine dead, and in February 1960 signed a trade agreement to exchange Cuban sugar for Soviet oil and machinery. Four months later the United States eliminated the Cuban sugar quota; in the first days of 1961 Eisenhower formally severed diplomatic relations with Cuba.

The search for a liberal alternative went on. Eisenhower gave the CIA permission to plan an invasion of Cuba and to begin training Cuban exiles to carry it out, with American support. Some of Castro's original liberal Cabinet members participated in the invasion scheme. Preparations were not complete when Eisenhower left office and the decision to go forward with the invasion or not became his successor's problem.

In 1960, young Democrats had taken over the party by nominating John F. Kennedy for the presidency. The Democrats were urging dynamism in foreign relations and a major increase in America's armed forces, as well as a totally new American relationship to the Third World. Kennedy and his advisers were most concerned with finding a liberal alternative to Castro. During the campaign Kennedy said his policy would be to give American support to "non-Batista democratic anti-Castro forces." But the major foreign-policy issue in the Nixon-Kennedy campaign of 1960 was Quemoy and Matsu. Kennedy doubted that the islands were worth defending. Nixon insisted that Quemoy and Matsu had to be held. Kennedy also stressed the missile gap, which Nixon denied existed. There were no other significant differences on foreign-policy issues between these two hot-blooded Cold Warriors who vied with each other over who would be tougher on the Communists. Kennedy won the election by a narrow margin.

In January 1961, Eisenhower delivered his farewell address. He was concerned about the internal cost of the Cold War. His ideals were those of small-town America. He was afraid that big government and the regimentation of private life were threatening the old American values. He pointed out that the "conjunction of an immense military establishment and a large arms industry . . . new in American experience, exercised a total influence . . . felt in every city, every state house, every office of the federal government. . . . In the councils of government, we must guard against the acquisition of unwarranted influence, whether sought or unsought, by the military-industrial complex."

The Democrats paid no attention. In the campaign, and in his inaugural address, Kennedy emphasized that

a new generation was coming to power in America.
Hardened by the Cold War, it was prepared to deal with
all the tough problems. He promised to replace Eisenhower's tired, bland leadership with new ideas and new
approaches. Since the generalities were not reinforced
by any specific suggestions, it was difficult to tell what
the new directions would be. What was clear was that a
forward-looking, offensive spirit had come to America.
Action was about to replace inaction. Kennedy promised
to get the country moving again. Where to, no one knew
precisely.

10

Kennedy and the New Frontiers

> Let every nation know, whether it wishes us well or ill,
> that we shall pay any price, bear any burden, meet any
> hardship, support any friend, oppose any foes, in order
> to assure the survival and success of liberty. This much
> we pledge—and more.
>
> JOHN F. KENNEDY,
> Inaugural Address

John Kennedy had a vision. He thought the United
States was the last, best hope of mankind. He wanted
prosperity and happiness for all the world's people and
believed the United States was capable of supplying the
leadership necessary to achieve those goals. He surrounded himself with the very best minds America had
to offer, appointing men who had the techniques and
the brains that would enable the new Administration to
solve any problem, indeed to go out and find new problems so that they could solve them.

Kennedy took office at the moment in time when
America's optimism was at its zenith. Kennedy believed,
and often said, it would be possible for the United States
to simultaneously take the offensive in the Cold War,
accelerate the arms race, eliminate poverty and racism
at home, lower taxes, all without unbalancing the budget
and starting inflation. His goals, in short, were as bound-
less as his pledge to "pay any price." Most Americans
agreed with him. Nixon had advocated an almost identical program in the 1960 campaign.

Kennedy and the men around him had been impatient
with Eisenhower's leadership. Eisenhower had not been
aggressive enough, he tended to compromise, he could

not stir the nation to great deeds. Fundamentally, Eisenhower had rejected the idea that there could be a military solution to Cold War problems or that America could shape the world's destiny. He had accepted limitations on America's role. Kennedy did not. Where Eisenhower had been passive, Kennedy would be active. Where Eisenhower had been cautious, Kennedy would be bold. Kennedy and his aides were especially interested in restoring the prestige and primacy of the presidency, which they felt had fallen under Eisenhower.

Republican rhetoric had consisted of unrestrained hostility to the Soviet Union and emphasized permanent war with Communism. But Democratic actions revealed a dynamic militancy.

The new President deeply believed that the United States was not doing nearly well enough in the Cold War. He said he was "not satisfied as an American with the progress that we are making." Kennedy wanted the people of Latin America and Africa and Asia "to start to look to America, to what the President of the United States is doing, not . . . Khrushchev or the Chinese Communists." Freedom was under the "most severe attack it has ever known." It could be saved only by the United States. And if the United States failed, "then freedom fails." The recurring theme, therefore, was, "I think it's time America started moving again."

In his first State of the Union address, on January 30, 1961, Kennedy warned, "Each day the crises multiply. . . . Each day we draw nearer the hour of maximum danger." He felt he had to tell the Congress the truth: "The tide of events has been running out and time has not been our friend." Finally, the grim prophecy: "There will be further setbacks before the tide is turned."

Kennedy wanted the United States to take the initiative. Although he emphasized that "a total solution is impossible in the nuclear age," he did not expect to "win" in any traditional sense. The military realities precluded victory, while America's view of the nature of the change and of Communism precluded peace. This tended to lock the nation into a policy of containment. Since stalemate was no more satisfactory to Kennedy than it had been to Dulles, however, Kennedy had to hold out a long-range hope. "Without having a nuclear war," he said, "we want to permit what Thomas Jefferson called 'the disease of liberty' to be caught in areas which are now held by the Communists." Sooner or later freedom would triumph. How? By waiting for the rotten system to implode from within and through the example of American vitality. Kennedy told the American people to expect a long, slow process of evolution "away from Communism and toward national independence and freedom."

The Third World provided the key. "The great battleground for the defense and expansion of freedom today," Kennedy said, "is the whole southern half of the globe . . . the lands of the rising people." Kennedy, like the Communists, believed in the inevitable victory of his system in the long run. Again like his enemies, however, he was not averse to speeding up the process. Fittingly, his first great opportunity, and his first crisis, came in a Third World revolutionary nation. For all the President's speeches about willingness to tolerate differences in the world, he was not ready to accept a Communist regime off the tip of Florida. In late 1960, the CIA, with Eisenhower's approval, had begun training anti-Castro Cuban exiles in the arts of guerrilla warfare. The plan was to land the counterrevolutionaries in a remote section of Cuba, with covert American assistance, so that they could set up a base of operations to overthrow Castro.

In mid-April 1961, Kennedy ordered the invasion to begin. Cuban exiles, carried in American ships and covered by American airplanes, waded ashore at the Bay of Pigs. Castro completely crushed them. He proved to be far stronger than the Americans had thought, the Cuban people showed little inclination to revolt against him, and the exiles were unable to find support in the Cuban mountains. Kennedy had played a delicate game, trying to give enough support to make the invasion work but not enough to make the American involvement obvious. He had failed on both counts.

Later, in analyzing the failure, Kennedy muttered that "all my life I've known better than to depend on the experts. How could I have been so stupid, to let them go ahead?" That the fault lay with the CIA and the Joint Chiefs beame the standard explanation. The President, young and inexperienced, had depended on their expert judgment and had been let down. He would, thereafter, know better.

That explanation was patent nonsense. The Bay of Pigs was hardly an operation carried out against the President's wishes or in opposition to his policy. He had advocated such activity by exile forces during the 1960 campaign, and the fact was that it fit perfectly into his general approach. The CIA had been wrong in predicting an uprising against Castro, but the prediction was exactly what Kennedy wanted to hear. The President believed there was a liberal alternative between Castro and Batista and that the exile counterrevolutionary group would supply the liberal leadership around which the Cuban people would rally. It was not the experts who got Kennedy into the Bay of Pigs; it was his own view of the world.*

Before he gave the final go-ahead, Kennedy had consulted with Senator William Fulbright. On March 29 the Senator sent a memorandum to the President. "To give this activity even covert support," Fulbright warned, "is of a piece with the hypocrisy and cynicism for which the United States is constantly denouncing the Soviet Union." The Bay of Pigs, the Senator said, would compromise America's moral position in the world and make it impossible for Kennedy to protest treaty violations by the Communists. Kennedy ignored Fulbright, partly because he felt that success would provide its own justification, more because to back down on the invasion would compromise America's position. Kennedy believed, as he

---

*Afterward, furious at Castro for so thoroughly embarrassing him, JFK ordered Castro assassinated. The CIA tried, but failed to carry out the orders.

later explained, that "his disapproval of the plan would be a show of weakness inconsistent with his general stance."

One of Kennedy's great fears was to appear weak. And, like most Cold Warriors, he thought the only way to deal with the Russians and their associates was from a position of strength. How much strength became the great question. The man Kennedy picked to answer it, Robert S. McNamara, the Secretary of Defense, maintained that "enough" meant great superiority. He set out to give America that superiority. McNamara described the result in some detail in a 1967 speech. McNamara recalled that when he took office, the Soviets possessed "a very small operational arsenal of intercontinental missiles," but they had the ability to "enlarge that arsenal very substantially." The Americans had "no evidence that the Soviets did in fact plan to fully use that capability," but the possibility existed that they intended to so expand. McNamara and Kennedy decided that "we had to insure against" a Soviet buildup by dramatically increasing American strength. After two years in office they had increased the defense budget from $40 to $56 billion. By 1967 America had forty-one Polaris submarines carrying 656 missile launchers and six hundred long-range bombers, 40 percent of which were always in a high state of alert. In ICBMs, Kennedy and McNamara had increased the American force level by a factor of five. They had inherited two hundred ICBMs from Eisenhower; by 1967 the United States had one thousand ICBMs.

The Kennedy-McNamara team had launched the greatest arms race in the history of mankind. It extended far beyond nuclear delivery weapons. The White House and the Pentagon cooperated in vastly increasing America's conventional war capability and, as a Kennedy favorite, guerrilla warfare forces. In 1954 Eisenhower had backed away from involvement in Dien Bien Phu because, unless he wished to inaugurate a nuclear exchange, he did not have the forces required. Kennedy wanted an ability to intervene anywhere. The new strategy was called flexible response.

As a reaction to the enormous American buildup, the Russians increased their ICBM forces. As McNamara put it in 1967, the Soviets may have had no intention of engaging in an arms race and might have been satisfied to accept the status quo of 1960, under which America had superiority but not enough to launch a first strike. The Kennedy-McNamara program, however, apparently convinced the Kremlin that America did in fact aim at achieving a first-strike capability, which forced the Soviets to increase their missile forces, which forced the United States to begin another round of expansion. But, as McNamara confessed, the whole thing had been a terrible mistake. America had been unwilling to take the risk of allowing the Soviets to achieve parity in nuclear delivery systems, but by building more missiles the Americans only increased their own danger. Given the inevitable Soviet response, the more missiles America built, the less secure America was.

McNamara himself recognized this when he admitted that "the blunt fact is that if we had had more accurate information about planned Soviet strategic forces [in 1961], we simply would not have needed to build as large a nuclear arsenal as we have today." McNamara concluded that American superiority in ICBMs by 1967 was "both greater than we had originally planned, and is in fact more than we require."

The political response to the Kennedy buildup was as important as the military reaction. Whereas the Republicans had been content to rest their military policy on the grounds that General Ike knew best, and make general, vague statements to the effect that there was no missile gap, the Democrats made specific statements in insistent tones about American superiority. Coupled with the Bay of Pigs, the new American military policy indicated to the Soviets that they had to deal with an aggressive, outward-looking Administration. The "hards" in the Kremlin found their direst prediction fulfilled, and they charged Khrushchev with having neglected Soviet military security. It seemed to them that the United States was trying to shift the military balance in its favor before reaching a worldwide settlement, part of which would be an agreement to keep military forces at the existing levels. Kennedy was always talking about arms limitation talks and at the end of his first year in office said his greatest disappointment was the failure to secure a nuclear test-ban treaty. The Russians saw Kennedy's expressed desire for arms limitation as a deliberate propaganda lie, coming as it did concurrently with the American military buildup, and believed it was a cover for the continuation of the status quo throughout the world, especially in Berlin, Vietnam, Korea, and Formosa. Kennedy, the Russians charged, would use superior American arms to block all change.

Kennedy said as much in the summer of 1961, when he met Khrushchev in Vienna. The President urged the Premier to preserve the existing balance of power in arms and geography. Kennedy insisted that the entry of additional nations into the Communist camp, or the loss of Formosa or Berlin, would alter the equilibrium and force the United States to react. Khrushchev rejected the concept. Even if he wanted to, he said, he could not stop change, and in any case the Soviet Union could hardly be expected to cooperate in enforcing stability on a world that was predominantly colonial and capitalist. Khrushchev complained that Kennedy "bypassed" the real problem. "We in the U.S.S.R. feel that the revolutionary process should have the right to exist," he explained. The question of "the right to rebel, and the Soviet right to help combat reactionary governments . . . is the question of questions." It was, he said, "at the heart of our relations" with the United States. He was sorry that "Kennedy could not understand this."

The American military buildup indicated that the United States would stop, by force if necessary, revolutionary movements in the Third World. It also indicated that the United States was willing to use force to maintain the status quo in Europe. But Khrushchev could not accept the situation in Berlin as permanent. The bone continued to catch in his throat. By the summer of 1961 he had to move quickly if he wished to do anything about it before the Kennedy-McNamara program gave the United States great superiority in strategic weapons.

Kennedy, for his part, seemed open to the reasonable accommodation. All through the summer of 1961 Khrushchev insisted that there had to be some settlement in Berlin before the end of the year. Kennedy's response was cold and firm: Nothing could be changed. Kennedy insisted, "If we don't meet our commitments in Berlin, it will mean the destruction of NATO and a dangerous situation for the whole world. All Europe is at stake in West Berlin."

Kennedy reacted boldly to Khrushchev's challenge. He put an additional $3.2 billion military budget through Congress, tripled the draft calls, extended enlistments, and mobilized 158,000 reserves and national guardsmen. Altogether, he increased the size of the armed forces by 300,000 men, sending 40,000 of them to Europe and making six "priority divisions" in the reserves ready for quick mobilization.

The two sides were now on a collision course: Khrushchev could not allow West Berlin to remain as an escape hatch; Kennedy could not accept any change in its status. Walter Ulbricht of East Germany announced that after he signed a peace treaty with the Russians he would close West Berlin's access to the Western world. The President prepared the American people for the worst. In a television address on July 25, 1961, Kennedy showed how determined he was to stay in Berlin by invoking heroic deeds from the past. "I hear it said that West Berlin is militarily untenable," he began. "And so was Bastogne. And so, in fact, was Stalingrad. Any dangerous spot is tenable if men—brave men—will make it so." He again said that if Berlin went, Germany would follow, then all of Western Europe. Berlin was essential to the "entire free world."

Khrushchev regarded the speech as belligerent and called Kennedy's arms policy military hysteria. Kennedy had made no new offers; indeed, he had made no offers at all to adjust the Berlin situation. East Germans continued to escape via Berlin; soon it threatened to become a country without people. Western propaganda continued to embarrass the Communists by loudly proclaiming that the flow of refugees proved the superiority of capitalism. By early August both world leaders had so completely committed themselves that no solution seemed possible. The crisis appeared destined to end in war.

The escapees were the sticking point. Khrushchev and the East Germans could not afford to continue to lose their best human resources to the West nor to give the West such an ideal propaganda advantage. For his part, Kennedy could hardly be expected to shut the doors to West Berlin or to refrain from using the refugee issue for propaganda.

On August 13, 1961, Khrushchev suddenly and dramatically solved his Berlin problem, and created a new one in the process. He built the Wall, presenting America and the West with a *fait accompli* and apparently permanently dividing Berlin. The flow of refugees was shut off and—after an initial reaction of outrage—the tension visibly eased. The Soviet building of the Wall, and the eventual Western acceptance of it, signified the end to all serious attempts in that decade to reunify Germany. Khrushchev was willing to live with West Berlin as long as it was isolated and did not drain East Germany. Kennedy was willing to live with the Wall as long as West Berlin stayed in the Western orbit. Khrushchev's Wall was a brilliant stroke.

It was also brutal and unprecedented. Never before in human history had a wall been built around a city to keep people *in*. Immeasurable human tragedy resulted.

The compromise solution in Berlin did not lead to a permanent end to tension. The American military build-up continued, after being expanded during the crisis. Kennedy had looked weak to many Cold Warriors in the United States because he had not torn down the Wall. Khrushchev looked weak to the Cold Warriors in the Communist world for building it. Khrushchev was in deeper trouble, however, because the Kennedy administration insisted on boasting about American military superiority. Kennedy officials and American strategic intellectuals were publicly sketching scenarios in which the United States would strike first. They justified the exercise by expressing their skepticism of Soviet missile credibility.

Khrushchev had to react. He could allow the United States its strategic nuclear superiority, and there was little he could do about it in any case, since the United States could and would outbuild him. But he could not allow the United States to be both superior and boastful about its superiority. He needed a dramatic strategic victory, one that would focus world attention on Soviet military capability and satisfy his own armed services. He found the answer with increased megatonnage. On August 30, 1961, he announced that he was breaking the three-year Russian-American moratorium on nuclear testing with a series of tests that climaxed with the explosion of a fifty-eight-megaton weapon, three thousand times more powerful than the bomb used against Hiroshima and many times more powerful than anything the United States had developed. The big bomb was good for propaganda, but it had little if any military use, as both sides already had bombs larger than they needed.

Khrushchev's series of tests did have the effect, however, of leading to strident demands that Kennedy begin his own series of tests. The President had given top priority to achieving a nuclear test-ban treaty and was despondent when he could not get it. He was furious with Khrushchev for breaking the moratorium, but he refused to be stampeded into a new series of tests. Kennedy was greatly worried about the radioactive fallout problem, and he realized that no matter how big Russian bombs grew the United States would remain strategically superior because of American delivery capability. He tried to compromise with a series of underground tests that began in September 1961. It was not enough, however, to satisfy his domestic critics or the atomic scientists or the Pentagon, and in April 1962 Kennedy ordered a series of American tests (thirty in all) in the atmosphere.

Khrushchev, frustrated in the nuclear field, unable to push the West out of Berlin, incapable of matching the United States in ICBMs, and increasingly irritated by the Chinese harping about Soviet weakness, began to look elsewhere for an opportunity to alter the strategic balance. He found it in Cuba. Since the Bay of Pigs, Russia had increased her aid to Castro and had begun to include military supplies. Kennedy had warned the Soviets not to give offensive weapons to the Cubans; Khrushchev assured the President that he had no intention of doing so. But in August 1962 the Soviet Union began to build medium-range ballistic missile sites in Cuba.

What did Khrushchev hope to accomplish? He could not have expected to attain a first-strike capability. The American delivery system was far too vast for the Russians to be able to destroy it. Nor could Khrushchev have wanted to expand the arms race, for the Russians would not be able to match the American productive capacity. Putting missiles in Cuba would not make Castro any more a Communist, but it was possible that Khrushchev thought the missiles were necessary to protect Cuba from invasion. The American Congress, military, and popular press were all talking openly of invading Cuba again, and the Russians insisted after the event that the missiles had been in response to the invasion talk. If this was his motive, however, Khrushchev badly miscalculated, for the missiles practically invited America to invade.

The issue in Cuba was prestige. Kennedy had taken from Khrushchev the fiction of the missile gap. The fifty-eight-megaton bomb had not been sufficiently impressive. The hard-liners in the Soviet Union and the Chinese continued to pressure Khrushchev to stand up to the United States. The Kennedy administration continued to boast about American military superiority. As Theodore Sorensen, Kennedy's chief speech writer, later put it, "To be sure, these Cuban missiles alone, in view of all the other megatonnage the Soviets were capable of unleashing upon us, did not substantially alter the strategic balance in fact . . . but that balance would have been substantially altered in appearance; and in matters of national will and world leadership . . . such appearances contribute to reality." The most serious crisis in history of mankind, in short, turned on a question of appearances. The world came close to total destruction over a matter of prestige.

On October 14, 1962, American U-2s photographed in Cuba a launchpad under construction that, when completed, could fire missiles with a range of one thousand miles. Kennedy was already under pressure from the Republicans for failing to stop the Soviet military buildup in Cuba. Congressional elections were less than three weeks away. The pressure to respond was overwhelming. When a high official in the Pentagon suggested that Kennedy do nothing and ignore the missiles since they constituted no additional threat to the United States, the President replied that he had to act. If he did not, he feared he would be impeached.

The President set the general goals: get the missiles out of Cuba; avoid a nuclear exchange; prepare for Russian moves elsewhere, as in Berlin; do not lose face. He appointed a special committee of a dozen or so members, which called itself the Executive Committee (Ex Comm), to give him advice. The leading figure of the Ex Comm was the President's younger brother, Attorney General Robert F. Kennedy. The Committee debated a wide range of alternatives, which soon narrowed down to launching a nuclear strike against the missile sites, launching a conventional air strike, followed by an invasion, or initiating a naval blockade that would prevent the Soviets from sending any further material into Cuba. Fear of Russian reprisal soon eliminated the talk of a nuclear strike; support for a conventional attack and an invasion grew. The missiles were a heaven-sent opportunity to get rid of Castro. Invasion forces gathered in Florida and Kennedy had the State Department proceed with a crash program for civil government in Cuba to be established after the occupation of that country.

Robert Kennedy, however, continued to insist on a less belligerent initial response. He refused to countenance a surprise attack, saying, "My brother is not going to be the Tojo of the 1960s." He wanted to begin the response with a partial naval bloackade, one that would keep out Soviet military goods but not force Khrushchev to react immediately. The great advantage of the blockade, as he saw it, was that the pressure could be stepped up if it did not work. Dean Acheson, who was called in for advice, vigorously opposed the blockade and voted for the air strike, as did the Joint Chiefs, but in the end Kennedy chose the blockade as the initial American response.

Having decided on what to do, JFK sent Acheson to Europe to inform the NATO allies. Although somewhat surprised at the extreme American reactions—the Europeans had lived under the shadow of Soviet medium-range missiles for years—de Gaulle, Adenauer, and the others supported the President. So did the Organization of American States. At 7:00 P.M., October 22, 1962, Kennedy went on television to break the news to the American people. He explained the situation, then announced that the United States was imposing "a strict quarantine on all offensive military equipment" being shipped to Cuba. He had placed American military forces on full alert and warned Khrushchev that the United States would regard any nuclear missile launched from Cuba against any nation in the Western hemisphere as an attack by the Soviet Union on the United States, requiring a full retaliatory response upon the Soviet Union. He appealed to Khrushchev to remove the offensive weapons under United Nations supervision.

Kennedy had seized the initiative. It was now up to Khrushchev to respond. His first reaction was belligerent. In a letter received in Washington on October 23, Khrushchev said the Soviet Union would not observe the illegal blockade. "The actions of U.S.A. with regard to Cuba are outright banditry or, if you like, the folly of degenerate imperialism." He accused Kennedy of pushing mankind "to the abyss of a world missile-nuclear war" and asserted that Soviet captains bound for Cuba would not obey the orders of American naval forces. The United States Navy meanwhile deployed five hundred

miles off Cuba's coast. Two destroyers stopped and
boarded a Panamanian vessel headed for Cuba carrying
Russian goods. It contained no military material and was
allowed to proceed. Soviet ships continued to steam for
Cuba, although those carrying missiles turned back.
Work on the missile sites in Cuba continued without
interruption, however, and they would soon be operational.

The threat of mutual annihilation remained high.
Kennedy stood firm. Finally, at 6:00 P.M. on October 26,
Khrushchev sent another message. Fittingly, considering
the stakes, it was long and emotional. The Premier
wanted the President to realize that "if indeed war should
break out, then it would not be in our power to stop it."
He said once again that the missiles in Cuba were for
defensive purposes only: "We are of sound mind and
understand perfectly well that if we attack you, you will
respond the same way. But you too will receive the same
that you hurl against us. . . . Only lunatics or suicides,
who themselves want to perish and to destroy the whole
world before they die, could do this." He said he did
not want an arms race. "Armaments bring only disasters.
When one accumulates them, this damages the economy,
and if one puts them to use, then they destroy people
on both sides. Consequently, only a madman can believe
that armaments are the principal means in the life of
society."

Then came the specific proposal. Khrushchev said he
would send no more weapons to Cuba and would withdraw or destroy those already there if Kennedy would
withdraw the blockade and promise not to invade Cuba.
He urged Kennedy to untie the knot rather than pull it
tighter.

The following morning, October 27, the Ex Comm
met to consider Khrushchev's proposal. Before the
members could decide whether or not to accept, a second
letter from the Premier arrived. More formal than the
first, it raised the price. Khrushchev, perhaps bowing to
pressure from his own military, said he would take out
the Cuban missiles when Kennedy removed the Amer-

ican missiles from Turkey. "You are worried over Cuba," Khrushchev stated. "You say that it worries you because it lies at a distance of ninety miles across the sea from the shore of the United States. However, Turkey lies next to us. . . . You have stationed devastating rocket weapons . . . in Turkey literally right next to us."

The Ex Comm was thunderstruck, even though, as Robert Kennedy later put it, "the fact was that the proposal the Russians made was not unreasonable and did not amount to a loss to the United States or to our NATO allies." The President had actually already ordered the missiles out of Turkey, but due to a bureaucratic foulup and Turkish resistance they were still there. To remove them now, however, under Soviet pressure, he regarded as intolerable. The blow to American prestige would be too great. The possibility of a nuclear exchange continued to hang in the balance.

The Joint Chiefs recommended an air strike the next morning against Cuba. The generals and admirals said they had always been against the blockade as being too weak and now they wanted immediate action. Their position was strengthened when a Soviet SAM knocked down an American U-2 flying over Cuba. At this point a majority on the Ex Comm agreed on the necessity of an air strike the next morning. The President demurred. He wanted to wait at least one more day. The State Department drafted a letter from Kennedy to Khrushchev informing the Premier that the United States could not remove the missiles from Turkey and that no trade could be made.

Robert Kennedy then stepped forward. He suggested that the Ex Comm ignore Khrushchev's second letter and answer the first, the one that offered to trade the missiles in Cuba for an American promise not to invade the island. Bitter arguments followed, but the President finally accepted his brother's suggestion. He sent an appropriate letter to Khrushchev.

Far more important, however, was an oral promise Robert Kennedy gave to the Soviet ambassador to the United States, Anatoly Dobrynin. Although the President would not back down in public on the Turkish missile sites, he evidently had begun to see the absurdity of the situation—the United States was on the verge of bombing a small nation with which it was not at war, and risking in the process a nuclear exchange with the Soviet Union, over the issue of obsolete missiles in Turkey that he had already ordered removed. Kennedy discussed the issues with his brother and asked him to talk to Dobrynin. On Saturday night, October 27, Dobrynin came to Robert Kennedy's office. The Attorney General first presented the Russian ambassador with an ultimatum: If the United States did not have a commitment by the next day that the missiles would be removed, "we would remove them." Dobrynin then asked what kind of a deal the United States was prepared to make. Kennedy summarized the letter that had just gone to Khrushchev, offering to trade the missiles for an American promise not to invade Cuba. Dobrynin turned to the sticking point—what about the American missiles in Turkey?

Robert Kennedy's answer, as given in his own account of the crisis, was: "I said that there could be no quid pro quo or any arrangement made under this kind of threat or pressure, and that in the last analysis this was a decision that would have to be made by NATO. However, I said, President Kennedy had been anxious to remove those missiles from Turkey and Italy for a long period of time. He had ordered their removal some time ago, and it was our judgment that, within a short time after this crisis was over, those missiles would be gone."

The statement was sufficient. The Russians had their promise. The next day Dobrynin informed Robert Kennedy that the Soviet missiles in Cuba would be withdrawn. The deal was done.

The world settled back to assess the lessons. Everyone learned something different. The Chinese, for example, told the Third World that the Cuban crisis proved one could not trust the Russians. The Russians learned that they could not have military parity with the United States, or even the appearance of it. Kennedy, having been to the brink and having looked into the yawning chasm of world holocaust, learned to be a little softer in his pronouncements, a little less strident in his assertions. His Administration took on a more moderate tone, at least with regard to the Soviet Union, and the need for peace and arms reductions replaced boasts about American military power.

At American University on June 10, 1963, Kennedy made a dramatic appeal for peace, which he characterized as "the necessary rational end of rational men." The Partial Test Ban Treaty was signed a few weeks later, prohibiting nuclear tests in the atmosphere. As Herbert S. Dinerstein notes, "The test ban treaty symbolically recognized that the accommodation between the Soviet Union and the United States would be made on the basis of American superiority."

The Chinese were furious. They called Khrushchev foolish for putting the missiles into Cuba and cowardly for removing them. Within the Kremlin, opposition to Khrushchev mounted. For all his dramatics he had been unable to deliver enough meaningful victories in the Cold War, while his brinksmanship had frightened nearly everyone. Within a year he was driven from power.

The easing of tensions that followed the Cuban missile crisis allowed de Gaulle and other Europeans to begin to think in serious terms about revising their relationship with the United States. De Gaulle wanted to restore European primacy; to do so, he realized, he had to break with NATO. After Cuba, he knew that the United States would not consult with its NATO partners before acting; he was convinced that the United States would not risk its own existence for the sake of protecting Europe; he doubted that the Red Army would ever march across the Elbe. He believed that the time had come for Europe to drop out of the Cold War and assert herself. He therefore prepared a Franco-German friendship treaty, moved to establish better relations with the Warsaw Pact nations, quickened the pace of French nuclear development, and decided to keep Britain out of the Common Market.

On January 14, 1963, de Gaulle announced his program. He vetoed British participation in the Common Market because it would transform the character of the European Economic Community and "finally it would appear as a colossal Atlantic community under American domination and direction." Kennedy had been pushing for a multilateral nuclear force within NATO, which supposedly would give the Europeans some say in the use of nuclear weapons while blocking any West German move to develop their own bombs. The trouble with the proposal was that under no circumstances would the United States give up its ultimate veto on the bombs. De Gaulle, therefore, denounced the plan. "France intends to have her own national defense," he declared. "For us . . . integration is something which is not imaginable." He concluded about the French nuclear force, "It is entirely understandable that this French enterprise should not seem very satisfactory to certain American quarters. In politics and strategy, as in economics, monopoly naturally appears to him who enjoys it as the best possible system."

De Gaulle then proceeded to withdraw French naval forces from NATO and soon asked NATO headquarters to leave France. His bold bid for European independence was not an immediate success, as West Germany decided to maintain her close ties with the United States, but certainly his general goals had enormous appeal. From Yalta in 1945 to Vienna in 1961, the Soviet Union and the United States had presumed to settle the affairs of Europe without any European leaders at the conference table. Those days were rapidly coming to an end. Europe was unwilling to be burned to a cinder because Russia and America disagreed about an island in the Gulf of Mexico.

The greatest lesson from Cuba was the peril of brinksmanship. Henceforth, Russia and America would strive to keep some control over their disputes, to avoid actions that could lead to escalations, to limit their commitments so that they could limit the other side's response. Struggle would continue, most obviously in the Third World, but preferably at a lower level. American goals remained the same, and Kennedy would continue to pursue them energetically, but he would try to do so with less military force and within the confines of the realization that the Third World had its own hopes and programs.

He had learned. An ability to grow was his most impressive asset and he was surely the honor graduate of the Cuban missile crisis class. "In the final analysis," Kennedy said in his American University speech, "our most basic common link is the fact that we all inhabit this planet. We all breathe the same air. We all cherish our children's future. And we are all mortal."

11

Vietnam: Paying the Cost of Containment

In the patriotic fervor of the Kennedy years, we had asked, "What can we do for our country?" and our country answered, "Kill V.C."

PHILIP CAPUTO,
A Rumor of War

Kennedy had forced Khrushchev to back down in Cuba because the United States had overwhelming superiority in nuclear weapons, delivery systems, and on the high seas. Following the crisis, the Russians vowed that never again would they be so humiliated. They began a crash program to modernize and strengthen their fleet and to build nuclear weapons with ICBMs to carry them. Kennedy and McNamara responded by increasing the pace of American production. The Russians then accelerated their program, and the arms race intensified.

As a presidential candidate, Kennedy had been critical of Eisenhower's defense policy because Ike put too much faith in the big bombs. Kennedy wanted to be able to respond to Communist aggression at any level. Kennedy set out to build a counterinsurgency force that could stamp out insurrection or revolution in the jungles of Asia or the mountains of South America. With his counterinsurgency force, Kennedy would prove to the world that the so-called wars of national liberation did not work. Through the Green Berets, as the force came to be called, the West would win the battle for the Third World.

Kennedy relied heavily on technology to overcome America's inherent manpower shortages, giving the Green Berets first call on all the Army's latest equipment.

The whole concept appealed strongly to the elitist strain in Kennedy, for the Berets consisted of the best young officers and enlisted men in the Army. They received extra training, better equipment, and special privileges. As the military equivalent to the Peace Corps, the Berets would apply American techniques and know-how in guerrilla warfare situations and solve the problems that had baffled the French. As Kennedy told a West Point commencement, he would apply "a wholly new kind of strategy." One of the great appeals of counterinsurgency, especially after the Cuban crisis, was that it avoided direct confrontation with the Soviet Union. The risks of an escalation to nuclear war were small.

In Kennedy's view, and in that of his advisers, and in the view of millions of American citizens, the United States would be able to do what other white men had failed to do in Vietnam and elsewhere partly because America's motives were pure, partly because America had mastered the lessons of guerrilla warfare. The United States would not try to overwhelm the enemy or fight a strictly conventional war, as the French had done in Vietnam. Instead the Berets would give advice to local troops while American civil agencies would help the governments to institute political reforms that would separate the guerrillas from the people. Kennedy's counterinsurgency would show the people that there was a liberal middle ground between colonialism and Communism.

The great opportunity came in South Vietnam. It had numerous advantages. Diem was more a low-grade despot than a ruthless dictator. He was relatively honest and a sincere nationalist. He had introduced a land-reform program that, on paper at least, was a model for others to follow. The Americans were already in Vietnam, with military and economic advisers. Finally, Vietnam was an ideal battleground for the Green Berets. Small-unit actions in the jungle or rice paddies suited them perfectly, as did the emphasis on winning the hearts and minds of the people through medical and technical aid. From Kennedy's point of view Vietnam was an almost perfect place to get involved. There he could show his interest in the Third World, demonstrate conclusively that America lived up to her commitments (the 1954 SEATO Treaty had extended protection to South Vietnam if it were attacked from without), and play the exciting new game of counterinsurgency.

The difficulty was the fuzzy legal situation. South Vietnam was a sovereign nation only because Diem said it was. Under the terms of the 1954 Geneva Agreements, which the United States had not signed but which it promised not to upset by force, South Vietnam was not a nation but a territory, to be administered by the French until elections were held. The 1954 agreements had also stipulated that neither Ho in North Vietnam nor Diem in South Vietnam should allow the introduction of foreign troops into their territories. The United States redefined the Geneva Agreements, deliberately creating the fiction that Geneva had set up two Vietnams, North and South. The Secretary of State, Dean Rusk, made the redefinition complete in 1963 when he claimed that "the other side was fully committed—fully committed— in the original Geneva settlement of 1954 to the arrangements which provided for South Vietnam as an independent entity."

The second major problem was the nature of the struggle. After Dulles wrote the SEATO Treaty and extended protection to South Vietnam, he assured the Senate that under no circumstances would the United States be required to put down an internal uprising or get involved in a civil war. Assuming that South Vietnam was a sovereign nation, the question then became one of ascertaining whether the opposition to the government came from within or without. The question was almost impossible to answer. After 1956 the North Vietnamese had concentrated on reconstruction in their own territory, and on building socialism there. After Diem refused to hold the elections in 1956, meanwhile, the Viet Minh in the South grew restive. Beginning in 1957, they carried on a systematic campaign to assassinate village chiefs and thus destroy Diem's hold on the countryside.

They suffered from political persecution, as did all Diem's opponents, for Diem was incapable of distinguishing between Communist and anti-Communist resistance to his government. In early 1960 eighteen national figures, including ten former ministers in the Diem government, issued a public manifesto protesting Diem's nepotism and the "continuous arrests that fill the jails and prisons to the rafters." They called for free elections. Diem threw them all into jail.

In March 1960 full-scale revolt began. Diem labeled his opponents Viet Cong, or Vietnamese Communists. The VC established the National Liberation Front (NLF) as its political arm. The bulk of the VC were recruited in South Vietnam and captured most of their arms and equipment from Diem's army. In September 1960, the Communist Party of North Vietnam finally bestowed its formal blessing on the NLF and called for the liberation of South Vietnam from American imperialism.

Under the circumstances, it was exceedingly difficult to prove that South Vietnam was the victim of "outside" aggression. The American Secretary of State, however, had no doubts. Rusk's views had changed not at all since 1950, when he decided that the Chinese Communists were "not Chinese." As he saw it, the war in Vietnam was sponsored by Hanoi, which in turn was acting as the agent of Peking. If the United States allowed the Viet Cong to win in South Vietnam, the Chinese would quickly gobble up the rest of Asia. Rusk warned his countrymen of the dangers of a Far Eastern Munich, thereby equating Ho Chi Minh with Hitler and raising the dreaded specter of appeasement.

Rusk was hardly alone in recommending the American involvement in Vietnam. Everything in the Kennedy record pointed to increased aid to Diem, and nearly everyone in the Kennedy administration supported the decision. The Joint Chiefs went along, but they did not push Kennedy into Vietnam, nor did American corporations with Asian interests, nor did the Asia-firsters in the Republican Party.

General William Westmoreland, who commanded the

American military effort in South Vietnam from 1964 to 1968, later said that before he left for Vietnam he discussed the situation there with every top official in the White House, the State Department, and the Pentagon. All agreed that the United States had to stand up to the aggressors from the north, using whatever means were necessary. He could not recall a single dissenter. There was also universal agreement on the need to prove to the Chinese that wars of national liberation did not work and to show the Third World that America stood by her commitments. These views were held most strongly by Kennedy's personal advisers, led by Walt Rostow and McGeorge Bundy. Westmoreland emphasized that America did not get into Vietnam, or stay there, because of a military conspiracy, or a military-industrial complex conspiracy, or any other conspiracy. America fought in Vietnam as a direct result of a world view from which no one in power dissented and as a logical culmination of the policy of containment.

Vietnam was the liberals' war. It was based on the same premises that Truman and Acheson had used. The United States, as Sorensen put it, "could supply better training, support and direction, better communications, transportation and intelligence, better weapons, equipment and logistics" to halt Communist aggression. With American skills and Vietnamese soldiers ("South Vietnam will supply the necessary men," Kennedy said), freedom would prevail.

In early 1961, Kennedy began sending his advisers to South Vietnam to report to him on what was needed and to teach Diem how to get the job done. The first to head a mission was the dynamic Texas politician Vice President Lyndon Baines Johnson. He returned in May 1961, determined to save the Alamo from the encircling enemy. "The basic decision in Southeast Asia is here," he declared. "We must decide whether to help these countries to the best of our ability or throw in the towel in the area and pull back our defenses to San Francisco and a 'Fortress America' concept." Johnson never explained how the fall of Diem could drive the United

States from its major Asian bases in the Philippines, Formosa, Okinawa, and Japan, not to mention Guam, Midway, and Hawaii.

The Kennedy team felt that America could not afford to back down anywhere. As Johnson put it in his report, if America did not stand behind Diem, "we would say to the world that we don't live up to our treaties and don't stand by our friends," which were almost the same words Kennedy was using with respect to the concurrent Berlin crisis. The Kennedy administration also assumed that if America set her mind to it there was no limit to what the nation could do, which made Johnson's conclusions inevitable: "I recommend that we move forward promptly with a major effort to help these countries defend themselves." American combat troops would not be needed and indeed it would be a mistake to send them because it would revive anti-colonial emotions throughout Asia. Johnson thought the South Vietnamese themselves could do the fighting, aided by American training and equipment.

Shortly after Johnson's trip Professor Eugene Staley, an economist from Stanford University, went to Saigon to advise Diem. Staley made a number of suggestions, the most important of which was that Diem institute a strategic hamlet program. The idea was that by bringing the peasants together it would be easier to protect them from the VC and prevent the VC from recruiting, raising taxes, or hiding in the villages among them. In practice, however, the strategic hamlets amounted to concentration camps. Diem's troops forced villagers to leave land their families had lived on for generations and thereby turned thousands of Vietnamese against the government. The war continued to go badly. Although the VC were concentrated in the least populated districts, they controlled nearly half the countryside.

In October 1961, Kennedy sent another mission to Saigon, headed by Rostow and Maxwell Taylor. Rostow was a Rhodes scholar, an M.I.T. professor, and an internationally famous economic historian. Taylor was a war hero, former superintendent of the U.S. Military

Academy, and one of the leading critics of Eisenhower's
reliance on massive deterrence. Between them, the professor and the soldier made a team that presumably
represented the best and the brightest in America.

The Rostow-Taylor mission reported that South Vietnam had enough vitality to justify a major United States
effort. Taylor said the major difficulty was that the South
Vietnamese doubted that the Americans really would
help them and he therefore recommended an increased
American intervention. He wanted the South Vietnamese Army (ARVN) to go on the offensive, with American
troops supplying the airlift and reconnaissance. Taylor
also urged Kennedy to send a combat unit of ten thousand men to South Vietnam. Rostow thought that Diem,
if pressed by the United States to reform, would be satisfactory. Both Rostow and Taylor agreed that the key to
victory was stopping infiltration from the north. If it
continued, they could see no end to the war. Rostow
argued forcibly for a policy of retaliation against the
north by bombing, graduated to match Hanoi's support
for the VC. Kennedy accepted the main conclusions (although he refused to bomb North Vietnam) and increased the shipment of troops and equipment to Diem.
When Eisenhower left office, there had been a few
hundred American advisers in South Vietnam; at the
time of the Rostow-Taylor mission, there were 1,364; by
the end of the following year, 1962, there were nearly
10,000; and by November 1963, there were 15,000.
Equipment, especially helicopters, came in at a faster
rate.

The American commitment to Diem was so strong, as
David Halberstam reported in *The New York Times,* that
Saigon "became more convinced than ever that it had
its ally in a corner, that it could do anything it wanted,
that continued support would be guaranteed because of
the Communist threat and that after the commitment
was made, the United States could not suddenly admit
it had made a vast mistake." The entire emphasis of the
Rostow-Taylor report had been on a military response,
and Kennedy concentrated on sending military hard-

ware to Saigon. The American ambassador did try to put pressure on Diem to institute political and economic reforms, but Diem ignored him.

Still, the war seemed to be going well. McNamara visited Vietnam in June 1962 and reported, "Every quantitative measurement we have shows we're winning this war." In March of 1963, Rusk declared that the struggle against the VC had "turned an important corner" and was nearly over. A month later he said there was "a steady movement in South Vietnam toward a constitutional system resting upon popular consent." The American generals on the spot made similar statements. The Buddhist uprisings against Diem in May of 1963, brought on by religious persecution, dampened the official optimism, but even the Buddhist display of dissatisfaction with Diem only caused embarrassment, not a reevaluation of policy. Kennedy continued to increase the size of the American military contingent and in one of his last press conferences declared, "Our goal is a stable government there, carrying on a struggle to maintain its national independence. We believe strongly in that. . . . In my opinion, for us to withdraw from that effort would mean a collapse not only of South Vietnam but Southeast Asia. So we are going to stay there."

But not necessarily with Diem. The CIA was soon involved in plots in Saigon to overthrow Diem and bring an efficient, honest government to power. Diem was a Catholic aristocrat, who had little support in his own army and no real ties with the non-Catholic majority of his people. His repressions were too blatant, his strategic hamlet and land-reform programs had too obviously failed. He had to go. In November 1963, ARVN, acting with the knowledge and approval of the CIA, although not at its prompting, overthrew and then killed Diem and his brother. A military regime that could hope to fight the war somewhat more efficiently, but that otherwise had neither program nor policy, took over. Three weeks after Diem's death, Kennedy himself was assassinated and Lyndon B. Johnson became President.

In Vietnam, as elsewhere, Johnson continued Kennedy's policies. In a 1964 New Year's Day message to South Vietnam, Johnson declared that "neutralization of South Vietnam would only be another name for a Communist take-over. The United States will continue to furnish you and your people with the fullest measure of support in this bitter fight. We shall maintain in Vietnam American personnel and material as needed to assist you in achieving victory." In July 1964 Moscow, Hanoi, and Paris joined together to issue a call for an international conference in Geneva to deal with an outbreak of fighting in Laos and with the war in Vietnam. China, the NLF, and Cambodia supported the call for a conference, as did the U.N. Secretary General, U Thant of Burma. Johnson replied, "We do not believe in conferences called to ratify terror," and the next day announced that the American military advisers in South Vietnam would be increased by 30 percent, from 16,000 to 21,000.

The American government continued to believe that it could win the war by applying a limited amount of force, primarily through ARVN. Throughout the summer of 1964 American officials continued to issue optimistic statements. Faith in the Kennedy-McNamara program of flexible response, counterinsurgency techniques, and the new theories of limited war remained high. Years later, when almost everyone was unhappy with the war, the American military and their supporters would charge that the failure in South Vietnam resulted from an inadequate application of force. America could have won the war, some generals and admirals claimed, had it put in more men sooner.

But at the time, at each step of escalation, the White House, the American military, the intelligence community, and the State Department, all believed that enough was being done. Ten thousand more troops, or a hundred thousand more, or five hundred more helicopters, or three more bombing targets would do the trick. The restraints on American action in Vietnam were self-imposed, and such factors as the public's unwillingness to pay a high cost for the war or fear of Chinese intervention played a role in limiting the use of

force. But by far the most important reason for the grad-
ualism was the deep belief within the Kennedy and Johnson administrations that enough was being done. There
was a consistent underestimation of the enemy.

Barry Goldwater, Republican candidate for the presidency in 1964, was one of the few politicians who disagreed. He thought that more had to be done, and soon.
Goldwater said he was prepared to go to the Joint Chiefs
and tell them to win, using whatever measures were necessary, including nuclear weapons. He also wanted to
carry the war to North Vietnam, starting with bombing
raids.

Johnson gleefully took up the challenge. In the 1964
campaign he ran on a platform promising major social
reforms at home and peace abroad. He presented himself as the reasonable, prudent man who could be trusted
to win in Vietnam while keeping the war limited. Johnson scornfully rejected Goldwater's bellicose suggestions.
Bombing North Vietnam, the President said, would
widen the war and lead to committing American troops
to battle. He was especially insistent about the last point:
"We are not going to send American boys nine or ten
thousand miles away from home to do what Asian boys
ought to be doing for themselves."

In the by now familiar pattern of American presidential campaigns in the Cold War, Goldwater was accusing
Johnson of not being tough enough with the Communists. Johnson had to show that he could be firm as well
as patient, hard as well as reasonable. He therefore
seized the opportunity that came on August 2 and 3,
1964, when he received reports that American destroyers had been attacked by North Vietnamese torpedo
boats in the Gulf of Tonkin. At the time few doubted
that the attacks had actually taken place, although *The
New York Times* and others suggested that the U.S. Navy
had provoked the attacks by escorting South Vietnamese
commando raids into North Vietnam. Later, in 1968,
Senator Fulbright's Senate hearings convinced millions
that the entire Tonkin Gulf affair was a fraud. In any
case, Johnson, without an investigation, charged North

Vietnam with commiting "open aggression on the high seas."

The result was the Gulf of Tonkin Resolution. Like Eisenhower in the Middle East, Johnson wanted and got a blank check that would allow him to expand the war as he saw fit without consulting Congress. The President asked Congress for authority to use "all necessary measures" to "repel any armed attack" against American forces. In addition, Congress gave the President the power to "prevent further aggression" and take "all necessary steps" to protect any nation covered by SEATO that might request aid "in defense of its freedom." The resolution sailed through the House on August 7, 1964, by a vote of 416 to 0. In the Senate, Fulbright steered the resolution through. He insisted that the Congress had to trust the President and turned back an amendment to the resolution that would have explicitly denied to the President authority to widen the war. The election was only three months away and Fulbright did not want to embarrass Johnson. The Senate then voted 88 to 2 in favor of the resolution (Wayne Morse and Ernest Gruening were the dissenters).

Hanoi, meanwhile, had sent out peace feelers. Perhaps encouraged by Johnson's charges that Goldwater was reckless, perhaps frightened by the Gulf of Tonkin Resolution, Ho Chi Minh secretly offered to negotiate. Neither Johnson nor his advisers nor the ARVN generals in Saigon were remotely prepared to accept a compromise solution to the war, however, for it would have meant a coalition government in South Vietnam with close ties to Hanoi. Elections almost surely would have eliminated the ARVN generals altogether. The new Saigon government would then reunite with the north and order the American troops out of Vietnam. These prospects were much too painful to contemplate and Johnson certainly did not want to make it possible for Goldwater to charge him with appeasement, or the loss of Vietnam. Johnson refused to negotiate, the war went on, and the American voters overwhelmingly voted for Johnson over Goldwater.

The key to victory remained hidden. The American military advisers before 1960 had trained ARVN to fight a conventional war, under the theory that if Hanoi decided to move against Saigon it would launch a North Korean-type assault. This was subsequently cited as a major factor in ARVN's difficulties, but it only hid the deeper malaise. The officer corps had no real connection with the troops. Half were Catholics, many from North Vietnam. Corruption was rampant. The desertion rate was the highest in the world. The truth was that in the face of a conventional assault, ARVN probably would have scattered even more than it did when faced with guerrilla warfare. There was simply no will to fight, for there was nothing to fight for.

ARVN's failure made Johnson's problem acute. He had to either negotiate or introduce American combat troops to retrieve the situation. If he continued Kennedy's policy of all-out material support plus Green Beret advisers, the Saigon government would collapse and the VC would take control of all South Vietnam.

The main debate in Washington after the Gulf of Tonkin and the election, then, was whether to escalate American involvement in the war or to negotiate. Either option was open. Hanoi had indicated in various ways its willingness to talk, but few American officials were interested. Johnson, Rusk, and the Kennedy aides who had stayed with Johnson consistently refused to negotiate. In the words of David Kraslow and Stuart Loory, "In 1964 the dominant view in official Washington was that the United States could not entertain the idea of talks or negotiations until after it applied more military pressure on the enemy." As a former White House aide later described the mood of that period, "The very word 'negotiations' was anathema in the Administration." Rostow, Taylor, and others argued that the military imbalance would have to be redressed before negotiations could be considered, which really meant that they wanted and expected victory. As Rostow explained the policy, "It is on this spot that we have to break the liberation war— Chinese type. If we don't break it here we shall have to face it again in Thailand, Venezuela, elsewhere. Vietnam is a clear testing ground for our policy in the world."

Johnson's great problem, after he rejected negotiation, was how to win the war without sending in American ground troops. The Air Force had the answer. Undaunted by the failure of interdiction bombing in North Korea, strategic–air-power advocates told the President they could stop Hanoi's aggression in a month. When a civilian aide asked the generals what would happen if Hanoi did not quit in a month, they answered that then another two weeks would do the trick. More specifically, Secretary of Defense McNamara, who also advocated taking the air war to North Vietnam, believed it would improve the morale of the South Vietnamese forces, reduce the flow and increase the cost of infiltration of men and equipment from North to South Vietnam, and hurt morale in North Vietnam. The net result would be to "affect their will in such a way as to move Hanoi to a satisfactory settlement." The third point was sometimes described as "ouch warfare." Sooner or later Ho Chi Minh would decide that his potential gain was not worth the cost, say "ouch," and quit. Another advantage to bombing was its peculiarly American flavor— the United States would win the war by expending money and material, of which it had an abundance, and avoid manpower losses.

In late 1964, Johnson decided to initiate a bombing campaign against North Vietnam. The Air Force and Navy made the necessary preparations. But to bomb a country with whom the United States was not at war, that had committed no aggressive actions against the United States, and against whom no one in Washington intended to declare war was a serious step. Johnson decided to make one last move to be certain the air campaign was really necessary to save the situation in the south. In late January, he sent a delegation headed by McGeorge Bundy, his special assistant for national security affairs and a Kennedy confidant, to Saigon to investigate.

On February 7, 1965, VC troops broke through the

defense perimeter around the American air base at Pleiku in South Vietnam and mortared the flight line and some American military barracks. Eight American soldiers were killed, six helicopters and a transport plane were destroyed. Bundy went to the scene to inspect the damage. As a White House official later recalled, "a man from the ivory tower was suddenly confronted with the grim horror of reality. Mac got mad and immediately urged a retaliatory strike." The ambassador to South Vietnam, Maxwell Taylor, and the American military commander, General William Westmoreland, joined Bundy in recommending instant retaliation. Within twelve hours a retaliatory raid began. The first major escalation had started.

On his way back to Washington, Bundy prepared a memorandum urging a steady program of bombing the north. He argued that within three months of the start of the bombing Hanoi would give up and seek peace. Bombing, he asserted, was the way to avoid the unpleasant decision to send combat troops. In Washington, planning went forward for a program of regular bombing of the north.

On March 2, 1965, American bombers hit an ammunition dump ten miles inside North Vietnam and a harbor fifty-five miles north of the demilitarized zone. The raids were the first to be launched without any alleged specific provocation by the North Vietnamese. Others quickly followed. Johnson himself picked the targets at luncheon meetings every Tuesday with McNamara, Rusk, and Rostow. Representatives of the Joint Chiefs and the CIA were sometimes present. They set limits based on a check list of four items: (1) the military advantage of striking the proposed target; (2) the risk to American aircraft; (3) the danger of widening the war by forcing other countries into the fighting; (4) the danger of heavy civilian casualties. The third point was the most important, for it was imperative to keep Russia out of the conflict, and Soviet ships were usually docked at Haiphong harbor, which was therefore not bombed.

Simultaneously with the bombing offensive in the

north, American airmen drastically stepped up their activity in South Vietnam. Indeed, according to Bernard
Fall, "what changed the character of the Viet-Nam war
was *not* the decision to bomb North Viet-Nam; *not* the
decision to use American ground troops in South Viet-
Nam; but the decision to wage unlimited aerial warfare
inside the country at the price of literally pounding the
place to bits." The sheer magnitude of the American
effort boggled the mind. First the headlines proclaimed
that America had dropped more bombs on tiny Vietnam
than in the entire Pacific Theater in World War II. By
1967 it was more bombs than in the European Theater.
Then more than in the whole of World War II. Finally,
by 1970, more bombs had been dropped on Vietnam
than on all targets in the whole of human history. Napalm poured into the villages while weed killers defol-
iated the countryside. Never had any nation relied so
completely on industrial production and material superiority to wage a war.

Yet it did not work. Hanoi did not quit or lose its
morale, the infiltration of men and supplies continued
(indeed increased), the VC still fought, and the political
situation in Saigon got worse. Johnson had rejected negotiation and given the Air Force its opportunity. The
Air Force had failed. New decisions had to be made.

Despite the bombing offensive, the option to negotiate
remained and Johnson came under heavy pressure from
the NATO allies and the neutral nations to talk to Hanoi.
Johnson gave his answer in a speech on April 7, 1965,
at Johns Hopkins University. He promised to launch a
massive economic rehabilitation program in Southeast
Asia once the conflict ended, a sort of Marshall Plan for
the area, and he claimed that he would go anywhere to
discuss peace with anyone. But far more important than
the olive branch the President waved was the sword he
flourished. The central lesson of the twentieth century,
he proclaimed, was that "the appetite of aggression is
never satisfied." There would be no appeasement in
South Vietnam as long as he was President. "We will not
be defeated. We will not grow tired. We will not with-

draw, either openly or under the cloak of a meaningless agreement." The next day American bombers launched a particularly severe series of air raids on North Vietnam, and fifteen thousand additional American troops started for South Vietnam.

The Air Force continued to strike North Vietnam, without success, and two months later, on June 8, 1965, Johnson announced that he was authorizing U.S. troops, formerly confined to patrolling, to search out the enemy and engage in combat. Three days later Saigon's last civilian government fell and Air Vice-Marshal Nguyen Cao Ky, who had fought for the French against the Viet Minh, became Premier. Ky soon announced that "support for neutralism" would henceforth be punishable by death. Despite the hard line in Washington and Saigon, however, the war continued to go badly. The VC had destroyed the railway system in South Vietnam. Acts of terrorism increased in the cities and more territory fell into Communist hands. Hanoi, meanwhile, working from its position of increasing strength, again attempted to open discussions by explicitly stating that approval in principle of American withdrawal, rather than withdrawal itself, was all that was needed to get the negotiations started.

In a major policy speech on July 28, Johnson repeated the untenable but customary claim that "there has been no answer from the other side" to America's search for peace. He, therefore, was compelled to send an additional 50,000 men to South Vietnam, bringing the total commitment to 125,000 men. It was clear that the American forces would actively engage in ground combat. America had decided to win in Vietnam by overwhelming the enemy. Johnson had already, on July 10, declared that there would be no limit on the number of troops sent to General Westmoreland.

From MacArthur onward, every responsible American military officer who had commented on the subject had warned against American involvement in a land war in Asia, yet the nation was now fully involved in one. Johnson had declared during the 1964 presidential campaign

that he did not want American boys dying in South Vietnam, doing what Asian boys ought to be doing for themselves, yet now the American boys were dying there. The
State Department had repeatedly stated that the United
States should never allow the Communists to claim that
America was fighting a white man's war against Asians,
yet that was exactly what had happened. Kennedy and
his aides had repeatedly pointed out that counterinsurgency was primarily a political task and that no guerrilla
war could be won without an appropriate political response, yet 90 percent or more of the material America
was sending to South Vietnam was military, and U.S.
troops were the only force that stood between a dictatorship and total collapse.

Why had the Americans not heeded their own warnings? Because they were cocky, overconfident, sure of
themselves, certain that they could win at a bearable cost,
and that in the process they would turn back the Communist tide in Asia. They expected to accomplish in Vietnam, in short, what Johnson had pulled off in the
Dominican Republic.

From 1916 to 1940 the U.S. Marines had controlled
the Dominican Republic, where American corporations
had large investments in plantations that provided fresh
fruits and vegetables to American markets during the
winter. President Roosevelt eliminated an overt American presence in 1940 when Rafael Trujillo won a rigged
presidential election and established a ruthless, efficient
dictatorship. Roosevelt characterized Trujillo as "an
s.o.b., but our s.o.b." In May 1961, Trujillo was assassinated.

With Trujillo gone, Kennedy saw three possibilities. In
"descending order of preference," they were: "A decent
democratic regime, a continuation of the Trujillo regime,
or a Castro regime. We ought to aim at the first, but we
really can't renounce the second until we are sure that
we can avoid the third." This typified Kennedy's—and
America's—approach to the Third World. Kennedy
wanted a democracy, but if the revolutionary govern-

ment had socialistic elements in it or there was a threat
that the country would go Communist, he would accept
a dictator and see what could be done later on about
restoring civil liberties. Above all he was determined to
keep the Soviets out and retain American economic and
political influence.

Kennedy did not have to make a choice between a
Castro and a Trujillo, for on December 20, 1962, following a series of transitory provisional governments,
the Dominican people elected Juan Bosch as their President. Bosch was a leftist, non-Communist visionary and
writer who had spent years as an anti-Trujillo exile and
who seemed to represent the liberal alternative Kennedy
was searching for. But Bosch was no match for the Dominican military and their conservative partners. Ten
months after his election, the military overthrew him in
a coup. Donald Reid Cabral took over, but he had almost
no following among the masses. By early April 1965, the
Republic was ready to explode again, even though the
United States had sent $5 million to Reid Cabral.

On April 24, young Boschist officers in the army
launched a coup that drove Reid Cabral from office, but
they were unable to restore order. Angry masses poured
into the streets of Santo Domingo. A junta of the regular
military, described in Washington as the Loyalists, decided to take power for themselves. The rebels armed
thousands of civilians and fighting began. The American
ambassador, W. Tapley Bennett, warned that a sudden
Communist takeover was one likely result of the civil war.

Johnson immediately decided that the revolt was part
of a larger conspiracy, probably masterminded by Castro, and that the challenge to American interests in the
Dominican Republic was a challenge to American interests throughout Latin America. He decided to intervene.
On April 28, Johnson sent in the Marines, to be followed
by the Army's 82nd Airborne Division. His initial rationale was to protect the lives of American citizens in
Santo Domingo, but on April 30 he announced a quite
different reason: "People trained outside the Dominican
Republic are seeking to gain control." The American

Embassy in Santo Domingo issued a documented list of fifty-eight "identified and prominent Communist and Castroite leaders" in the rebel forces, a list that was obviously, even outrageously, false—it came from one initially prepared years earlier by Trujillo himself. Bosch's assessment was more widely accepted: "This was a democratic revolution smashed by the leading democracy in the world."

Johnson had acted unilaterally, partly because of the need for speed, partly because of his opinion of his partners in the Alliance for Progress. "The OAS," he remarked, "couldn't pour piss out of a boot if the instructions were written on the heel." Once the Marines had restored some order and prevented Bosch from taking office, however, it was necessary to deal with the OAS. Johnson was able to persuade the Latin Americans to join him in the Dominican Republic and by May 28 an OAS peacekeeping force had reinforced and taken control from the U.S. troops. The search for a middle ground in the government went on. Eventually, in September, a government was formed and in June 1966 moderate rightist Joaquin Balaguer defeated Bosch in a presidential election.

Johnson had won. The intervention had been limited in time, number of troops involved, cost, and lives lost. American Marines and paratroopers had prevented the rise of either a Castro or a Trujillo in the Dominican Republic and the OAS had been mollified.

At the height of the crisis, Johnson had been besieged by liberal critics. *The New York Times* editorialized: "Little awareness has been shown by the United States that the Dominican people—not just a handful of Communists— were fighting and dying for social justice and constitutionalism." Robert Kennedy protested that Johnson had failed to notify the OAS before acting. Johnson ignored the critics and his eventual success proved justification enough. He may have concluded that he could do the same in Vietnam and that success there would also silence the critics.

Meanwhile, Johnson had problems in the Middle East, brought on by the intensity of nationalism in the region, and its possession of the lion's share of the world's oil reserves. In the 1960s, the Arab states, one by one, took control of their oil, owned by the British before World War II. During and after the war, American oil companies had forced the British to share the riches with them. But the postwar Arab governments, along with Iran, began demanding more for their precious, limited, and only important natural resource. Premier Mossadegh in Iran was the first to attempt a full-scale nationalization of the oil fields (1951), and he was toppled (1953) by the CIA. In 1959 the producing states—Venezuela, Iran, Saudi Arabia, Kuwait, and Iraq—together formed the Organization of Petroleum Exporting Countries (OPEC). OPEC's first objective was to ha' a worldwide slump in the price of crude oil. The United States was still an exporter of oil in 1959, and there was such a glut on the market that it took ten years to raise the price of oil back to its pre-1959 levels. In the meantime, each of the producing states had nationalized its oil fields, whether by agreement with the British and American oil companies or by the simple exercise of their sovereign power.

As other Arabs got rich, Nasser was unable to bring about any miracles in Egypt. Despite his commitment to socialism and Arab unity, neither really existed as the Egyptian people remained mired in nearly the worst poverty in the world, despite Soviet aid. His United Arab Republic was falling apart. By 1967 Nasser needed a dramatic victory to restore his sagging fortunes. He had an opportunity because ever since the 1956 war the Russians had been supplying Egypt, Syria, and Iraq with advanced weapons, while following a strongly anti-Israel policy. The Arabs greatly outnumbered the Israelis and were now better armed. By 1967 the Russians were encouraging the Arabs to attack Israel, although they made it clear there would be no open Soviet backing for the

Arabs, who could not expect help if their military adventure failed. Still, with thousands of Russian technicians and their families in Egypt, working on the Aswan High Dam or with the Egyptian military, Nasser may have assumed the Russians had to support him.

In May 1967, goaded by the Russians and by Arab extremists, Nasser demanded the removal of the United Nations Emergency Force (UNEF), which had stood between the Egyptians and Israelis since 1957. Secretary General U Thant, noting that he could hardly keep U.N. troops in place in opposition to the host government, promptly pulled the UNEF out of the Sinai. This seems to have surprised both Nasser and the Russians. The Soviets now changed their position, urging caution on Nasser, as they feared the outbreak of a war that they could not control and that might lead to a United States–U.S.S.R. confrontation. But Nasser could not back down at this juncture; Egyptian troops took possession of Sharm al-Shaikh, overlooking the Strait of Tiran, and closed Israel's access to the Gulf of Aqaba and thus to the port of Elath.

The United States was preoccupied with Vietnam at this time, becoming more dependent on Arab oil, and above all anxious to avoid another war, particularly one in the Middle East, with possible repercussions too frightening to think about. But it could not simply abandon Israel to Nasser and the Russians. President Johnson tried to organize international attempts to run the Egyptian blockade, but the Western European nations, fearing Arab oil embargoes, would not cooperate. Israel believed the American efforts were half-hearted at best and decided to take matters into her own hands, before she was slowly strangled.

At this juncture General de Gaulle gave Israel's foreign minister, Abba Eban, some perceptive advice. "Don't make war," de Gaulle declared. "You will be considered the aggressor by the world and by me. You will cause the Soviet Union to penetrate more deeply into the Middle East, and Israel will suffer the consequences. You will create a Palestinian nationalism, and you will never get rid of it." De Gaulle's last prophecy proved to be especially accurate. The Russians and Americans were meanwhile urging Egypt and Israel, respectively, not to strike the first blow.

But on the morning of June 5, 1967, the Israeli Air Force struck. By flying over the Mediterranean rather than over the Sinai, the planes avoided Egyptian radar and consequently achieved complete tactical surprise. They demolished most of Egypt's planes and left its airfields inoperative, then turned and repeated the operation against the Jordanian, Syrian, and Iraqi air forces. It was a dazzling demonstration of the superiority of the Israeli fliers and gave them control of the air. Nasser sank ships to block the Suez Canal. Soviet Premier Aleksei Kosygin got on the Hot Line that morning to inform President Johnson that the Soviet Union would not intervene unless the United States did. Israeli tanks and infantry columns were already marching into the Sinai, seizing the Golan Heights, and capturing from Jordan the West Bank and Jerusalem. Johnson told Kosygin that America was ready to demand a cease-fire, which the U.N. Security Council did the next day, June 6. Meanwhile, Johnson had put the U.S. Sixth Fleet in the Mediterranean on full alert and had sent two aircraft carriers toward Egypt.

Inadvertently, Johnson had given Nasser a perfect excuse for the miserable showing of the Egyptian armed forces. Although the Soviets had the American Sixth Fleet under tight surveillance, and thus knew perfectly well that no American combat aircraft had been launched on either June 5 or 6, Nasser falsely charged that American planes from the Sixth Fleet and British planes from Cyprus had participated in the initial waves of attack. He was widely believed in the Arab world. By the morning of June 7, Egypt, Algeria, Iraq, Sudan, Syria, and Yemen had broken relations with the United States and Britain. But Nasser was unable to bring the moderate Arab states along with him—relations were preserved between the United States and Jordan, Libya, Morocco, Kuwait, Tunisia, and Saudi Arabia. The Arab petroleum ministers did proclaim an embargo of oil shipments to Israel's backers, especially Britain and the United States, but it had little effect.

Israel, meanwhile, had won a stunning victory. When she accepted a cease-fire on June 10 (giving the conflict its name, the Six Day War), Israel had conquered all of Egypt's Sinai Peninsula and the Gaza Strip, driven twelve miles into Syria, seizing the Golan Heights, and taken all of Jerusalem plus the West Bank of the Jordan River.

For both Russia and the United States the results of the Six Day War were melancholy. Russian arms had been blasted by French arms (the French Mirage was the backbone of the Israeli Air Force), and the huge buildup of Russian tanks in the Arab world had come to naught—indeed, those tanks not destroyed were now part of Israel's captured booty. The Arabs, generally, were furious with the Russians for not helping them more directly during their time of troubles. The Americans had tried to deter war and had failed. Now Suez was blocked, the Arabs had placed an embargo on oil, the Soviet Union was more entrenched than ever in the Middle East (because, much as they hated it, the Arabs were more dependent than ever on Russia for rebuilding their armed forces), and half the Arab states had broken diplomatic relations with the United States.

Worst of all, Israel now occupied territory that was indisputably Arab* (Sinai has been an integral part of Egypt for more than five thousand years), and the Palestinian refugee problem had grown from an irritant to a cancer. There were tens of thousands of new refugees, who spilled over into Jordan, Lebanon, Egypt, and Syria, and other thousands of Palestinians now living under armed Israeli occupation. The immediate consequence was the expansion of the Palestine Liberation Organization (PLO) and a dramatic increase in the scope and number of terrorist acts carried out by the desperate

---

*Before 1967 Israel occupied only territory once a part of the British Palestine Mandate.

Palestinians. Israel had won, but in the process it had added enormously to its problems and put off into the indefinite future the day when it could live at peace with its Arab neighbors. Nevertheless, the Israelis believed that territory was security, and they refused to pull back to the June 4, 1967, borders.

France, meanwhile, acceding to demands by the oil-holding Arabs, announced that it was imposing an embargo on all arms sales to the Middle East. DeGaulle even blocked delivery to Israel of fifty Mirages on order and already paid for. The Russians rushed new aircraft to Syria and Egypt. Under the circumstances, Johnson was under intense pressure, because for the first time an American President had to choose between supplying Israel with weapons on a large scale* or taking the domestic political consequences of seeing Israel lose her military superiority. Johnson decided he had to support Israel, and the United States became her chief supplier of sophisticated weaponry with the 1968 sale of fifty Phantom F-4s (supersonic jet fighter-bombers).

The Arabs, badly defeated, began a slow retreat. In July 1967 they rejected a draft resolution prepared by the United States and the Soviet Union for the U.N. General Assembly that called upon Israel to withdraw from all territories occupied after June 4 and urged all parties to acknowledge the right of each to maintain, in peace and security, an independent national state. The Arabs refused to recognize Israel's status as a sovereign state, but they did tacitly abandon the call for the extinction of the Zionists and committed themselves to diplomatic efforts to solve the problem. In August they lifted the embargo on oil shipments to America and Britain. In October Egyptian missiles sank an Israeli destroyer and Israeli artillery fire destroyed Egypt's two principal oil refineries. Both sides by then had had

*The United States had sold surface-to-air antiaircraft missiles to Israel in 1962, Patton tanks in 1965, and A-4 Skyhawks in 1966.

enough and requested action by the U.N. Security Council to bring about a meaningful cease-fire.

The result was the famous Security Council Resolution 242, drafted by Lord Caradon of Great Britain and adopted on November 22, 1967. An evenhanded document, 242 attempted to reconcile the vital interests of the opposing sides. For Israel it promised peace with her neighbors, secure and recognized boundaries, and free navigation of regional waterways. For the Arabs it promised Jewish evacuation of the conquered territories and a national homeland for the Palestinians. Both the Arabs and the Israelis accepted 242, but Israel with the understanding that firm, guaranteed peace treaties must be signed before there would be any withdrawal, while the Arabs insisted that 242 meant full Israeli withdrawal must precede any other diplomatic move.

Thus the two main results of the Six Day War, which most Israelis and Americans interpreted as a great victory for Israel, were Israeli occupation of Arab national territory and the creation of a fully developed, and fanatic, Palestinian nationalism. The Arabs could not rest until they had their territory back, and the Palestinians would not rest until they had their own national state.

A third result of the war—military overconfidence—allowed the Israelis to feel that they could safely ignore these threats. They began to think of themselves as invincible. So did other observers, including the CIA. These impressions were strengthened in 1970 when President Richard Nixon began selling arms to Israel on a wholly unprecedented scale. A fourth result was to drive the most moderate of the Arab states solidly into the anti-Israel column, because of the occupied territory, the Palestinian problem, and because Israel now had possession of the old city of Jerusalem, as holy to the Muslims as to the Jews and Christians. Most Arabs agreed that the Israelis could have peace, or they could have territory, but they could not have both.

For Americans it was Vietnam that provided the setting for Lyndon Johnson's agony, indeed for the agony of an entire nation. From 1965 on, Vietnam brought up the old questions about America's position in the world, questions that had lain dormant since Senator Taft had first raised them in response to the Truman Doctrine. America had been called upon to pay up on an insurance policy written in 1947 for Europe and extended from 1950 to 1954 to Asia. The price proved to be far higher than anyone had expected. Eventually the almost universal commitment within the United States to the policy of containment began to give way. Senators, intellectuals, businessmen, and millions of citizens launched a massive attack on some of the fundamental premises of American foreign policy during the Cold War, especially the definition of America's vital interests and the domino theory. The tendency had been to define the nation's vital interests as any area in which the United States had political, economic, or military influence, which meant that America's vital interests were always moving outward. There had been little serious opposition to this trend until Vietnam. But by 1968, for the first time since the late forties, the State Department had to defend the definition of vital interests.

In Vietnam the American people had been forced to face up to the true cost of containment. In 1965 most Americans agreed that it was necessary to hem in China and Russia militarily, that America had vital interests in Western Europe, Japan, Latin America, and certain sections of the Middle East, that the United States would have to do whatever was required to prevent any of these areas from going Communist, and that to protect these areas it was necessary to defend the regions around them. This was the original escalation—the escalation of what America considered its vital interests. It was also assumed that America's needs included worldwide stability and order, which too often meant the preservation of the status quo. These had been the broad general aims of all the Cold War presidents, and although there had been differences in degree, Truman and Eisenhower and Kennedy had been prepared to take the risks and pay the cost involved in maintaining them.

It was Johnson's bad luck that he got stuck with Vietnam.

At bottom, Vietnam differed from the Dominican Republic intervention only in the cost. The Vietnamese intervention was not, in Johnson's view, the misapplication of an otherwise sound policy but rather one possible outcome that had always been implicit in the policy of containment. On every possible occasion, the President emphasized that he was only following in the footsteps of Truman, Eisenhower, and Kennedy, and he never saw any good reason to question the basic assumptions.

Others did. As the American commitment mounted, from $10 billion to $20 billion to $30 billion a year, from 150,000 to 300,000 to 500,000 and more men, as the casualties mounted, as the bombs rained down on the people of both North and South Vietnam, Johnson's critics began to wonder not just about Vietnam but about containment itself. Riots in America's cities, air and water pollution, the persistence of racism, the revolt of young people against the draft all added to the force of the questioning. The college students of the fifties had not questioned the policy of containment for many reasons, but the most important was probably that, after the Korean War, containment did not entail the death of thousands of young American men, the squandering of billions of dollars. In the late sixties, as the war in Vietnam went on and on and on, students and others began not only to ask about the war in Vietnam, but more significantly, to ask what kind of a society could support such a war. This led to an examination of all aspects of American life. As a result some students came to believe that they lived in an evil, repressive society that exploited not only foreigners but Americans as well.

The campus revolt, however, was not as immediately significant as the broader questions raised by older men who had a stake in the society and a commitment to preserving it. Many came to believe that containment, and the specific expression of that policy in Vietnam, was not saving America but destroying it. They returned to an older vision of America, best expressed by Lincoln at Gettysburg, which saw America's mission as one of setting an example for the world. "America can exert its greatest influence in the outer world by demonstrating at home that the largest and most complex modern society can solve the problems of modernity," Walter Lippmann wrote. "Then, what all the world is struggling with will be shown to be soluble. Example, and not intervention and firepower, has been the historic instrument of American influence on mankind, and never has it been more necessary and more urgent to realize this truth once more." Senator Fulbright added, "The world has no need, in this age of nationalism and nuclear weapons, for a new imperial power, but there is a great need of moral leadership—by which I mean the leadership of decent example." But for Johnson it was in America's self-interest—and it was her duty—to use military force to stop the spread of Communism, whether in the Dominican Republic or in Vietnam.

Johnson's foreign-policy advisers, almost to a man Kennedy appointees, agreed. Secretary Rusk took the lead. In private as well as in public, Rusk argued that China was actively promoting and supporting the war in Vietnam, which in his view did not differ in any significant way from Hitler's aggression in Europe. "In his always articulate, sometimes eloquent, formulations," as Townsend Hoopes, Under Secretary of the Air Force, put it, "Asia seemed to be Europe, China was either Stalinist Russia or Hitler Germany, and SEATO was either NATO or the Grand Alliance of World War II." Johnson echoed Rusk's theme. "The backstage Johnson," Philip Geyelin reported, "was quite capable of telling one of the Senate's more serious students of foreign affairs that 'if we don't stop the Reds in South Vietnam, tomorrow they will be in Hawaii, and next week they will be in San Francisco.' "

There was an obvious difficulty with the approach, a difficulty inherent in the policy of containment. If the threat were really as pervasive as Johnson and Rusk said it was, if the stakes were actually as cosmic as they claimed, it made little sense to fight the tip of the spear and leave the spear chucker alone. The only possible justification for the death of fifty thousand American soldiers and twenty times or more that many Vietnamese was to win, which meant defeating the spear maker in Peking. But no one dared risk taking the war to China, or even to Hanoi (except in the air). The Vietnam War differed from the Korean War in many ways, but one of the most important was that the Administration never attempted to liberate North Vietnam. Yet unless Hanoi itself were occupied by American troops, the North Vietnamese and the VC could carry on the war for a very long time. Bombing could not harm their source of strategic materials, since the source was in China and even more in Russia, and the U.S. Air Force could not seriously disrupt a line of communications that depended in large part on trails and men on bicycles. Nor could the United States impose an unacceptable toll on the enemy's manpower or material resources on the battlefield, for whenever the VC wished to cut their losses they could withdraw into the jungle or across the Cambodian or Laotian borders and avoid further combat.

The war could not be won without expanding it. The influx of American combat troops meant that it would not be lost. Hanoi would not negotiate until the bombing ended, nor until America promised to withdraw her troops, nor on the basis of elections held under the auspices of the Saigon government. America would not negotiate until Hanoi "stopped her aggression" by withdrawing her troops and material support for the VC, nor would America withdraw until she was assured that the Saigon government would remain in power. Since who ruled in Saigon was what the war was all about, and since neither side would surrender, America was committed to a long war in the East.

The Kennedy liberals, meanwhile, turned against Johnson, although as much because they were offended by his style as because they disagreed with the policy. The Senate doves began holding frequent meetings to complain about the President. At the meetings, as in their public statements, they tended to personalize the issues. At one of the private sessions, Senator Eugene McCarthy of Minnesota was reported to have said, "We've got a wild man in the White House, and we are going to have to treat him as such," and Senator Albert Gore of Tennessee (father of current Vice President Al Gore) called Johnson "a desperate man who was likely to get us into war with China, and we have got to prevent it."

Much of the criticism missed the point. Johnson was flamboyant, he did overreact to events, and he was at least as guilty of personalizing everything as the doves were, but his policies were simply a logical outgrowth of those pursued by his predecessors, as he himself pointed out on every possible occasion.

By 1967, however, style seemed to be the issue. The doves called Johnson a monster. He called them "chickenshit." "I'm the only President you have," he was fond of declaring, with the implication that any criticism was unpatriotic. "Why don't you get on the team?" he would demand of the few critics who got into the White House to see him. In November of 1966, Johnson told assembled officers at the Officers' Club in Camranh Bay, "Come home with the coonskin on the wall." Dean Rusk kept on talking about Munich and appeasement, a theme Johnson picked up, thereby linking the doves with Chamberlain and the Administration with Churchill. Fulbright's private rejoinder was, "We go ahead treating this little piss-ant country as though we were up against Russia and China put together."

The opposition mounted, but Johnson was probably right in asserting that its strength was overstated. America had never fought a war without some internal dissension and it would be impossible to prove that the doves' dissatisfaction with Vietnam was deeper or more vocal than the Whig dissatisfaction with the Mexican War or the Copperheads' opposition to Lincoln, or even than the opposition FDR had faced before Pearl Harbor. There was not, in any case, a straightforward dove position. All Johnson's critics on the left agreed on the need to halt the bombing of the north, but beyond that they could not rally behind a program. Some wanted to get out of Vietnam altogether, admitting defeat, but continuing the general policy of containment. Their criticism was tactical—America had overextended herself. Other doves wanted to struggle on in South Vietnam—they remained wedded to an all-out containment and objected only to the bombing of the north. A growing number wanted not only to get out of Vietnam but to go further and reexamine the entire containment policy. The deep divisions within the opposition allowed Johnson to hold to his course.

As the public criticism mounted, Johnson fought back with predictions that victory was just around the corner. Rostow was in the vanguard of the effort. He fed the press carefully selected figures from the American computers in Vietnam that proved the Administration was on the high road to victory. The "weapons loss ratio" was 4.7 to 1 in favor of the Americans, as opposed ot the unfavorable 1 to 2 ratio in 1963. Enemy desertions were up from 20,000 in 1966 to 35,000 in 1967. ARVN desertions were down from 160,000 to 75,000. The VC were incapable of mounting any large-scale attacks. The number of people under Saigon's control had jumped from 8 million to 12 million, or nearly 75 percent of the south's population.

The overwhelming application of American power, the Johnson administration insisted, was having a cumulative effect that would, in time, bring Hanoi and the VC to their knees. The enemy's losses in the south were little short of catastrophic, yet Hanoi was not sending more troops from North Vietnam to the south to make up the losses because the bombing campaign in the north tied down enormous numbers of workers and troops. Captured documents indicated that VC morale was low. There was light at the end of the tunnel. America was winning the war of attrition.

When Rostow's brave analysis failed to silence the critics, Johnson tried a harder sell. He brought General Westmoreland back to the States to explain how and when the victory would be won. At the National Press

Club, Westy declared, "I am absolutely certain that whereas in 1965 the enemy was winning, today he is certainly losing." On national television, the general predicted victory within two years; Johnson, meanwhile, to give the one last shove needed to force Ho Chi Minh to surrender, again expanded the bombing. In mid-November 1967, the heaviest attacks yet against the Hanoi-Haiphong complex began.

Through it all ran a single thread—military victory was possible and necessary. Although the Administration presented the war as limited in scope and purpose, in fact the only satisfactory outcome for America was the maintenance in power of the Saigon regime, which meant the total frustration of Hanoi and the VC. America was committed, as Townsend Hoopes put it, "to the preservation and anchoring of a narrowly based government in the South, which could not survive without a large-scale U.S. military presence, whose constitution ruled out all political participation by the main adversary, and which was diligently throwing in jail even those non-Communists who advocated opening a dialogue with the National Liberation Front."

It could not have been otherwise. Containment meant containment. Any compromise solution would have led to an NLF participation in the politics of South Vietnam, which would have carried with it the very great risk of an eventual Communist victory, which would have meant that the Communists had not been contained, which would have meant that all the sacrifices had been made in vain. Hoopes sums it up nicely: "In short, President Johnson and his close advisers had so defined our national purposes and so conducted the war that a compromise political settlement would be tantamount to a resounding defeat for U.S. policy and prestige. Accordingly, it could not be faced. Military victory was the only way out." Throughout 1967, and into 1968, the Administration insisted that victory was possible.

Then came Tet. The Communist offensive in late January 1968, launched with brutal swiftness and surprise on the religious holiday of Tet, showed in a direct if

painful fashion that everything Rostow and Westmoreland had said and everything the computers had reported was wrong. The VC drove the Americans and
ARVN out of parts of the countryside and into the cities,
thereby making a shambles out of the pacification program, and even took some of the cities. In Saigon a VC
suicide squad actually took temporary possession of the
American Embassy grounds. The Americans, it turned
out, did not control the situation. They were not winning. The enemy retained enormous strength and vitality.

The American response to Tet illustrated much about
the American view of the war and of the American attitude toward the people of Vietnam. As one example,
the VC took control of the ancient cultural capital of
Hue. David Douglas Duncan, a famous combat photog-
rapher with long experience in war, was appalled by the
American method of freeing the city. "The Americans
pounded the Citadel and surrounding city almost to dust
with air strikes, napalm runs, artillery and naval gunfire,
and the direct cannon fire from tanks and recoilless
rifles—a total effort to root out and kill every enemy
soldier. The mind reels at the carnage, cost, and ruth-
lessness of it all." An artillery officer explained, "We had
to destroy the city to save it."

The Administration claimed that Tet represented a
last-gasp effort by the enemy, but the interpretation
found few adherents. Senator Eugene McCarthy, meanwhile, challenged the President in the presidential primary campaign in New Hampshire and almost defeated
him. The junior Senator from New York, Robert Kennedy, then announced that he was entering the campaign. McNamara had left the Cabinet after failing to
persuade Johnson to stop the bombing, but to Johnson's
great surprise the new Secretary of Defense, Clark Clifford, widely considered to be a hawk, also wanted to stop
the bombing. Faced by the crisis in confidence in his
Administration, informed by the polls that he faced almost certain defeat in the upcoming Wisconsin primary,
deserted by all but a small handful of the most extreme

hawks within his own Administration, shocked by a request from Westmoreland for 200,000 additional troops
for Vietnam (which would have required calling up the
reserves and expanding the draft), Johnson finally decided to change his military policy. On Sunday evening,
March 31, 1968, Johnson announced on national television that he was stopping the bombing in North Vietnam, except for the area immediately north of the
demilitarized zone. To everyone's astonishment, he then
withdrew from the presidential race.

It was a humiliating end. Certainly Johnson had been
the most powerful man in the world, and quite possibly
he had the strongest will, yet a relative handful of VC
had resisted and overcome his power and broken his
will. The man who had done more for black Americans
than any President since Lincoln found himself accused
of fighting a racist war with racist methods. A truly tragic
figure, Johnson had overreached himself. He had
wanted to bring democracy and prosperity to Southeast
Asia but he had brought only death and destruction. By
early 1968 he had learned the painful lessons that the
power to destroy is not the power to control, and that
he had reached and passed the limits to his own power.

12

Nixon, Détente, and the Debacle in Vietnam

Give us six months, and if we haven't ended the war by then, you can come back and tear down the White House fence.

> HENRY KISSINGER to a group of
> Quakers, March 1969

Let me speak to you honestly, frankly, openheartedly. You are a liar.

> LE DUC THO to
> Henry Kissinger, 1972

I'm not going to be the first President to lose a war.

> LYNDON BAINES JOHNSON, 1967
> RICHARD MILHOUS NIXON, 1972

In the summer of 1968 the Republicans nominated Richard Nixon for the presidency. The Democrats chose Hubert Humphrey, Johnson's Vice President, and adopted a platform that pledged to continue Johnson's policies in Vietnam. As one of the original and most ferocious of the Cold Warriors, Nixon hardly offered an alternative to the doves. There was, therefore, no opportunity to vote "yes" or "no" on the Vietnam War in the 1968 election, a fact that contributed heavily to the extreme bitterness of that presidential campaign. The third-party ticket in that year, the one that did offer an alternative to the two old parties, was headed by Governor George Wallace of Alabama and adopted as its foreign policy a program designed to "bomb North Vietnam back into the stone age." Thus the doves, representing nearly half the population, were left without a candidate for President in 1968.

Precisely because their numbers were so great, however, the doves did have an influence, because both Nixon and Humphrey had to go after their votes. Nixon did so when he announced that he had a "secret plan to end the war," without explaining what it was. Humphrey, meanwhile, hinted that he was secretly a dove, but could not reveal his true position until safely elected, for fear of offending Johnson.

Earlier, in May of 1968, preliminary peace talks between the United States and North Vietnam had gotten under way in Paris. Between that time and the campaign, the two sides argued about the shape of the table around which the final peace conference would meet. The real issue was whether the VC and Siagon would be represented. Both Johnson and Ho Chi Minh were more interested in making propaganda than progress toward peace, at least until the results of the election were known. Throughout the campaign there was no progress in Paris.

As the campaign neared its climax, Johnson needed to reach out to the doves, for Humphrey's sake. He did so on October 31, five days before the election, when he announced that serious peace talks would start shortly in Paris, with all four parties represented, and that he was halting "all air, naval and artillery bombardment of North Vietnam."

Humphrey, who had been closing steadily on Nixon, went ahead of him in the polls. A desperate Nixon then played his trump. He had Mrs. Claire Chennault, widow of the famous commander of the World War II Flying Tigers, tell President Nguyen Van Thieu* that South Vietnam would "get better treatment from me than under the Democrats." Responding to this promise, two days before the election Thieu undercut Humphrey and Johnson by announcing that he would *not* participate in the peace talks, which made Johnson's bombing halt appear to be a last-minute political ploy rather than a real move toward peace. On Election Day, Nixon won with

*Ky's successor as leader of South Vietnam.

43.4 percent of the vote to Humphrey's 42.7 (Wallace got 13.5 percent).

With his narrow victory, Richard Nixon earned the right to decide American policy in the Vietnam War. He had numerous options. He surely recalled how Eisenhower had added to his popularity by ending the Korean War six months after taking office. He could do the same in Vietnam by simply bringing the boys home. Or he could continue Johnson's policy of all-out war in the south, hands off the north. Or he might decide to turn the war over to the Vietnamese, making them do the fighting with American equipment. Or he could extend the bombing campaign to the north, devastate Hanoi, mine Haiphong harbor, and invade with ground troops. Or, the final option, he could use nuclear weapons. Given the nature of the campaign, Nixon might have adopted any one of the above options or a variation thereof, saying that it was his "secret plan to end the war." And, except for the last option, he could have worked up significant, even majority, support for any one of them.

The trouble with the first option, to simply end the war, was that Hanoi would not cooperate. In Korea in 1953, Eisenhower had gotten the Chinese to accept a truce after threatening to use atomic weapons if they did not. But in 1969, Nixon was not dealing with the Chinese; he had to deal with Ho Chi Minh, who was more stubborn than Johnson and who would *not* agree to a compromise peace, as the Chinese had done in Korea.* Ho wanted all of Vietnam. For him (as for Johnson and Nixon) the issue was: Who will rule in Saigon? ARVN officers wedded to the United States, or Ho Chi Minh and the Communists? On that question, there

---

*Another reason the Chinese were willing to call it quits in 1953, as the North Vietnamese were not in 1969, was that the South Koreans had built an army capable of defending the nation, while ARVN had made little progress despite arms shipments from the United States nearly four times as great as those that went to Korea.

could be no compromise. That did not prevent Nixon from pulling out, but it did mean that a complete American withdrawal would be followed by a Comi.. 'nist victory.

The second option, continuing Johnson's policies, had nothing to recommend it. All the Kennedy-Johnson assumptions about Vietnam and the nature of the war there had been proven wrong and expensive. Something new had to be tried.

The third possibility, turning the war over to the Vietnamese, had the most appeal. It avoided defeat. It kept alive some hope of an ultimate victory. It would relieve the pressure from the peace groups in the United States and mollify many of the doves. And it left open the fourth option, to step up military action against Hanoi and otherwise escalate the war.

The final option, to use nuclear weapons, although discussed seriously from time to time among high civil and military officials, was never very tempting. Aside from the moral opprobrium it would bring on the United States, and the intense internal opposition it would arouse, the use of the big bomb made little military sense. If the United States dropped one on Hanoi, it was possible that the Chinese or the Russians, or both, would retaliate by dropping one on Saigon. What would happen next was anyone's guess, but no one, including Nixon, wanted to find out.

So it came down to the program Nixon called Vietnamization. Six months after taking office, he announced that his secret plan to end the war was in fact a plan to keep it going, but with lower American casualties. He proposed to withdraw American combat troops, unit by unit, while continuing to give air and naval support to ARVN and rearming ARVN with the best military hardware America had to offer.

American policy had come full circle. Three decades earlier, when Franklin Roosevelt began his third term as President, he had declared that the United States would serve as the great arsenal of democracy. American boys ought not be fighting in Europe, he said, doing what

European boys ought to be doing for themselves (Johnson had said the same thing about American and Asian boys). Instead, the Americans would supply the tools of war so that others could contain the Axis aggressors. In 1969 Nixon proposed to contain the Communist aggressors by extending lend-lease to South Vietnam.

It proved to be a disastrous choice, one of the worst decisions ever made by a Cold War President. Some of the direct results were: a prolongation of the war by four years, at immense cost in lives and treasure; double-digit inflation, previously unknown in the United States; more bitterness, division, and dissension among the American people; the flouting of the Constitution by the President as he secretly extended the war to Laos and Cambodia, with tragic results for the people of both countries; and the eventual loss of the war. The best that could be said of Vietnamization was that it bought Nixon some time and helped him avoid having to answer, in his 1972 reelection campaign, the question, "Who lost Vietnam?"

Of course, Nixon had high hopes for his policy when he started out. His brilliant National Security Adviser, and later Secretary of State, Dr. Henry Kissinger of Harvard University, had convinced him that there was a path to peace with honor in Vietnam and that it led through Moscow and Peking. If the two Communist superpowers would only refrain from supplying arms to the North Vietnamese, Kissinger argued, Hanoi would have to agree to a compromise peace, a policy ploy that he called "linkage." The United States would withhold favors and agreements from the Russians until they cut off the arms flow to Hanoi. Peace would follow.

There were all sorts of problems with linkage, the first being that it was hardly new, that it was in fact exactly the policy every Administration since Roosevelt's had followed (when Truman withheld a loan from Stalin in 1945, it was with the hope that this would make the Russians behave in East Europe) without success. Dean Rusk had already tried it with regard to Vietnam. Linkage ignored the obvious fact that if the United States stopped supplying Saigon, there would also be an immediate peace, and that in any event the Russians and Chinese were sending into North Vietnam considerably less military hardware than the United States was shipping into the south.

Linkage assumed that world politics revolved around the constant struggle for supremacy between the great powers. Like Dulles and Acheson and Rusk, Kissinger regarded North Vietnam, South Vietnam, Cambodia, and Laos as pawns to be moved around the board by the great powers. He insisted on viewing the war as a highly complex game in which the moves were made from Washington, Moscow, and Peking (Beijing). He could not believe that Hanoi had its own aims and objectives, more or less unconnected to Russia's or China's.

Linkage fed Kissinger's megalomania. His self-confidence knew no bounds. Kissinger wanted to make peace, not just for his generation, nor just for his children's generation, but for his children's children. This impossible dream drove Kissinger to seek the broadest possible agreement with Russia. Everything was linked—the industrial nations' oil shortage, the Vietnam War, American wheat sales to Russia, China's military capacity, and so on. Kissinger sought nothing less than an all-ecompassing agreement that would bring worldwide, permanent peace. Through linkage, Kissinger would out-Metternich Metternich.

The first step would be an arms-control agreement with the U.S.S.R. From it would flow a more general détente, trade with Russia, lowered tensions in the Middle East, and peace in Vietnam with President Nguyen Van Thieu still in power. For these reasons and because the Strategic Arms Limitation Talks (SALT) were inherently the single most important issue facing the United States and the U.S.S.R., who between them were spending large sums of money on unbelievably destructive weapons, Kissinger put a mighty effort into arms control. The Johnson administration had started the talks but had given them such a low priority that Nixon and Kissinger were, in effect, starting anew.

They came to SALT with some sobering realizations, chief of which was that the days of American unchallenged superiority were finished. The United States had 1,054 intercontinental ballistic missiles (ICBMs), 656 submarine-launched missiles, and 540 long-range bombers, a force sufficient to kill each Russian fifty times over. The Russians, however, had built, in a crash program, 1,200 ICBMs, 200 submarine-launched missiles, and 200 big bombers. As Morton Halperin, one of Kissinger's assistants, noted in a staff study, "It was impossible to escape the conclusion that no conceivable American strategic program would give you the kind of superiority that you had in the 1950s."

Halperin's conclusion was hard to take and hardly taken. Nixon announced that sufficiency, rather than superiority, would be the new American strategic goal, Kissinger acknowledged that "an attempt to gain a unilateral advantage in the strategic field must be self-defeating," and the Americans placed a high priority on SALT. Nevertheless, Nixon still hoped to keep the American lead in strategic weaons, and he succeeded.

One of Nixon's first acts as President was to send the nuclear nonproliferation treaty (which prevented the "have-nots" from getting nuclear weapons), negotiated by the Johnson administration, to the Senate for approval. The day after that approval came—supposedly clearing the way for meaningful SALT talks—Nixon announced a new antiballistic-missile (ABM) program. His purpose was to create "bargaining chips" for SALT. In other words, like bombing in Vietnam to insure peace, Nixon was building new weapons so that the United States would not have to build new weapons. The President also endorsed the Multiple Independently Targeted Reentry Vehicle (MIRV), which could give each ICBM three to ten separately targeted nuclear warheads. Most military experts considered MIRV to be a quantum leap comparable to the switch from conventional to nuclear weaponry. Despite his talk about "sufficiency," Nixon still pushed on, determined to keep the United States in first place. He would not allow the American negotiators at SALT to bring up the subject of MIRVs; he wanted the United States to develop, perfect, and deploy the MIRVs before he would consider a freeze on them.

The SALT I agreement that was finally signed in 1972 froze ICBM deployment but not MIRV, which was about as meaningful as freezing the cavalry of the European nations in 1938 but not the tanks. Throughout the period of the Nixon administration, the Pentagon added three new warheads per day to the MIRV arsenal, a policy the Gerald Ford administration continued. By 1973, according to the State Department, the United States had six thousand warheads to the Russians' twenty-five hundred. By 1977 the United States had ten thousand warheads, the Russians four thousand. It was a strange way to control the arms race. As Laurence Martin, Director of War Studies at the University of London, noted, "So far the SALT exercise has done more to accelerate than to restrain strategic arms procurement on both sides."

SALT was the only arms-control agreement signed by any President in the first four decades of the Cold War. It was therefore of some symbolic importance, but it was badly flawed. It did not institute a freeze at 1972 levels. The Americans refused to swap MIRV for ABA,* to even consider a ban on antisatellite weapons (later called Strategic Defense Initiative). In the words of Raymond Garthoff, a scholar and participant in the arms-control talks, the President and the Secretary "were very skeptical of

---

*The Russians were well ahead of the Americans in ABMs, while the Americans were prepared to make their MIRVs operational at a time when the Russians had not gotten far in their research. A simple swap—no MIRVs, no ABMs—was possible, but the generals on both sides were horrified at the thought of giving up their respective advantages, and no deal was struck. Kissinger later stated that had he thought it through, he would have made the swap, and wished that he had.

arms control as a means of establishing greater stability and relied much more on political strategies."

Détente was supposed to lead to mutual trust, and SALT contained a declaration of principles in which both sides pledged not to attempt to take a unilateral advantage, but the day they left Moscow, after signing the treaty, Nixon and Kissinger went to Iran, where they offered the Shah unlimited access to American arms. Along with the opening to China, discussed below, and the strengthening of the American arsenal and of the NATO allies, and the encouragement Nixon, via the Shah, gave to rebels in Afghanistan, the Russians saw themselves being hemmed in militarily and politically, which was exactly what Nixon intended to do. The irony was that Nixon's critics charged he was letting the Russians lull him into a false sense of security, when that was exactly what he was doing to the Russians.

SALT did place limits on the ABMs, two per side, signifying Nixon's acceptance of the concept of Mutually Assured Destruction, or MAD. He explained in his memoirs that a "major effect of the ABM treaty was to make permanent the concept of deterrence through mutual terror: By giving up missile defense, each side was leaving its population hostage to a strategic missile attack. Each side therefore had an ultimate interest in preventing a war that could only be mutually destructive." The statement is a good example of how short a time "permanent" is in politics.

Nixon's policies, unlike his rhetoric, were designed to keep America ahead, which he managed to do with SALT. Still, Kissinger had to fight for the ratification of the interim agreement that SALT I produced. Senators charged that he was allowing the Russians superiority, an absurd position to take. Kissinger finally got the interim agreement through the Senate, thereby completing the first step in linkage. The next move was to bring Peking in on the game.

Since 1949 the United States had had no relations with the People's Republic of China, pretending all the while that the Nationalist Chinese on Taiwan, not the Communists in Peking, represented the "real" China. As a policy, nonrecognition had little to recommend it (aside from its value on the domestic political scene); certainly it had not made China any less Communist. When Nixon and Kissinger took office, China was not an issue they had to face. Democrats were afraid to raise the subject for fear of being labeled soft on Communism, and Republicans—led by Nixon himself—claimed to feel an intense loyalty to the Nationalist Chinese. Neither the public, the press, nor the Congress had the slightest hint that the new President might reexamine the old policy, with which he had been intimately associated throughout his career.

Suddenly, in July 1971, Nixon announced that he was going to visit China at the invitation of China's leaders. Kissinger had arranged the trip during a series of secret meetings with Chou En-lai, China's second in command. The trip would take place in February 1972. There had been no public pressure to change the China policy, and no public debate had taken place on the subject for years. Why had it been done? Who stood to gain what from it? Commentators speculated that perhaps Nixon and Kissinger wanted to use the opening to China as a way to squeeze both Moscow and Hanoi.

It appeared that Nixon saw vast possibilities for the United States in a Sino-Soviet split. He specifically believed that he could so manage the split as to force both Communist powers to abandon North Vietnam, which in turn would let the United States safely exit from Vietnam. The way to get China and Russia to cooperate, Nixon reasoned, was to keep them guessing about actual United States intentions. Nixon's active pursuit of détente could not help but make China worry about a possible U.S.-U.S.S.R. alliance against China. Nixon's opening to China, meanwhile, made Russia's leaders fearful of a U.S.-China alliance directed against them. There were many nuances to Nixon's policy, but always a consistent aim: to get Moscow and Peking to force Hanoi to allow the United States to extract itself from

South Vietnam and to refrain from toppling Thieu until a "decent interval" had gone by (presumably until Nixon left the White House in 1977).

But whatever their fears and worries about Nixon's moves, neither Moscow nor Peking changed their Vietnam policy. They continued to send supplies to their beleaguered fellow Communists, especially antiaircraft artillery. Neither Communist nation helped Nixon in any way with his Vietnam problem.

Nixon wanted to make history, and recognition of China, especially by Nixon himself, would most assuredly be historic. It was the right thing to do, he believed, and he was the right man to do it, his anti-Communist credentials being what they were. In 1978 Nixon said he believed no other American politician could have gotten away with it. The move was good politics. The right wing might (and to some extend did) complain, but it had no one but Nixon to cling to. The left wing could only applaud. The boldness and drama of the new policy, the basic common sense in recognizing China, and the magnificent television coverage of the trip itself, with Nixon always at the center, helped him win millions of votes. Just the sight of Nixon shaking hands with Chou or chatting with Mao Tse-tung gave him stature.

Nixon had taken a historic and sensational step. In a joint communiqué, issued from Shanghai, the governments of China and the United States agreed to take further steps toward normalization of relations between themselves, and further agreed that Formosa was a part of China. The next move came six years later, when in December 1978 President Jimmy Carter announced that the United States was establishing full diplomatic relations with China while simultaneously ending its mutual defense treaty with the Nationalist Chinese on Formosa. In the eighties the two countries began to establish trade relations.

The Nixon-Kissinger policy of détente and linkage had some successes in other parts of the world. An essential part of détente was wrapping up some of the old problems left over from World War II. One such was divided Berlin, the city where so much of the Cold War drama had taken place. In September 1971 the winners in World War II—Britain, the United States, the U.S.S.R., and France—signed the Berlin Accord, which was also endorsed by both Germanies. It provided for improved communications between sectors of the divided city. It became part of a comprehensive Berlin Agreement signed in June 1972 in Berlin, which also provided for an American recognition of East Germany. Formal diplomatic relations between the United States and East Germany were established in 1974.

At Helsinki, Finland, meanwhile, accords were signed in 1972 that recognized the boundaries of the various Russian satellites in East Europe and committed all signatories (including the Russians) to the defense of human rights (there was no enforcement machinery).

In the Pacific, too, Nixon was able to eliminate a problem left over from the war, the status of Okinawa. America had been in command on the island since 1945; under the terms of an agreement made in November 1969 between Nixon and Japanese Premier Eisaku Sato, Okinawa reverted to Japanese sovereignty in 1972. The United States retained its extensive military facilities but agreed to remove its nuclear weapons from the island.

The various settlements gave the Japanese what they wanted in the Pacific, the Communists what they wanted in East Berlin, East Germany, and East Europe. America had backed down from demands for democracy and free enterprise in the areas overrun by the Red Army. This retreat reflected, in turn, the coming of a new era in the world's history. The enormous American preponderance of power of 1945 was gone. This was on a relative scale, of course, as America's destructive power in 1975 was far greater than it had been in 1945, but in comparison to the rest of the world it was much less. So too with the American economy, which in the seventies was booming as never before, but which was also dependent on foreign sources as never before. In 1972, for the first

time in the twentieth century, the United States had a
deficit in its international trade accounts. Once a major
exporter of raw materials, America had become an
importer of copper, lead, zinc, and most of all oil. Meanwhile, the United States was also importing manufactured goods at record rates (in 1970, 71 percent of
American imports were manufactured goods, only 31
percent raw materials—including oil—and foodstuffs).
Fortunately, American agriculture remained the most
productive in the world, and in 1972 and again in 1979
the United States was able to make a major dent in its
balance of payments situation by selling massive quantities of wheat to the Russians. The exports were subsi-
dized by the U.S. government. The wheat deal was
perhaps the most direct payoff Nixon got from détente.

A way still had to be found out of Vietnam. The basic
difference between the Johnson and Nixon administrations was that Johnson believed in military victory,
whereas Nixon knew that the United States could not
win the war, at least not at a price the nation would
accept. Nixon realized that for economic reasons (the
war was simply costing too much) and for the sake of
domestic peace and tranquillity he had to cut back on
the American commitment to Vietnam, which meant in
turn accepting an outcome short of victory. The best
Nixon could hope for, and this was his aim, was a gradual
United States withdrawal, complemented by an improvement in ARVN's fighting qualities. Then, at best, South
Vietnam could maintain its own independence, rather
like South Korea; at worst, there would be a decent interval between American withdrawal and Communist
victory.

To buy the time needed to build up ARVN, Nixon
had to moderate the domestic dissatisfaction with the
war. Less than two months after he took office, the North
Vietnamese added to that dissatisfaction by launching
(February 23, 1969) a general offensive in which the
541,500 American troops in Vietnam (the peak level in
the war) took heavy casualties. Television newscasters

announced that the American combat death toll in the
Vietnam War had passed that of the Korean War, with
more than 40,000 dead.

Nixon responded to the offensive by moving in two
directions simultaneously. On the tough side, to let the
North Vietnamese know he could not be pushed around,
Nixon launched his secret war against the North Vietnamese supply routes in Cambodia. The "secret," obviously, was well known to the Cambodians and
Vietnamese, but Nixon managed to keep it from the
American public (and Congress) through four years of
intensive bombing. It was a bold, risky policy, with much
at stake. Unfortunately, the return on investment was
low. At their best, America's B-52s caused a 10 percent
falloff in movement of men and supplies from North to
South Vietnam via Cambodia. As in Korea, interdiction
could not work against an enemy who moved his goods
on human backs, along foot or bike trails.

In addition to the bombing of Cambodia, Nixon
sharply increased the level of bombing in South Vietnam. But he offered not only an iron fist to Hanoi—
there was a velvet glove also. On June 8, 1969, after
meeting with President Thieu of South Vietnam on Midway Island, Nixon announced the first United States
troop withdrawals from Vietnam. By August 1, he said,
twenty-five thousand American soldiers would be returned to the United States. Further reductions would
follow, as ARVN's fighting quality improved.

It was a historic turning point. Johnson's policy of
escalation in Vietnam had been reversed. It was the first
important American strategic retreat in Asia since
MacArthur fell back from the Yalu in 1950. That it was
an act forced on Nixon by public opinion made it no
less significant. And it was a great help in appeasing the
doves. So, too, was Nixon's promise to end the draft and
institute an all-volunteer army. The first step came in
November 1969 with the creation of a lottery system to
determine who would get drafted, which made the selective-service process fairer to all classes and groups,
and let a young man know where he stood with the draft.

The all-volunteer army was excellent politics, because the antiwar movement, as a political event, was essentially a student movement, and an all-volunteer army seriously weakened the political impact of the doves by robbing them of their major support, male college students. So, while constantly proclaiming that he would not allow policy to be dictated in the streets, Nixon allowed just that to happen, giving the protesting students exactly what they had been demanding: no more conscription. Nixon believed that there was not enough idealism in the antiwar movement to sustain it once college students were no longer threatened with the draft, and he was right. Except for a brief period following the Cambodian invasion of May 1970, Nixon had less trouble with street demonstrations than had his predecessor.*

Meanwhile, Nixon was supplying ARVN on a wholly unprecedented scale, to such an extent that when the final surrender came in 1975, ARVN was the fourth-ranking military power in the world.† Nixon warned Hanoi that the speed of American withdrawal from Vietnam would depend on progress in the Paris peace negotiations, and upon the levels of enemy activity, which meant that he was taking the position that while he was sending more weapons into South Vietnam, Hanoi should send less.

*It should be added that Attorney General John Mitchell came down very hard on all antiwar groups. He had the FBI infiltrate, then disrupt or sabotage or destroy, numerous student groups; he hauled others into court on trumped-up charges that were never sustained by a jury anywhere but that did have the effect of keeping such organizations as the Vietnam Veterans Against the War tied up in court, spending all their energy and time and money defending themselves. These, and numerous other actions taken by Mitchell, were an important factor in limiting the effectiveness of antiwar groups.

†In 1979 Communist Vietnam used these weapons to overrun Cambodia in two weeks.

That was the Administration's public posture. Privately, Kissinger had started, in August 1969, a series of secret negotiating sessions in Paris with Le Duc Tho, a member of Hanoi's Politburo. In these sessions Kissinger sought to bring about an armistice that would lead to the return of the American POWs, President Thieu's remaining in power in Saigon (at least for a decent interval), and a cease-fire. In return, the United States would withdraw all its troops from Vietnam and would recognize Communist possession of large sections of the South Vietnamese countryside. From Hanoi's point of view, the offer was an attempt to buy the Communists off with half a loaf just when they had the whole loaf in their grasp. From Thieu's point of view, it was a sellout, handing over parts of his country to the enemy just so the Americans could extract themselves without too much loss of face. From Kissinger's point of view, it was a reasonable compromise, and he put his tremendous energies and unbounded enthusiasm into the task of bringing it off. It took him almost four years, but he finally made it. In the process his patience was sorely tested. Le Duc Tho would return time and again to the tiniest point, which had been settled over and over in previous sessions. Kissinger would sigh deeply, then take it up once again.

While Kissinger prepared to divide South Vietnam between the contending parties, the war went on. Nixon had to justify it to an increasingly restive Congress and public. He used a series of different justifications. He said he had inherited the war and was fighting on only to extract American troops safely, or he argued that an American defeat in Vietnam would seriously affect American interests elsewhere. At times he referred to America's treaty commitments and the overwhelming need to prove to friend and foe alike that America stood by her word.

Nixon also warned the American people that if they quit and the Viet Cong won, there would be a terrible bloodbath in Saigon and the blame would rest with the United States. In his foreign-policy message to Congress in January 1970, Nixon declared, "When we assumed the burden of helping South Vietnam, millions of South Vietnamese men and women placed their trust in us. To abandon them would risk a massacre that would shock and dismay every one in the world who values human life." Most of all, Nixon justified the continuation of the war by raising the issue of the POWs held by Hanoi. We will fight on until we get them back, he declared, and it was a rallying cry with enough emotional content to convince most Americans that the war must go on.

The POW issue could not, however, win the war for Thieu. Vietnamization meant, first of all, vastly increased military aid for the Government of South Vietnam (GVN). Backed by the sudden, massive inflow of money and arms, Thieu ordered a general mobilization. By inducting all men between eighteen and thirty-eight into the service, Thieu expanded the GVN armed forces from 700,000 to 1,100,000, which meant that over half the able-bodied male population of South Vietnam was in uniform. As Frances FitzGerald points out in her award-winning *Fire in the Lake,* counting the militia, the civil service, and the 110,000-man police force, "the United States was arming and, in one way or another, supporting most of the male population of Vietnam—and for the duration of the war."

The sudden expansion of ARVN produced a temporary but real military advantage for the U.S.-GVN side. FitzGerald describes the results: "Now all, or most, of the Vietnamese were swept up into the American war machine. 'Vietnamization' preempted the manpower base of the country and brought it into a state of dependency on the American economy. And the results were spectacular. The major roads were open to traffic; the cities flourished on American money and goods; those peasant families that remained in the fertile areas of the Delta grew rich on bumper crops of 'miracle' rice. The country was more 'pacified' than it had ever been before."

From the American (and Thieu's) point of view, Vietnamization seemed to be working. By 1972, 50 percent of the population lived in cities (Saigon's population alone had jumped from 300,000 to 3,000,000 in ten years), where the refugees from the countryside became dependent upon the Americans. South Vietnam had the population distribution of an industrialized state, but it had no industry, except for the war and the Americans. Vietnamese refugees made their living either in the ARVN (where they were paid by the Americans) or by working directly for the Americans. In the cities the refugees were safe, certainly better off than they had been when living in the "free-fire zones," and they were fed by the American government—but they had no real economy.

From 1961 onward, American presidents never tired of proclaiming that the United States was making sacrifices in Southeast Asia only for the good of the people of the region. The United States had no territorial objectives, nor did it wish to replace the French as the colonial masters of the Vietnamese. It was true that the United States took no wealth out of Vietnam; in fact, it poured money in. "And yet," FitzGerald points out, "it has produced much the same effects as the most exploitative of colonial regimes. The reason is that the overwhelming proportion of American funds has gone not into agricultural or industrial development but into the creation of services for the Americans—the greatest service being the Saigon government's army. As a whole, American wealth has gone into creating and supporting a group of people—refugees, soldiers, prostitutes, secretaries, translators, maids, and shoeshine boys—who do not engage in any form of production."

The GVN was a government without a country. The people were dependent on it—or rather on the Americans—but they felt no loyalty to it. South Vietnam, once a major world exporter of rice, now produced almost nothing. The GVN had guns and money. The other side had a cause and brutal discipline. North Vietnamese morale went up and down over the decade of active American involvement, as would be true in any army in such a long war, but even at its lowest point Communist morale was so much higher than that of ARVN that no comparison was possible. The Americans talked incessantly about "pacification" and "winning the hearts and minds of the people," while Nixon dropped new record tonnages of bombs on their heads. Those who escaped the bombing offensive went to the cities to become unwilling conscripts in ARVN or resentful servants to the Americans. In the army they would not fight, for the good reason that they had nothing to fight for. Meanwhile, the VC and the North Vietnamese held on against the world's most powerful air force, thereby providing—in FitzGerald's words—"an example of courage and endurance that measures with any in modern history."

Throughout 1969 and into 1970, the Americans regularly released figures to prove that Vietnamization was working. ARVN, according to the Pentagon, could "hack it." Body counts were higher than ever; ARVN had more troops, more and better leaders and equipment. Then, on April 30, 1970, Nixon made a surprise announcement that a large force of U.S. troops, supported by major air strikes and backed by a major ARVN force, had invaded Cambodia. Nixon said the purpose was to gain time for the American withdrawal. The invasion of Cambodia resulted in the deaths of some Communist troops but otherwise had only negative results. It hardly even slowed the flow of supplies to the VC and North Vietnamese in the south. It turned Cambodia into a battleground and eventually prompted a successful Communist insurgency there, thereby making the domino theory come true.

The Cambodian invasion extended the list of nations the United States was pledged to defend, despite Nixon's solemn promise that he was not making any pledges to the Lon Nol military regime, which had recently (March 18, 1970) overthrown the government of Prince Norodom Sihanouk, a neutralist who had tried to keep the war away from Cambodia. The invasion temporarily revived the antiwar movement at home, especially after four students were shot dead on May 4 by the Ohio National Guard at Kent State University.

The American people, however, were not willing to see their boys fighting in yet another country. It was not just the students at Kent State and elsewhere who protested; Congress passed a bill forcing Nixon to remove American ground and air forces from Cambodia by July 1970. Nixon continued to bomb Cambodia while continuing to deceive the public and the Congress about it. He did have to pull the troops out, announcing as he did so that the operation had been a great success. In fact, he had put himself in the position of having another government to defend that could not possibly defend itself, and he had left ARVN with a new responsibility that it could not meet.

In announcing the invasion, Nixon had said, "If, when the chips are down, the world's most powerful nation . . . acts like a pitiful, helpless giant, the forces of totalitarianism and anarchy will threaten free nations and free institutions throughout the world." The almost totally negative results of the great risk he had taken in expanding the war showed in fact that the United States, in a guerrilla war in Asia without popular support, was nearly helpless.

A new force in the making of American foreign policy, meanwhile, was beginning to exert itself. Throughout the Cold War and the Vietnam War, the Congress had been a cipher. It had ignored its Constitutional duties on the grounds that in the modern age the President had to be free to act immediately against aggressors. From the mid-forties onward Congress legislated for the domestic front while the President acted on the foreign front. The system was mutually satisfactory as long as America was winning. But the absence of victory in Vietnam, the drawn-out nature of the struggle there, caused a change. Congress began to assert its authority. Democracies, as Lincoln and Wilson and Roosevelt knew, cannot fight long wars, because long wars inevitably become unpopular wars. That unpopularity will first show up in Congress, the branch of government closest to the people.

Like the people, Congress was frustrated by the war, and like them, it hardly knew what to do about it. The instinct to trust the President when the nation is at war is very strong; Nixon always counted on the prestige of his office in carrying through his policy. Some argued that there was nothing Congress could do, because the President is Commander in Chief of the armed forces and thus held all the power.

Under the American Constitution, however, the ultimate power resides not in the White House, but in Congress. At the starkest level, Congress can impeach and remove from office the President, but the President cannot remove Congress or individual Congressmen. On questions of foreign policy, only Congress can declare war or appropriate the money necessary to fight it. Here the trouble was more a practical one than one of Constitutional theory. The United States was already *at* war with North Vietnam. On December 31, 1970, Congress repealed the Gulf of Tonkin Resolution, but Nixon simply ignored this action, saying the resolution was not necessary to justify the continuation of the war. As to money, few Congressmen were willing to risk their careers by voting against the Defense Department budget under ordinary circumstances, much less when American boys were engaged in combat and had to have arms, ammunition, and other equipment to protect themselves.

Congress did find an ingenious way to use the appropriation power to exert its will, without stripping the fighting men of their means of defense. It declared that none of the money it was appropriating for military purposes could be used to widen the war, and specifically forbade the use of American ground troops in Cambodia or Laos. The restriction prevented Nixon from sending American troops into Laos on February 8, 1971, when ARVN launched a major invasion of Laos. Because Congress had failed to restrict his use of the Air Force, however, Nixon did have American bombers and helicopters fly missions to protect the ARVN invaders. Despite the air cover, Hanoi's forces sent ARVN reeling. It suffered 50 percent losses in the forty-five-day operation. It was a major embarrassment. As FitzGerald noted, it convinced the South Vietnamese that Vietnamization "meant increased Vietnamese deaths in pursuit of the American policy objective to extract the American troops from Vietnam without peace negotiations."

On March 30, 1972, Hanoi launched its own major offensive across the demilitarized zone. Two weeks later Nixon responded by resuming the intensive bombing of the north, hitting Haiphong and Hanoi on April 16, for the first time since 1968. He also mined Haiphong harbor. He had taken great risks—he was jeopardizing détente with the Russians and the opening to China, a clear indication that Vietnam was always his first priority. Despite the loss of a ship in Haiphong harbor, the Russians acted as if nothing had happened, and a month later Nixon visited Moscow for a summit meeting. Kissinger credited linkage and détente for this success; others attributed it to Russia's need for America's wheat and corn. Peking's reaction was limited to verbal denunciations.

Nixon had gotten away with a major escalation of the war, but by no means did that solve his problems. To win reelection in 1972 he had to have some semblance of peace in Vietnam, but he also had to have Thieu still in power in Saigon, or he would become "the first President to lose a war." Nixon decided to force Le Duc Tho to accept a compromise peace that would leave the Communists in control of much of South Vietnam's countryside (but not the cities, especially Saigon), by further escalating the war. While Kissinger took a hard line in his continuing secret talks with Le Duc Tho, Nixon stepped up the military offensive against North Vietnam, Cambodia, and Laos.

It was primarily an air offensive, because by the spring of 1972 Nixon had reduced the American ground-troop level in Vietnam to 70,000, far below the 540,000 that had been there when he took office four years earlier. American combat deaths were down from three hundred per week to one per day. Vietnamization was working, from Nixon's point of view, if only Hanoi would sign a peace agreement.

The Kissinger–Le Duc Tho talks were dragged out and terribly complex. Incredibly small points were haggled over while each side blamed the other for insincerity. There was some shifting of positions. What stood out, however, was a real consistency. Throughout, Hanoi was willing to allow the Americans to get out, and to turn over the POWs when they did. From that point on Hanoi insisted that what happened in Vietnam was none of America's business, which meant Le Duc Tho would sign no binding contract as to Hanoi's behavior in the future. Washington consistently argued that Hanoi had to abandon the use of force in settling the problem of a divided Vietnam. Such an agreement, of course, would have insured Thieu's position for some years to come, given that he controlled the army, the police, the civil service, and most importantly, the ballot boxes in South Vietnam.*

Eventually, Le Duc Tho indicated his willingness to sign an agreement. His motives remain unclear. Perhaps he realized that once the Americans were gone, Nixon and Kissinger would find it difficult to influence events. Perhaps he responded to a bribe; Nixon promised a massive program of reconstruction for North Vietnam once the shooting stopped. In any event, on October 26, 1972, just in time for the election, a triumphant Kissinger announced that "peace is at hand," and Nixon claimed that his policies had brought "peace with honor." The Democratic candidate, Senator George McGovern, who had rotten luck throughout his inept campaign, lost the only issue he still had going for him. Despite McGovern's last-minute plea to the American people,

---

*Thieu had become an "elected" president in 1971 when he held an election forced on him by the United States, but as he was the only candidate on the ballot he hardly had a mandate.

"Don't let this man fool you again," more than 60 percent of the voters chose Nixon, who scored one of the greatest victories in modern American electoral history.

Immediately after the election, astonishingly, the talks broke down again. At Nixon's insistence Kissinger had raised the price just when Le Duc Tho was ready to sign. Nixon demanded an ironclad guarantee that Thieu would remain in power. In part, this was a response to Thieu's intransigence. Thieu knew that he was being sold out, that an American withdrawal would sooner or later lead to his downfall, no matter how many promises Le Duc Tho made, and so Thieu threatened to ignore any cease-fire agreement that Kissinger might sign. Kissinger made extravagant promises to Thieu and Le Duc Tho about American military support in the event of a Communist offensive and about American reconstruction funds that would be available to both sides after peace came. Nixon meanwhile began the Christmas bombing campaign against Hanoi. It quickly made Hanoi the most heavily bombed city in the history of warfare.

Nixon's publicly stated reason for the air offensive was to force Hanoi to release the American POWs, but the campaign itself led to the loss of at least fifteen B-52s and eleven fighter-bombers (Hanoi claimed much higher American losses), increasing by ninety-three the number of POWs held by Hanoi. The losses, meanwhile, were more than the U.S. Air Force could afford. The generals had never liked the idea of sending costly B-52s over Hanoi, a city heavily defended against air attack by Soviet SAMs. As the losses mounted, the generals wanted out. Nixon must also have been aware of the worldwide opposition to the bombing, and Kissinger may have convinced him that the October agreement was the best the United States could get. Perhaps most important, despite Nixon's personal triumph in the election, the Democrats still controlled Congress and were finally ready to assert themselves. Nixon knew that the new Congress, coming into office in January 1973, was going to cut off all funds for bombing. Nixon therefore called off the bombers and agreed to sign a cease-fire agreement. On January

23, 1973, all active American participation in Vietnam
ended.

Nixon claimed that the Christmas bombing had done
the trick, but two of his own officials gave that story the
lie when they were interviewed by Marvin and Bernard
Kalb. "Peanuts," said one official when asked what difference the Christmas bombing had made. "That enormous bombing made little critical difference. What the
B-52s did was to get the margin in January pretty much
back to where it was in October." Another official explained, "Look, we were in an embarrassing situation.
Could we suddenly say we'll sign in January what we
wouldn't in October? We had to do something. So the
bombing began, to try to create the image of a defeated
enemy crawling back to the peace table to accept terms
demanded by the United States."

For the next two years Kissinger claimed that he had
managed to achieve the impossible. "It took me four
years to negotiate peace in Vietnam," he told the Arabs
and the Israelis, indicating that although he was indeed
a miracle man, even he could not bring an immediate
peace to the Middle East. Nixon, meanwhile, spoke and
acted as if the United States had won a decisive victory
under his command.

The claims had a hollow ring, because fighting continued in South Vietnam while it increased in Cambodia.
The huge American Air Force in Asia concentrated on
Cambodia in a series of heavy assaults. Congress reacted
by cutting off funds for such bombing. On June 27,
1973, Nixon vetoed the bill cutting the funds. Two days
later he assured Congress that all United States military
activity in Cambodia would cease by August 15, and on
July 1 he signed a bill ending all American combat activities in Indochina by August 15. Most observers believed that he caved in only because of his weakened
political position due to the Watergate scandal.

The cease-fire in Vietnam, meanwhile, broke down.
Nixon rushed more arms to Thieu ($3.2 billion in 1973),
who already had the fourth-largest military force in the

world. Indeed, all four sides to the final cease-fire agreement (Saigon, Hanoi, the VC, and the United States), so painfully negotiated over such a long period of time, violated it in every imaginable way, as everyone had suspected beforehand they would. All that had really been agreed to was that the United States would pull its fighting men out of Vietnam, and that Hanoi would give back the American POWs.

Over the next two years the battle raged, with relatively little shifting in positions. Congress refused to appropriate additional funds for Thieu's army, despite increasingly strident pleas from Kissinger, Nixon, and eventually President Gerald Ford. The final collapse of the Thieu regime began in January 1975, when Phuoc Binh, capital of Phuoc Long Province, fell to the Communists. Thieu decided to shorten his lines—until this time he had been trying to hold onto as much territory as possible—but the attempted retrenchment to more defensible lines proved to be a disastrous mistake. Once ARVN started retreating, it never stopped. Panic among the troops spread to the civilian refugees, who soon clogged the roads. Hue fell on March 26, Da Nang on March 31. On April 22 ARVN withdrew from Xuan Loc, forty miles east of Saigon. A week later the VC captured the huge air base at Bien Hoa, fifteen miles from Saigon.

On April 21 President Thieu delivered an emotional speech on Vietnamese radio and television. He accused the United States of breaking its promises of support and blamed the debacle on American cuts in military aid. He then resigned and got out of the country, most of his relatives and money and friends going with him. On April 28 President Ford ordered the emergency helicopter evacuation of all Americans remaining in South Vietnam. In a dreadful scene, U.S. Marines kept panic-striken Vietnamese (who had fought alongside the Americans and had much to fear from the Communists) away from the helicopters as the Americans and a select few Vietnamese were evacuated. On April 30, 1975, the remnants of the South Vietnamese government announced its unconditional surrender to the Communists. Saigon was renamed Ho Chi Minh City, and Vietnam was again united into one country. That same month the Lon Nol regime in Phnom Penh fell to the Khmer Rouge. America's most disastrous foreign-policy adventure, the intervention into the Indochinese war, had come to an end.

Nixon's dire predictions about all the dominoes that were going to fall to monolithic Communism proved to be wrong. Within a year Communist Vietnam was at war with Communist Cambodia; by 1978 it was at war with China. But any doves who believed that the Communists of Southeast Asia were agrarian reformers who only wanted to redistribute the land were in for a great shock, as the Khmer Rouge instituted in Cambodia one of the most repressive regimes in the world's history; it was so bad, in fact, that Senator McGovern—one of the original doves—advocated military action by the United Nations in order to do something about what was going on in Cambodia. In Vietnam, meanwhile, tens of thousands tried desperately to get out, by any means possible. For all the faults of the Diem/Ky/Thieu regimes in Saigon, the city was a veritable paradise of free speech and assembly while they were in charge, as compared to what was happening under the Communists. As Nixon noted with some satisfaction in 1978, no one was trying to break into Communist Vietnam.

The Americans were finally out of Indochina. Except in Hong Kong and South Korea, in fact, the white troops were now out of mainland Asia, the Americans being the last to leave. The process begun by the Japanese one generation earlier, when they had proclaimed that Asia should be run by Asians, was nearly complete. America's long relationship with Asia, begun with the acquisition of the Philippines three quarters of a century earlier, had reached a divide. America had been involved in war in Asia for twenty-two of the thirty-four years between 1941 and 1975. Over 120,000 American boys had died in combat there (41,000 in World War II, 33,000 in

Korea, 46,000 in Vietnam), and 530,000 were wounded (130,000 in World War II, 100,000 in Korea, 300,000 in Vietnam).*

And what did America have to show for all the treasure spent, all the lives lost, all the bodies crippled for life? Democracy in the Philippines, South Korea, and Japan, but Communism in China, Laos, Cambodia, and Vietnam. And for the immediate future, Americans did not want to hear about Vietnam. President Ford set the tone when he called for amnesia, not analysis. "The lessons of the past in Vietnam," Ford declared in 1975, "have already been learned—learned by Presidents, learned by Congress, learned by the American people—and we should have our focus on the future." He never said what the lessons were, but the American people responded gratefully to his invitation to forget the whole nightmare. Later, Vietnam came under intense scrutiny as a new generation of college students tried to understand how tiny, backward North Vietnam had defeated the mighty United States.

It seemed that one likely legacy was an increased congressional role in the making of foreign policy. One of the major themes in the American rise to globalism after 1938 had been the immense growth in the power of the presidency, especially in foreign affairs. To get the country out of Vietnam, Congress had been forced to assert itself. How long it would continue to do so remained to be seen; in the nature of the American political system, Congressmen are much more concerned with domestic than with foreign affairs, unless the United States is at war.

Another Vietnam legacy was the 1973 War Powers Act, which required the President to give an accounting of

---

*The ratio of combat deaths to wounds was much lower in Vietnam than in previous wars, thanks to helicopter evacuation of the wounded and to magnificent progress in field medical techniques.

his actions within thirty days of committing troops to a foreign war. After that time, Congress had to approve the presidential action.

It was an awkward way for Congress to assert its Constitutional right and duty to declare war. The last time the President consulted Congress over war powers was in 1964, when Johnson sent the Gulf of Tonkin Resolution through the legislature virtually without opposition. Congress had played absolutely no role in the major decisions of the Nixon White House: Vietnamization, the air and later the ground offensives against Cambodia and Laos, the China trip, détente, linkage, the mining of Haiphong harbor, the Christmas bombing, or the cease-fire agreement. The War Powers Act, by starting with the assumption that the President had to be free to move quickly in a crisis, gave the game away. Once the President, acting in strict accord with the law, had troops committed, could anyone believe that the Congress would force him to pull out?

By wrapping himself in the flag and appealing to the patriotism—and the jingoism—of the public, the President could keep his war going. That the public still yearned, even after Nixon, for strong leadership, that it would still respond enthusiastically to American saber rattling, became clear in May 1975, when President Ford sent the Marines into Cambodia to rescue a captured merchant vessel. The affair revealed that the quickest path to popularity for a President remained a *successful* military adventure. In such situations, hopes for a less active, more cautious and realistic, less expansive foreign policy were slim.

The agony of Vietnam has had innumerable repercussions. The Vietnam syndrome has caused Presidents, the Joint Chiefs, the Congress, and the people to be far more cautious about undertaking foreign adventures that involve a military commitment. There is a continuing debate over the wisdom and justice of the cause for which 50,000 American boys died (President Ronald Reagan proclaimed it a "noble cause"), and an even more intense debate over the way the war was fought. "What if" questions abound. Hawks argue that the war could have been won if Johnson had escalated sooner and more decisively and had expanded the war to Laos and Cambodia. Doves argue that such policies would not have worked and might have started World War III. Nixon supporters assert that had Congress not hamstrung the Commander in Chief, the United States would have used its Air Force to stop the 1975 North Vietnamese offensive and South Vietnam would still be free today. Since no one can know, the debate will go on. It should because it involves fundamental questions about the role of the United States and its military forces in the world.

13

America in the Middle East and Africa

The United States is committed to defend Israel's existence, but not Israel's conquests.

HENRY KISSINGER, 1970

Since 1945 the eastern end of the Mediterranean, where
Western civilization began, has been a theater of intense
activity. Both the United States and the Soviet Union
have tried to impose on the scene their own Cold War
mentality and habits—movement and response, bluff
and counterbluff—as each superpower has attempted to
gain a temporary advantage. The Turks, Arabs, Iranians, Jews, and others who live in the region have tried,
with fair success, to play one side against the other, but
essentially the Cold War was irrelevant to them. They
took advantage of the American and Russian obsession
with each other, but they never felt that Communism
versus anti-Communism was their problem or that it in
any way defined their choices. Consequently, there has
been a bewildering shift in alliances over the past generation, with both the Americans and the Russians enjoying brilliant successes, then suffering devastating
setbacks.

War, as always, has been the supreme arbitrator. There
have been six major Middle Eastern conflicts since World
War II, in 1948, 1956, 1967, 1973, 1980–89 and 1990–
91, with endemic border warfare in between the big
wars. The United States, the Soviet Union, Britain,
France, China, and Czechoslovakia have all sent massive
shipments of arms and fighting men to participate in
the area's struggles.

The stakes are enormous. The Arab world is important to America and Western Europe because the Arabs sit astride the Suez Canal and beside the Straits of Gibraltar, and they control the northern approaches to the Indian Ocean; because they are the sacred guardians of one of the world's largest religions and its great shrines; and because there are so many of them. Most important to the West is the fact that a small percentage of Arabs control a large percentage of the world's oil.

The non-Arab countries in the Middle East include Turkey, Iran, and Israel. The Turks have little oil, but they do have a strategic location because they block Russia's only warm-water port, and of course they have one of the world's oldest civilizations. In 1972, they invaded Cyprus, taking the northern half of the island and thus exacerbating their centuries-old conflict with the Greeks—who are their allies in NATO. Only in the Middle East could allies also be enemies! The Iranians are strategically weak, due to their long border with Russia, but they have abundant oil, which allowed them to buy from the United States a modern and large air force.

Israel, by way of contrast, has neither oil nor population nor strategic advantage, is without easily defended borders, and is surrounded by her much more numerous enemies. What she does have is an army with the highest morale of any in the world, a highly educated, intense, hard-working people, a moral claim on the world's conscience, and the active support of the American Jewish community, which is tiny in numbers but mighty in political strength and a major prop of Israel's economy.

It is the presence of the Jewish state of Israel on territory that was once Palestine that causes the basic Middle Eastern political problem, whose magnitude cannot be exaggerated. It has been and remains the most intractable problem of world diplomacy.* From 1948 on, most Arabs have refused to agree that the state of Israel has

*The Northern Ireland problem is equally intractable, but it concerns only Ireland and the United Kingdom.

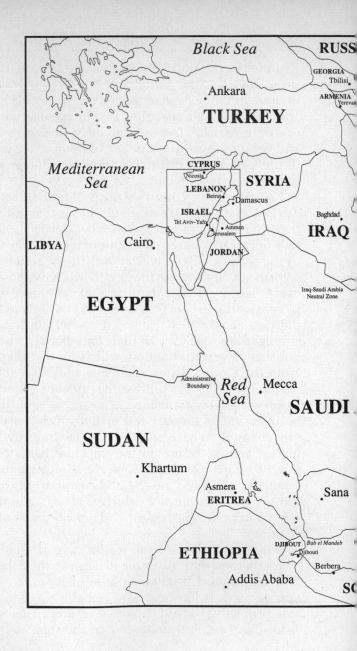

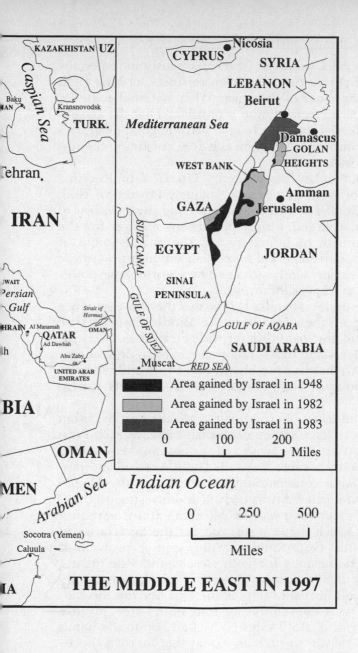

KAZAKHISTAN UZ

Caspian Sea

Baku
IAN

Kransnovodsk

TURK.

Tehran.

IRAN

JWAIT

*Persian
Gulf*

HRAIN   Al Manamah

QATAR
Ad Dawhah

OMAN

Abu Zaby.

UNITED ARAB
EMIRATES

BIA

OMAN

MEN

Arabian Sea

Socotra (Yemen)

Caluula

IA

CYPRUS   Nicosia

SYRIA

LEBANON

Beirut

Mediterranean Sea

Damascus

GOLAN

HEIGHTS

WEST BANK

GAZA

Amman

Jerusalem

EGYPT

JORDAN

SINAI

PENINSULA

GULF OF AQABA

SUEZ CANAL

GULF OF SUEZ

Strait of
Hormuz

SAUDI ARABIA

Muscat   *RED SEA*

Area gained by Israel in 1948

Area gained by Israel in 1982

Area gained by Israel in 1983

0   100   200

Miles

Indian Ocean

0   250   500

Miles

THE MIDDLE EAST IN 1997

a right to exist, while the Israelis have insisted (especially
since 1967) that the Palestinian refugees have no right
to a national state of their own. When national existence
is at stake, no compromise is possible. That the Israelis
and Arabs will someday have to become good neighbors
seems as impossible to them as it does obvious to the rest
of the world.

Robert Stookey has written, "The land of Palestine
belongs of right to a people uniquely favored of God,
the vehicle of His revelation respecting the salvation of
mankind, charged with a permanent mission for the
enlightenment of humanity and the establishment of
justice, long the object of repression and injustice, whose
enemies are presently sustained by a world superpower
for its own imperial interests."

Israelis and Arabs alike believe that the above sentence
is describing them. In short, the Middle East sets true
believer against true believer with survival as the issue.
No wonder, then, that solutions are hard to find, or that
the warfare has been so bloody and costly and, worst of
all, continuous. No wonder, too, that hatreds run so
deep.

For American policymakers the Middle East has often
been a headache, sometimes a nightmare, as each President has tried, in his own way, to pursue an even-handed
policy, if only because he needed both Arab oil and Jewish campaign contributions. By the 1970s the United
States also needed Arab goodwill and investment. Com-
plicating everything was the American anti-Communist
crusade, which made it difficult for the Secretaries of
State to deal realistically with the essential problem of
national homelands for both Israelis and Palestinians.
Nor were the Secretaries altogether wrong to see Communism as a threat to the Middle East, for the Russians
certainly were constantly meddling in the area, just like
the Americans. Both sides poured arms into the hands
of their friends, to such an extent that in 1973 the Israelis, Egyptians, and Syrians fought the second-biggest
tank battle in history. The Arabs lost 1,800 tanks, the
Israelis more than 500.

Neither of the superpowers has had much interest in ideological purity. At various times the Russians have supported the most reactionary of the richest Arab rulers, while the United States gave aid to the most radical of the poorest Arab governments. American and Russian involvement was on a day-to-day, or at best month-to-month, basis, because neither side had a well-thought-out program for the region. They could not have one, because they had no solution to the problem of national homelands. So each played it by ear, with resulting policy shifts that often appeared to be not only sudden but incomprehensible. One looked in vain for consistency, except that both sides insisted that the other had no right to intervene in the Middle East (except when war broke out, when each demanded that the other exert its influence to stop the fighting).

As was shown by the events following Nasser's death in 1970, Nasser's successor, Anwar el-Sadat, was painfully aware that Egypt was held in contempt or pity by much of the world. This included the Russians, who were supplying him with military hardware and financial support, but who treated him indifferently at best, with contempt at worst. Because of the huge military budget, what little money the Russians did provide was hardly enough to stave off national bankruptcy in the poverty-stricken land (Israel was also approaching bankruptcy due to military expenses). Furthermore, Sadat doubted that the Russians would ever be able to move the Israelis out of Sinai, while the Americans might be able to force them back. Also, it was obvious that the United States did a far better job of supplying its friends than Russia did. But the United States could hardly be expected to come to Egypt's aid when Soviet soldiers and technicians were swarming over the country.

So in 1972 Sadat presented the United States with one of its greatest victories in the Cold War: Without informing Secretary Kissinger in advance of his intentions or extracting anything from Washington in return, he expelled the 20,000 Russians from Egypt. It was a foreign policy setback to the Russians of the first magnitude.

Nothing remotely like it had happened previously. At a stroke Russian influence in the Middle East was cut back, her presence dramatically reduced. But because there had been no preparation, and because Kissinger (and Nixon and the CIA and the Israelis) continued to believe that Sadat would not dare take up arms to rectify the situation in the Sinai, the United States did nothing to follow up on Sadat's bold initiative. Kissinger made no serious attempt to force Israel to compromise; indeed, he looked the other way as Israelis began building permanent settlements in the occupied territories. Sadat, meanwhile, knew that with every passing day the Israeli occupation of Arab lands would come to seem more acceptable, even normal. Soon the world would accept it as a fact. He could not abandon his homeland. Again and again Sadat warned that war must come if the Israelis did not withdraw. Again and again he was ignored.

The Israeli Army, in the meantime, had overextended itself. By occupying all of the Sinai up to the east bank of the Suez, it had gone far to the west of the natural defensive line on the high ground running north and south through the middle of the Sinai. Further, the presence of Israeli soldiers along the Suez was a standing affront to the Egyptians.

Sadat had set 1971 as the "year of decision." It came and went, with no action. Egypt looked more pathetic than ever. In 1972 Sadat kicked out the Russians. In March 1973 Sadat sent his security adviser, Hafez Ismail, to Washington. Kissinger later told Prime Minister Golda Meir, "What did I do in those conversations? I talked with Ismail about the weather . . . just so we wouldn't get to the subject. I played with him. . . . Ismail told me several times that the present situation could not continue. He asked me whether the United States did not understand that if there weren't some agreement then there would be war. . . . There wasn't even a slight smile on my face, but in my heart I laughed and laughed. A war? Egypt? I regarded it as empty talk, a boast empty of content."

So empty, in fact, that the United States seemed to go out of its way to insult Ismail. Although Nixon promised him that the United States would use its influence with Israel, a few days after he left Washington the United States announced that it was supplying Israel with forty-eight additional Phantom jets.

Sadat gave up on a political approach. The only way to get back Egyptian territory was to drive the Israelis from it. Since the Americans would not take him seriously, Sadat swallowed his pride and turned to the Russians, after first arranging with Syria for a coordinated attack on Israel, and with King Faisal of Saudi Arabia for a simultaneous imposition of an oil embargo, which would presumably have the effect of paralyzing the United States. When the Kremlin heard Sadat's plan, the Russian leaders decided in turn to swallow their pride and supply the Egyptians and Syrians with enough hardware—especially missiles—to launch an attack.

On October 6, 1973, during the Jewish religious holiday of Yom Kippur, the Egyptian and Syrian armies struck with tanks, missiles, and planes. The Israelis were caught by surprise. On the Syrian front they were driven off the Golan Heights; along the Suez the Egyptians destroyed the much-vaunted Bar-Lev defensive line, which the Israelis had thought impregnable, then drove several miles deep inside the Sinai and entrenched.

These stunning victories came as a surprise to everyone except possibly Sadat. Israel may not have been quite on the verge of extinction, but her national existence was threatened as it had never been before, and her leaders knew that without outside assistance she was doomed. Only the United States could provide the necessary help in the form of new planes, tanks, and missiles.

Thus began one of the most controversial events in Dr. Kissinger's controversial career. Because of the role he chose to play, and because of the way in which he played it, he was vilified by both sides at various times, cursed, hanged in effigy, accused of having neither morals nor common sense, denounced as a man who was incapable of responding to the misery of millions of Palestinians, and perhaps worst of all, charged with not caring a fig for his own Jewish people.

The first requirement was to save Israel from a complete military disaster. A second was to avoid, if at all possible, an oil embargo, which would be much more effective in 1973 than in 1967, because in the intervening six years the United States had switched from being a net exporter of oil to a net importer. A third requirement was to find some formula, such as 242, to bring peace to the Middle East. Kissinger failed to solve the problem of how to help Israel without goading the Arabs into an oil embargo, and he was unable to bring peace to the area, but what Kissinger did manage to accomplish was impressive enough.

Kissinger was the first to recognize that the Israeli loss of tanks and planes during the early hours of the fighting, coupled with the now demonstrated fact that Egyptian and Syrian soldiers could fight and kill, shifted the strategic balance away from Israel. His first step was the traditional proposal of a cease-fire in place, but Israel would not accept it because she was losing and Sadat would not accept because he was not winning enough. Recovering from their surprise, the Israelis began to hold their own, but to retake lost ground they needed new weapons. They began making frantic demands on Kissinger for supplies, especially after October 10, when the Russians launched a large-scale airlift of supplies to Syria and Egypt, replacing the arms lost in battle. The Russian objective was to support a cease-fire after the Arabs had won the maximum advantage from their surprise attack and before Israel had time to mount an effective counteroffensive.

Kissinger was under heavy pressure. The American public and the Congress regarded Israel as the victim of aggression (ignoring the obvious fact that the Arabs were only trying to recover territory conquered by Israel in 1967). The Soviets, by shipping arms after promising restraint, had directly challenged the United States in a crucial spot on the globe. The Israeli Ambassador to the

United States punctuated his demands for help with explicit threats to mobilize American Jews against the Nixon Administration.

The Secretary of State gave in to the pressure, perhaps most of all because of his determination that Russian guns should never be allowed to prevail over American guns. On October 13 Kissinger got Nixon to order an all-out airlift by American military aircraft direct to Israel. In the end American deliveries substantially exceeded those of Moscow to the Arabs, proving that America's military capacity in time of crisis was superior to that of the Russians. On October 15, with the American equipment, the Israelis began their counterattack, crossed the Suez at two points, and encircled the Egyptian Third Army while driving the Syrians back from the Golan Heights.

The shift in the tide of battle brought the Russians back onto the scene, this time as promoters of a cease-fire in place. Kissinger agreed. He did not want to let the Israelis win a big victory and certainly did not want to humiliate Sadat. In addition, he now had to deal with his worst nightmare become reality: The Arab oil states, led by Faisal of Saudi Arabia, had imposed an effective embargo on oil shipments to the United States and to Israel's friends in Europe.

The Great Oil Embargo of 1973 was as important an event in the awakening of the Arabs as the Egyptian/ Syrian victory in the first week of the Yom Kippur War. From Kissinger and Nixon on down, Americans had assumed that the Arabs could never stick together, that any attempt at coordinated action would break down into petty bickering in a matter of days, and that therefore Arab threats about making political use of oil were not to be taken seriously. This was a great mistake, because in 1973 the Arabs did impose an embargo and made it stick. Americans discovered, to their collective chagrin, that they needed the Arabs more than the Arabs needed them.

Kissinger's first step, in what he called step-by-step diplomacy, was to get the shooting stopped and the talking started. He therefore joined with the Russians on October 22 to put through the Security Council Resolution 338, which called for a cease-fire in place and the implementation of Resolution 242.

Israel ignored it. General Moshe Dayan, Israel's Minister of Defense, kept the pressure on the surrounded Egyptian Third Army, because, as he later told *The New York Times,* he wanted to capture thirty thousand Egyptian soldiers, "and Sadat would have had to admit it to his people. We might only have held them for a day and let them walk out without their arms, but it would have changed the whole Egyptian attitude about whether they had won or lost the war." Kissinger, fully aware of Dayan's intentions, was furious. There could be no productive talks if the Egyptians were humiliated again, and without talks there would be no oil. So, Dayan complained, "the United States moved in and denied us the fruits of victory." Kissinger handed down "an ultimatum—nothing short of it." Of course, Kissinger's ultimatum was the threat to stop the flow of arms that had made the victory possible in the first place.

Simultaneously with Kissinger's pressure on Dayan, the Russians made a startling move. On October 24 Soviet Party Chairman Leonid Brezhnev proposed to Nixon that they send a joint Soviet-American expeditionary force to Suez to save the Third Army from Dayan. If Nixon was not interested, Brezhnev added, the Soviet Union would go in alone. The CIA meanwhile reported that the Russians had seven airborne divisions on alert, ready to go.

Kissinger responded in the strongest terms possible, short of actual war.* He persuaded Nixon to proclaim a worldwide alert of American armed forces, including nuclear strike forces. The Pentagon prepared plans to

---

*He later called the alert "our *deliberate* overreaction." Nixon, all but consumed with his Watergate woes, was leaving the tactical moves to Kissinger, but he was setting the main policy lines.

fly American troops to the Suez to confront the Russian paratroopers, if necessary. Kissinger then made certain that Brezhnev understood that the United States would go to the limit to keep Russian troops out of the area. The U.N. peacekeeping force must be drawn from the armies of non-nuclear powers, Kissinger insisted. Brezhnev agreed and the American alert, which had alarmed everybody, was called off. Dayan ended the pressure on the Third Army and the war was over.

Now Kissinger could step onto the center stage, previously occupied first by the contending armies, then by the American nuclear forces on alert. It was time for diplomacy, and never had the world seen a diplomat quite like the Secretary of State. It was true that the United States had previously acted as honest broker in the Middle East, bringing the Egyptians and Israelis together to arrange local cease-fires or border adjustments, but Kissinger added his own special touch to the process. Flying from Israel to Arab capitals in his specially equipped jet airliner, surrounded by the world press corps, appearing on the evening news with a different monarch or head of state each night, dazzling reporters with his wit and statesmen with his charm, overwhelming everyone with his detailed knowledge (he knew the height, in meters, of every hill in Sinai), the Jewish refugee from Hitler's Germany became a genuine worldwide superstar.

His essential role was more modest—as he himself often declared, all he could do was explain to one side the constraints under which the other side operated. He did so with impressive patience, thoroughness, goodwill and skill. To the Israelis he said: All the world is against you, and you cannot stand against the whole world. To the Arabs he said: Only the United States can persuade Israel to retreat from the conquered territory, but you cannot expect the United States to invest so much time and energy in an operation that is so clearly in the Arab interest as long as you withhold your oil. To both sides he said, You must compromise.

But he said it in the context of step-by-step diplomacy,

which meant that instead of taking on the big questions, such as the status of Jerusalem or a homeland for the Palestinians, he began with the little problems, mainly disengaging the armies, which were badly intermixed on both sides of Suez and in the Golan Heights. The trouble with step-by-step, according to Kissinger's numerous critics, was that it was myopic, precisely because it ignored the real issues. How could you have peace in the Middle East if you ignored the PLO? According to Kissinger's numerous defenders, it was obvious that if you began by discussing the PLO, the talks would end right there.

Kissinger also took advantage of his position as spokesman for the world's richest nation. Although the evidence is inconclusive, and no details are known, he evidently made vast promises about the American economic and technical help that would be available to both sides in the event of genuine peace in the region.*

Step one began on November 7, 1973, when Kissinger flew to Cairo to meet with Sadat. The United States and Egypt reestablished diplomatic relations, broken since 1967. Next Kissinger arranged for an exchange of prisoners of war and the lifting of the Israeli sieges of the

---

*He had done the same in Vietnam. Kissinger's willingness to make promises became the subject of a popular joke in Israel: Kissinger goes to see a poor man and says, "I want to arrange a marriage for your son." The poor man replies, "I never interfere in my son's life." Kissinger responds, "But the girl is Lord Rothschild's daughter." "Well, in that case . . ."

Next Kissinger approaches Lord Rothschild. "I have a husband for your daughter." "But my daughter is too young to marry." "But this young man is already a vice president of the World Bank." "Ah, in that case . . ."

Finally Kissinger goes to see the president of the World Bank. "I have a young man to recommend to you as a vice president." "But I already have more vice presidents than I need." "But this young man is Lord Rothschild's son-in-law." "Ah, in that case . . ."

city of Suez and of the Third Army. He set up a Geneva conference that met in December and accomplished nothing; in private he arranged for an Egyptian-Israeli accord (signed January 18, 1974) that provided for a mutual disengagement and pullback of forces along Suez and the establishment of a U.N. Emergency Force buffer zone between them. The Russians, like everyone else, watched in amazement as Kissinger moved the pieces around the chessboard.

His great triumph, the reward for all his hard work, came on March 18, 1974, when the Arab states lifted the oil embargo. During May 1974 he shuttled back and forth between Syria and Israel, finally (May 31) achieving a cease-fire and complex troop disengagement agreement on the Golan Heights.

In the remaining two and a half years of the Nixon-Ford administrations, the United States provided Israel with more than $3 billion worth of weapons. These included precision-guided munitions, cluster-bomb units, tanks, armored personnel carriers, self-propelled artillery, cargo trucks, cargo aircraft, rifles, helicopters, antitank guided rockets, electronic counterradar boxes, Phantoms, and Skyhawks. One Pentagon official declared, "Israel wants one thousand percent security and she's getting it. She can decisively defeat any combination of Arab armies at least through 1980."

This commitment to Israel's defense was not Kissinger's doing alone. By the mid-1970s Congress was beginning to exert itself in foreign affairs (see chapter twelve). It was usually an interference on the side of caution—pull out of Vietnam and Cambodia, stay out of Angola, and so on—but in the Middle East, where everything gets turned around, the Congress was determined to stand by Israel. Thus on May 21, 1975, seventy-six members of the Senate wrote a collective letter to President Ford to endorse Israel's demand for "defensible" frontiers. The letter was spiced with such phrases as "the special relationship between our country and Israel," "witholding military equipment from Israel would be dangerous," and "the United States . . . stands firmly with Israel." This was an impressive demonstration of the strength of the Jewish lobby in Washington. It was followed in the summer of 1975 by a Senate vote that blocked the sale of defensive Hawk missiles to King Hussein of Jordan.

Kissinger was caught in his own trap by the Senate when Senator Henry Jackson of Washington turned Kissinger's concept of linkage against him. Jackson linked Jewish emigration from Russia with American trade deals with the Kremlin. Kissinger, never one to see consistency as a virtue, was furious at this linkage, because it jeopardized the trade agreements that were to be the payoff for détente. He tried to explain to Senator Jackson that emigration and trade were not and should not be linked, but he failed to convince the Senate.

Jackson successfully blocked the granting of Most Favored Nation (MFN) status to the Russians, which would have allowed greatly increased trade between the United States and the Soviet Union, over the issue of the "exit tax." This was, in effect, a tuition the state charged Jews who imigrated to Israel, taking their education and skills with them. Senator Jackson said this was blood money and an outrage. Brezhnev, who was eager for the trade but unwilling to have it thought that he had been forced to back down by a U.S. Senator, offered a compromise to Nixon. He would privately suspend the exit tax, and would continue to allow an annual level of Jewish emigration of 40,000. But when Nixon brought this compromise to Jackson, he discovered that rather than wanting the best achievable arrangement, Jackson wanted an issue. Jackson refused to remove his objections. In retaliation for failure to obtain MFN status, Brezhnev sharply curtailed Jewish emigration, cutting it down to less than 1,000 per year, and charged the full "exit tax." Yet Senator Jackson remained the favorite of the American Jewish lobby!

This is as good an example as any of the difficulties that ensue when the Congress gets involved in foreign policy, and of the kind of thinking Nixon and Kissinger had to contend with while they tried to erect their new world order. It provides a startling point for a discussion of the widespread belief that Richard Nixon was a brilliant maker of foreign policy.

There is a basis for the belief. In the face of great obstacles one of which was the Senate, the Nixon administration had some major foreign policy triumphs. First, it managed to extract the United States from Vietnam. Second, it opened the door to China. Third, it promoted a policy of détente with the Russians. Fourth, it reached an arms-control agreement with the Soviets. No other Cold War administration could claim even one such accomplishment.

But there is another side to the story. Nixon's retreat from Vietnam came only after four horrible years of war, and when he did pull out he got no better a deal than he could have had in 1969. If he was the man most responsible for opening the door to China, he was also the man most responsible for keeping it closed for the preceding thirty years. Détente, for all its promise, was substantially flawed by Nixon's inability to convince the Senate of its desirability, and his own refusal to trust the Russians to the slightest degree. As a consequence, détente was coldly rejected by the subsequent Administration. The limits set by SALT have long since been passed. There was, in short, little that was lasting in Nixon's foreign policy, certainly nothing like the Truman Doctrine.

Nixon had some brilliant ideas, but he did not build the constituency necessary to carry them out. Perhaps, as the example of Senator Jackson and Jewish emigration indicates, it would have been impossible to overcome a quarter century of Cold War habits. Perhaps, as Nixon's admirers argue, if he had had a full four-year second term, he could have prevailed.* Perhaps, as Nixon ar-

*Richard Nixon resigned in August 1974, and Gerald Ford became President.

gues, had he been at the helm in 1975, the North Vietnamese would never have dared overrun Saigon. Perhaps.

The final reckoning is that Nixon and Kissinger failed to reach their major foreign policy goals. They did not extract the United States from Vietnam without losing Vietnam to the Communists; they could not solve the problem of Formosa and thus establish full diplomatic relations with the Chinese; they could not establish a lasting détente; they did not put any controls on the arms race; they did not bring peace to the Middle East. Judged by their own standards, they came up short.

In the Middle East, Nixon and Kissinger had little to show for shuttle diplomacy, except that the Arabs were selling oil—at a fourfold price increase—to the United States and Europe. The Senate's letter on the defense of Israel made the Israelis immune to American threats of the withdrawal of American support, enabling them to continue to take a tough line in the peace negotiations. The Israelis still occupied most of the Sinai, the Golan Heights, and the West Bank of the Jordan. The PLO problem was worse than ever, punctuated by a confusing civil war in Lebanon between Christians and Muslims, with Syria deeply involved, the PLO in the thick of it, and Israeli-manned, American-built modern weapons devastating Lebanese suspected of harboring the PLO.

Peace in the Middle East remained a goal, rather than a reality, of American foreign policy. Permanent solutions still were out of reach. The Middle East overall remained, as it had been so often described by American presidents, a tinderbox, ready to set the world afire from a single spark.

In Africa, too, in the 1970s, these was no peace. In Zambia, Rhodesia (Zimbabwe), Angola, Southwest Africa (Namibia), Mozambique, and South Africa, 4 million whites ruled 30 million blacks. These states were roughly united by their minority government status and by a shocking exploitation of black labor* by an elite of fabulously wealthy whites.

But just as the white-ruled states followed different traditions, so would they take different paths. By 1979 Zambia, Angola, and Mozambique had achieved majority rule, and Rhodesia was on the way toward the cremation of a democratic state based on a one-man, one-vote principle. In Nambia, on the other hand, the situation worsened, as South Africa tightened her grip on her colony. And in South Africa itself, independent since the turn of the century, the most racist white-ruled state in the world grew even more racist. The white minority had a monopoly of force that it did not hesitate to use and of power that it would not yield or share.

All the states of southern Africa had some economic importance to the United States. Consequently American policy, as summed up by NSSM 39,† was "to try to balance our economic, scientific and strategic interests in the white states with the political interest of dissociating the U.S. from the white minority regimes and their repressive racial policies." The problem was that this was less a policy than a hope and thus contributed to the relative paucity of American influence on developments in southern Africa.

NSSM 39 predicted a continued stalemate in the Por-

---

*In South Africa workers had to live in camps next to the mines for twelve to eighteen months and could not see their families during that time. Wages in the mines, which were seventy-two cents per day in 1910, had fallen to fifty-seven cents per day in 1975. But the situation was so much worse in other parts of the southern third of Africa that blacks were trying to get *into* South Africa in search of jobs.

†National Security Study of Memorandum 39 was a comprehensive National Security Council review of American policy in Africa, and an analysis of American economic and political interests in Africa, done in 1969 at Henry Kissinger's request.

tuguese colony of Angola,* where black liberation forces
waged a guerrilla war against the government. Angola
differed from South Africa and Rhodesia in that all overt
racial discrimination had been eliminated by the Portuguese, who in the sixties started a crash program to
educate blacks and integrate them into the economy.
Many black leaders rejected this program as an attempt
to retain white control.

There were three major movements demanding full
independence for Angola, namely, the Popular Movement, or MPLA, the National Front, or FNLA, and
UNITA (National Union for Total Independence). All
received some aid from Russia and/or China, but the
MPLA leaders had Marxist, antiimperialist views and
had denounced the United States for its support of Portugal. American newspapers spoke of the "Soviet-
backed" MPLA and the "moderate" FNLA.

The United States had attempted to remain an observer of the problems of Angola and Mozambique (also
a Portuguese colony), while maintaining a posture of
coolness toward Portugal itself, until 1971 when Nixon
moved in a pro-Portuguese direction. Kissinger wanted
a strong NATO and access to Portugal's strategic base in
the Azores. In exchange for the latter, Nixon signed an
executive agreement that gave Portugal a $436 million
loan. The next year Nixon authorized the sale of military
transports to Portugal, then lent more money, which the
Portuguese used to buy helicopters for use against the
guerrilla warriors in their colonies. The payoff for Kissinger came during the Yom Kippur War of 1973, when
Portugal was the only NATO ally to allow American
planes bound for Israel to refuel on its territory.

In April 1974 a military coup in Lisbon created a new
situation. Tired of fighting unending and unsuccessful
wars, the Portuguese military leaders decided to give the

*Held by the Portuguese to be legally a part of Portugal, as
the French once held Algeria to be part of France.

colonies their independence. In January 1975 a transitional government was established in Luanda, the capital of Angola, with each of the liberation movements sharing in the preparations for independence and each group campaigning throughout the country for the elections scheduled for October 1975. Independence day would be November 11, 1975.

The FNLA, the MPLA, and UNITA found it impossible to work together; according to the big powers, because of ideological splits over Communism versus capitalism, but according to African sources, because of major ethnic and tribal cleavages. In any event, the chaos in Luanda invited outside intervention.

The United States was the first to respond. Kissinger and CIA Director William Colby argued that the United States entered the Angolan civil war only to counter a Russian threat there, but John Stockwell, the chief of the CIA Angola Task Force, later charged that the United States made the first actual move.* Given Angola's political options, the CIA's choice was the FNLA. Also acceptable was UNITA. The MPLA was thought to be radical, Communist, and Russian-backed, so it had to be stopped. In fact, great-power rivalry was the motivating factor, for outsiders moved in on Angola almost before the Portuguese could get out of the way. It was not merely the great powers, either; at one time or another the FNLA and UNITA received support from not only the United States and China, but also Rumania, North Korea, France, Israel, West Germany, Senegal, Uganda, Zaire, Zambia, Tanzania, and South Africa. The MPLA was supported by the Soviet Union, Cuba, East Germany, Algeria, Guinea, and Poland, surely a record of some sort for politics making strange bedfellows.

South Africa entered the conflict with regular army troops in September 1975. This was the first time South

---

*China was a close second, sending 112 military advisers and some equipment to help the FNLA.

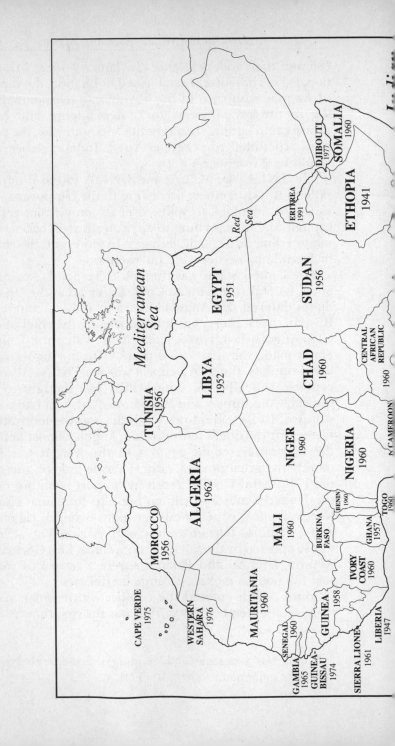

SOMALIA 1960

DJIBOUTI 1977

ERITREA 1991

ETHIOPIA 1941

Red Sea

EGYPT 1951

SUDAN 1956

CENTRAL AFRICAN REPUBLIC 1960

Mediterranean Sea

LIBYA 1952

CHAD 1960

CAMEROON

TUNISIA 1956

NIGER 1960

NIGERIA 1960

ALGERIA 1962

MALI 1960

BENIN 1960

MOROCCO 1956

BURKINA FASO

GHANA 1957

TOGO 1960

MAURITANIA 1960

IVORY COAST 1960

CAPE VERDE 1975

WESTERN SAHARA 1976

SENEGAL 1960

GUINEA 1958

LIBERIA 1947

GAMBIA 1965

GUINEA-BISSAU 1974

SIERRA LEONE 1961

*In di***

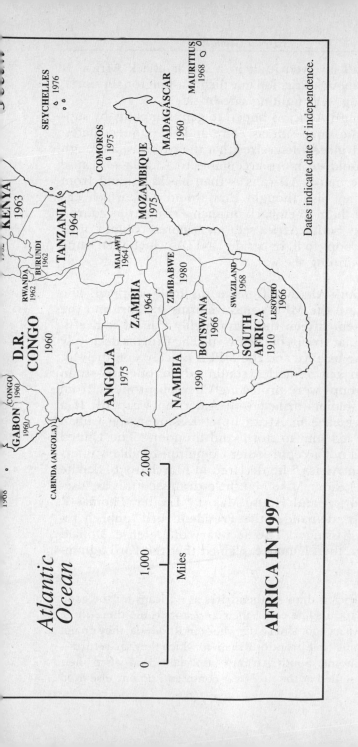

Atlantic
Ocean

GABON
1960
CONGO
1960

CABINDA (ANGOLA)

D.R.
CONGO
1960

RWANDA
1962
BURUNDI
1962

KENYA
1963

TANZANIA
1964

SEYCHELLES
◊ 1976

ANGOLA
1975

ZAMBIA
1964

MALAWI
1964

COMOROS
◊ 1975

MADAGASCAR
1960

MAURITIUS
1968

NAMIBIA
1990

ZIMBABWE
1980

MOZAMBIQUE
1975

BOTSWANA
1966

SWAZILAND
1968

LESOTHO
1966

SOUTH
AFRICA
1910

Dates indicate date of independence.

0   1,000   2,000

Miles

AFRICA IN 1997

Africa had involved itself in a war in Black Africa. It brought about a situation in which Washington, Pretoria, and Peking were fighting side-by-side.

The South Africans hoped to gain sympathy by supporting the same side as Zaire and the United States. They convinced themselves that their troops, although white, would be more acceptable to Angola—because they were native Africans*—than blacks coming from Cuba. They also thought they would win, which encouraged them to embark on such a dangerous course. Eventually South Africa sent an armored column of its regular troops to fight beside UNITA, which then came close to winning the war.

The South African offensive was finally stopped. The Soviets gave the MPLA massive arms support and the Cubans sent fifteen thousand highly trained and efficient regular troops of their own. The Cubans decisively tipped the balance and the MPLA quickly won the war. American oil refineries continued to operate—soon Cuban troops were protecting Chevron property from UNITA soldiers armed with American weapons. If a Soviet presence in Africa upset Kissinger, the Cuban presence led him to storm and thunder. "The United States will not accept further Communist military intervention in Africa," he declared in March 1976. Senate Majority Leader Mike Mansfield dismissed this as "useless rhetoric," and House Majority Leader Thomas P. O'Neill, Jr., demanded that President Ford "publicly repudiate" Kissinger. The Secretary of Defense, Donald Rumsfeld, then lamely explained that the Ford admin-

---

*South Africans think of themselves as Africans for the good reason that, in some cases, their ancestors came there three hundred years ago. Unlike the whites in Rhodesia, they do not have a "home" in Europe or Britain to which they can return— Africa is home. South Africans also claim that when their ancestors settled at the tip of the continent, no one else lived there.

istration was reviewing "only economic or political action against Cuba, not military."

It was another example of Congress taking charge of foreign policy in a way unthinkable in the Truman, Eisenhower, Kennedy, or Johnson years. Congress used the same power it had exercised to force Nixon to pull out of Vietnam, the power of the purse. On January 27, 1976, despite last-minute appeals from Ford and Kissinger, the House voted 323 to 99 to ban covert military aid to Angola. A frustrated President Ford accused the Congress of having "lost its guts."

Perhaps so, but to many Americans it seemed that Congress was finally living up to its responsibilities and in the process exerting a much-needed restraining influence on the adventurers in the CIA and the White House. That the MPLA won in Angola scarcely seemed a crucial development to a Congress that was less worried about American prestige in Africa, more concerned with costs, and less willing to charge at the sound of the trumpets than the CIA. In 1976, for example, when Ethiopia and Somalia were on the verge of war, the CIA was ready to intervene on the Ethiopian side, on the grounds that the Soviets were arming Somalia with modern weapons and that Cuban advisers had joined the Somali forces. Kissinger agreed with the CIA, but Congress was suspicious, and with a new Administration's coming to power in Washington, nothing was done. A year later, in the fall of 1977, the Russians were expelled from Somalia and began to arm Ethiopia. The CIA then urged the Carter administration to intervene on behalf of Somalia.

At the southernmost tip of Africa is the Republic of South Africa, almost in another world, a world that the ruling whites said they were determined to defend forever. Around the rest of the world, since 1945, the main political movement had been either in the direction of majority rule or toward socialist collectivism. Colonial rule had all but disappeared (outside the Soviet Union). It was true that one-party rule in the socialist states was a far cry from any real democracy, but it is also true that in the past forty years the world had managed to rid itself of many monarchies and one-man dictatorships. And the socialist states were committed, in theory at least, to such principles as equality of opportunity, education, and basic rights.

South Africa moved in the other direction, away from democracy and away from the idea of equality of all citizens under the law. Since World War II, South African racial policies had steadily hardened. As her economy boomed, she needed more black labor. As black participation in the economy increased, the level of repression to enforce apartheid was stepped up. Real wages were lowered, black political dissidents were arrested and murdered; absolute separation of the races vigorously enforced. South Africa came to be a police state that, if it did not rival Hitler's death camps or Stalin's labor camps, its bitter realities, like modern Russia's psychiatric wards, were still abhorred by the rest of the world.

South Africa, though an international pariah, was also a marvelous investment opportunity because of cheap labor and the mineral wealth of the country. Profits were high, risks low. Some private American investment money had inevitably found its way into South Africa, but not to be compared with the levels of American investment in Europe, the Middle East, or Latin America. Total American investment in South Africa in 1973 was $1.2 billion, representing a 73 percent increase in the years of the Nixon administration, which was not much greater than the rate of inflation. The $1.2 billion was about one third of the total American investment in Africa, and about 15 percent of the total foreign investment in South Africa. The United States also sold South Africa roughly 17 percent of her imports. South Africa produced 60 percent of the Western world's gold, and was the third-largest supplier of uranium. In addition, the United States had a NASA satellite-tracking station and an Air Force tracking station in South Africa, and the Navy wanted port facilities on or near the Cape, one of the most strategic points in the world.

Taken altogether, that was not a large investment. The United States had no vital interest in South Africa. Further, on the grounds of civil rights, it was obviously impossible for any American politician to take a pro-South African stance (the last to do so was Dean Acheson, who was notoriously pro-South Africa). It was nearly as difficult to propose policies that would force South Africa to move toward majority rule. Consequently, American policy toward South Africa was mixed and confused. On the one hand the United States did maintain diplomatic relations; on the other hand Ambassador Adlai Stevenson in the early sixties took the lead in the United Nations in denouncing apartheid. The United States government had never forbidden investment in South Africa, and Nixon came close to actually encouraging it, despite the fact that the United States had led the effort in 1963 to establish a U.N. arms embargo on South Africa.

To the south of Angola lies Namibia (Southwest Africa), a colony of South Africa. The United States had insisted that South Africa's continued domination of Namibia was illegal,* to the point that President Nixon, acting at Kissinger's insistence, informed potential American investors that the United States would henceforth discourage investment in Namibia. In any event, Namibia's major—almost only—export is manpower for the South African mines. Pretoria was not willing to give up this source of cheap, reliable, hard-working labor. As NSSM 39 summed up the problem in Namibia: "No solution in sight. South Africa is entrenching its rule and

---

*Namibia was mandated to South Africa by the League of Nations in 1920. It is the only mandated territory that did not become independent (or a U.N. trust territory) after World War II. South Africa has ignored all U.N. demands that it withdraw.

has extended its application of apartheid and repressive measures. South Africa considers the area vital to its security and an economic asset."

Africa's cultural and economic ties are with Europe. The great bulk of African students are enrolled in Western European universities, not in American or Russian schools, and the level of Western European trade with and investment in Africa is much higher than that of either superpower. English and French are the "modern" and common languages of Africa, and African English is spoken with a British, not an American, accent. Africa is more a European than an American problem.

14

Carter and Human Rights

Human rights is the soul of our foreign policy.
JIMMY CARTER, 1977

Iran is an island of stability in one of the more troubled areas of the world.
JIMMY CARTER, 1977

In November 1976, Jimmy Carter narrowly defeated Gerald Ford for the presidency. Carter had conducted a skillful campaign that took full advantage of the public's response to Nixon's Watergate scandal, widespread resentment of big government in Washington, D.C., and the general perception of a need for a less-active, less-involved foreign policy. In effect, Carter promised no more Watergates and no more Vietnams.

What he was *for* was less certain. A Georgia businessman and former governor of the state, in terms of foreign affairs Carter was the least-experienced President of the post-World War II era. In sharp contrast to the realpolitik of the Kissinger years, Carter's chief characteristic was his idealism. Unlike his predecessors, he did not regard Communism as the chief enemy; he said repeatedly that Americans had become too fearful of the Communists while giving too little attention to the greater danger of the arms race and too much support to repressive right-wing dictatorships around the world.

In his inaugural address, Carter said his ultimate goal was the elimination of nuclear weapons from the earth. He wanted to start immediately to limit arms and to decrease America's arm sales overseas because he did not want the United States to remain the arms merchant to the world. And he made a firm commitment to the defense of human rights everywhere, later calling human rights "the soul of our foreign policy" and making them the touchstone of American relations with the other nations of the world. All were noble goals, nobly stated. They raised hopes worldwide, especially the emphasis on human rights, which struck a responsive chord among the oppressed everywhere.

But all the goals were wildly impractical and none were achieved. Far from making progress toward eliminating nuclear weapons, the Carter administration continued to increase the American nuclear arsenal at about the same rate as had the Nixon and Ford administrations. American arms sales abroad actually increased during the Carter years. Furthermore, Carter's emphasis on human rights badly damaged America's relationship with many of her oldest allies; it caused resentment in the Soviet Union and other Communist countries that contributed to the failure to achieve such major goals as arms control or genuine détente; it contributed to the downfall of America's oldest and staunchest ally in the Middle East, the Shah of Iran, with consequences that were also disastrous for Carter himself. There was a huge gap between aim and achievement in the Carter administration. The principal causes of the gap were an excess of idealism, a lack of experience, and an overreaction to Russian actions.

"We can never be indifferent to the fate of freedom elsewhere," Carter declared in his inaugural address. "Our commitment to human rights must be absolute."

The concept that every human being has certain unalienable rights is essentially Jeffersonian and American, but it had received worldwide backing in the U.N. Charter (1945) and again in the Helsinki Accords of 1975, when all the participants, including the Soviet Union, solemnly agreed to respect and protect the human rights of their own citizens.* Unfortunately, there was no enforcement machinery. Congress had endorsed the policy in the early 1970s, before Carter's inauguration. In reaction to Kissinger's realpolitik and embarrassed by America's support of dictators around the world, Congress forbade American aid to countries that engaged "in a consistent pattern of gross violations of internationally recognized human rights." Thus Carter was not advancing an original idea, but no President before him had gone so far in the area of human rights.

Carter felt the issue deeply himself and, in addition, it provided an opportunity for him to distinguish his foreign policy from that of Nixon and Kissinger. Further, it offered something to both the Cold Warriors (who could and did use it to criticize the Soviet Union for its abominable record on human rights) and to idealists (who could and did use it to criticize Chile, Brazil, South Africa, and others for their abominable records on human rights). Carter established a Bureau on Human Rights in the State Department and gave or withheld economic aid, trade advantages, weapons, and other forms of aid on the basis of a nation's human rights record.

The campaign for human rights brightened Carter's image, but had little discernible positive effect and did considerable harm. He preached to the converted; the sinners deeply resented Carter's sermons on human rights and either ignored his pleas for improved treatment of their political prisoners or actually increased the repression. Still, the human rights advocates were convinced that the campaign was positive and helpful. As one of them put it, "The former reputation of the United States as a supporter of freedom was being restored, replacing its more recent image as a patron of tyranny."

A major difficulty, however, was that inevitably the campaign was directed against America's allies and

*Credit for the Helsinki Accords belongs to President Ford, who pushed hard for them, over strong protests.

friends rather than its enemies, if only because such allies as South Korea, Argentina, South Africa, Brazil, Taiwan, Nicaragua, and Iran were vulnerable to Carter's pressure, since they relied upon the United States for military sales and economic assistance. To critics, it made little sense to weaken America's allies because of objections to their morals while continuing to advance loan credits, sell grain, and ship advanced technology to the Soviet Union, which had one of the worst human rights records in the world and was clearly no friend of the United States.

In his relations with the Soviet Union, Carter's major goals were to free America from its "inordinate fear of Communism" and to complete a SALT II treaty that would reduce the chances of nuclear war. His Secretary of State, Cyrus Vance, a New York lawyer with long government experience, was a leading advocate of détente and took a moderate and conciliatory approach toward the Russians. Carter and Vance believed that it was time to redefine the relationship between the United States and the Soviet Union. Vance stressed that the new approach to the Soviets had to be based upon "positive incentives" rather than a policy of containment. He rejected the notion that "the United States can dominate the Soviet Union" or otherwise "order the world just the way we want it to be." The United States had to accept a more limited role in world affairs.

The first "positive inducement" took place within twenty-four hours of Carter's inaugural, when he ordered the immediate withdrawal of American nuclear weapons from South Korea. This major step did not elicit any Soviet response (and was in fact ultimately blocked by the Pentagon bureaucracy). This outcome was highly disappointing to Carter, who had, it must be noted, shown his inexperience by taking such a bold step without first discussing it with his own military leaders and without first informing the Kremlin and obtaining some promises for reciprocal action in advance. In general, during his first year in office, Carter was distressed by

Soviet failure to respond to his signals. As America backed off from some of its more advanced positions around the world, the Soviets, far from responding in kind, became more adventuresome. They continued and even increased their arms buildup, became involved in both the Horn of Africa and in southern Africa, using Cuban troops as their advance agents. The Russians evidently saw Carter's "positive incentives" as signs of weakness and indecision and they responded by becoming more aggressive.

The Russian actions strengthened the position of Carter's Special Assistant for National Security Affairs, Zbigniew Brzezinski, a political scientist who immigrated to the United States from Poland in 1953. Brzezinski was in the Kissinger-realpolitik tradition, and he competed with Vance for influence over Carter. Brzezinski made powerful arguments for not trusting the Soviets, arguments that were strengthened by Russian actions. For example, in early 1979 the Russians began placing jet-fighter aircraft, a combat unit, and a submarine pen in Cuba. Carter was furious with Leonid Brezhnev for this apparent violation of the 1962 Cuban missile crisis accord, and went on national television to denounce the Soviet Union for its actions.* Brezhnev, predictably and correctly, replied that the airplanes and other equipment were not offensive weapons by their nature and thus did not violate the 1962 Kennedy-Khrushchev informal arrangement. Nor did Brezhnev remove the weapons or the troops. For Carter the experience was a stage in his

---

*This "crisis" had its origins in the political ambitions of Senator Frank Church, chairman of the Senate Foreign Relations Committee. He was coming up for reelection in Idaho and his opposition charged that he was soft on Communism. So at a press conference on August 30, 1979, he "revealed" the presence of a Soviet brigade of 2,500 men in Cuba, and "demanded" that the President "insist" on the removal of "all Russian combat troops from Cuba." Actually, the brigade had been there since 1963.

journey from idealism to a hard line with regard to the Soviets.

The most important result of Carter's growing hostility toward and fear of the Soviets was the demise of SALT II. Carter was unwilling to go more than halfway in meeting the Russians; indeed, Carter eventually demanded more arms for the United States, and less for the Soviets, than Kissinger and Nixon had been willing to accept. Carter's demands, plus Soviet resentment at his public support for Russian dissidents and his linking of SALT talks to human rights, set back the negotiations for more than a year. Carter had said he wanted to complete the treaty in 1977, but not until June 1979 did Carter meet with Brezhnev in Vienna to sign the SALT II treaty. By then, Carter had already ordered the construction of cruise (Pershing II) missiles, and an enhanced radiation (neutron) bomb. Brezhnev had responded by accelerating Soviet production of the Backfire Bomber and the new SS-20 missiles.

The SALT II treaty that the two leaders signed in Vienna was a strange accord. As had been the case with SALT I, it set upper limits toward which both sides could build rather than freezing nuclear weapons and delivery systems, and it failed altogether to even mention the Pershing II missiles or the Backfire Bomber or the MIRV problem (multiple warheads for individual ICBMs). Salt II, in short, was far behind the current technology. Specifically, the treaty limited each side to 2,400 launchers of all types. At that time, in mid-1979, the two sides were roughly equal: The United States had 1,054 ICBMs, of which 550 were MIRVed, while the Russians had 1,398 ICBMs, of which 576 were MIRVed. The United States had 656 submarine-launched ballistic missiles, of which 496 were MIRVed, while the Russians had 950, of which 128 were MIRVed. In addition, the United States had 574 heavy bombers carrying the largest nuclear weapons, while the Soviets had 156 such bombers. As both sides were free to build as many nuclear warheads as they wished, and to MIRV all their launchers, SALT II, for all practical purposes, put no limits at all on the arms race.

Nevertheless, the treaty was sharply criticized in the United States, especially in the Senate, where it was charged that it gave too much away and allowed Russia's supposed strategic superiority to continue and even to grow. Carter himself, as one part of his hardening attitude toward the Soviets, lost faith in the treaty. He did not press for ratification. Instead, in December 1979, the Carter administration persuaded its NATO partners to agree to a program of installing Pershing II missiles with nuclear warheads in Western Europe as a response to the Soviet installation of hundreds of new medium-range SS-20 missiles in Eastern Europe. This was hardly a move forced by the Americans on reluctant Europeans. The West Germans, British, Dutch, and other NATO members were greatly alarmed by the SS-20 threat and insisted upon an American response. NATO members made a "two-track" decision—to install American cruise missiles in Western Europe while simultaneously urging arms control talks on the Russians. The NATO states promised that if the Russians would remove SS-20s in Eastern Europe, the cruise missiles would not be installed. These steps were a major escalation in the arms race and had, as one immediate effect, the bringing to life of the moribund antinuclear movement in Europe, which soon spread to the United States. People throughout the world, from every walk of life and every political persuasion, found it increasingly difficult to understand how building more bombs enhanced their security. In an era in which each side had tens of thousands of nuclear warheads and overkill capacity was measured in factors of forty to fifty, it was equally difficult to see how adding to that capacity improved a nation's strategic position. Nevertheless, the arms race went on.

In December 1979, some 85,000 Soviet troops invaded Afghanistan. The event seriously jolted Carter. He said that "the implications of the Soviet invasion of Afghanistan could pose the most serious threat to world peace since the Second World War," and argued that "aggression unopposed becomes a contagious disease." The United States curtailed grain sales to Russia, suspended high-technology sales, and—at Carter's insistence—boycotted the 1980 Olympic Games in Moscow. In addition, Carter told the Senate to defer indefinitely consideration of the SALT II treaty. These were all most serious steps—except for the Olympic boycott, which was purely symbolic and for which the Russians got their revenge in 1984—and represented a reversal of long-standing policies that went back to the Kennedy years. Indeed, by 1980 Carter was taking a generally harder line toward the Soviets than any President since Eisenhower. He explained that Afghanistan was the reason, saying: "This action of the Soviets has made a more drastic change in my own opinion of what the Soviets' ultimate goals are than anything they've done in the previous time I've been in office." He called the invasion "a stepping-stone to their possible control over much of the world's oil supplies."

Carter's critics saw his response as an overreaction. They argued that the Soviets went into Afghanistan for defensive reasons. There already existed in Afghanistan a pro-Moscow government, put in power after a coup in April 1978; that government, however, was unable to suppress Muslim insurgency and the Russians—evidently fearful that the Muslim uprising that had already swept through Iran would spread to the millions of Muslims within the Soviet Union—reacted by invading.

But Carter insisted that the Red Army was on the march—and it was true that this was the first time the Soviets had sent their own troops into an area not conquered by the Red Army in 1945. Fearful for the West's oil supplies, Carter backed away from SALT II and increased defense spending; he also announced that restrictions on the activities of the CIA would be lifted and proclaimed a Carter Doctrine for Southwest Asia. Defining the Persian Gulf area as within the zone of American vital interests, Carter declared that the United States would repel an assault in that region by the Russians "by any means necessary—including military force." Critics asked how the United States could defend, singlehand-edly, an area thousands of miles from any American military base, except through the use of nuclear weap-ons, and expressed the wish that Carter had consulted with the Persian Gulf states and the NATO countries before promulgating the Carter Doctrine.

When Carter left office, relations with the Soviet Union were worse than they had been when he was in-augurated. Soviet dissenters were persecuted more ac-tively and severely in 1980 than had been the case in 1976. The nuclear arsenals of the superpowers had in-creased. Soviet SS-20s threatened Western Europe as never before, while America was producing cruise mis-siles so as to equally threaten Eastern Europe and Russia. Trade between the United States and the Soviet Union had fallen off sharply.

Carter had begun with a firm policy, a policy that in many ways held hope for a new beginning—lowered expenditures for armaments, greater trust between the two sides, more trade and more cultural exchanges, in short, a genuine détente. But he had been unable to hold to that policy, in largest part because of the failure of the Soviets to respond to his "positive incentives," but also because of internal political pressure to "get tough," because his own inexperience led him to overreact to events, as in Cuba and Afghanistan, and because the momentum of the arms race could not be even slowed, much less halted, as each side reacted to its fears of technological or numerical breakthrough by the other. And because, too, Carter was not a strong enough cap-tain to set a course and hold to it. By 1980, the word most often used to describe his foreign policy was "waf-fle." It was a stinging indictment.

Aside from the human rights campaign, Carter's ide-alism had its greatest impact on policy in relations with Africa, Latin America, and China. In Africa, Ambassa-dor Andrew Young's outspoken support in the United Nations for the merging nations of the continent, plus

his insistence on majority rule in southern Africa, won
many new friends for the United States. In Latin America, Carter withdrew support from the repressive military junta in Chile, thus reversing Nixon's policy. In
February 1978, Carter also cut all military and economic
aid to one of America's oldest allies, Anastasio Somoza
of Nicaragua, because of Somoza's odious record on
human rights. In June 1979, the United States supported
an OAS resolution calling for Somoza's resignation.
Without American assistance Somoza could not with-
stand the attacks of the Sandinista guerrilla movement.
In July 1979, Somoza fled to Miami; a year later, he was
assassinated in Paraguay. The United States immediately
recognized the new Sandinista government and provided it with $16 million in economic aid. A year later,
Carter signed a $75-million aid package for Nicaragua.
Insofar as the Sandinistas were left wing, with a strong
Communist element in the government, Carter's re-
sponse to the revolution represented a major shift in
United States' relations with Central America.

In May 1980, left-wing guerrillas in El Salvador, encouraged and aided by the Sandinista victory in Nicaragua, and by Castro, began a civil war. The El Salvador
government fought back with brutal, but inefficient,
search-and-destroy missions. El Salvador's army sent out
right-wing death squads to slaughter civilian opponents
in the hundreds, indeed ultimately in the thousands.
Following the murder of three American nuns and a lay
worker by government troops, Carter suspended military and economic aid to El Salvador, although on January 14, 1981, in one of his last acts as President, he
announced the resumption of limited aid.

One of Carter's great triumphs in foreign policy came
in 1978, when he took a bold and courageous stand on
the Panama Canal Treaty, which returned to Panama
full sovereignty over the Canal Zone. By no means could
Carter take full credit—negotiations had begun during
the Johnson administration and were brought to near-
completion under the Republicans in the seventies. But

when it came time for the crucial Senate vote, a highly charged, emotional opposition nearly blocked it. Ronald Reagan, campaigning for the presidency, denounced the treaty. One Senator said irritably, "We stole it [Panama] fair and square." But both Ford and Kissinger gave the treaty their support, and Carter put the full weight of the presidency behind ratification. The treaty narrowly passed.

Carter also followed the Republican lead with regard to China. Nixon's 1972 trip had opened the door to a new United States-Chinese relationship, but the problems of full recognition of Communist China and what to do about America's treaties with Nationalist China still had to be overcome. Carter announced in 1978 that as of January 1, 1979, the United States and China would extend full recognition to each other and exchange ambassadors. Further, the United States unilaterally ended its 1954 mutual defense treaty with Taiwan and withdrew diplomatic recognition of the Nationalist regime there, simultaneously recognizing Taiwan as part of China. Senator Barry Goldwater and presidential candidate Reagan led Republican criticisms of this "betrayal" of one of America's staunchest allies, but Carter forced the new policy through anyway, primarily because it was a logical outgrowth of the Nixon-Kissinger initiative in China, a fact that strongly muted Republican criticism.

Carter also followed Kissinger's lead in the Middle East, where he played a central role in bringing about a peace treaty between Egypt and Israel, something almost no one—including Kissinger—had thought possible. In the process, Carter raised his own prestige both in the United States and around the world. Carter's success was possible, primarily, because of Nasser's successor, Anwar el-Sadat. Sadat recognized that Egypt could afford no more war and was, in any case, incapable of driving the occupying Israeli army out of the Sinai. He decided to offer Israel peace and recognition in return for the occupied Egyptian territory. In December 1977, Sadat went to Israel to speak to the Israeli Parliament, an act of great courage and drama that captured the imagination of the world. Sadat was risking not only denunciation by his fellow Arabs but assassination as well. He also risked being misunderstood by the Israelis. He was forthright in what he told the Parliament, insisting that any agreement between Israel and Egypt would have to include an Israeli retreat from the West Bank of the Jordan River and from the Golan Heights, a homeland for the Palestinians and a recognition of the PLO as their government, and a relinquishment of Israel's unilateral hold on the city of Jerusalem. Such objectives seemed impossible, as the new Israeli Prime Minister, former terrorist and right-wing politician Menachem Begin, was unwilling to compromise on Jerusalem or the PLO. Nor would Begin make concessions on the Golan Heights or the West Bank. But Begin was willing to sign a separate peace with Egypt (it had long been an aim of Israeli foreign policy to divide the Arabs). Sadat could not abandon the other Arabs, especially the PLO, not even for the return of the Sinai, but he was willing to talk. This gave Carter his opportunity.

In the fall of 1978 Carter invited Begin and Sadat to meet with him at the Presidential retreat at Camp David, Maryland, with the United States acting as a "full partner" in the negotiations. For nearly two weeks the three men carried on intensive discussions. They could not reach a final agreement, however, because they could not settle the issues of Jerusalem, the West Bank, the Golan Heights, or the PLO. By December, they had reached an impasse. Carter called it "the most frustrating experience of my life."

Still, he persisted. In early 1979 he made a sudden, dramatic journey to the Middle East, where he met with Sadat in Egypt and Begin in Israel, and eventually persuaded them to sign a peace treaty. Essentially it was an agreement for Egyptian recognition of Israel, and peace between the two nations, in return for a staged Israeli withdrawal from the Sinai. The future of the PLO was also mentioned, but in a vague way that allowed conflicting interpretations as to what was meant. The agreement did not mention the Golan Heights or Jerusalem (indeed, Begin incorporated the Golan Heights into the State of Israel in 1982, and Jewish settlers in large numbers moved into the West Bank). The treaty was therefore unacceptable to the other Arab states, who vigorously denounced Sadat. But the treaty did lead to an Israeli withdrawal from the Sinai, completed in April 1982, and the opening of diplomatic economic relations between Egypt and Israel. Sadly, it also led to Sadat's assassination, by Egyptian soldiers, in October 1981.

Ironically, it was events in the Middle East, site of Carter's greatest triumph, that led to his downfall. In one of the most bizarre incidents of the twentieth century, the Iranian revolution almost brought American government, in 1980, to a standstill. Events in Iran played a major role in the presidential election that year and led to Carter's electoral defeat.

Since 1953, the year in which the CIA participated in a coup that restored the Shah of Iran to his throne, American relations with the Shah had wavered. Eisenhower had been an enthusiastic supporter of the regime, but both Kennedy and Johnson had limited arms sales and economic assistance to Iran on the grounds that the Shah was a reactionary dictator who could not be trusted. Nixon and Kissinger, however, returned to the Eisenhower policy, and indeed expanded it. In their view, Iran was America's best friend in the Middle East, a principal partner in the policy of containing the Soviets and the only reliable supplier of oil to the West. The Shah was a prime customer for America's military hardware during the early seventies, purchasing up to one third of all arms sold by the United States abroad, and thus was a major factor in solving America's balance-of-payments problems. He was also a staunch foe of Communism, and Iran's geographical position on Russia's southern border made it a strategically crucial nation. The Shah was a voice of moderation in OPEC. In addition, the

Shah allowed the Americans to station sophisticated electronic listening devices along Iran's border with the Soviet Union.

Iran was much more clearly an American vital interest than South Vietnam or South Korea had ever been. On his frequent trips to the United States, the Shah was given royal receptions. Tens of thousands of young Iranians came to the United States to study; Iranian military officers were trained at the various American war colleges; SAVAK, the notorious Iranian secret police force, received its training and equipment from the CIA; American oil companies provided the Iranians with technicians, financing, and general guidance, while sharing in the huge profits; and thousands of American businessmen operated in Teheran. Relations between the United States and Iran, in short, could not have been closer or better.

Or so it seemed. But in fact, except among the ruling elite in Iran, anti-American feeling was strong and growing. Iranians blamed the United States for putting the Shah back in power in 1953, and keeping him there afterward. They believed that the United States encouraged the Shah as he increasingly gathered all power in Iran into his own hands; they felt that the United States was responsible for the Shah's enormous expenditures on the armed forces, expenditures that were out of all proportion to Iran's security needs and were designed to protect the Shah's position rather than improve the condition of the Iranian people. Countless Iranians believed that the United States was responsible for the Shah's modernization programs, which in their view violated fundamental Islamic law and traditional Persian customs. But because the Americans got their information about Iran from the Shah, SAVAK, the Iranian military, and the oil companies, the seething unrest among the Iranian masses was either unknown, ignored, or dismissed.

Carter, despite his human rights policy, accepted the Nixon-Kissinger thesis that the Shah was a bulwark of American interests in the Middle East, and he continued the practice of selling the Shah military equipment at a record pace. (American arms sales to Iran, which had totaled $1.2 billion over the twenty-two years since 1950, increased almost sixteen-fold to a total of $19.5 billion from 1972 to 1979.) At the end of 1977, his first year in office, Carter went to Iran, where he was the guest of honor at a glittering dinner on New Year's Eve. The President proposed a toast: "Iran, because of the great leadership of the Shah, is an island of stability in one of the more troubled areas of the world." Carter failed to mention the massive anti-Shah demonstrations that had occurred that day in Teheran and which had led to hundreds of arrests. The CIA was equally myopic. In August 1978, by which time strikes and demonstrations had virtually paralyzed Iran, the CIA issued a sixty-page analysis of "Iran in the 1980s," in which it concluded, "Iran is not in a revolutionary or even a 'prerevolutionary' situation."

But by this stage Iran in fact was full of revolutionary activity. The Shah was under attack from both the left (the Fedayeen, which was closely connected to the PLO) and the right (the Mullahs, or Islamic clergy, who were demanding an Islamic republic and a retreat from modernization). The CIA failed to see the seriousness of the challenge or understand the depth of Iranian hatred for the Shah, even though it had more agents in Iran, per capita, than anywhere else in the world. American intelligence also failed to uncover a crucial fact: The Shah had an incurable cancer and was being treated with massive doses of drugs by French doctors. His will was shattered; he was indecisive at critical moments; he had no stomach for turning his magnificently equipped army, or his secret police, against the rioters, who consequently grew increasingly bolder. But neither Carter nor the CIA could believe that an absolute monarch, in command of a wealthy oil-producing nation, with huge armed forces and secret police giving him their enthusiastic support, could be overthrown by unarmed mobs led by bearded Mullahs. Indeed, so contemptuous was Carter of the Shah's political opponents that he made no attempt to open lines of communication with them. It was a momentous miscalculation.

By mid-1978, a single leader of the Iranian opposition had emerged. He was the Ayatollah Khomeini, an aged fanatic who was living in exile in Paris, from which place he sent instructions and exhortations to his followers in Iran. His message was to strike, disrupt, riot, and create chaos until the Shah was forced to abdicate. Hundreds of thousands of Iranians did as he instructed; soon Iran was not producing enough oil even for its own internal needs, and the country was indeed in chaos. The Iranian army, forbidden by the Shah to fire on the rioters (the Shah feared that a bloodbath would ruin his son's chances of succeeding him), was demoralized. Finally, on January 16, 1979, the Shah left the country for an extended "vacation." Two weeks later, the Ayatollah Khomeini returned to Iran, where crowds of supporters, numbering in the hundreds of thousands, greeted him with wild enthusiasm. Although Khomeini never took a formal position in the government, he immediately became the de facto ruler of Iran.

The Carter administration hardly knew what to make of the Ayatollah. Accustomed, like its predecessors, to thinking exclusively in terms of the Cold War, it was unable to adjust to a fundamentalist religious revolution that denounced the United States and the Soviet Union equally. Discounting the Ayatollah's rabid hatred of Communism, Carter tended to hear only Khomeini's vicious assaults on the United States which he called "the great Satan." Thus Carter's fear was that Khomeini would allow a Soviet penetration of Iran. This was seen as a possible first step in a Soviet penetration of the entire Middle East, with incalculable consequences for the entire Western world. Once again, in other words, Carter was seeing dangers that did not exist, while ignoring those that did.

What the United States government never fully recognized was that the cement holding the otherwise incompatible Fedayeen and Mullahs together was anti-Americanism and hatred of the Shah. The two sentiments merged into one because the Shah had not abdicated (he went first to Morocco, then to the Bahamas), because the United States continued to maintain a large diplomatic corps and business community in Iran, and because Iranians still blamed the United States for the events of 1953. It was almost universally believed in Iran that the CIA would attempt a repeat performance. In fact, Carter had no intention of trying to restore the Shah, as indicated by his recognition in February 1979 of the new Islamic government. Carter's hope was instead to restore normal relations with Iran and make it, once again, a pillar of stability in the Middle East. The Iranians, however, could not believe that the United States would abandon the Shah, and so long as he was alive they anticipated another CIA coup.

In July 1979, the Shah's sixty-day visa in the Bahamas expired. The Carter administration, after many aborted talks with a number of countries, finally persuaded the Mexican government to grant him a six-month tourist visa. Meanwhile, however, Carter was under intense pressure from David Rockefeller, Henry Kissinger, and other old friends of the Shah to admit the Shah to the United States. Kissinger said it was disgraceful that the United States had turned its back on one of her oldest and closest friends. Carter resisted this pressure, but he was moved ultimately by humanitarian motives, the most important being the argument that the Shah could receive proper medical treatment for his cancer only in a New York hospital. Carter agreed to allow the Shah to come to the United States for treatment. The Shah entered the United States in late October 1979; the Carter administration had taken the precaution of obtaining assurances from the Iranian government beforehand that it could protect the American embassy in Teheran. How Carter could have believed these assurances is somewhat of a mystery; it seemed obvious to most observers that allowing the Shah into the United States would have the effect of waving a red flag in front of an already fever-pitched bull.

On November 4, 1979, enraged Iranian "students"

overran the United States embassy in Teheran and took some 100 hostages. The Ayatollah Khomeini condoned the takeover, saying that "if they do not give up the criminal then we shall do whatever is necessary." It was an outrageous action, the worst violation of the basic principle of diplomatic immunity in modern history. Prime Minister Mehdi Bazargan, head of a "government" that existed only at the sufferance of Khomeini, tried to secure the release of the hostages, failed, and resigned. Carter ordered the Pentagon to prepare a contingency plan for military action to rescue the hostages. He also told Attorney General Benjamin Civiletti to inform the fifty thousand Iranian students in the United States to report to the nearest immigration office. Any student found to be in violation of the terms of his or her visa was to be deported. (Little came of this threat, as American courts consistently upheld the rights of the students.) Carter suspended arms sales to Iran, froze Iranian assets in American banks, and announced an embargo on Iranian oil. As Iran no longer wanted American arms anyway, and was not even producing enough oil for her own needs, these actions had no immediate effect.

More important than his actions were Carter's public statements, which had the effect of enormously enhancing the value of the hostages to the Iranians. By word and deed, the President made it clear to the Iranians and the world that the lives of the hostages were his first priority. He met repeatedly with the families of the hostages and prayed publicly with them at the National Cathedral; he confessed to reporters that virtually his every waking moment was spent worrying about the fate of the captives; to the great frustration of Senator Edward Kennedy, Carter refused to participate in the preconvention political campaigning for the Democratic nomination on the grounds that he needed to devote his full time to the hostage crisis, which helped Carter in his contest with Kennedy but later hurt him badly in the general election; he allowed the hostage crisis to dominate American foreign policy for the next fourteen and a half months. At the time, few questioned his priorities, although probably no other nation in the world would have put the fate of the fifty-three hostages (Khomeini had ordered the release of most black and female hostages) ahead of all other considerations. The media, by giving the crisis an extremely high level of coverage, including nightly TV "specials" on the situation, added to the emotional response of the American people, and Carter's popularity soared every time television showed huge mobs of crazed Iranians in Teheran crying "Death to Carter." Carter's choices—to allow the Shah to remain in an American hospital, to continue recognition of the Iranian "government," to put mild economic pressure on Iran, and to attempt to negotiate a solution—originally won wide support.

Negotiations, however, required a stable government in Iran, one that was really in power, and such a government did not exist. The Iranians were in a revolutionary situation, attempting to draw up a new, basic Islamic constitution; meanwhile there were a series of Prime Ministers, none of whom could stay in office a day without Khomeini's blessing. As a consequence, not until February 1980 did the United States have a list of Iranian demands to consider. As announced by the newly elected President of Iran, Abol-Hassan Bani-Sadr, the conditions were the return of the Shah to Iran for trial, the return of the Shah's wealth to the Iranian people, an admission of guilt by the United States for its past actions in Iran, plus an apology, and a promise not to interfere in Iran's affairs in the future. These were clearly unacceptable demands, especially the first one, as the Shah had already (in December 1979) left the United States to take up residence in Panama. In response to Bani-Sadr's demands, Carter threatened harsh new sanctions against Iran and against Iranian citizens in the United States unless some progress was forthcoming. In March 1980, the Shah left Panama, one day before Iran was to present formal extradition papers, and accepted a long-standing offer of safe haven from President Sadat of Egypt. With the Shah now in an Islamic country and with Bani-Sadr promising an early release of the hostages, Carter's spirits soared.

But Carter's elation was short-lived. Bani-Sadr stalled, then ruefully admitted that he did not have the power to effect the release of the hostages, and Khomeini's demands were unchanged. Carter was furious at this double-cross. On April 7 he announced the severing of diplomatic relations with Iran, the implementation of a complete economic embargo against Iran, an inventory of financial claims against Iran to be paid from Iranian assets in the United States, and told Iran's diplomats to be out of the country within twenty-four hours.

Carter also gave a go-ahead for a military attempt to rescue the hostages. The military operation, on April 25, 1980, was poorly planned and badly executed. Long before any of the American helicopters got anywhere near the hostages, Carter had to cancel the operation because of equipment failure. The botched operation made the United States appear to be a "pitiful helpless giant" and Carter more of a waffler than ever. Hard-liners condemned him for not having mounted a rescue operation sooner, not putting enough military force into it when he decided to go, and then backing down at the first sign of difficulty. From the wait-and-negotiate camp, Secretary of State Vance resigned his post in protest. Vance believed the attempted rescue, even if successful, would inevitably lead to the shooting of many of the hostages, would deepen the chasm between the United States and Iran, and might lead the Soviets to intervene, with dangerous consequences for American policy in the Middle East. In short, whether seen from the left or the right, Carter's abortive rescue mission was a disaster.

The President was widely perceived, by this time, as having gone from blunder to blunder. In an admittedly difficult situation, his decisions had been consistently wrong—his failure to support the Shah when the revolution began, his failure to open lines of communication with Khomeini, his recognition of a government in Iran that could not govern, his decision to allow the Shah into the United States, his highly emotional response to the taking of the hostages, his long-delayed and then botched use of the military rescue option. Carter's standing in the polls declined sharply.

An impasse in the hostage crisis had been reached, to continue through the summer of 1980. On July 27, the sixty-year-old Shah died of cancer, but any hope that his death would improve the hostage situation was soon dashed. In September, Khomeini stated four conditions for the release of the hostages: The United States must (1) return the Shah's wealth; (2) cancel all financial claims against Iran; (3) free Iranian assets frozen in the United States; and (4) promise never to interfere in Iranian affairs. Since the Iranian demand for an apology from the United States for its past behavior was not mentioned, there was now at least a basis for talk. Chances for a settlement also improved after September 22, when Iraq invaded Iran's Khuzistan Province and full-scale war began between the two countries.

The possibility of the dismemberment of Iran was highly disturbing to the United States, because the Soviets would be sure to take advantage of it, so in October Carter announced that he would release Iran's assets, end economic sanctions, and normalize relations if Iran would release the hostages. On November 4, Ronald Reagan defeated Carter in the presidential election, thereby putting additional pressure on Khomeini. In public Reagan was denouncing the Iranians as "barbarians" and "common criminals" and hinting that he would take strong and direct military action against them. Actually, Reagan had made a private deal with Khomeini. If the Iranians would hold the hostages until after the election, the new Reagan Administration would pay ransom for them in the form of arms for Iran. Khomeini badly needed the weapons for his war with Iraq, so the deal was struck.

After the election, but before Reagan's inauguration, Khomeini tried to make a separate deal with Carter. On December 21, Iran demanded a specific ransom for the captives—$24 billion—deposited in Algeria. The new Secretary of State, Edmund Muskie, said the demand was "unreasonable" but indicated that it formed a basis for negotiations. On January 6, Iran reduced the demand to $20 billion, and a week later made another reduction, to $8 billion. Complex negotiations followed, in an atmosphere of haste, as Reagan would take office on January 20. Finally, on Carter's last morning in office, the Iranians agreed to a deal that gave them $8 billion worth of Iranian assets that had been frozen (but $5 billion was set aside to pay off Iran's debts to American and European banks) in return for the release of the hostages, who flew out of Teheran that day. The crisis was finally over.

Except for the return of its assets, Iran got nothing from the episode—no apology, no international tribunal to hear Teheran's grievances against the United States, no promises about the future, no return of the Shah's wealth. The outcome was nevertheless hardly a triumph for the United States, which had been humiliated for more than fourteen months and shown to be impotent even in defending its vital interests. Khomeini was left with a bankrupt and divided country that was involved in a dangerous and expensive war with Iraq. Carter suffered the worse electoral defeat of any incumbent President ever, including Herbert Hoover in 1932. The only real winner was Reagan, whose huge margin of victory was due in no small part to Carter's inept handling of the crisis. Indeed, most observers felt that had Carter secured the release of the hostages before the election, he might well have won; Ronald Reagan certainly thought so, which was why he made the arms-for-hostages deal with Iran. Nearly everyone agreed that had the military rescue worked, Carter would have been triumphantly returned for a second term.

15

Reagan and the Evil Empire

The Soviet Union is the focus of evil in the modern world.
RONALD REAGAN, March 1983

With the advent of the Reagan administration, American foreign policy underwent another of its periodic swings. The new team of President Reagan, former governor of California and movie actor, and Secretary of State Alexander Haig, former NATO commander and assistant to Kissinger, was far tougher in its public statements than the Carter-Vance team had been. The Republicans said they were determined to restore the shattered American prestige and position around the world. They talked tough to the Russians, took a firm anti-Communist line in Central America, and dramatically escalated the arms race. Reagan charged that Carter (and by implication Nixon and Kissinger before Carter) had allowed the Soviets to achieve strategic superiority, and insisted that the SALT II agreements would have to be revised before they could be considered for ratification. Reagan ordered the B-1 bomber, cancelled by Carter, put into production; he stepped up the preparations for basing Pershing II missiles in Western Europe; he sharply increased defense expenditures for both conventional and nuclear forces within the United States; he scrapped the human rights policy; and he allowed American arms manufacturers to sell arms at a record level.

As a consequence, the arms industry became the leading growth industry in the United States. The level of armaments reached unprecedented proportions. By the early 1980s, worldwide military spending was nearly $550 billion annually, or $150 for every person on earth.

The Russians were actually exporting more arms than the United States, while France, Britain, Germany, and other industrialized countries were paying for their oil and other imports with arms sold to the Third World exporters of raw materials.

But just as Carter had discovered in the Iranian crisis that being the Commander in Chief of the greatest armed forces ever assembled on this earth (or the second-greatest, depending on which statistics about the Soviet armed forces one believed) did not give him sufficient power to enforce his will, so did Reagan discover in the Polish crisis in late 1981 that for all America's missiles and bombers and submarines and NATO partners, he was no more able to influence events in Eastern Europe than Truman and Eisenhower had been in the first years of the Cold War. When the Soviet Union forced the Polish army to impose martial law in order to crush Solidarity, a trade union that had nearly half the Polish population in its ranks, and which was moving Poland toward a genuine democracy, Reagan was outraged. But he was also disconcerted to discover that he was helpless. He dared not risk war with the Soviets over Poland; he could not persuade his NATO allies to join in an economic blockade of either Poland or Russia; he was, in the end, reduced to verbal denunciation and the most limited and ineffective economic sanctions. The only effects were to make life even more difficult for Polish citizens while strengthening the resolve of the Polish generals. In August 1984, after the Polish military released some of its hundreds of political prisoners, the Reagan administration lifted most of the sanctions.

By the early eighties, there were more wars going on, in more places. By 1984, Europe, which had seen so many wars over so many centuries, and which had twice in the twentieth century dragged the rest of the world into war, was the only continent where no active fighting was going on. Everywhere else wars were raging. Many of them had no connection with the Cold War, or with political or religious ideology. In Southeast Asia, Communists were at war with Communists (China versus Vietnam; Vietnam versus Cambodia). In the Middle East, Muslims fought Muslims (Iran versus Iraq) as Jews fought Arabs and Lebanese Christians fought Lebanese Muslims. The United States was involved in these conflicts, sometimes as a mediator, always as a supplier of arms. So were the Russians.

Virtually all Third World countries were spending enormous sums on war or preparation for war, despite staggering debts and dreadful poverty. In the Western economic boom of the second half of the 1970s, excess capital had piled up in American and European banks, and so large sums were loaned to the Third World. The money was used to purchase either arms or consumer goods, rather than as investment capital to increase production facilities. As a consequence, when the worldwide economic recession set in during the early 1980s, bringing with it a drop in the price of Third World exports (oil, minerals, commodities) and a rise in interest rates (caused in part by the previously unimaginable level of American deficits, as Reagan simultaneously cut taxes while increasing defense spending dramatically), many Third World nations faced bankruptcy. Billions of dollars in potential defaults were involved, putting the entire Western banking structure at risk. The world faced an economic crisis that was potentially worse than the Great Depression of the 1930s.

There was no easy solution. A temporary respite—loaning more money so that the Third World countries could at least meet the interest payments—only made the long-term problem worse. By 1984, the American economy was again expanding, at near-record rates, but because of Reagan's success in holding down inflation (4 percent in 1984), prices of commodities, oil, and other Third World products were not rising.

Another threat to worldwide stability was the continuing Iran-Iraq war. In 1984 the two sides began to attack oil tankers in the Persian Gulf with modern missiles. In 1979, the United States had proclaimed, in the Carter Doctrine, that it would use military force to prevent the

Russians from controlling the region or disrupting the flow of oil. But in 1984, the United States watched helplessly as Iraq and Iran disrupted the oil flow. In 1987, an American ship, the U.S.S. *Stark*, was hit by a French-made Exocet missile fired by an Iraqi plane. Iraq apologized and paid damages; Reagan's critics asked why the United States had a warship in a war zone without a specific task in the first place.

In the other major war in the Middle East, in Lebanon, the United States had no economic interest of any consequence, but nevertheless it became deeply involved. The war was exceedingly complex (it pitted Lebanese Muslims against Lebanese Christians, Syria against Lebanon, the PLO against everyone, and Jew against Arab), but the reason for American involvement was simple—to contain the Soviet Union. Reagan saw Syria as a client state of the Russians, and Israel as a potent Cold War ally in the Middle East. Secretary Haig and Defense Secretary Caspar Weinberger wanted close military ties with Israel, because they regarded Israel as the strongest and most reliable power in the region. The difficulty was that the Israelis, although eager to accept American arms and willing to cooperate with the Americans on military intelligence, viewed Arab nationalism and the PLO, not the Russians, as the chief threat.

Alliances are almost impossible to make when the potential partners do not agree on a common enemy. Haig and Weinberger realized that before they could persuade Israel to concentrate on an anti-Russian alliance, Israel had to be assured of peaceful, stable borders. Thanks to Carter's Camp David agreements, such borders had been achieved on Israel's Egyptian front. But on the West Bank of Jordan, on the Golan Heights, where Israel faced Syria, and on the northern front, where Lebanon provided a base for the PLO fighting forces, Israel had major problems, which Israeli leaders believed had to be solved before they could turn their energies and power to an anti-Soviet alliance with the United States.

American policy aimed to provide Israel with security,

primarily by eliminating the PLO base in Lebanon, partly through military action, partly by giving the Palestinians a homeland on the West Bank. Such a two-track policy was necessary, Reagan believed, because the moderate Arabs could not simply stand aside as Israel eliminated the PLO. Until the Palestinians had a homeland, they would be a permanent source of turmoil, terrorism, and war in the Middle East. The West Bank provided the best opportunity for such a homeland, if only the PLO, Jordan, Syria, and Israel would agree.

None would, however. The PLO could not accept the American formula of a Palestinian state tied to Jordan and unable to set its own foreign and military policy. Jordan had no desire to take responsibility for the PLO. Syria aimed at a regional predominance that had no room for an independent PLO. And Israel would not agree to a Palestinian nation on the West Bank no matter how tightly controlled by Jordan. On the contrary, Prime Minister Begin and his government continued to believe that Israeli security depended on seizing and holding territory, and on military might, rather than on political compromise. Thus in direct defiance of strongly stated American wishes, Begin continued to encourage Jewish settlement on the West Bank, turning it from a potential homeland for the Palestinians into a perhaps permanent part of greater Israel.

Reagan and Haig believed that if the PLO could be eliminated as a fighting force, Israel would be willing to be reasonable about a Palestinian homeland on the West Bank. The military base of the PLO was in southern Lebanon. Because Lebanon was torn by an endemic civil war, the government in Beirut was incapable of asserting its authority over the PLO. As a first step in getting the Israelis to be reasonable about the Palestinian question and to turn Israel's attention to the Soviet threat, Haig decided to encourage Israel to solve the PLO problem with a massive military stroke. On May 26, 1982, in Chicago, Secretary Haig delivered a major foreign policy address. Israel had just completed on April 25 her withdrawal from the Sinai, in accordance with the Camp

David agreement. With a peaceful and stable southern border, Begin felt free to concentrate on his northern front. In his Chicago speech, Haig called for "international action" to end the Lebanese civil war. This was, most observers agreed, a signal to Israel to invade Lebanon.

On June 6, 1982, Israel did invade. Israeli troops drove northward and then beseiged West Beirut, where refugee camps held tens of thousands of Palestinians and provided a base for PLO soldiers. Officially, the United States did not welcome the invasion, but neither would it condemn it. The immediate aim of the invasion was to crush the PLO, but the immediate result was a de facto Israeli occupation of southern Lebanon, thus adding to Israel's conquered territory. Haig stated publicly that the invasion created "new and hopeful opportunities" for a political settlement in Lebanon, which presumably meant the elimination of the PLO, but by this time the confused situation had the Reagan administration working at cross-purposes. American Ambassador Philip Habib was laboring, with impressive energy, skill, and patience, to find a diplomatic solution. The Israelis were apprehensive that Habib would put together a compromise that would give the PLO a permanent place in Lebanon (a solution supported by Saudi Arabia, Jordan, and Syria, as well as by Defense Secretary Caspar Weinberger).

In August 1982 Israel began the systematic and heavy shelling of the PLO camps in West Beirut. This action led to a general public demand that Reagan dissociate the United States from Israeli action and contributed to the resignation of Secretary of State Haig, who was replaced by George Shultz, a California businessman and former professor with long experience in government. By September, Ambassador Habib produced a political compromise. Israel agreed to lift the siege while a trilateral force of French, Italian, and American troops supervised the withdrawal of the PLO army from Beirut to Jordan and Tunisia, countries Habib had persuaded to give refuge to the PLO soldiers.

Reagan then tried to get the Camp David process in motion once again. He delivered a major foreign policy speech that committed the United States to the general principles agreed to by Begin, Carter, and Sadat in 1979—a homeland and self-determination for the Palestinians on the West Bank and in Gaza in return for a guarantee from the Arab states of the inviolability of Israel's borders and its right to exist. But immediately upon the removal of the PLO troops from Beirut and the withdrawal of the trilateral force, the Israeli army moved into Beirut again—just as PLO leader Yasser Arafat had warned that it would—and took control of the city. The Christian militia of Lebanon, working closely with the Israelis, sought revenge for the assassination of the Christian leader, President Gemayel. They entered the Palestinian refugee camps and slaughtered hundreds of women and children. The bloodbath horrified the world and forced Reagan once again to send in the U.S. Marines (along with the returning French and Italian troops), in an attempt to restore some semblance of peace in Beirut.

The peacekeepers, however, found themselves virtually besieged in Beirut and completely unable to influence events. There were not enough Marines, French, and Italian forces to enforce their will on any of the various warring factions, but the mere presence of Western troops, especially American Marines, in Beirut was infuriating to the Muslims. Every political party in Lebanon now had its own militia; Syria occupied eastern Lebanon, Israel occupied southern Lebanon, what remained of the PLO (by 1983 itself divided in warring factions) occupied northern Lebanon, while U.S. Marines, with neither a clear objective nor the necessary force (there were only 1,500 of them) to accomplish anything, were isolated at the Beirut airport.

Far from solving anything, much less leading to a U.S.-Israeli alliance directed against the Soviets, the Israeli invasion of Lebanon had made a bad situation worse for everyone involved—most of all for Israel itself. The war was costing the Israelis billions of dollars and heavy casualties; the occupation of southern Lebanon brought worldwide denunciation; Israel's inflation rate was 400 percent annually; and Israel's body politic was badly split between hawks and doves. Still, Israel would not retire from Lebanon.

In February 1983, Reagan attempted to induce Israel to pull back by promising "this administration is prepared to take all necessary measures to guarantee Israel's northern borders in the aftermath of the complete withdrawal of the Israeli Army." It was an historic pledge— never before had an American President made an offer to guarantee any of Israel's borders—but the Israelis would not respond, primarily because the following day Reagan, in an attempt to maintain an evenhanded policy, called for "something in the nature of a homeland for the Palestinians." Meanwhile American Marines began taking casualties from sniper fire. Reagan told the Israeli foreign minister of the "necessity and urgency" of an Israeli withdrawal, again to no avail. Reagan also refused to release some 75 F-16 fighters to Israel, again without results.

In May 1983, with Secretary of State Shultz himself acting as mediator, an Israeli-Lebanese agreement was finally reached. But it was a paper accord, without substance. The new Lebanese President, Amil Gemayel, controlled only one small faction in his country and was not in a position to make good on any agreement, much less one that allowed the Israeli Army de facto control of southern Lebanon. The Shultz formula called for the simultaneous withdrawal of all Israeli, Syrian, and PLO forces from Lebanon, but it allowed the Israelis to remain in southernmost Lebanon until the others had withdrawn. Worse, neither the Syrians nor the PLO had agreed to either this or any other of Shultz' propositions, and indeed denounced the agreement immediately. Neverthelss, Reagan, grateful for Israeli "cooperation," lifted the embargo on the F-16 fighter planes, and in June 1983 Defense Secretary Weinberger announced that the prospective U.S.-Israeli alliance against the Soviet Union could now be revived. The Israelis, meanwhile, shortened their lines in Lebanon, but insisted they would not completely withdraw until Syria and the PLO also withdrew.

By August 1983, six distinct armies were fighting throughout Lebanon—Syrians, Israelis, Christian Phalangists, Muslim militia factions, the Lebanese army, and the PLO (also divided into factions). Beirut was under constant shelling; the Marines at the airport were taking more casualties. It was increasingly difficult to see what point there was to keeping the Marines in Lebanon, and Congress was threatening to invoke the War Powers Act, which would force Reagan to withdraw them within ninety days. Secretary Shultz, in response, restated the Administration's position that although the Marines in Lebanon "are involved in a situation where there is violence," they were not "in combat" and thus the War Powers Act did not apply. His statement confused more than it elucidated and satisfied almost no one.

In truth, the Reagan administration had blundered in Lebanon as badly as Carter had blundered in Iran. Encouraging the Israeli invasion had turned out to be a dreadful mistake, made worse by sending in the Marines in such insufficient force that they became hostages rather than peacekeepers. The attempts at evenhandedness—denouncing Israeli settlement on the West Bank, placing an embargo on the sale of airplanes to Israel, speaking out for a "sort of" homeland for the Palestinians that frightened Israel while still leaving the PLO far short of its aspirations, demanding a Syrian and PLO withdrawal while allowing the Israelis to maintain their position in southernmost Lebanon, putting the Marines into a hostage situation at the airport—made all the participants angry at and suspicious of the United States. It was difficult to see how American diplomacy could have done worse.

Reagan tried to retrieve the situation by sending in more force, in the form of U.S. warships stationed off the Lebanese coast. In September 1983, as fighting in Beirut escalated and the Marines took still more casualties, the Navy began shelling Druse militia positions. This

only exacerbated the problem and led many people to
wonder who on earth was in charge of American foreign
policy, and especially of the use of the military to support
that policy. Firing sixteen-inch naval guns into the Lebanese countryside hardly seemed a proper application
of force in a civil war in which the United States professed to be neutral and a seeker of peace.

The violence increased with every salvo from the huge
battleships, reaching a culmination on October 23, 1983,
when a suicide truck loaded with TNT drove into Marine
Headquaters and killed 230 Marines. Vice President
George Bush, visiting the site three days later, declared
that such terrorist acts would not be allowed to shape
American foreign policy. Reagan denounced the "des-
picable" act, promised to find and punish those repon-
sible, and forthrightly declared that it was "central to
our credibility on a global scale" to keep the Marines in
Lebanon. Naval shelling of Muslim positions increased,
supported by air strikes.

But for all the brave words and deeds, the situation
had in fact become intolerable. Reagan had no choice
but to withdraw the Marines, and in effect admit a terrible mistake. In January 1984, just as the campaign for
his reelection was getting under way, he began the preparations for the withdrawal. On a minor scale, it was like
Nixon's withdrawal from Vietnam—slow, painful, full
of threat and bluster, punctuated by random bombing
and shelling, and marked by misleading statements and
downright lies. Reagan insisted, in December 1983, that
U.S. Marines and Navy vessels (by then forty in number,
including three aircraft carriers) would stay in Lebanon
until the Lebanese government was in full control of the
situation. The battleship *New Jersey* and the Naval aircraft
openly took the side of Gemayel's government in the
raging civil war—a strange action for a "peacekeeping"
force—but even as he was thereby stepping up American
involvement, Reagan announced on February 7, 1984,
that he was "redeploying" the Marines to ships off
Beirut.

That same day, the White House announced that the

bombardment of Muslim militia positions was done for the purposes of "protecting" the Gemayel government; two days later it declared that the shelling was for "the safety of American and other multinational force personnel in Lebanon." Such contradictory pronouncements were a fitting way to end the American involvement in Lebanon, where no one, most of all Reagan himself, ever seemed to be clear on the purpose of that involvement.

By February 26, 1984, the Marines were gone. The Navy soon followed. The war went on. Completing the debacle, in March, Lebanon canceled its agreement with Israel. The Israelis still held southern Lebanon, but at a high cost; Syria still held eastern Lebanon; civil war still raged; there was no U.S.-Israeli alliance; there was, in brief, nothing good to say about the Reagan administration's policies in Lebanon, and much to denounce. But as had been the case in Vietnam after American withdrawal in 1973, no one wanted to learn the lessons of failure. Lebanon was not even an issue in the 1984 presidential campaign.

Far more satisfactory to the Reagan administration, and to the public, was a successful piece of gunboat diplomacy on the tiny Caribbean island of Grenada. In October 1983, a military coup in Grenada (a British Commonwealth nation) deposed and then killed Prime Minister Maurice Bishop, himself a leftist who had already greatly alarmed the Reagan administration because he was allowing Cuban construction workers to build an airfield on the island, and had signed military agreements with Communist bloc countries. The military council that took power, headed by General Hudson Austin, was thought to be even more Communist than Bishop. When Austin murdered Bishop, the United States decided to intervene. On October 25, Reagan announced that he had ordered 1,900 Marines to invade Grenada and depose General Austin. The Cuban workers and troops, some eight hundred altogether, fought back, but had no chance of successful resistance and were quickly overwhelmed. A new government was formed, under Governor General Sir Paul Scoon. The Cubans were ordered off the island, the Soviet embassy was closed and all members expelled. Land redistribution policies carried out under the Bishop regime were cancelled.

Reagan called the invasion a "rescue mission," an interpretation that got vivid visual support when American medical students, returning to the United States from Grenada, kissed the ground upon arrival at the airport. Latin Americans, fearful as always of the Colossus of the North, condemned the invasion as Teddy Roosevelt Big Stick tactics. The United Nations General Assembly approved a resolution that "deeply deplored" the American action. Much of the American press was outraged, not so much by the invasion as by the fact that the Pentagon did not permit newsmen to cover it. Reagan personally saw it as a major triumph. It showed he could be tough and decisive; it enhanced American credibility in the Caribbean; it prevented the Russians from gaining a strategic airfield; it added to the President's popularity; it served as a warning to revolutionaries in Central America.

The British were upset about the invasion, not because they disapproved, but because they were not consulted, and Grenada was a Commonwealth member nation. Reagan and the State Department simply ignored the British, a particularly gratuitous insult because, if they had been asked, the British almost certainly would have given reluctant consent. This slighting gesture by the Reagan administration caused a setback in Anglo-American relations, which had reached a high point only a year and a half earlier, during the Falklands War.

In March 1982, the Argentine junta seized the Falkland Islands, a barren and sparsely inhabited British possession off the tip of South America. Those islands were of no significance to the world, with neither stategic nor economic importance or potential. But they did have tremendous political significance, enough to cause a war and once again illustrate the power of nationalism as the strongest of all political forces. What made the Falklands War the dramatic and incredible event that it became was that it was fought with the most modern weapons, which fascinated everybody, over the oldest issue of all: Whose territory is this? Whose flag flies here? It had absolutely nothing to do with any of the issues dividing mankind and causing wars, the modern issues such as Communism versus capitalism, or the colored world versus the white world, or the Muslims versus the Jews. Such issues were irrelevant to the British-Argentine War of 1982.

The Falkland Islands had long been claimed by Argentina, but the British had always refused to negotiate seriously on the issue, which gave the military junta a reason for action. Patriotism was thus stirred up, diverting the public's attention from the botch the generals had made of the economy, not to mention their horrific record on human rights. The generals who twitched the British lion's tail became heroes. What the generals had not anticipated was the tough British reaction, because they ignored the obvious fact that British nationalism was at least every bit as strong as Argentinian, and the fact that the serving Prime Minister herself could use a boost in the public opinion polls.

When the Argentines took the islands, Margaret Thatcher's response was tough and immediate. She ordered a large naval task force to the Falklands, including using the ocean liner *Queen Elizabeth II* as a troop carrier—the largest fighting task force since the end of World War II. The public was overwhelmingly enthusiastic. The British were also delighted at the American reaction. Reagan told his military to give the British task force covert support, especially invaluable intelligence. Reagan also had his United Nations Ambassador, Mrs. Jeane Kirkpatrick, support the British in heated debates in the United Nations. British gratitude was widespread; when Britain won the short war, not without taking heavy losses, there was an outpouring of pro-American sentiment in the United Kingdom, where many public figures remarked that the strain on U.S.-U.K. relations created by Eisenhower's actions during the 1956 Suez crisis was now eliminated.

As noted, Reagan sacrificed much of this goodwill in 1983, when he invaded one of the Queen's possessions without informing, much less consulting, Prime Minister Thatcher (it must be noted that she was in a secure position, having recently won a quickly called election that took full advantage of her victory in the Falklands War). To Reagan, however, the positive results of invading Grenada far outweighed the negative repercussions. The reason was that the Caribbean and, even more, Central America were central to Reagan's thinking.

Central America was almost an obsession with Reagan. Unlike previous Presidents, who have looked east and west for the dangers and challenges, toward Europe and the Soviet bloc, and toward Japan and China, Reagan has looked south for his challenges. He was not very persuasive in getting others to join him in regarding Central America as *the* critical area. This stemmed, in part, from a lack of experience; when he took office, Reagan was as inexperienced in foreign affairs as Carter had been. He knew only what he was against. In Central America, he was very much against any expansion of the Sandinista movement. What he was for was less clear.

What Carter had been for was extending a helping hand to the Sandinista regime, in the hope that this really would bring about a viable social democratic government in Nicaragua, with political and economic justice. What Reagan was for was a 1980s version of Churchill's cry in 1919, "We must strangle Bolshevism in the cradle."

In Reagan's view, the threat from the Sandinistas and their partners, the rebels in El Salvador, was twofold. First, that Nicaragua would become another Cuba, providing the Russians with a base in Central America that they would use both to export revolution to their neighbors, north and south, and as a naval and military base. The second threat Reagan saw was that either continued chaos, or even worse a Communist victory throughout

Central America, would lead to a massive flight of refugees from Central America into the United States itself. America already had serious problems with illegal immigrants from Mexico; the propect of countless Central American refugees crossing the Rio Grande caused Reagan to view the situation with the greatest alarm. Far better, Reagan reasoned, to support the existing governments in El Salvador, Guatemala, and Honduras, however distasteful, than to abandon the region to the Communists.

Reagan moved immediately. Within days of taking office, he froze the last $15 million of Carter's aid package to Nicaragua because, he said, Nicaragua was "aiding and abetting violence" in El Salvador. Reagan also extended extensive military aid to a government in El Salvador that was, many charged, as objectionable as Somoza's in Nicaragua had been. According to his critics, Reagan grossly exaggerated both the extent of Communist infiltration and Cuban-Russian support for the guerrillas in El Salvador. In March 1981, Reagan nevertheless increased military aid to the military government in El Salvador by $25 million and soon sent in American military advisers. Reagan dismissed any analogy with Vietnam in the early sixties and pointed to the free election held in El Salvador in March 1982.

Still, Reagan could not rally support sufficient to get the Congress behind the effort. Too many politicians, and too large a segment of the public, believed that Reagan was seeing the wrong threats and applying the wrong solutions, for Reagan to get a consensus behind him. His critics thought that it was precisely the governments themselves, the ones Reagan was supporting with military aid, that were the danger and the problem. Narrowly based military regimes that perpetuated right-wing violence and a grossly unfair economic status quo based on a colonial relationship with the United States, such as the governments of El Salvador, Honduras, and Guatemala, could never bring stability to an area that cried out for change. Reagan's critics further charged that Reagan exaggerated the number and quality of arms supplied by the Communists to the rebels in El Salvador, the size of the Cuban contingent in Nicaragua, and even the degree of influence of Communists in the Sandinista movement. The critics thought that the United States should be working with the Sandinistas, not against them, in order to promote the kind of social and economic democracy that is a prerequisite for stability. Economic aid to the forces of the left, rather than military aid to the forces of the right, was the proper policy. As to the "wave of refugees" Reagan so feared, the critics responded that an improvement in the political and economic situation in Central America, not more military rule, was what was needed to meet that threat.

Certainly the threat of deepening military involvement was there, and hanging over it, always, was the memory of Vietnam. In Congress and among the public there were widespread fears that Central America would become "another Vietnam." No matter how often Reagan explained that there was no comparison between the situations in Vietnam and Central America (a judgment that was more right than wrong), he could not dispel the fear. Congress proved extremely reluctant to meet Reagan's demands for military aid for the army of El Salvador, even after the State Department asserted that El Salvador had curbed its right-wing death squads and "made progress" in human rights. In March 1983, a year after the elections in El Salvador, fears of "another Vietnam" were markedly increased when Nicaraguan counter-revolutionaries ("Contras"), based in Guatemala and supported and trained by the CIA, crossed the border and began an insurgency operation against the Sandinista government. Reagan asked for more money to support the operation, but Congress remained hesitant.

Reagan tried to raise the level of alarm. He justified CIA support for the Contras in his press conferences as necessary to overthrow the Sandinistas, calling the Contras "freedom fighters." Secretary Shultz asserted that support for the El Salvador government was "moral" because the United States was preventing a "brutal military takeover by a totalitarian minority." In April 1983,

Reagan went before a Joint Session of Congress to ask support for his Central American policy, asserting that the "national security of all the Americas is at stake in Central America." But to his dismay, the only sustained applause he received, from Republicans as well as Democrats, was when he promised to send no American combat units to the scene.

In the fall of 1983, Reagan nevertheless increased the pressure. The CIA-sponsored Contras expanded their activities, to the bombing of oil storage and other facilities in Nicaragua. The U.S. Army held major maneuvers in Honduras and began construction of a permanent military base near the Nicaragua border. But Congress remained unconvinced, not only because of painful memories of Vietnam, but also because Congress represented the split in the country as a whole over Central America. No other issue in the world—not even arms control, the Middle East, or relations with Russia— caused such a deep and broad split in American opinion. The result was congressional stalemate. Reagan could not get the funds that were necessary to prosecute the war against the Central American revolutionaries successfully, but Reagan's critics could not force him to withdraw from the area, much less support the forces of change. This stalemat made it difficult for the United States to influence events in Central America, even though, as always, Uncle Sam was blamed by both the left and the right in Latin America for everything that went wrong.

In March 1984, presidential elections in El Salvador gave the Reagan administration some cause for optimism. The leader of the death squads, or so it was charged, Roberto d'Aubuisson, was the candidate of the right wing. He was defeated by the somewhat more moderate candidate, the man the United States supported, José Napoleon Duarte, who quickly set about trying— with some success—to improve El Salvador's image in the world.

Simultaneously, however, the Contras—using CIA-supplied equipment—began mining Nicaragua's harbors, and some Russian ships were damaged. Reagan was forced to announce that he was withdrawing his requests for additional military aid to El Salvador until after the elections. In other words, the hopelessly divided American perceptions of the nature of the threat in Central America continued to make it difficult for the United States to set, and hold to, clear policy goals. Violence and turmoil in Central America continued.

In his relations with the Soviet Union, Reagan had much clearer goals than he did in Lebanon and the Middle East, and a much broader and deeper consensus supporting him than he did in Central America. Reagan's goals were peace, limitations on the arms race, an actual reduction in the size of the nuclear arsenals, good trade relations with Russia, cooperation in solving such problems as acid rain and water and air pollution, and generally a mutually beneficial détente. Almost all Americans wanted the same general goals achieved. Where the consensus broke down was over the means used to achieve the goals.

Reagan's tactics for achieving peace and controlling the arms race included hurling insults at the Soviet Union. In March 1983, he characterized the Soviet Union as an "evil empire" and "the focus of evil in the modern world." Outside of Japan and Western Europe, few people around the world accepted Reagan's analysis. In the southern half of the globe, the general perception was that poverty, imperialism, and racism were the true focus of evil. In the Middle East, the Israelis saw the radical Arabs as the focus of evil. The Arabs saw the Israelis as the source, while in Iran the perception was that the United States was equally a focus of evil with the Soviet Union.

Fewer Americans disagreed with Reagan, but many wondered how such accusations could further the cause of peace or détente. The argument was that there was no point to hurling gratuitous insults against the other superpower, because the United States had to live with the Soviet Union, like it or not.

With regard to arms control, by far the most important real issue challenging the superpowers, Reagan rejected Carter's policy of offering the Soviets restraint and even accommodation, because, as he pointed out, Carter's policy had not worked. The Russians simply did not respond; indeed they took advantage of Carter. Reagan reverted to Nixon's policy of buildup, the old Cold War tactic of never bargaining with the Russians except from a position of strength (i.e., superiority). In his first three years in office, Reagan increased defense spending, in real terms, by 40 percent. This massive buildup did indeed alarm the Russians, but to Reagan's dismay it did not cause them to negotiate seriously. Instead, as they had always done in the past, they matched (and in some areas exceeded) the American increases.

Europe remained the area of greatest concern and danger. The most serious destabilizing factor in Europe was the Soviet emplacement, in the late seventies, of more than 345 SS-20 missiles (modern intermediate-range weapons with three nuclear warheads each). NATO decided, in December 1979, to match this threat with some 500 American cruise missiles based in Western Europe. Carter, at the urging of the NATO allies, had made the cruise decision; Reagan heartily endorsed it, despite intense opposition within many of the NATO countries, an opposition that was well financed (from Russian sources, it was charged by opponents), well-organized, and highly motivated.

To many Europeans, the most frightening aspect of the situation was that it appeared that the United States and the Soviet Union had agreed that if war ever broke out between them, Europe was the battleground on which it would be fought. If that happened, then there surely would be no more Europe. This realization put a great strain on NATO and the individual countries involved. But all the governments remained steadfast behind the original decision, despite massive protest demonstrations in London, Bonn, Paris, Rome, and West Berlin.

On November 23, 1983, deployment of the cruise missiles began in Great Britain and West Germany. The

Russians immediately discontinued the arms control talks in Geneva. Russian-American relations were at one of their lowest points since the Cold War began. There was widespread alarm, and there was good cause for it. The arsenals of both sides had reached huge, indeed unbelievable proportions (except that they were all too real). In strategic weapons, the United States had more than 9,000 nuclear warheads on bombers and missiles, the Soviet Union more than 7,000. These were aimed at targets inside the other superpower's homeland. In theater nuclear weapons, the Soviet Union had 3,580 of all types (land- and sea-based) directed at targets in Western Europe, while NATO had 4,445 aimed at Eastern Europe and the western sections of the Soviet Union (including 98 French and 64 British theater nuclear missiles). Aside from the dangers to human existence, the cost of these arsenals, and of the conventional forces in the Warsaw Pact and NATO, was horrendous. By 1985 the United States was spending $300 billion per year on defense, the West Europeans nearly $150 billion. (Accurate figures for the Warsaw Pact nations are impossible to come by, but were somewhat less than the total for Western Europe.)

"This is not a way of life at all," President Eisenhower had declared in 1953, when the costs and the dangers of the arms race were one tenth or less of what they had become thirty-two years later, but no one could find a way out of the arms race. Both sides made proposals—the Russians offered to reduce their SS-20 deployment to the size of the French and British missile forces if NATO agreed to deploy no cruise missiles; Reagan offered a "zero-zero" option, in which NATO would forgo the deployment of cruise missiles if the Soviets dismantled all the SS-20s—but in each case the offer was seen by the other side as propaganda, not to be taken seriously.

A principal Soviet aim, Western leaders agreed, was to divide and weaken NATO, and certainly the huge costs were putting a great strain on the alliance. Europeans protested against the prospect of Europe becoming the battleground in a superpower nuclear war; Americans protested against paying so much for what was widely regarded as the defense of Europe. By 1985, one half or more of the American defense budget went for NATO defense. It was, therefore, galling to hear West Germans refer to the American troops in their country as an occupying force, rather than West Germany's defenders; it was irritating that the Europeans would not spend more on their own defense.*

In Congress, there was growing sentiment for the United States to reduce its NATO commitment and costs, unless the Europeans did more for their own defense. In 1984, Senator Sam Nunn, Democrat of Georgia, proposed that ninety thousand of the three hundred sixty thousand U.S. troops stationed in Europe be withdrawn within five years if the Europeans declined to increase their share of the burden. The Reagan Administration opposed Nunn's proposal, and it lost in the Senate, but only by a vote of fifty-five to forty-one. Obviously Nunn had struck a responsive chord. In 1953, Eisenhower had said that American troops could not remain in Europe indefinitely, because America could not afford to maintain a "Roman wall" forever. By 1985, it appeared that the Senate, and millions among the public, agreed with

*With regard to Japan, which paid practically nothing for its defense, but rather relied completely on American arms, the situation was maddening. The Japanese were free to put their scientists and technicians to work on consumer goods and to use their funds for research and investment, thus gaining a clear advantage over the United States in the competition for world markets, while the United States had to put its scientists and technicians, and tax dollars, to work on military programs partly for Japan's defense. The situation got worse in 1987, when the Americans paid the cost, in blood and treasure, to protect oil tankers in the Persian Gulf that were headed for Japan, while the oil-producing states in America struggled along with depression-type conditions because of the cheap Arab oil.

Eisenhower's assessment. The consensus on both sides of the Atlantic as to what NATO was, what it should do, and how it should do it, was under severe strain.

Reagan's economic policies toward the Soviet Union contributed to the difficulties. Originally, Reagan had supported Carter's decision to put an economic blockade against the Soviets into effect in response to the invasion of Afghanistan. Indeed, Reagan went beyond refusing to sell grain to the Russians, as he attempted to prevent America's European allies from trading with the Eastern bloc. In the late seventies, the Western Europeans had concluded an agreement with the Soviet Union that allowed them to purchase Soviet-produced natural gas in return for building a pipeline from Siberia. But the pipeline was dependent upon American technology, which was to be supplied by European-based multinational corporations. Reagan, outraged by this, attempted to block the construction of the pipeline by imposing economic sanctions on those corporations that sold American-produced equipment to the Soviets. But the sanctions were insufficient to deter the Europeans.

Furthermore, Reagan himself was eager to trade. For all his "evil empire" talk, Reagan had a huge grain surplus and a major balance of payments problem. By 1985, although the Soviets were still very much involved in attempting to subdue Afghanistan (where they had taken nearly fifty thousand casualties, roughly equal to American losses in Vietnam, and where they had used poison gas and chemical weapons), Reagan had abandoned nearly all the restrictions and embargos Carter had instituted against the Soviets. To Europeans, Reagan's actions seemed contradictory, as he was simultaneously selling more wheat and corn to the Soviets while insisting that they *not* sell pipeline technology. Reagan responded that the pipeline was a strategic issue (presumably food sales were not). More to the point, Reagan argued that the Soviets could buy grain elsewhere, but they could only get the technology for the pipeline from the United States. His arguments, however, convinced few if any Europeans, and the pipeline, like the grain sales, went forward. Indeed, by 1984 Reagan was actually encouraging pipeline and other high-tech sales to the Soviets, completing the reversal of Carter's policies. Amazingly, most of the public continued to regard Jimmy Carter as "soft on Communism," Ronald Reagan as "hard."

Reagan's actions confused many Americans. They wondered why, if the U.S.S.R. was their enemy, the United States was selling it badly needed commodities and goods. And if the U.S.S.R. was not America's enemy, then why was the United States spending such enormous sums on missiles directed against Russia?

During the 1984 presidential campaign, Democrats called Reagan the "Teflon" President, because none of his mistakes ever seemed to stick to him. Events preceding the election illustrated the point. In early September 1984, the Sandinistas shot down a helicopter in Nicaragua, killing two Americans who were members of the Civilian Military Assistance group, a private organization—or so it was claimed. Still, Reagan's policies in Central America did not become an issue. The debacle in Lebanon was also ignored, even when in mid-September terrorists drove a truck carrying explosives into the U.S. Embassy in Beirut and blew it up, killing twenty-three people. Reagan responded to critics by charging that the blame for the disaster lay with "previous administrations" for the "near destruction of our intelligence capabilities." By this time, Reagan had been in office three and one half years!

In October, the Associated Press revealed that the CIA had prepared a manual for the Contras that suggested assassinations and kidnappings as techniques for use in Nicaragua. This was part of a total program of using terror to overthrow the government, carried on by an Administration that had been the most forthright in the world in denouncing terrorism. Meanwhile, in Beirut, Reagan was as unsuccessful in obtaining the release of American hostages held by Muslim extremists as Carter had been in Iran during the 1980 election. Yet none of these contradictions and embarrassments reduced Reagan's great popularity; he got three out of every five votes cast, and was triumphantly reelected.

But Reagan was unable to transfer his great personal popularity into support for his policies. For example, the Congress, in the so-called Boland Amendment, defied the President and ordered a ban on military support of the Contras. It began in October 1984 and continued for two years. During that time, Reagan devised and executed a series of programs and actions designed to circumvent the clear intent of the Congress, or—more bluntly—to violate the law.

He did so in any number of ways. He solicited contributions from King Fahd of Saudi Arabia, other Arab potentates, Texas oil men, and rich right-wing American widows. Aides to the President, including Lieutenant Colonel Oliver North of the NSC staff and Robert McFarlane, the National Security Adviser, also solicited funds. These funds were then used to buy arms for the Contras. The CIA, meanwhile, in specific violation of the law, provided the Contras with military assistance, including intelligence, weapons, and supplies. The law also required the CIA to disclose to the congressional oversight committees the nature and scope of its activities, but CIA Director William Casey, perhaps the strongest supporter of the Contras within the Administration, simply ignored the law.

Thus was a private terrorist army raised and equipped and supported from the White House and CIA headquarters. Its objective was to overthrow the Sandinista government. But the Contras were unable to make progress. They had no popular base; they controlled no cities or even towns; they consisted of a mixture of former Somoza National Guard officers and mercenaries; they could not rally behind a single leader or a program; and they would not take on the Sandinista army in open battle, but rather made their war against villages and the civilians.

Reagan tried to make up for the shortcomings of the Contras through overblown rhetoric. In February 1985, he called the Contras "our brothers," and said that Nicaragua had become "a Communist totalitarian state." On March 1, he called the Contras the "moral equal of our Founding Fathers" and insisted that "we owe them our help."

Congress could not be moved. The ban on military assistance to the Contras remained in place. Adding to Reagan's woes, the private fundraising efforts were proving inadequate to the need. The collapse of the Contras, and thus of Reagan's policy in Centray America, was imminent.

Reagan's credibility and prestige were also at risk in another region of the world rife with guerrilla warfare, the Middle East. In Lebanon, in his second term, Reagan faced a problem similar to the one that had destroyed the Carter presidency, namely the holding of innocent American hostages by the crazed revolutionary Muslim followers of the Ayatollah Khomeini, who demanded a ransom for their release. Reagan had been scathing in his criticism of Carter's softness on Khomeini, and absolutely convincing in his repeated promises to never pay a ransom. He also, wisely, avoided Carter's mistake of overstressing the hostages and thus kept the subject off the front pages. He was helped by the differences in the situations: The terrorists in Lebanon held less than ten hostages, as opposed to more than fifty in Teheran five years earlier, and in Teheran the terrorists had overrun and held the U.S. Embassy, while in Lebanon they took private citizens and held them in secret places.

But Reagan's public face, calm and confident, concealed a terrible inner anxiety about the fate of the hostages. Soon he was as obsessed by them as Carter had been. The anxiety became unbearable when the terrorists took the CIA station chief in Beirut, William Buckley, and began torturing him.

Reagan decided to act. In the spring of 1985, he began putting into motion a master plan that he had devised, one that if it worked would solve simultaneously his problems in Central America and in the Middle East, bring the hostages home, chase the Communists out of Central America, and win a new ally for the United States in the Middle East.

Reagan's plan was a bold one, but it was not well thought out, and indeed showed an absence of understanding of the most basic events of the immediate past. Anyone who had made the slightest study of Carter's problems with the Ayatollah Khomeini could have warned Reagan, "You can't trust any of those people." And anyone who had lived through the Watergate scandal could have told Reagan, "In this country it is next to impossible for the President to get away with breaking the law."

Reagan's master plan was to sell arms to Iran, as he had promised Khomeini he would during the 1980 election campaign. Iran's military equipment, purchased by the Shah, was nearly all made in America, and the war with Iraq gave Iran an insatiable appetite for American arms and ammunition. Reagan believed that by selling arms to Iran, he could create a new beginning for U.S.-Iranian relations, perhaps reestablish the closeness that prevailed in the days of the Shah. As a second benefit, the sales would be a ransom for the hostages in Lebanon (which assumed that the Ayatollah Khomeini could and would order them released, in gratitude). The bonus was that the Iranians would pay double and triple the value of the weapons; the profits could be diverted to the Contras in Nicaragua and provide them with a permanent source of funding. Long-term funding, in fact, as Reagan was simultaneously supplying Iraq with critical military intelligence, gathered by America's spy satellites, which would help ensure that even with the American arms, Iran could not win the war. Her need for arms might never end.

In implementing his plan, Reagan operated in the utmost secrecy. He failed to inform the State Department or his Secretary of State of the new policy. Thus he failed to build a base in the bureaucracy for the policy. In public, rather than attempting to build a constituency for paying a ransom or selling arms to Iran, he continued to insist that he would never, ever pay a ransom, and to call on all nations to impose an arms embargo on Iran, as he said the United States was doing.

What could have led the President to tell such tales? Evidently, his anxiety about the hostages became unbearable and led him to insist on immediate action. Lieutenant Colonel North and others began selling arms to Iran, through a variety of channels, mainly Israel. The Iranians offered to release a hostage to show their good faith. The President asked that it be CIA agent Buckley, but Buckley had by then been tortured to death. American clergyman Benjamin Weir was then released, the first—and as it turned out, the only—payoff Reagan got for his new policy.

The Iran-Iraq war, meanwhile, had become by 1985 the third-largest and most expensive war of this century, with no end in sight. Reagan continued to sell arms to Iran, whose leaders tantalized him with promises, as they provided North with millions of dollars in profits, a part of which was used to fund the Contras (the bulk of it went into private hands as profit). Still, the Contras were losing.

So, at the beginning of 1986, Reagan increased his pressure on Congress to get behind a policy of aid to the Contras. He demanded $100 million for "humanitarian aid" and military support. On March 16, he delivered a national television address warning about the consequences of allowing the Communists to win in Nicaragua. He made telephone calls to swing Congressmen right up to the roll call. But he failed. After two days of bitter debate, cries of "no more Vietnams" and assertions that if the United States did not stop the Communist menace in Nicaragua "then we will soon be fighting them along the Rio Grande," the Congress narrowly defeated the Administration package.

Reagan funded the Contras anyway, through the arms sales to Iran and money privately raised. He granted tax deductions to American donors, and made favorable decisions about high-tech sales to foreign governments for corporations that pitched in with a contribution for the

Contras. Thus did Reagan force a confrontation with
the Congress and the Constitution. By ignoring the Boland Amendment, the Administration challenged Congress in a fundamental way over an ultimate question:
Who controls the foreign policy of the United States?

The question was asked in an atmosphere that was
unprecedented: The Congress had told the President
what he could *not* do in foreign affairs, while the President was engaged in willful and continuing violations
of the law.

It was a startling development, this congressional assertion of its authority over foreign policy, but it had
been building for two decades. Since the end of the
sixties, the Congress had attempted to take control of
foreign affairs in ways quite unimaginable during the
first two decades of the Cold War. The Boland Amendment was a culmination, not an aberration. Still Reagan
ignored it, but in the first two years of his second term
no one in Congress knew this.

What Reagan wanted was the kind of consensus that
developed behind FDR in 1941, or behind Harry S. Truman at the time of the containment doctrine and the
Marshall Plan. When the President leads a united country, he can safely ignore the Congress, because with a
consensus behind him the President is clearly in control
and capable of acting boldly, as Reagan had demonstrated when he ordered the invasion of Grenada, and
showed again in his handling of international terrorism.

In October 1985, the nation gave its full and enthusiastic approval to Reagan's use of aircraft from the U.S.
Sixth Fleet in the Mediterranean to force the hijackers
of the cruise ship *Achille Lauro* to land in Italy. Reagan
warned terrorists everywhere, "You can run, but you
can't hide."

Two months later, terrorists attacked civilian passengers in the Rome and Vienna airports; the State Department called the perpetrators "beyond the pale of
civilization." In January 1986, Reagan accused Libya of
aiding the Palestinians who had mounted the airport
assaults and ordered the severance of all U.S. economic

ties with Libya. Libyan leader Colonel Muammer el-Qaddafi defied the United States, hurled insults at Reagan, and drew a "line of death" across the Gulf of Sidra. In January and February 1986, there were clashes in the area between elements of the U.S. Sixth Fleet and the Libyan air force. Hostilities escalated in March, with a climax coming when Reagan ordered a major air strike on Tripoli, evidently with the aim of killing Qaddafi, whose residence was the aiming point of the bombers. Qaddafi escaped, although his daughter was killed and his prestige was badly hurt. Predictably, the Arabs denounced the United States, the Europeans were concerned over Reagan's trigger-happy approach, while the American people heartily approved.

The intense public interest in Reagan's war against the terrorists was in sharp contrast to the relative indifference the public showed to the Iran-Iraq war, or the Contra war, a contrast that in turn showed how difficult it is in a democracy to concentrate on the main event while avoiding side shows. Americans in the spring of 1986 put international terrorism high on the list of their greatest concerns, and tourism to Europe dropped by half. But, in fact, terrorism had hardly touched the Americans—of the 950 people killed by terrorists in 1985, only 23 were Americans. Terrorism was important, mostly because the Reagan administration said it was. Reagan, in other words, was repeating Carter's mistake of attaching far too much importance to terrorism and hostage-taking.

In the spring of 1986, Reagan's prestige was at its zenith, due in part to his offensive against the terrorists, and he was able to use his popularity to get the Congress to lift its ban on aid to the Contras, as it rescinded the Boland Amendment and appropriated $100 million to support them. So in the summer and fall of 1986, the Contras were receiving aid overtly from the Congress, covertly from the CIA; Arab potentates were contributors, as were American millionaires; the Israelis chipped in, as did Lieutenant Colonel North with some of the profits from the arms sales to Iran. Never have so many contributed so much to so few with less results, for despite everything, the Contras made no progress. But almost to the end of 1986, there were no questions asked about the legality of the President's actions, because the actions remained unknown.

When Reagan began his second term, in January of 1985, there were hopes expressed that he would use the opportunity to become the President who brought arms control into reality and thus achieved historic standing as the peacemaker. Just as Nixon was the only American politician who could have opened the door to China, it was said, so Reagan was the only one who could achieve arms control with the Russians, as no one could accuse Reagan of being soft on Communism or of having neglected the nation's defenses.

As a second-term President, with his last election behind him, Reagan stopped calling the Soviet Union an "evil empire" and began indicating that he might be willing to sit down with the new Soviet leader, Mikhail Gorbachev, to discuss arms control.

Gorbachev was eager to meet with Reagan, as a part of his overall policy of *glasnost*, or openness. The policy involved reforms at home and an easing of tension abroad, and featured Gorbachev's presentation of himself as trustworthy, reasonable, open, and peaceloving. Reagan wanted to project the same image of himself. But however great their desire, the path to arms control and détente was strewn with unanticipated obstacles. Chance happenings, like the Russian shooting down of a Korean Air Lines (KAL) passenger jumbo jet in 1983, set back progress. The event demonstrated how deeply seated were the suspicions of both sides, and how far apart their views. To the Americans, the KAL incident showed what bloodthirsty monsters the Russians were; to the Russians, it showed that the capitalists would stop at nothing, not even putting spy equipment on a civiliam airline and sending it over highly sensitive Soviet military intelligence centers. The truth of the matter, as has so often been the case in these Cold War incidents, was elusive. Eventually, a summit was set up for Geneva in November 1985. Going into the meeting, Reagan was simultaneously calling for a 50 percent reduction in nuclear weapons and an expanded Strategic Defense Initiative, or SDI. He said that what he feared most was a nuclear Pearl Harbor, and argued that the way to prevent it was to eliminate all offensive missiles through arms-control talks and to push SDI in order to erect a defensive shield in the event the arms control talks failed.

SDI was the most expensive weapons system ever devised. Many scientists argued that the thing simply would not work, that it could be overcome through offensive countermeasures that were much cheaper, and that it could only provoke the Russians, who would have to match American expenditures on the off chance of success. But Reagan insisted that it was purely defensive and that it would be unforgiveable of him to pass up an opportunity to provide a defense for the American people. His critics replied that SDI, if carried out, would leave America more insecure than ever, and trillions of dollars in debt to boot.

In short, at the time of the Geneva summit, the superpowers were on the brink of a stupendously big jump in the expenditures on the arms race, and each side had overwhelmingly powerful reasons to wish to avoid that outcome—in the United States, the federal deficit, incomparably larger than it had ever been as a direct consequence of Reagan's arms race, loomed over the American way of life more dangerously than did the Soviet missiles; in the Soviet Union, expenditures for defense had made a mockery out of the original Communist promise to improve the lives of the Russian people.

Thus hopes were high, engendered by the mutual need for restraint and the high cost of pushing ahead with the arms race. Reagan spoke to those hopes in a nationally televised address on the eve of his departure for Geneva. The meeting with Gorbachev, he said, "can be a historic opportunity to set a steady, more constructive course in the twenty-first century."

But the following day, even as the President was departing, Defense Secretary Caspar Weinberger leaked a letter he had given to the President, in which he gave a list of supposed Soviet treaty violations, asked the President not to agree to observe the terms of the never-ratified SALT II, not to give an inch on SDI expenditures, and in short not to enter into any agreement at all. It was sabotage, pure and simple. Weinberger had given every Senator opposed to any sort of arms control a perfect peg on which to base opposition to whatever agreement Reagan and Gorbachev might reach. At Geneva, meanwhile, Reagan did as Weinberger had recommended. He would not back down on SDI and no agreements were reached.

Three months late, the Joint Chiefs released a paper entitled "United States Military Posture," in which they said that the Soviet Union "continues to comply with the SALT II treaty by dismantling strategic systems as new systems are introduced." This directly contradicted statements made by both Reagan and Weinberger.

Contradictions were fast becoming the chief characteristic of the Reagan administration. As his expenditures for arms went to new record heights, especially for SDI, he astonished everyone, including some of his closest advisers, by revealing a letter he had written to Gorbachev, in which he proposed to share SDI with the Soviets once America had completed the research and development phases. Which was harder to believe—that the United States really would give away the fruits of the most expensive program in history, or that Gorbachev would consent to trust that Reagan (and his successors) would live up to Reagan's promise if SDI did work—no one could say.

Through 1986, Gorbachev maintained a unilateral ban on nuclear testing. He used every opportunity to obtain maximum propaganda advantage from the ban, primarily by asking the United States to join the Soviets in refusing to test. But Reagan, who like Carter had said repeatedly that his goal was the elimination of all nuclear weapons from this earth, insisted that meanwhile he had to test new weapons. In January 1987, the Russians, citing America's frequent tests, resumed their own program.

Gorbachev's much-touted *glasnost*, meanwhile, underwent a severe test. On April 26, 1986, a nuclear accident occurred at Chernobyl in the Soviet Union. Gorbachev failed to inform the world about the mishap. Radioactive poison spread over much of Europe. Everyone, everywhere, was furious with the Russians. But Gorbachev had a bit of the "Teflon" quality that Reagan enjoyed, and subsequent Russian cooperation with nuclear scientists from the international community restored his image rather quickly.

One reason for Gorbachev's success in courting world opinion was his obvious eagerness for an arms-control agreement, as opposed to Reagan's apparent hesitancy. Thus it was Gorbachev who took the lead in promoting the next summit, using rather bizarre tactics to bring it about.

In August 1986, American officials arrested Gennadi Zakharov in New York and charged him with espionage for the KGB. The Soviets responded by arresting Nicholas Daniloff, a reporter for *U.S. News.* They charged Daniloff with espionage for the CIA. The White House insisted that Daniloff was innocent (although he was the grandson of a Czarist general and spoke fluent Russian, and anyway was asking the same questions as a reporter that a CIA agent would have asked, such as how many Russian troops were in Afghanistan, how were they equipped, what was their morale, and so on). Reagan said that under no circumstances whatsoever would there be a swap—Daniloff for Zakharov—because Zakharov was clearly guilty, Daniloff innocent.

Two weeks later, Reagan made the swap. He then told the American people that he had not made a deal for Daniloff. The next day the White House announced that Reagan had agreed to a Gorbachev proposal for a summit meeting in Reykjavík, Iceland, in two weeks—this from an Administration that had always insisted it would never go to the summit without adequate preparation.

The Reykjavík summit was as barren as the windswept countryside of Iceland. At its conclusion, a sad and haggard-looking Secretary of State Shultz reported that Reagan and Gorbachev had agreed on the elimination of all nuclear weapons and the missile systems to deliver them and that this process of disarmament was to be completed in ten years. It seemed much too good to be true, and it was—Shultz went on to explain that these agreements in principle had been abandoned because Reagan refused to accept one of Gorbachev's demands, that the United States give up its SDI program.

There were howls from around the world. The left wing wanted to know how on earth Reagan could squander such an opportunity for a defensive system that experts said would not work. The right wing wanted to know how on earth Reagan could agree to eliminate nuclear weapons and the missile systems when the Soviets had a commanding lead in conventional warfare capability. A series of conflicting statements from the White House further confused everyone. No one could say with any authority, evidently not even the President himself, what the American policy on arms control was or was not. Efforts to revive the talks, in the first half of 1987, consisted primarily of propaganda statements by both sides, with no real progress.

In the fall of 1987, Reagan and Gorbachev agreed on a much more modest arms reduction, the elimination of short-range missiles in Europe. Although these constituted but a small fraction of the total arsenal, this was potentially a major event, as it was the first time the two sides actually agreed to reduce their missile strike forces. Signed in Washington in December 1987, the treaty did not end the arms race, nor did it reduce the dangers significantly, but it did promise some hope for more meaningful progress in the future.

Reagan's foreign policy in his second term was not completely without success. He got through a crisis in the Philippines in 1986 that was fraught with danger. In elections in February, President Ferdinand Marcos, a dictator who had enriched himself beyond all imagination at the expense of the Filipino people, ran against Mrs. Corazon Aquino, widow of an opposition leader who had been gunned down by Marcos's military. Marcos, who counted the ballots, declared himself the winner. The Filipino people took to the streets in an astonishing and unique display of what they called "People Power." The held what amounted to a general strike. Marcos attempted to tough it out, counting on American support.

Initially, Reagan was willing to provide that support. He asserted that there had been a fair and free election with an honest count and said that despite the charges of fraud "there is evidence of a strong two-party system now in the islands." But as the demonstrations continued, Reagan found it necessary to endorse a report from Senator Sam Nunn, in which Nunn insisted that Mrs. Aquino was the winner by actual vote count and that Marcos was engaged in an "all-out effort to steal the election."

When even the Philippine Defense Minister and the Chief of Staff joined in the demand for Marcos's resignation, Reagan gave up the effort to maintain Marcos in power. He telephoned Marcos to ask him to resign and leave the Philippines, and made it pssible for Marcos to do so by promising to provide U.S. Air Force transportation to Hawaii, where Marcos could live permanently, and—not incidentally—keep his fabulous riches. By the end of February 1986, Marcos was in Hawaii, and Aquino was the President of the Philippines.

Reagan had little choice under the circumstances, but nevertheless his actions were critical to this happy outcome. It was Reagan who prodded Marcos into resignation and exile; had Reagan not made the offers he did, it is possible Marcos would have stayed in Manila and thrown his country into a savage civil war. Fear on Reagan's part that Aquino would not be tough enough on the Filipino Communists made it even more difficult

for him to support her, but support her he did when
the incontrovertible evidence proved she was the choice
of the people of the Philippines.

In another Spanish-speaking region of the Third
World, Central America, Reagan continued to lead the
counteroffensive against the Sandinistas. In the first ten
months of 1986, the offensive took many forms, including major military maneuvers by U.S. troops on Nicaragua's borders and diplomatic efforts to enlist
Nicaragua's neighbors, Honduras and Costa Rica, as allies in the counterrevolution. Their reluctance to get
involved, however, put more of the burden on the
Contras.

In the fall of 1986, the Sandinistas shot down a transport airplane flying supplies to the Contras. Three
Americans were the crew; one of them survived and
confessed that he was working for the CIA. A month
later, an Arab journal published an article that gave some
of the details of the arms sales to Iran; at a quickly called
press conference, Attorney General Edwin Meese revealed some parts of the Iran/Contra scam, and suddenly
Reagan had a scandal within his Administration that rivaled Watergate for importance and press attention. It
could not have come at a worse time for Reagan, as the
Democrats had swept the fall elections and were about
to take control of the Senate; with commanding major-
ities in both Houses, the Democrats were in an ideal
position to reap the full benefit of any Republican
scandal.

Shocking disclosures were followed by incomprehensible statements. Reagan initially claimed that only a "few
strictly defensive weapons" were shipped to Iran, denied
that any third country had been involved, asserted that
"no U.S. law has been or will be violated," and insisted
that "our policy of not making concessions to terrorists
remains intact." Two days later he confessed that he had
entered into discussions with the Iranians in the hope
that they could lead to the release of the American hostages in Lebanon. The following day he said it was "ut-

terly false" to charge that the weapons he sent to Iran were a "ransom."

From this low point, things got worse. Secretary of State Shultz said he had opposed sending any arms to Iran, that he had not been consulted about this major shift in American foreign policy, and that American ambassadors in the Middle East were reporting directly to the White House, ignoring the State Deparment. A week later, on November 25, 1986, Reagan relieved his National Security Adviser, Admiral John Poindexter, and his assistant, Lieutenant Colonel Oliver North, who directed the Iran/Contra program for the NSC, because "serious questions of propriety" had been raised. Simultaneously, Reagan praised North as "an American hero."

North immediately began shredding documents in his White House office, while the FBI called for a special prosecutor. Reagan's approval rating fell 21 points to 46 percent. In early December, Poindexter and North appeared before the Senate Intelligence Committee and invoked the Fifth Amendment in refusing to answer questions. Reagan, meanwhile, insisted that he knew nothing about anything; when pressed, his defense was "I don't remember." He said that like everyone else he was eager to find out what Poindexter and North had been doing; Democrats pointed out that he was Commander in Chief, and if he really wanted to know, all he had to do was order the admiral and the lieutenant colonel to tell him.

By the spring of 1987, a series of investigations were under way. Former Senator John Tower was the head of an independent committee, appointed by Reagan, to look into the affair. The Tower Commission reported that laws had been violated, pointed to various serious flaws in the Reagan administration's foreign policy structure, found the President negligent in meeting his duties, but stopped short of charging him with illegal actions. The Congress meanwhile created a select joint committee to conduct hearings. These hearings soon rivaled the Watergate hearings for public attention, as they were telecast daily and continued to reveal additional details of the scam. It was a sorry and sordid sight. Eventually, the congressional Iran/Contra committee concluded that in selling arms for hostages and in diverting some of the profits to the Contras, the Administration had brought "confusion and disarray at the highest levels of government, evasive dishonesty and inordinate secrecy, deception and disdain for the law." President Reagan, the committee charged, abdicated his "moral and legal responsibility to take care that the laws be faithfully executed."

Strong words, in some ways stronger than the impeachment charges brought against Richard Nixon. Why, then, did Congress make no move to impeach Reagan? One reason was timing—he had less than two years to go and it hardly seemed worth the effort. Besides, the Democrats did not want to run in 1988 against an incumbent President George Bush, nor did the Democrats want to be known as the party that went around impeaching Republican Presidents.

So Ronald Reagan survived, barely, but his Administration had been seriously crippled.

Reagan had failed to achieve his basic goals in foreign policy. In Poland, nothing he had done had made the slightest difference; in the arms race, he had been unable to eliminate a single nuclear bomb, much less all of them; his buildup of the American armed forces had had little effect on the Soviets. In terms of foreign trade, America had the largest trade imbalance in her history, by far, and it came simultaneously with the largest deficit in the federal budget in history, by far. These circumstances in turn led to a stock market collapse in October 1987, which was itself a result of worldwide financial crisis. The crisis resulted, in part, from Reagan's policy of borrowing money from the Japanese to pay for America's military expansion, in order to protect oil for Japan coming out of the Persian Gulf. Reagan did not have the hostages out of Lebanon, he had not improved U.S. relations with Iran, and he had abandoned neutrality in the Iran-Iraq war when he chose to protect Kuwait's oil tankers (because Kuwait, Iraq's ally, used some of its oil profits to support Iraq's war costs). He did manage to successfully challenge the War Powers Act, not directly but simply by ignoring Congressional demands that he invoke it. Congress was incapable of forcing the President to follow its wishes, partly because of the inherent difficulties in the Act, mainly because of divisions in the Congress itself.

In the spring of 1987, Reagan implemented the Carter Doctrine (without citing it) when he sent U.S. Navy warships into the Persian Gulf to protect tankers from Kuwait that had been reflagged with American colors. The tankers, which were carrying oil for Japan, were threatened by missiles made in France and China, fired by Iranians and Iraqis. On May 17, the *U.S.S. Stark* was hit by two missiles fired by Iraqi jet fighters; thirty-seven sailors were killed. Reagan responded by sending minesweepers and helicopters to the Gulf; in October, after Iranian missiles had hit tankers flying the U.S. flag, U.S. navy destroyers shelled Iranian offshore oil platforms. Former president Jimmy Carter said that the U.S. had become an ally of Iraq and was engaged in hostilities and called for Reagan to invoke the War Powers Act. Reagan ignored him.

The war escalated, on the ground, in the air, and at sea. The U.S. Navy convoys got through, usually successfully, although in April 1988, an American frigate was damaged by a mine. The navy destroyed two Iranian oil rigs in retaliation and damaged or sank six Iranian vessels. As more mines were laid and more tankers came under missile fire, Reagan ordered U.S. forces in the Gulf to extend protection to all neutral vessels.

On July 3, the *U.S.S. Vincennes* mistakenly shot down an Iranian passenger jet, killing all 290 passengers and crew. Reagan called the incident "tragic" but said it "appears that it was a proper defensive action." Later he sent a message of "deep regret" to Iran and compensated the families of the victims.

Terrible though this action was, it does seem to have helped propel the two sides in the second-longest and third-bloodiest war of the century to seek peace. Two weeks after the incident, Iran agreed to a U.N. call for a cease-fire; the Ayatollah Khomeini gave the agreement his personal endorsement, thereby accepting the "poison" of ending the war without winning it. In effect, he admitted he had sacrificed hundreds of thousands of young Iranians, and uncountable treasure, for nothing. Indeed, Iraq had gained some territory at Iran's expense. In August, the cease-fire went into effect.

Reagan's goal of overthrowing the Sandinista government in Nicaragua continued to elude him. In the summer of 1987, the presidents of the Central American republics, led by Oscar Arias Sanchez of Costa Rica, drafted a peace plan to which the Sandinistas agreed. Reagan gave it grudging suppport while continuing to supply and encourage the Contras. Nicaraguan President Daniel Ortega proposed direct talks between the U.S. and Nicaragua, but Reagan refused. Ortega nevertheless implemented the various steps called for in the peace plan, including lifting the ban on the opposition newspaper *La Prensa* and allowing Catholic radio stations to broadcast without censorship. To most observers, Reagan looked like the main obstacle to peace in Central America, even more so when the Nobel Peace Prize went to Sanchez.

Another small country that was able to taunt and defy the Colossus of the North was Panama. In June 1987, students staged a riot in Panama, accusing General Manuel Noriega of involvement in the death of the nation's former leader, General Omar Torrijos. Noriega managed to turn the demonstrations against the U.S. Embassy; in response, the State Department protested strongly, then announced a suspension of all aid to Panama. Noriega began arresting his political opponents and otherwise causing embarrassment to the United States, which had worked closely with him on intelligence and covert activities over the past few years—among those involved was then vice president and former CIA director George Bush.

By early 1988, the Panamanian opposition, mostly in exile, was charging Noriega with murder, drug trafficking, and money laundering for drug lords. On February 5, the U.S. Justice Department brought two indictments against Noriega on drug-trafficking charges. He was accused of providing airstrips for drug smuggling and receiving $350 million for his efforts. President Eric Arturo Delvalle then dismissed Noriega as commander of the defense forces; Noriega, in turn, ousted Delvalle and put his own man in as president. Delvalle went underground but continued to be recognized by the United States.

In March, Noriega turned down a U.S. offer to drop the criminal charges against him if he would leave Panama to live in exile. Reagan then imposed economic sanctions on Panama, ordering American firms to withhold all payments to the government. This hurt the people of Panama, but had no effect on their new dictator. It destroyed the economy and converted some members of the internal opposition to Noriega into critics of the United States.

By the fall of 1988, Reagan's Central American policy was in a shambles. Ortega was still in power and Noriega was openly defying the U.S. government. The Republicans, who had been touting Reagan's policy as a great success, were doing everything possible to avoid mentioning the region during the presidential campaign.

In its policy toward South Africa, the Reagan administration was also running into difficulties. There was a high level of concern in the United States, especially on the college campuses, with the increasing brutality of the South African regime. Student protesters demanded an end to American investment there, and at schools like the University of California at Berkeley they were able to force the trustees to divest the university's South African holdings. Reagan's policy, which he called "constructive engagement," was to encourage American investment on the basis that American policy toward South Africa ought to be to support corporations that provided jobs for black workers, paid a fair wage, and made some room in management for blacks. The argument was that this would have a more beneficial effect on the vast majority of the blacks than pulling out and leaving them to the mercies of the white South Africans.

That sounded fair and reasonable, but the problem was that it simply did not work. Things got worse rather than better. Still, the Reagan administration stuck to its policy of constructive engagement, even as some of the major U.S. corporations divested their South African holdings. In South Africa, meanwhile, the divestments were beginning to hurt the economy, raising some hope that there could be a change in the government's policies toward blacks in general and the African National Congress (ANC) specifically.

The Reagan administration did have a major breakthrough to the north of South Africa. On December 22, 1988, the United States and the Soviet Union announced support for an agreement worked out by the United Nations regarding the future of Angola and Namibia. It stipulated that Cuban troops would leave Angola within two years and provided for independence of the last colony in Africa, Namibia, within that time. Although Reagan continued to provide military support for UNITA, the African equivalent of the Contras, in Angola, the U.N. agreement nevertheless was significant, as it involved more active collaboration between Moscow and Washington than there had ever been on any other regional conflict in which the superpowers were at odds.

The cooperation at the southern tip of Africa was part of the great triumph of Reagan's foreign policy, an arms-reduction treaty with the Soviets. Achieved in the Administration's last eighteen months in office, it held out hope for a genuine easing of tensions in the world, perhaps even the end of the Cold War. This was a startling turnaround for Reagan, and highly welcome. It appeared to justify his tough-guy approach of the previous six years and gave him his strongest claim to success in foreign affairs. How much of the credit belonged to

Reagan, how much to Gorbachev, and how much to events outside their control cannot be judged with any precision. What can be said is that it happened while they were in power.

U.S.–Soviet relations had reached a low point in the late summer of 1986, following the breakup of the Reykjavík summit, after Reagan had rejected Gorbachev's bold proposal to eliminate all nuclear weapons. For the next year, the two sides snarled at each other. On June 12, 1987, in Berlin, Reagan goaded Gorbachev when he challenged him to "tear down this wall." To most observers, it seemed to be an irresponsible provocation, as almost no one in the world expected the Berlin Wall to come down in the twentieth century or even the twenty-first.

One month later, however, in Geneva, the Soviets presented a new arms-reduction proposal, to which the United States almost immediately agreed. It called for the worldwide elimination of all U.S. and Soviet short- and medium-range missiles. In December 1987, at a summit meeting in Washington, Reagan and Gorbachev signed the Intermediate Nuclear Force (INF) treaty, which called for the dismantling and destruction of all short- and medium-range missiles, with provisions for a system of independent, on-site verification and weapons inspection.

The INF treaty was a great breakthrough in the Cold War. Ever since the first arms-control proposals were made—back in the Eisenhower administration, with the 1955 offer of "Open Skies"—the Soviets had refused to even consider on-site inspection of their missile capabilities. Further, none of Reagan's or Gorbachev's predecessors had ever dared to consider actual arms reduction; instead, they tried—unsuccessfully—to achieve some measure of arms control. But in 1987, the INF treaty provided for the actual elimination of major weapons systems, with on-site inspection.

By no means were all the world's problems solved with the INF treaty. Reagan continued to invest huge sums in SDI; Gorbachev continued to maintain the world's largest ground forces and a huge navy; U.S. and Red Army forces continued to face each other on opposite banks of the Elbe River; the strategic arsenals of the superpowers—long-range missiles, submarine-launched missiles, bomber-carried nuclear weapons—remained intact. Still, INF did lower the destructive capability of each side, it loosened the taut bowstring in central Europe—where the Pershing missiles had reduced the warning time for a nuclear attack to a few minutes—and, most important of all, it was a symbolic achievement of the first order.

Who to praise? Reagan's admirers claimed that Gorbachev had crumbled because the Soviet Union could not keep pace with the Americans in the arms race, that Reagan's policy of building more and more weapons so that we would not have to build more weapons in the future had worked brilliantly. He had forced the Soviets to accept peace and accommodation because the Soviet attempt to match America, missile for missile, had left the Soviet economy in a shambles. The Soviets had paid for their SS-20s and other new weapons by denying their citizens not only consumer goods but even food and shelter. Gorbachev could not simultaneously engage in an arms race and implement *glasnost* and *perestroika,* so he gave up on the arms race.

There is some truth in that analysis. There is also truth in the observation that the Americans had paid for their military buildup with money borrowed from the Japanese. Reagan was leaving his grandchildren with a $3 trillion debt. Prophets warned that some day that debt would have to be paid, and when it was it would be the American people who would be sacrificing not only consumer goods but even food and shelter to pay for SDI. As Eisenhower had observed way back in 1953, "Every gun that is made, every warship launched, every rocket fired, signifies, in the final sense, a theft from those who hunger and are not fed, those who are cold and are not clothed."

Such criticism should not obscure the fact that the Washington summit of December 1987 was one of the most successful and hopeful of the Cold War. Gorbachev rightly called it "a major event in world politics." Beyond INF, Reagan and Gorbachev talked about further arms reductions in strategic and conventional weapons. In addition, Gorbachev indicated that he was preparing to withdraw Soviet troops from Afghanistan. All previous summits had ended with a claim that although little or nothing concrete had been accomplished, at least the meeting had "reduced tensions." The Washington summit actually eliminated major causes of tension, and promised to inaugurate a new world structure.

It also promoted "Gorby's" already high worldwide popularity. He proved to be a natural at American-style public relations as he met with leaders from Congress, the media, and business. He met with schoolchildren. At one point, he dramatically ordered his limousine to stop on Connecticut Avenue, got out, and plunged into the crowds, shaking hands and talking. Even Reagan was captured by his charm.

There were disagreements between the two men. Reagan lectured Gorbachev on human rights, which led the Soviet leader to tell the American leader, "You are not the prosecutor and I am not the accused." But Reagan had needed to provide something for his right-wing supporters, who were furious about INF. For his part Reagan, who for almost two decades had been the chief spokesman for American Cold Warriors, the leading opponent of *any* arms accord of *any* kind with the Soviets, charged that the conservative opponents of INF wanted to believe "that war is inevitable." That Ronald Reagan would criticize the hawks indicated just how different the new world he and Gorbachev were creating was going to be. That he could get the Senate to quickly ratify the INF treaty showed how popular both he personally and arms reduction in general were with the American people.

In April 1988, Reagan announced an agreement with the Soviets over the withdrawal of the Red Army from Afghanistan—the first time in thirty-three years that the Red Army would pull back from anywhere—and on May

18, the first Soviet unit left Afghanistan. Eleven days later, Reagan arrived in Moscow for his second summit meeting in less than six months. To appease the right wing back home, he continued to criticize Gorbachev for human rights violations, meeting with ninety-six Soviet dissidents and demanding reform. Gorbachev struck back by inviting North American Indians to Moscow; they asserted that they were political prisoners in the land the whites had stolen from their ancestors. Reagan gave Gorbachev some lessons of his own in PR, as he took an unscheduled walk along the famous Moscow street Arbat, mixing with the crowds. He obviously enjoyed using the Soviet people and Red Square as a backdrop for his kind of politics. The American television networks, meanwhile, gave unprecedented and quite fascinating coverage to the Russian people, their culture and history.

The networks gave less coverage to the meetings themselves because the two leaders were unable to reach their stated goal: a reduction of strategic arms. The failure showed the latent persistence of conservatives on both sides, the strength of the legacy of mistrust, and the limits on the powers of the two presidents. Gorbachev bemoaned the "missed opportunities" and indicated he would wait for Reagan's successor to try again. Reagan stopped in London on his way home to confer with Prime Minister Thatcher. There he made a statement that took much of the sting and disappointment out of the failure to reach agreement in Moscow: Gorbachev, said Reagan, "is a serious man seeking serious reform. We are beginning to take down the barriers of the postwar era . . . and this is a time of lasting change in the Soviet Union."

That certainly was true, on all fronts. In Russia, *glasnost* was opening up the government to severe criticism across the board and encouraging the unwilling members of the Soviet empire—of whom there were many millions— to protest and demand their independence. Three months after the Moscow summit, there were mass demonstrations in Estonia, Latvia, and Lithuania, the three Baltic republics forcibly incorporated into the Soviet

Union by Stalin in 1940. Other demonstrations soon followed in Armenia, Azerbaidzhan, Georgia, and Ukraine. Not only that, the coal miners throughout the Soviet Union went on strike. Western experts made almost daily predictions that Gorbachev could not survive the growing domestic turmoil, but somehow he did.

He survived, in part, because he was an astute politician who outmaneuvered all his internal opposition, and in part because of his successes in dealing with Reagan. Dramatic evidence of those successes came in September, when the Americans destroyed two Pershing missiles as a first step in implementing the INF treaty, and U.S. officials in the Soviet Union witnessed an underground nuclear test, measuring it with their own instruments. Both actions had been unthinkable just two years earlier, when the Americans were installing Pershing II missiles in Germany and the Russians were insisting, as they had done for forty years, that they would never, ever, allow American inspection teams on their soil.

When Reagan left office in January 1989, the world was much different from what it had been when he had moved into the White House. Cuban troops were withdrawing from Angola, where the cease-fire was taking effect. The Soviets were retreating from Afghanistan. The Iran-Iraq war had ended. In Central America a peace plan was under way and armed hostilities were diminishing. International terrorism was on the decline (although terrorists still held a dozen Americans hostage in Lebanon, where fighting continued, while in the Arab areas occupied by Israel—the West Bank, Gaza, and East Jerusalem—a peoples' uprising led by teenage boys was forcing the Israeli armed forces to act in a brutal and bloody manner). Most of all, Reagan's second term had seen more progress in ending the Cold War and achieving a genuine détente between the U.S. and U.S.S.R. than had any other administration. Around the world, peace had broken out. There were fewer wars, and less killing, in 1989 than in any year since 1938.

Not in half a century had a president handed over to

his successor an American foreign policy in better shape. This came about in some part thanks to Reagan's consistent refusal to compromise with Communism in any way ("tear down this wall"). But because he had refused to pay the cost of the arms race he had escalated he was handing over to his successor a debt greater, by far, than that incurred by all his predecessors put together.

Further, much of the change in the world had come about despite, rather than because of, Reagan. The United Nations was more instrumental in bringing about the cease-fire in the Iran-Iraq war than was anything done by Reagan. So too for the Soviet withdrawal from Afghanistan and the Angolan-Namibian disentanglement. Indeed, Reagan had often stood in the way, especially when he had undertaken to undercut the U.N. by stopping payments to UNESCO (an ideological decision, brought on by domestic policies; it was connected to the birth control policies of UNESCO) and by threatening to stop payments to the U.N. proper because of the votes on Israel. Under Perez de Cuellar's stewardship, U.N. peacekeeping forces were working successfully in the Golan Heights, in Namibia, Cyprus, and Lebanon. The quiet diplomatic successes of the U.N. in the Reagan years were part of a process that would become clearer in the 1990s: the growing loss of influence of the United States in the international arena. The U.N. kept on working, even prospering, despite U.S. complaints and obstructionism.

Perhaps the most amazing thing about Reagan was his immense popularity after eight years as president, despite the national debt, despite Iran-Contra, despite domestic scandals as bad as any seen in fifty years, despite his flip-flops from arms builder to arms destroyer and from seeing the men in the Kremlin as the focus of evil in the world to becoming the number-one fan of Gorbachev. Reagan's popularity is all the more remarkable when it is recalled that six of his nine predecessors who had guided America through the tumultuous half century of the Depression, World War II, and the Cold War had been judged to be failures by their contemporaries.

When they left office, Herbert Hoover, Harry Truman, Lyndon Johnson, Richard Nixon, Gerald Ford, and Jimmy Carter had all fallen to the point that three out of four voters disapproved of the way they were doing their job. Insofar as John F. Kennedy was in office for too short a period to allow for any meaningful assessment, it appears that only Franklin Roosevelt, Dwight Eisenhower, and Ronald Reagan were judged competent by their contemporaries. That illustrates a number of points: the difficulties of the times; the high expectations people have of the president; the unfairness of contemporary judgments, among others. But it also indicates that Reagan, despite the sneers of sophisticated critics, who regarded him as an object of ridicule, was somehow doing something right. Or perhaps he was just lucky.

16

The End of the Cold War

A new world is within our reach.

GEORGE BUSH

On November 8, 1988, Republican candidate George Bush easily defeated Democrat Michael Dukakis in a presidential race in which foreign policy had not been a major issue. The Democrats retained their hold on the Senate, 55–45, and increased their margin in the House, to 262–173, continuing the pattern of Republican presidents and a Democratic Congress.

Bush was pledged to continue the policies of the man he had served under for eight years. That meant a commitment to the Contras, to SDI, to a strong NATO, to a peace process in the Middle East, to liberalization in South Africa but without imposing further sanctions, to trade adjustments with Japan, to improved relations with China, and to a continuation of détente with the Soviets, among other things. The incoming administration—with James Baker 3d, Reagan's former chief of staff and secretary of the treasury, replacing George Shultz as secretary of state—indicated there would be no sudden shifts in policy. Prudence would be the guiding principle.

It was Bush's fate to take office in what proved to be the most momentous year in world history since 1945. So sweeping were the changes around the globe in 1989 that it seemed appropriate for the momentous transformations to occur in the year of the 200th anniversary of the French Revolution. There was much that was remarkable about 1989, including unprecedented, unpredictable, and unimaginable events in China, in Eastern Europe, in the Soviet Union, in South Africa, and in

Central America. But what was perhaps most remarkable was that, except in Central America, the United States played almost no role in the worldwide revolution.

The United States at the beginning of the last decade of the twentieth century—the century Henry Luce had proclaimed would be "the American Century"—was the most powerful military nation in the world, capable of destroying the planet. The country had the largest gross national product of any nation. Yet it was almost irrelevant to the events taking place in Europe, Asia, and Africa. Forty years earlier, Dean Acheson had observed that the United States was the locomotive at the head of mankind and the rest of the world the caboose. In 1989 the American president was a bystander, observing as the train sped down the tracks toward who knew what destination.

The absence of an American response to the world revolution of 1989 was in part a consequence of self-imposed limitations placed by President Bush, but in many ways he had no real choice. He was the leader of the leading debtor nation; one of the heritages he received from Reagan was the simple fact that there was no money in the bank. He could not offer help to emerging democracies desperate for the kind of aid the United States had extended after World War II in the Marshall Plan because the U.S. treasury was empty. Nor was there much prospect of generating capital to replenish it, because another legacy from Reagan was a pledge from the Republican party to never raise taxes under any circumstances. "Read my lips," Bush had said during the campaign: "No new taxes." This in a country in which the tax rates were the lowest of all industrial countries.

On January 20, 1989, in his inaugural address as the forty-first president, Bush had little to say about foreign policy, except that he intended to take strong measures to stop the flow of illegal drugs into the United States. With regard to the Soviet Union, he indicated that he would be reassessing relations.

That same month, eighty-seven-year-old Emperor Hirohito died. In his first foreign trip as president, Bush went to Tokyo for the funeral. While there, he conferred with Japanese leaders. Bush urged them to open their market to American-made goods, to allow American farm products to come into Japan duty free, and to stop subsidizing Japanese goods sold in America. These were themes that had dominated American–Japanese talks for more than a decade; as usual, Bush got some promises and no action.

From Tokyo, Bush went to the Asian mainland. In Seoul, he promised that "there [were] no plans to reduce United States forces in South Korea." In Beijing, where he spent two days, he conferred with Chinese leaders on increasing trade and said that the upcoming Chinese–Soviet summit, the first in thirty years, would not be "detrimental to the interests of the United States." As a former ambassador to China, Bush had good relations with the Chinese leaders and high hopes of creating a warmer, closer relationship. American Congressmen, however, were making progress difficult because of their criticisms of Chinese policy.

There was much to criticize. The Chinese had imposed martial law in Tibet (where they had seized control in 1959) in response to rioting by Tibetans demanding independence. The U.S. Senate passed a resolution denouncing the imposition of martial law; the Chinese responded by objecting to the resolution as a "gross interference" in China's domestic affairs. The Chinese also objected to Congressional critics who were making an issue of Chinese policies with regard to family planning and the Chinese record on human rights.

All this was but a prelude to the events of the spring of 1989. In April, students began staging mass demonstrations in Tiananmen Square in Beijing to demand more freedom, an open government, an end to the privileges enjoyed by the elite, and democracy. The government issued a ban on public demonstrations; the students defied it and began to boycott classes. Police moved in on Tiananmen Square, but instead of breaking up the demonstrations, the number of protesters increased, to 200,000 and more. On May 15, Gorbachev arrived for the summit meeting with Deng Xiaoping. In Tiananmen Square, intellectuals, workers, and bureaucrats joined the students, some of whom were engaging in hunger strikes. The number of demonstrators swelled to over one million. Innumerable posters praised Gorbachev and his reforms. The Soviet leader called the student uprising part of a "painful but healthy" process leading Communist countries to greater democracy.

That was not a direction in which Deng Xiaoping and his cohorts wanted to go. It was embarrassing to their regime to have so many of their people praising a foreign leader; it was dangerous to them to have such broadly based demonstrations demanding democracy; it was humiliating to have the massive protests witnessed by the entire world, as television cameras from the United States, Europe, and Japan were in Beijing to cover the summit. The government responded to the challenge by imposing martial law on May 19 and banning live Western TV coverage. The following day, in open defiance of martial law, crowds of about one million demonstrators blocked troops and tanks attempting to take control of Tiananmen. The scene was reminiscent of Hungarian students defying Red Army tanks in 1956, only on a much larger scale.

On June 2, Deng made his decision. The following day, the unarmed protestors were shot and killed as troops and tanks moved into Tiananmen Square to break up the protests. Submachine guns mowed down students by the hundreds, perhaps by the thousands. We cannot know the full toll, as the government immediately began a massive cover-up, blaming the demonstrators for the bloodshed, praising the army for upholding law and order, and arresting and executing student leaders.

These shocking events horrified the entire world. Free world and Communist leaders alike condemned Deng and his government. Bush stated that he "deplore[d] the decision to use force against Chinese citizens who were making a peaceful statement in favor of democracy." On June 5, he suspended military sales to China and three

days later said that the United States and China could
not reestablish normal relations until China's leaders
"recognize the validity of the prodemocracy movement."
On June 20, the White House announced the suspension
of high-level exchanges between U.S. officials and the
Chinese government.

But within weeks, Bush secretly sent his national security adviser, Brent Scowcroft, to China to confer with
the government. When this was discovered some months
later, there were howls of outrage from many Democrats
and some Republicans, both at the lies from the Administration and the fact of resumed relations with a criminal
regime. Bush nevertheless continued to defuse the tension between the two governments as he pursued a
course designed to mollify the Chinese. When Congress
passed a bill designed to protect Chinese students in the
United States—students who were at risk because they
had supported the demonstrations and who were clearly
going to be punished by the government when they were
forced to return to China—Bush vetoed it. In December,
Bush waived a congressional ban on loans for companies
doing business in China, and he agreed to allow the
export of satellites to China. When China lifted martial
law in Beijing at the beginning of 1990, most observers
regarded it as a cosmetic device at best, but Vice President Danforth Quayle said it showed the "dividends" of
Bush's policy of accommodation, while Bush called it "a
very sound step." It was his policy to maintain relations
with the Chinese government, no matter how it used
that power.

That was his policy toward China. Toward another
Communist government closer to home, he was not so
accommodating. In Nicaragua, he continued the Reagan
policy of unremitting hostility. Despite the peace plan
that had been accepted by Ortega and other Central
American leaders, which called for disbanding the Contras as a precondition to elections promised by the Sandinistas, Bush continued to supply the Contras and
helped to keep them intact as a constant threat to the

government of Nicaragua. He also maintained the economic embargo, which was having a dreadful effect on the Nicaraguan economy, where inflation was about the worst in the world, production was at disastrously low levels, and the economy in shambles. Ortega was forced to put into place a new austerity plan that called for a 44 percent reduction in the budget and the layoff of 35,000 government employees.

Such measures badly hurt Ortega's popularity, even as he moved toward reconciliation with his internal foes and attempted to improve relations with the United States. In March 1989, the government announced the pardon of 1,800 former members of the Nicaraguan National Guard, in accord with the peace plan. The Bush administration response was to reaffirm American commitment to the Contras. Although all Central American presidents (except for Jose Azcona Hoyo of Honduras) had called for the immediate disarming of the Contras and their removal from Honduras, the United States announced that it was continuing "humanitarian aid" and requested that the Contras be allowed to remain in their Honduran base camps for another year. In August 1989, Ortega suspended the military draft until the conclusion of elections. He also signed an agreement with the internal opposition that asked the Contras to disband and set February 25, 1990, as election day. Still Bush supported the Contras in Honduras. Vice President Quayle, speaking in Honduras, predicted that the promised elections would be a "sham."

In November, Ortega called off the nineteen-month-long cease-fire with the Contras because of Contra attacks in Nicaraguan villages. He offered to drop the demand that the Contras disband in Honduras if the Contra forces in Nicaragua would return to their bases in that country. Two months later, a Contra force ambushed and killed two nuns. Nevertheless, Ortega went ahead with the election. Despite the economic disaster that had befallen his country in the decade he had held power, he was confident of victory. He believed the people would blame the American economic blockade, not the Sandinistas, for their plight. Former president Jimmy Carter led a team of international observers to certify the fairness of the election, which was called the most closely watched in history.

The result was a stunning surprise. Violeta Barrios de Chamorro, leader of the opposition coalition, won easily. Almost as surprising, at least to the Bush administration officials who had been predicting that Ortega would never give up power, was Ortega's immediate statement to respect the result and his declaration of a cease-fire. Four years earlier Ortega's deputy foreign minister, Alexjandro Bendana, had told American reporters that the Sandinistas believed in democracy and would certainly abide by the results of a free and fair election, even if they lost. No one had believed him. But he had spoken the truth. The transfer of power from Ortega to Chamorro was an inspiring moment. It is a rare event when power changes hands peacefully in Latin America; it is a unique event when a revolutionary Marxist government abides by the rules, allows a free election, and hands over power as a result of an election called and conducted by that government.

The Bush administration had been expecting the worst. The American contribution to these unanticipated developments had been to keep the Contras supplied in Honduras, which had almost wrecked the peace process and endangered the elections. The damage that the American embargo did to the Nicaraguan economy helped make Ortega vulnerable to the voters; American financial contributions to the opposition coalition may have helped Chamorro; in general, however, it must be said that the American role was sterile if not negative, and that the credit for the triumph of democracy in Nicaragua goes to President Arias of Costa Rica, his fellow Central American presidents, but most of all to Daniel Ortega and the Sandinistas.

In another Central American republic, Panama, elections were held on May 7, 1989. Unlike Nicaragua, international observers, led by former president Carter, denounced the election process; Carter said that the Noriega government was "taking the election by fraud." General Noriega defied world public opinion; he seized the tally sheets and proclaimed his candidate the victor. On May 9, Bush charged that the election was marred by "massive irregularities" and urged the people of Panama to overthrow Noriega. But on September 1, Francisco Rodriguez was sworn in as president of Panama; the State Department called him "Noriega's latest puppet president."

Bush was not ready to deal with Rodriguez. The traditional American response to dictators in Latin America has been to organize a coup to overthrow them; the Bush administration did so in Panama in October, when it urged officers in the Panamian Defense Force (PDF) to overthrow Noriega. They tried, but the coup was put down by troops loyal to Noriega; the dictator then ordered the immediate execution of the officers involved. Bush came in for severe criticism, first for encouraging the coup, then for failing to support it.

On December 15, 1989, the National Assembly of Panama named Noriega head of state, and he declared that "a state of war" existed with the United States. This gave Bush a heaven-sent opportunity, which he seized four days later when he sent a division-sized force of army and marine troops to invade Panama. He called it Operation *Just Cause*. After some days of confusion, in which 24 U.S. and 139 PDF troops were killed, along with some fairly heavy civilian casualties and widespread looting in Panama City, the Americans managed to capture the fugitive Noriega, who had found his last refuge in the Vatican mission. They had already installed as president Guillermo Endara, who had been the apparent winner of the May elections.

Reactions were predictable. Noriega, who was taken to Miami as a prisoner of war and held in a civilian jail, awaiting trial on his indictment for drug dealing, charged Yankee imperialism. So did Bush's domestic political opponents and critics. Liberals who in the past had decried the use of the CIA for coup and assassination plots now asked why Bush had to use so much force to remove one man. Latin American leaders made *pro forma* complaints about the unilateral action. Soviet spokesmen wondered why it was that the United States assumed the right to dictate to the government of Panama and use its armed forces in that country, even as it denounced the Kremlin for using force in dealing with nations on its borders, such as Afghanistan.

Western European commentators found it ironic that the United States was practicing old-fashioned "Big Stick" diplomacy in its back yard at the moment when the Soviets were showing remarkable restraint during the unraveling of Communist regimes in the traditional Soviet sphere in Eastern Europe. American conservatives, meanwhile, praised the president for his bold and daring action. The American people generally gave Bush enthusiastic support: his approval rating went up to an astonishing 80 percent.

In January 1990, Bush announced a program to provide $1 billion in economic aid to Panama. In March, he asked for additional money to send aid to the Chamorro government in Nicaragua. He was already providing funds to the governments of Colombia to fight drug lords and to El Salvador (where President Alfredo Cristiani admitted in January 1990 that "elements of the armed forces" had massacred six Jesuit priests and two civilians in the previous November) to fight left-wing rebels. From 1985 on, the United States had provided economic aid to Honduras in exchange for Honduran support of the Contras. Taken together, these relatively tiny Central American countries were getting more American economic aid than all the countries of Europe.

Most American foreign aid was going to one small and one large Middle Eastern nation: Israel and Egypt, respectively. This was the consequence of a Democratic, not Republican, policy initiative. When Jimmy Carter persuaded Begin and Sadat to sign the Camp David Accords in 1979, bringing peace between Egypt and Israel, he had promised billions of dollars in ongoing aid to the two countries. Reagan and Bush continued the policy. Ten years later, when the total American foreign aid program, economic and military, was a little less than $16 billion, more than one-third was going to Israel and Egypt (almost $6 billion). About $4 billion of that aid was in the form of military equipment, evenly split.

Israel and Egypt were willing to take American money, but not American advice. In February 1989, in its annual report on human rights around the world, the State Department charged that there had been "a substantial increase in human rights violations" by the Israelis in the occupied territories. American policy, as proclaimed by Secretary of State Shultz and his successor, James Baker, was to promote local elections in Gaza, the West Bank, and East Jerusalem and to encourage the Israelis to talk directly to PLO leaders, but the Israelis consistently and even insultingly refused. When the Americans complained about Israel putting Russian Jews into permanent settlements in the occupied territories, the Israelis simply ignored the complaints.

The inability of the Bush administration to force Israel to negotiate with the PLO and to seek accommodation with its Arab neighbors must be seen in context: none of Bush's predecessors had been any more successful. The Middle East remained an armed camp, with most of the arms supplied by the United States. In the spring of 1990 there was little basis for any hope or optimism about the end of the bloodshed there any time soon, especially as the *Intifada,* the uprising of the Arab teenage (and younger) boys on the West Bank and in Gaza continued.

The Middle East thus stood in sharp contrast to South Africa, where for the first time in decades there was hope for a genuine peace and real progress toward democracy. On February 2, 1990, yielding to the economic pressure of sanctions and the moral pressure of world public opinion, President F. W. de Klerk lifted a thirty-year ban on the ANC. Nine days later, in a dramatic event witnessed on television by millions of people around the world, ANC leader Nelson Mandela walked out of prison, after

twenty-seven years in captivity. Apartheid had not come
to an end, and South Africa was still far from one-man,
one-vote; nevertheless those of goodwill everywhere
could but cry tears of joy at this development, with its
promise of a brighter future.

Even more joyful and startling events were taking
place in Central and Eastern Europe, the area in which
the Cold War had begun and where it finally came to
an end. They were linked to developments in the Soviet
Union; they were unanticipated because they were unpredictable; they brought about momentous change.

What caused the demise of Communism in Poland,
East Germany, Czechoslovakia, Romania, and Hungary?
In part, it was the culmination of four decades of patient
containment by the NATO alliance and especially the
NATO leader, the United States. In part, it was the burden of the arms race, which was bankrupting the Soviet
Union to the point that the Kremlin could no longer
afford to maintain its grip on the satellites. In part, it
was the people of Eastern Europe themselves and their
refusal to ever abandon their hopes for freedom. Mostly
it was the objective fact that Communism is a rotten
system. The people who lived under it hated it. Marx
and Lenin had predicted that their system would produce a new socialist man, but it was precisely the young,
who have lived all their lives under Communism, who
hated it the most.

Still, a desire to be free is not enough, not when the
government holds the guns—as the Chinese students
had discovered in Tiananmen Square on June 3. Opportunity must be matched with desire. Gorbachev provided the opportunity. So the lion's share of the credit
must go to Gorbachev, who understood that he could
not realize a revolution of *glasnost* and *perestroika* at home
if he did not allow Eastern Europe to go its own way.

The process began in January 1989, when Gorbachev
reduced the Soviet military budget by 14 percent while
cutting spending on weapons by 20 percent. He also
announced the withdrawal of 200,000 troops from Asia.

The Estonian legislature, meanwhile, voted to give Estonian preference over Russian as the official language of the small republic. While relatively insignificant by themselves, these actions pointed to a future that would be much different from the previous seventy years of Soviet rule.

On February 14, 1989, the last Soviet soldiers withdrew from Afghanistan. That same month, dissident playwright Vaclav Havel was convicted of inciting a riot in Prague and sentenced to nine months in jail. In April, the Polish government signed an agreement with the Solidarity labor union, making the union legal and setting open elections for June. Gorbachev called for more arms reductions in Europe; the U.S. secretary of defense, Dick Cheney, said that the United States would not begin to negotiate at any time in the near future and said Gorbachev's call was a "dangerous trap."

In May the Hungarian government, for some time the most liberal in the Warsaw Pact, dismantled the 150-mile-long barbed-wire fence along the Austrian border. The "Iron Curtain," erected in 1946, was finally coming down. The most immediate consequence was the flight of hundreds, then thousands, of East Germans to Hungary, where they crossed over to Austria and then into West Germany. A mass exodus was under way, the likes of which the world had never seen. In the Soviet Union, meanwhile, ethnic unrest led to riots in virtually all the republics, accompanied by demands for more freedom from Moscow.

That same month, speaking in West Germany, President Bush called for an end to the political division of Europe and the destruction of the Berlin Wall. Gorbachev, who for some time had been speaking of Europe as "our common home," took up the challenge. Speaking in Bonn while on a four-day visit to West Germany, he said that the Wall "can disappear when those conditions that created it fall away." Meanwhile Solidarity candidates won a decisive victory over the Communists in elections for the Polish Parliament. General Wojciech Jaruzelski remained president, but a Solidarity leader became prime minister, while Lech Walesa, the hero of the Solidarity movement of 1980–81 that had unleashed it all, stood hopefully in the wings.

While visiting France in June, Gorbachev told reporters that the political future of Poland and Hungary was "their affair." Those two words effectively put an end to the Brezhnev Doctrine and all but invited the other East European nations to take their affairs into their own hands. It was a development of sufficient significance to justify Bush's remark that "a new world is within our reach."

It came with breathtaking suddenness. All summer thousands of young East Germans fled their country as if the black death had struck. In August, Solidarity took over the government of Poland, giving postwar Poland its first ever non-Communist government. When it asked for economic aid from the United States, Bush responded that the $119 million already promised was sufficient. One week earlier he had pledged $8 billion for drug control.

Despite American passivity, the pace of change of Eastern Europe speeded up. In October, demonstrations in Prague, Budapest, Leipzig, and East Berlin swelled to immense size, with half a million and more Czechs, Hungarians, and East Germans taking over the streets and chanting "We are the people." In the Soviet Union, the Baltic republics demanded independence, while ethnic and economic unrest threatened to dismember the Soviet empire. Foreign Minister Eduard Shevardnadze told the Supreme Soviet that the Red Army invasion of Afghanistan was a violation of Soviet and international law, and he confessed that the radar complex in Siberia was "an open violation" of the ABM treaty with the United States. Demonstrators outside KGB headquarters in Moscow demanded democratic changes.

Soviet confessions of wrongdoing and demonstrations in Moscow—these were events no one ever expected to see in the twentieth century. But even greater changes were at hand. November 1989 brought more shifts in the basic structure of the world system than had been seen since the summer of 1945. In Czechoslovakia, Vaclav Havel came out of prison on his way to becoming president, as the Communist party gave up its monopoly of power after a week of massive demonstrations. The Warsaw Pact nations, including the Soviet Union, issued a statement condemning the Soviet-led 1968 invasion of Czechoslovakia as "illegal" and promised not to interfere again in each other's affairs. That was the official end to the Brezhnev Doctrine.

On November 9, the most astonishing, least expected, and most welcome event of all took place. The East German government, completely unable to stem the tide of the flight of its people, announced that "it is now possible for all citizens to leave this country through East German crossing points." Within hours of the announcement, tens of thousands of East Germans had overrun the Berlin Wall.

It was one of the most remarkable days of the twentieth century. For twenty-eight years, the Wall had been *the* symbol of the Cold War. Suddenly it was gone. The unthinkable had become reality.

At the beginning of 1989, the Communists had been in complete—and seemingly permanent—control of Eastern Europe. At the end of the year, they were gone. Democratic coalitions, promising free elections in the immediate future, had taken power in East Berlin, Prague, Budapest, Warsaw, and even Bucharest (where the Rumanian tyrant Nicolae Ceausescu was overthrown on December 22, then executed on Christmas Day). As a result, the Warsaw Pact had been, in effect, dismantled. The Soviet Union had withdrawn inside its borders, which were themselves shrinking. The Cold War in Europe was over.

The United States had not played an active role in these events. The Bush administration stood on the sidelines. The CIA was not involved. No American guns were fired. But although the Americans and their European allies had "won"—or so at least American conservatives claimed—victory in 1989 was not at all like victory in 1945. American troops did not occupy the Soviet Union.

The Soviet government, although weakened, confused, and groping toward an uncertain future, was still intact. The U.S.S.R. did show some of the signs of a defeated power—widespread unrest, severe economic dislocation, separatist movements of serious scope, general demoralization—but in other ways it did not. The Red Army, although retreating from Eastern Europe, remained the largest in the world. The strategic forces were still there—the navy, the missiles, the nuclear warheads—and the Soviets remained capable of destroying the world in a flash.

Nor was the United States the dominant world power it had been in 1945. President Bush's response to the world revolution of 1989 and the end of the Cold War was passive or prudent, depending on the point of view. He managed to restrain whatever emotion he felt as the Berlin Wall came down. He and the Pentagon continued to call for very high levels of defense expenditure. He refused to consider bringing the troops home from their forward NATO positions. He gave Lech Walesa of Poland and President Havel of Czechoslovakia a warm welcome in Washington but very little money. He continued to send large sums to Israel and Egypt (where no changes were taking place) and to Central America, but only a pittance to Eastern Europe.

On a per capita basis, Israel was the top recipient of American aid by far, but close behind were El Salvador and Honduras. The United States in 1990 was sending $588 million in military aid to Pakistan to oppose a Red Army in Afghanistan that had left two years earlier. The fourth-largest recipient of American aid was Turkey; next came Greece. They made up NATO's "southern flank," and supposedly the aid was designed to counter a Soviet threat that seemed to have disappeared; actually the Greeks and Turks used the weapons to threaten each other. The allocation of American foreign aid illustrated the way in which domestic politics, not foreign policy realities, dictated the policy. In 1990, when Senate Republican leader Robert Dole proposed redirecting 5 percent of the aid that went to Israel and Egypt to Eastern

Europe, the Israeli lobby mobilized 73 Senators to oppose the idea.

Bush's critics wanted him to reverse his priorities, to stop funding an unwinnable drug war, an unreasonable Israel, and unimportant Central American republics, and to start funding the creation of a new, democratic Central and Eastern Europe. His supporters thought that his go slow, go steady, don't make any mistakes in a hurry approach was appropriate to fast-changing, confusing events.

Bush, like Reagan, regarded Gorbachev not only as preferable to any alternative in sight, but as a positive statesman whose reforms were as welcome as they were necessary. Bush wanted Gorbachev to prosper. Secretary of State Baker put it well when he told the Foreign Policy Association that the United States wanted to see *"perestroika* succeed" because improvements in the U.S.S.R. would lead to "Soviet actions more advantageous to our interests." In that spirit, Bush announced an "informal" summit, quickly called. It took place in Soviet and U.S. naval vessels off the coast of Malta in the Mediterranean on December 2–4, 1989. The tone of the meeting was positive. The two leaders agreed to attempt to conclude a treaty on strategic nuclear arsenals and a treaty on conventional arms limitations in 1990—both sets of negotiations had been going on for many years—and to try to integrate the Soviet Union into the world market economy.

Even as Bush talked arms limitations with Gorbachev, he pursued a hard line on defense. Two weeks after the Malta summit, he rejected the recommendation of Defense Secretary Dick Cheney and the Air Force Strategic Air Command (SAC) to reduce round-the-clock airborne nuclear command surveillance. The SAC recommended the reduction because, it said, there was less risk of a surprise Soviet nuclear attack than had been the case since Khrushchev's day.

The Bush defense budget for 1990, while it did not call for the big increases that had marked Reagan's budgets, did not call for any significant reductions, either.

The Pentagon's insistence on holding the line on forces in being and pushing ahead with such new and terribly expensive weapons systems as the B-2 bomber was severely criticized by Congressmen from both parties. The politicians wanted a "peace dividend" to spend on their favorite projects—the American poor, the American environment, reducing the deficit, economic aid to the emerging democracies in Europe, or whatever—but they evidently were not going to get it from Bush. Even though the Warsaw Pact was, at best, a hollow shell of its former self, even though the Red Army was pulling back from Eastern Europe, even though no one could imagine a Soviet ground offensive into Western Europe, Bush insisted on maintaining a large American army in Germany.

East and West Germany, meanwhile, were moving rapidly toward unification. American General John Galvin, the Supreme Allied Commander in Europe, told a news conference that he no longer knew what line he was supposed to defend. Before 1990, it had clearly been the Elbe River, which divided the two Germanies, but now the river united Germany, leaving NATO in an advanced stage of confusion about its role. The prospect of one Germany, meanwhile, aroused deep concern in France, Poland, and, indeed, throughout the world. There was much discussion about whether the new Germany would be neutral or a part of NATO. The Soviets preferred a neutral Germany, but West German politicians said it would undoubtedly remain a member of NATO; Western European politicians, and some from America, said it was necessary to keep U.S. forces in Germany as a way of reassuring her neighbors that Germany would not repeat the history of the 1930s. Moreover, as in Japan, which also was no longer threatened by the Soviets, it was necessary to maintain the alliance so that Germany and Japan could not feel a need to acquire their own nuclear weapons.

Such talk assumed that NATO would still be a functioning military alliance in the twenty-first century—a somewhat doubtful proposition, if only because it was difficult to see who the enemy would be. Alliances, after all, have to be directed against someone, especially defensive ones. In the 1950s, NATO may have had a mission of "double containment"—i.e., containment of both the Soviets and the Germans. But by the 1990s it was difficult to see the point of an alliance that was directed against one of the allies, or at least designed to hold one of the allies in check to reassure the others. What seemed more likely was that the Germans would exercise their rights of self-determination and decide their own future, whatever the Americans or the other NATO nations wanted.

The ongoing discussions highlighted the basic change that had taken place in the world. For nearly forty-five years, the two superpowers had dominated international politics, alliances, and trade arrangements. But by 1990 the world was no longer bipolar, except in strategic nuclear weapons and delivery systems. In economics, the three major parts of the world were forming regional economic blocs—superblocs. Western Europe was the clearest case of a group of sovereign nations moving deliberately to form a closer union, with the goal of a single European market in 1992.

The second superbloc was forming across the Pacific in East Asia. From Melbourne to Seoul, intraregional trade and investments were rapidly expanding. In virtually every country except the Philippines, there was rapid economic growth. The dynamo propelling East Asian economic integration was Japan, the instrument was the strong yen.

The third superbloc was forming in North America, around the United States and including Canada, Mexico, and the Caribbean Basin. In 1988, the United States signed an important free-trade agreement with its neighbor to the north, creating a single integrated economic market. By 1990, one-third of all American investments abroad was in Canada. The United States was trading more with the province of Ontario than with Japan, while the Canadians had far more investment in America than did the Japanese. With free trade coming between the United States and Canada, the border had become—economically—meaningless.

By 1992, a free-trade agreement with Mexico and Canada was possible. As has been noted, insofar as the United States had a foreign aid program in the Bush years (outside of Israel and Egypt), it was directed toward Central America. The national mood was clearly to lessen the burdens of international leadership and to ask others to accept more responsibility for military security, foreign aid, and support for international organization. It was only a short step from that attitude to isolationism, 1930s style.

A chief characteristic of isolationism is not caring very much about what happens elsewhere. This is reflected in an unwillingness to spend on foreign affairs. Exactly that had happened in the United States. Although the national economy had doubled between 1960 and 1980, by 1980 the country was spending less in real terms on defense and foreign aid than in 1960. And while military expenditures had increased in the Reagan years, American outlays for other aspects of international affairs had declined, from $12.7 billion in 1981 to $10.5 billion in 1988. In the Bush years the outlays declined even further.

But if the U.S. was having financial problems that made it difficult for Bush to maintain the level of foreign aid of his predecessors, the Soviet Union was in a financial collapse that made it impossible for Gorbachev to maintain any level of assistance to his client states in the Third World. The competition between the superpowers to purchase the friendship of developing nations was over.

So too was the arms race between the superpowers. Gorbachev's government was bankrupt while Bush was under relentless pressure to reduce the defense budget; with the Warsaw Pact gone and the Red Army in retreat, there was no reason to continue an American program of building newer, more expensive, and more destructive weapons; with Gorbachev looking to the U.S. for loans and grants, it made no sense for the Soviets to expand, or even to maintain, their threatening posture against Western Europe and the U.S. On June 1, 1990, the two leaders met at Camp David to sign arms control agreements. They pledged to reduce their reserves of long-range nuclear weapons by 30 percent and their chemical weapons stockpile by 80 percent. Within a year they had agreed to verification procedures that included on-site spot inspections at weapons sites. Existing nuclear warheads being destroyed instead of new ones being built, with on-site verification, meant that President Eisenhower's hopes when he announced his Atoms for Peace and "Open Skies" proposals in the early 1950s had finally become reality.

This development vindicated four decades of American policy. In November, 1990, Bush announced, "The Cold War is over," something Gorbachev had been saying for the past year. Credit for the victory went to all the Cold War presidents, who had maintained Truman's containment policy with the expectation that sooner or later the Soviet Empire would collapse because of its own internal contradictions. The West, and especially the U.S., had shown remarkable patience and had practiced prudence in its statecraft to bring about the victory, which was much less expensive—despite the cost of the arms race and the cost to two generations of Poles, East Germans, Russians, and others who suffered under communist rule—than the victory in World War II had been (not to mention what the cost of World War III would have been).

For forty-five years, the people of the Western world had lived in dread of the day the Red Army marched across the Elbe River to undertake the conquest of Germany, France, and England. But by 1990, the Red Army was moving in the opposite direction, out of Central Europe, out of its never-digested gains from 1945. The Baltic States opted out of the Soviet Union; Gorbachev was unable (or unwilling) to stop them. Once the process of disintegration began, it could not be stopped.

Bush had given no support to the seceding Balkan

States, except to criticize Gorbachev when the Red Army used force against nationalists in Lithuania and Latvia. Nor did he support separatists in Ukraine, Georgia, and the southern republics in the Soviet Union. He did support Gorbachev, with limited financial and food assistance, and with words. At the end of July 1991, following a summit meeting in Moscow in which he addressed Gorbachev as a friend and virtual ally, Bush told the Ukrainian Parliament in Kiev that the U.S. would not choose sides between the Soviet government and the independence-seeking republics. He was much criticized for fence-straddling, but he was faced with a difficult dilemma. He liked Gorbachev, was accustomed to working with him, believed Gorbachev meant predictability and stability in foreign affairs, and feared the consequences of disunion. But he was an American: How could he not support peoples who wanted independence and freedom, especially when the independence of the various republics would further weaken the already badly damaged Soviet Union, America's enemy for forty-five years?

Another factor making Bush hesitate to choose between Gorbachev and the republics was the help Gorbachev had given Bush in the 1990–91 crisis with Iraq (see chapter 17). Without Gorbachev's cooperation, Bush almost surely could not have carried out his policy in that situation. The disappearance of the Soviet Union could only be good for the remaining superpower, but even better would be a reformed Soviet Union no longer posing a military threat but able to act as a great power in support of American policies.

For hard-liners, on both sides, the rapid movement toward a new world structure was alarming. In addition, on both sides the major form of employment was in defense and security-related industries that depended on the Cold War that had created them to sustain their existence. Between the true-believers and the job-seekers, there was a powerful potential to block change.

Less than three weeks after Bush's departure from Moscow, in August 1991, reactionaries in the Red Army and the Communist Party staged a coup. On taking power and after arresting Gorbachev, they announced that the signing of the new union treaty, scheduled for the next day, would not take place. The treaty would have shifted power from the central government to the nine republics that had agreed to sign it. Blocking the union treaty may have been the proximate cause for the coup (if so, the plotters had surely made one of the all-time great mistakes); the larger cause was the desire to return to a Brezhnev-era—not Stalinist-era—style Communism.

Bush spoke out at once in support of Gorbachev and the established government. In Moscow, Russian President Boris Yeltsin called for a general strike and resistance to the coup. Citizens threw up roadblocks around the Kremlin and tens of thousands maintained a continuous vigil to keep the tanks away and to protest against the coup.

Thanks to Yeltsin, the coup collapsed in three days. Rather than stopping change, it accelerated change. Gorbachev returned to Moscow to proclaim, "I am in full control of the situation." But he was not. That same day, August 21, Yeltsin told the Russian Parliament that he was issuing decrees establishing Russia's economic sovereignty, taking control of Soviet agencies, and abolishing the Communist party. Before the year was out, Gorbachev had resigned and the leaders of Russia, Belarus, and Ukraine declared that "the USSR as a subject of international law and geopolitical reality is ceasing its existence."

It was a declaration of independence of the republics from the union; it was also a declaration of independence by the people of the old union from communism. Yeltsin took drastic steps to move his country toward a market economy, steps that required severe sacrifice for millions of people. Bush recognized and established relations with the new republics on December 25, 1991. Insofar as the republics were pledged to create a democratic, market-oriented state, it was a wonderful Christmas present for them and for the world.

The problem was, there was not much follow-up. The republics were poor, in a state of virtual economic catastrophe. Yeltsin and the other leaders wanted money, credits, high-technology skills, investment. Bush was only willing to offer food. Former president Nixon strongly criticized Bush for failing to respond to the crisis in the republics with a massive aid program.

This was the beginning of a debate over fundamentals—What should the foreign policy of the U.S. be in a totally new situation? The Cold War was over, no one threatened the security of the United States, indeed the Gulf War of 1990–91 made the United States and Russia virtual allies. All the great "isms" of the twentieth century against which the United States had fought—colonialism, fascism, Communism—had been defeated.* This represented what Francis Fukuyama, in a widely read and highly influential article, called "the End of History." Fukuyama postulated that the collapse of communism meant that liberal democracy had been proved superior to all its competitors. Everyone had not gotten there yet, but everyone strove for a democratic political system and a market economy. This meant the end of history, in the sense of searching for the best system. It also meant, Fukuyama indicated, the end of large-scale war.

If these predictions are true, the future is going to be radically different from the past. There are no guideposts. In this new world, Germany and Japan—premier examples of liberal democracies—pose more of a challenge to the well-being of the American people than any military power or enemy possibly could. Those who make better trucks are more of a threat than those who make better tanks. This brings us back to the subject of the debate—What foreign policy should the U.S. adopt in facing the new world situation?

With no conceivable threat to the United States, many people, including former CIA Director William Colby, called for a 50 percent reduction in defense and security

*Except for Communism in Cuba, China, and Southeast Asia.

funding. They pointed out that the United States already had more military might than the rest of the world combined. Others, led by President Bush, rejected any cuts. They argued that disarmament was always wrong and pointed to the Gulf War and to the possibility of a reactionary coup succeeding in Russia, which still, after all, had sufficient nuclear weapons and missiles to destroy the world.

The military question existed side-by-side with the political question: Should the U.S. make a major effort to help the republics? McGeorge Bundy, former special assistant for national security to Presidents Kennedy and Johnson, said yes. He pointed out that for one-tenth of one-percent of the $4,000 billion dollars spent on the Cold War, "we could play our part in the Russian turn to freedom." The United States could not possibly invest money more wisely than in helping Russia achieve a democratic future.

Opponents doubted that sending financial and technical aid to Russia would be affordable or would work. Beyond that, they wanted to keep the money at home. Thus, the debate went back to the most persistent question in American foreign policy for two centuries: Should the United States be isolationist or internationalist? An important corollary question was, should the nation be protectionist or free trade? Truman had faced the same questions as he met the responsibility of defining a new American foreign policy to meet the new situation of 1946. He chose internationalism. His doctrine, containment, proved to have been a wise choice over the long haul.

But in a world of economic rather than military threats, the machinery Truman had created to support his foreign policy choice was drastically out of date. The National Security Council is not organized to frame policy options regarding trade, resources, the environment, and so forth. The Department of Defense cannot defend the nation from drugs or Japanese imports. By their nature, these two great Cold War organizations, the ones most concerned with the formation of American foreign policy, were least prepared to lead a debate about it. Because the United States had made Cold War considerations the touchstone of its policy in all foreign relations, all relationships in a post-Cold War world required a new foreign policy.

Some of the basic elements that require debate included free trade versus protectionism, regional economic blocks, the role of the military, the role of the United Nations, the response to civil war and aggression around the world, the level of foreign aid, the endemic problems of the Middle East, the role of a NATO that has no enemy and perceives no threat, the relationship with the democracies in Central and South America and with South Africa, the relationship with China and Russia and the new republics, and more.

They are all complex questions. On all of them there are strong arguments on each side. Free trade with Mexico, for example, arouses the fear in organized labor that American manufacturers will move their plants south of the border to lower labor costs. But surely the United States will benefit, supporters point out, from a prosperous Mexico, not least because if there are no jobs for Mexicans in Mexico, the United States might as well abolish the border altogether, because nothing will be able to stem the flow of Mexicans to where the jobs are.

In the new world, arms sales abroad are a more critical problem than superpower arms control. The nuclear weapons and missile race came to an end not through negotiation but through the collapse of the Communist superpower. As that happened, and as the Soviets eliminated arms shipments to client or anti-American nations, the United States dramatically increased its arms sales, more than doubling the total (from $7.8 billion in 1989 to $18.5 billion in 1990) in the first year of the new world order. This was a great help, second only to agriculture, in meeting the nation's balance of payments bill. Nevertheless, it made a world torn apart by nationalist and ethnic feuds far more dangerous, even dangerous to the seller, as Bush discovered when American forces had to face American armaments held by an Iraqi army he had helped to build.

Relations with the great powers, Russia, Germany, and Japan, are at the center of the question of isolationism versus internationalism. All three were defeated in this century by the United States in a hot war (Germany twice) or a cold war. The relationship with Germany and Japan, now nearly a half-century old, is solid and sustaining for all concerned. As William Colby said, "I'd rather have them as economic competitors than as military foes." The relationship with a defeated Russia has yet to be worked out. As the debate continues, it ought to include some of the lessons from history. The coming to power of Hitler, followed by World War II, taught Americans that it had been a mistake to subject a defeated nation to a vindictive peace settlement and to walk away from the responsibilities of victory. After World War II, the United States treated the defeated nations of Japan and Germany with magnanimity and stayed on the job to lead the defeated totalitarian states into a democratic future. Would the United States do for Russia what it did for Germany and Japan?

The question of the Russian relationship was a part of the broader question about the role of America in the new world. Within less than a year of Bush's declaration that the Cold War was over, two crises erupted, one in the Persian Gulf and one in Yugoslavia. The crises gave Bush an opportunity to establish a new foreign policy, and beyond that a new world order. But his responses to Iraqi aggression in Kuwait and Serbian aggression in Yugoslavia were starkly different—massive intervention in the first case, studied indifference in the second.

President Bush called the crisis that began when Iraq invaded Kuwait in August 1990 the "defining moment" in setting a new foreign policy for a "new world order." It was the first post–Cold War crisis. Although it took place in that home of crises, the Middle East, it had many new elements to it, the first of which was that the United States was able to operate freely as the only superpower.

There were so many new elements, in fact, that the crisis may have been unique, which would mean there were no lessons that could be applied to other parts of the world and that therefore the debate on the American role in the world had to go on.

Bush insisted that his policy was clear: the United States would punish aggression to insure the new world order. In other words, the United States would act as world policeman defending the status quo.

Robert Tucker and David Hendrickson call this response "the Imperial Temptation." Precisely because America's military might is so great relative to that of everyone else, meaning America can today defeat any armed forces anywhere in the world using high technology and thus by suffering few American casualties, Americans will be tempted to intervene, to punish, then to walk away from the consequences and ignore the responsibilities of victory. To give into that temptation, Tucker and Hendrickson warn, would be to lose our soul.

Tucker and Hendrickson advise using economic sanctions in the post–Cold War world. They argue that the end of the Cold War transformed the world, and state that "The principal features of this transformation were the declining utility of force—above all, in the relations among the major developed states—and the increasing importance of economic power."

In addressing the crisis in Yugoslavia, Bush did rely on economic sanctions and ruled out military intervention. His actual policy was far more pragmatic than his rhetoric about punishing aggression. The policy was selective isolationism, meaning only tepid, absolute minimal support for freedom and order in Yugoslavia or for Russia and other struggling democracies, balanced by selective internationalism, meaning quick and massive military intervention to protect genuine national interests (read "oil"). In short, a traditional statecraft rooted in the pre-Cold War era, a statecraft based on case-by-case judgments with the sole guiding principle being American national interests.

By their natures, then, the Gulf crisis of 1990–91 and the Yugoslavian crisis of 1990–95 raised basic questions in a way they would not have in the seventies or eighties. Because they were the first post–Cold War crises and because one occurred in the area most critical to the world economy, the other in an area of little concern to outsiders, how they were handled and what the lessons might be are precedent-setting. With the booming razzle-dazzle of a Tomahawk missile launch, Bush would unleash the full firing of the U.S. military on Iraq to protect Kuwait's sovereignty and oil reserves. But by allowing genocide to take place in Yugoslavia Bush exposed the lack of U.S. resolve to intervene abroad on moral grounds. Nevertheless, the way they were handled and some of the repercussions need to be considered.

First, however, it needs to be noted that these first crises of the new world order took place in a world much different from what it had been at the time of the first crises of the Cold War. History does not repeat itself. The direction of the new world order will be greatly affected by chance. But history and chance take place in a context, a structure, a reality. Harry Truman worked from a position of overwhelming strength; George Bush was and his successors will continue to be in a position of weakness. Still, Truman had another superpower to deal with, unlike Bush and his successors.

The 1980s were a terrible decade for America's position in the economic world. Even as her military forces were strengthened and were winning the Cold War, her power in the marketplace shrank. Consider that at the beginning of the 1980s, as had been the case since World War II, the United States was the world's largest creditor nation. At the beginning of the 1990s, the United States was the largest debtor nation in history. Germany and Japan were the creditors.

In 1980, as had been true for forty years, the United States was the world's largest exporting nation of manufactured goods. By 1991, West Germany, with a work force one fourth the size of America's, had taken the lead. In 1980, Citicorp and Chase Manhattan were the two largest banks in the world. By 1991, the world's ten largest banks were all Japanese. The biggest American bank, Citicorp, ranked twenty-seventh in the world.

This relative decline may be slowed, or even stopped, but its meaning for American foreign policy is permanent. Never again will the United States dominate the world economy as it did in the early Cold War. The United States will not be able to generate another Marshall Plan.

In the twentieth century, the United States turned back the forces of totalitarianism—the Kaiser's Germany, Hitler's Nazi Germany, Japan's militarist and expansionist government, Mussolini's Fascist Italy, and Soviet Communism. Surely justice has never been better served. The legacy of the American Century is a world in which more people are relatively freer to make their own choices, certainly far freer than they were under any of the isms, than ever before. That is a splendid legacy.

The counterpart is American hubris. The experience of the Cold War gives Americans a sense that they can run the world because their military power is so much greater than that of any other nation or group of nations. But the nation's economic base is smaller than ever, so resources do not support expectations. In addressing the first crises of the new world order. Bush had to respond to both the expectation and the reality.

17

Bush and the Gulf War

"This Will Not Stand."

GEORGE BUSH

On August 1, 1990, Iraqi troops invaded Kuwait, thereby setting off the first post–Cold War international crisis. It came in a part of the world that was neither communist nor capitalist, but feudal; a part of the world that did not belong to any of the three superblocs, but was critical to the industrial nations of Europe, the Pacific, and North America; a part of the world that had seen more fighting and killing than any other region since 1945. The crisis came as a surprise and caused many new surprises.

The proximate cause of the crisis was the seizure of Kuwait by the army of Iraq's dictator, Saddam Hussein, followed by Hussein's announcement that Iraq had annexed Kuwait and by the movement of much of the Iraqi army to the border between Kuwait and Saudi Arabia. Hussein's quarrel with Kuwait was that the tiny nation had exceeded its OPEC quota and thereby driven down the world price of oil. Insofar as the Saudis could manipulate the oil prices more or less at will by increasing or decreasing their production, Saudi Arabia appeared to be a logical next target for Hussein.

He seemed to be threatening to take over Saudi Arabia by force. The Iraqi army in Kuwait numbered in the hundreds of thousands. It had more than 5,000 tanks. The Saudi army was minuscule, more a police force than an army. Hussein had taken over Kuwait because his army was the overwhelming power in the region. The

balance of power between the Arab states of the Middle
East had been badly upset.

This was the fault of the superpowers, who had sold
arms to and otherwise supported Iraq throughout the
1980s in its war with Iran. Kuwait and Saudi Arabia had
paid most of the bill. Iraq bought Soviet-built tanks and
American technology. The Bush administration provided Hussein $5.5 billion in loans; some was money
hidden in the Agriculture Department budget. Hussein
used the money to accelerate his program to build a
nuclear bomb. In the early summer of 1990, United
States policy toward Iraq was to assist in improving the
Iraqi armed forces, with the purpose of deterring Iran.
So close were Iraq and the United States in July 1991,
that joint military maneuvers were being planned for
later in the year. With regard to Iraq's border dispute
with Kuwait, the American ambassador told Hussein the
United States took no position.

This policy had not been thought out nor was any part
of it based on principle. But Iraq's invasion of Kuwait
and its suddenly threatening posture on Saudi Arabia's
northern border inspired a lot of immediate thought
and principled action. There were many firsts; most important it was the first time the United States and the
U.S.S.R. acted together in a Middle East crisis. The result, in the U.N. Security Council, was spectacular.

The day after the invasion, Bush condemned it and
asked world leaders to join him in action against Iraq.
The following day Secretary Baker and Soviet Foreign
Minister Eduard Shevardnadze issued a joint statement
from Moscow that called for a worldwide embargo on
arms for Iraq because of its "brutal and illegal invasion
of Kuwait." Meanwhile the action at the United Nations
was stunning. On August 2, the Security Council condemned Iraq and demanded a retreat on pain of man-
datory sanctions. Four days later, sanctions were
imposed, including an embargo against Iraqi and Kuwaiti oil.

Meanwhile, in another first, Secretaries Baker and
Cheney flew to Saudi Arabia, where they convinced King

Fahd that his country was threatened and persuaded him to agree to the deployment of large numbers of American troops into his kingdom. The next day, August 7, American paratroopers, an armored brigade, and fighter airplanes were on their way to Saudi Arabia to begin Operation Desert Shield. They were quickly joined by token forces from Egypt, Morocco, and Syria. The U.N. Security Council supported the operation.

These actions marked a potential turning point in world history, the point at which the U.N. finally began to realize its potential and to fulfill the hopes of its founders. The overwhelming reason for the relative failure of the U.N. during the Cold War had been superpower hostility. With that factor gone, the U.N. was bound to be different.

Other developments associated with the end of the Cold War were also pointing to a new world structure, but as always the portents for the future were contradictory. In one case, Germany, people were coming together again in a peaceful manner; in the other, Yugoslavia, the Serbian/Communist-dominated federation Tito had erected, people were splitting up in a violent manner.

Ever since 1945, Germany had been divided, but in the fall of 1990 she was reunited and the occupying powers gave up their rights in that country. This meant, among other things, that the bipolar world of the previous forty-five years had given way to a multipolar world. So long as the Cold War between the superpowers had dominated world politics, the U.N. could do little more than debate. But with the disappearance of the Iron Curtain, the destruction of the Berlin Wall, the unification of Germany, the demise of the Warsaw Pact; with the emergence of new problems in the U.S.S.R. and the U.S. that had no relation to the Cold War or to the communist-capitalist confrontation; with the spread of advanced weapons from the developed to the undeveloped world (including such elements of the poor man's arsenal as gas warfare, bacteria, hostages, and terrorism); with the rise of an industrial Asia that was dependent for its energy on an undeveloped Middle East; with all this, the superpowers, for all their ability to destroy the planet hundreds of times over, were irrelevant to many of the world's problems.

So was the U.N., it turned out, at least to the peoples of Yugoslavia. There a civil war broke out in 1991 that involved the worst fighting and highest casualties Europe had seen since 1945. The war pitted Serbia against Croatia and Bosnia. The U.N. ordered sanctions against Serbia, but without an American commitment to support the use of force, the U.N. was unable to do to the Serbs what it had done to the Iraqis. In a world with only one superpower, the U.N. could not play a prominent role without American leadership. So although the U.N. sent a peace-keeping force to Yugoslavia in 1992, it was too small to enforce a cease-fire without the cooperation of the warring parties.

Almost everything in the situation made American intervention dangerous. The racial, ethnic, and religious differences that were tearing Yugoslavia apart were centuries old. An irony here; these problems were the ones Woodrow Wilson had attempted to deal with when drawing a post-Hapsburg Empire map of Europe at the 1919 Versailles Conference. The century had come full circle; with imperialism, fascism, and Communism turned back, the world returned to the problem of nationalism. As it will almost certainly turn out to be *the* great cause of instability, poverty, and disorder in the world, and far more likely to be a glimpse into the future than the Iraqi crisis was, the response to the Yugoslavian civil war was more precedent-setting than the Gulf War.

Beyond the apparent impossibility of persuading Muslims and Christians, Croats and Serbians to get along with each other (short of using the methods of Marshal Tito), Yugoslavia was unappealing to the Bush administration as a place to get involved for many reasons. It had little economic significance. It was not a major crossroads of world trade. Its front-line position in the Cold War era was of no importance by 1991. It was a European problem requiring a European, not a United States or U.N., solution.

In Yugoslavia, therefore, aggression went unpunished. The United States was content to denounce Serbia but not to act against her. The Russians joined President Bush in condemning Serbia and imposing economic sanctions, but that did not affect Serbian policy.

This was unexpected. For nearly half a century, when a superpower spoke, its client states obeyed. It had been unthinkable that either one of them could be ignored, much less the two acting together. Yet in 1990, Iraq defied both the Soviet Union and the United States. So did Serbia. Hussein and the Serbs were confident that the power to destroy (after all, with less than one percent of their nuclear arsenals, either the United States or the U.S.S.R. could have wiped out Baghdad and/or Belgrade in a split second) was not the power to control. Iraq and Serbia doubted that the United States or the U.N. would act. One was right, the other wrong.

President Bush sent a little food to Yugoslavia and much of the armed might of the United States to Saudi Arabia.

On August 8, less than a week after the invasion of Kuwait and a day after putting Operation Desert Shield in motion, Bush announced the principles on which he was acting. Appeasement does not work; aggression must be punished. He had a four-point program: First, "The immediate, unconditional and complete withdrawal of all Iraqi forces from Kuwait"; second, the restoration of "Kuwait's legitimate government"; third, an American-enforced guarantee of "the security and stability of the Persian Gulf," which meant disarming Hussein; fourth, to protect the lives of American citizens abroad, which meant the hostages held in Kuwait. Bush made no mention of the defense of Saudi Arabia.

Bush stuck to this position through many ups and downs over the following six months; when he added new points to it, they were even tougher on Iraq (chiefly that Iraq pay reparations). It was a response that carried considerable risk. Sanctions were hurting Iraq and would become more effective as time passed, but Hussein could make up for his losses by requiring further sacrifice from his people and blaming their misery on the United States. He could pose as the champion of the PLO, which would make it difficult to hold the Arab members of the coalition (Egypt, Syria, and Saudi Arabia, above all) together. Meanwhile, he was working on building a nuclear weapon and was expanding his poison gas arsenal (and he had used gas against the Kurds during the Iran-Iraq war). And how long would the U.S. be willing to maintain a quarter of a million troops in the desert? Especially to defend the feudal, filthy-rich, easy-to-despise, and impossible-to-like Arab royal families?

Bush's stated cause was above criticism. Hussein's aggression had to be stopped, as there could be no reward for naked aggression. That had been the clear lesson of the crisis that is described at the beginning of this book, Munich in 1938. Bush, a World War II veteran, harked back to his youth to find principles to guide his actions. But he had also been through the great oil shock of 1973. Although he did not stress the point, he intervened to hold down the price of oil. This was a necessary but not a noble cause.

The immediate response to Bush's August 8 speech was overwhelmingly positive, but within a month the constant tension in American foreign policy between interventionists and isolationists began to reassert itself. Critics wondered if Iraq really had been threatening Saudi Arabia. General Norman Schwarzkopf, commanding the U.N. forces in Operation Desert Shield, said that in the first three weeks of the crisis Iraq could have overrun Saudi Arabia without opposition. That Hussein had not done so perhaps indicated that he never intended to do so. In that case, what difference did it make which of the Arab sheiks got the oil profits? The critics were not proposing to cut a deal with Hussein. They supported sanctions. But they were not willing to see American boys dying for the emir of Kuwait. By fall, oil prices had settled down at their precrisis level; the world was getting along quite well without Iraqi or Kuwaiti oil.

In this confused situation, all sorts of unimaginable developments took place. Iran, two years after the end of an eight-year war with Iraq in which each side had lost a million men, became Iraq's ally. Secretary Baker went to Syria, branded a terrorist nation by the U.S., to seek cooperation in the Persian Gulf. Saudi Arabia and Kuwait agreed to pay most of the cost of the American presence in the Middle East; Germany and Japan pitched in.

Hussein remained defiant. He held thousands of hostages from the U.S. and Western Europe and he proclaimed he was prepared to use them as a human shield against an American attack. He annexed Kuwait and closed the embassies in Kuwait City. He prepared defensive positions along the border with Saudi Arabia and increased his army there. He spoke of "the mother of all battles."

Bush was just as defiant. From the first day of the crisis, he insisted that "this will not stand." To a remarkable degree, he personalized the dispute—Bush versus Hussein. "I've had it." "I am getting increasingly frustrated." "Consider me provoked." "I am not ruling out further options." "I don't want to say what I will or will not do." "I will never—ever—agree to a halfway effort." Jean Edward Smith comments, "It was as if foreign policy had become presidential autobiography."

Bush began comparing Hussein with Hitler. It was a brilliant way to fend off pressure to negotiate; one could not negotiate with a Hitler. But it was a two-edged sword. By comparing Hussein with Hitler, and by calling for war crimes trials, Bush was committing the United States to a policy of unconditional surrender by Iraq. He was further implying that after the war the United States would take responsibility for Iraq and try to build there a secure state governed by men chosen by the people. But he did not want to do that. He wanted Iraq out of

Kuwait and her military capabilities destroyed, but he had no intention of marching to Baghdad and occupying all of Iraq. At no time did he call for authority, from either the U.N. or the Congress, to invade and overrun Iraq. But by insisting on the Hitler analogy, he invited people to believe that such was his policy.

Bush pushed ahead with plans for punishing Iraq on a World War II scale. On September 16, *The Washington Post* published an interview with Air Force Chief General Michael Dugan. He disclosed that the Joint Chiefs had decided to use "massive bombing" to defeat Iraq. He said that the Iraqi Air Force had "very limited capability," that the pilots were inferior, that the Iraqi army was "incompetent." He wanted to target Saddam Hussein and his family and personal guard as a way of ending the war quickly.

Although Dugan was dismissed for his indiscretions, what he said was true. Joint Chiefs Chairman General Colin Powell had told the President that if war came, the United States should fight all-out using overwhelming resources. From the field, Schwarzkopf was demanding a greater deployment and warning against a premature order to attack. So the military leaders wanted time, as they meanwhile planned how to use the overwhelming force to bring about the quickest possible victory at the lowest possible cost in American casualties. That was exactly what Bush wanted them to do.

In shaping his response, President Bush drew on his recollections of Munich 1938 and the 1972 Middle East war, and many other memories, but the one that haunted him, and the American people, was Vietnam. The legacy of Vietnam was a nation deeply resistant to sending American boys off to fight long, drawn-out wars in faraway places for murky causes. Bush was the chief inheritor of that legacy. He swore that if he went to war, it would not be at all like Vietnam. In place of hesitation, the gradual application of force, and target restraint, there would be all-out war, quick, massive, and decisive.

To carry out such an operation, General Schwarzkopf

needed more troops, especially the U.S. VII Corps stationed in Stuttgart, combat ready, built to fight the Red Army. On October 30, 1990, Bush ordered a major reinforcement of the Desert Shield force, more than doubling it, from 250,000 to 550,000. The reinforcements would come from the reserves, the National Guard, and most of the combat ready active duty forces in the United States and Germany. A large proportion of the Air Force and Navy, also built to fight the Soviet Union, became part of Desert Shield. It was a bigger commitment than the United States made to South Vietnam. It was not made for defensive purposes, but to drive Iraq out of Kuwait and to destroy Iraq's military capability.

Bush's reinforcement of Desert Shield, and its clear implication that there would be war, brought forth criticism from both the left and the right. Pat Buchanan, Jeane Kirkpatrick, and Edward Luttwak, all important conservative commentators on foreign policy, joined such liberals as Arthur Schlesinger, Jr., Ramsey Clark, Daniel Patrick Moynihan, and George McGovern in asking whether America's vital interests were at stake. The Bush administration answered yes, and produced new evidence in support. On the television talk shows the Sunday after Thanksgiving, Secretary Cheney suggested that Iraq was on the verge of developing a nuclear bomb.

If true, that made action imperative. But the time table was not clear; previous estimates had run from three to ten years before Iraq acquired a bomb. But Cheney was talking about weeks, at most months. Hussein with a bomb was unthinkable. This was one place where the Gulf crisis may be a precursor of the future: the mad dictator of a medium-sized country with nuclear bombs. It could be the most destabilizing element imaginable, and it appeared to be a possibility in any number of countries.

If the Bush administration exaggerated the imminent nuclear threat from Iraq to force action, the President was successful. In November, the United States got the Security Council to set a deadline for Iraq to withdraw from Kuwait and to accept other U.N. demands or face attack under a resolution that permitted "all appropriate measures." The deadline was January 15, 1991.

The military was leery of the rush to war. The generals and admirals had been in Vietnam as junior officers. Admiral William Crowe, former chairman of the Joint Chiefs, counseled sanctions, not war. He told the Senate Armed Services Committee, "It is curious that just as our patience in Western Europe has paid off and furnished us the most graphic example in our history of how sanctions is sometimes the better course in dealing with problems, a few armchair strategists are counseling a near-term attack on Iraq. It is worth remembering that in the 1950s and 1960s, individuals were similarly advising an attack on the USSR. Wouldn't that have been great?" Former Secretary of Defense and CIA Chief James Schlesinger told the Committee that sanctions were working.

The Bush Administration's answer was that sanctions would take a year to work, perhaps longer. Time was Bush's enemy. Leaving aside the nuclear threat, there were the unpublicized but also critical factors of holding the alliance together and maintaining 550,000-plus American troops in the desert indefinitely. Highly publicized and sometimes suspect stories about Iraqi outrages inside Kuwait added to the sense of urgency. So it was necessary to give an ultimatum to Hussein: Get out in 47 days or there will be war. Many observers, at the U.N. and elsewhere, thought the ultimatum would work, that Hussein would withdraw.

Bush and Hussein were under intense pressure to open negotiations, Bush from the opponents of war, Hussein from his fellow Arab leaders. Both presidents made gestures. After the Security Council ultimatum was issued, Bush offered to enter into direct negotiations. On December 1, Hussein accepted, but he insisted that the Israeli–PLO situation be on the agenda, a part of his attempt to link the Iraqi takeover of Kuwait with the Israeli-occupation of Arab territory. He also insisted that he was too busy to meet with Secretary Baker before

January 12, 1991. Bush replied that the conditions were unacceptable and no meeting took place.

In another effort to sway international opinion, Hussein announced on December 6 that all hostages held in Baghdad and Kuwait City would be freed within a week. This gained him nothing—his use of innocent civilians, many of them oil engineers working for the Iraqi government, as human shields evoked outrage around the world and cost him much. It exposed Baghdad to an air attack that Bush might not have ordered had the city held thousands of Westerners.

As the deadline approached, a fierce debate raged in the United States. It concerned timing. Opponents of war argued that the sanctions were working. CIA Director William Webster testified to the House Armed Services Committee that if sanctions continued, within three months the Iraqi air force would lose its ability to fly and within nine months Iraq's ground forces would lose their combat readiness. Secretary Cheney countered; he told the Senate Armed Services Committee that "there is no guarantee that sanctions will force Hussein out of Kuwait" and warned that if military action were delayed, the multinational coalition might falter.

While the debate within the United States went on, the French came up with a peace proposal: Iraq out of Kuwait, Israel out of the West Bank and Gaza. On January 6, 1991, Baker rejected the proposal because of the link with Israel, which the Bush administration insisted was a separate subject to be addressed only after an unconditional Iraqi withdrawal from Kuwait. Two days later, Bush asked Congress to adopt a resolution supporting the use of force against Iraq if Iraq did not comply with the January 15 deadline.

Bush did not ask for a declaration of war, but his request for a resolution supporting the use of force was the functional equivalent. Congress conducted an intense debate with strong arguments being made for continuing sanctions and for striking immediately. The final vote, on January 12, was close. Fifty-two Senators, mainly Republicans, voted for war, forty-seven opposed. In the

House, where the division was also mainly along partisan lines, 250 voted for, 183 against. This was a triumph for Bush.

The president had been careful and impressive in pushing his policy. He had lined up an international coalition for taking the offensive; he had held the Arab states together; he had consulted with Congress in advance; he had built up a tremendous striking force in the desert; he left the conduct of the war to the military. He had, in short, avoided the mistake Truman had made in Korea (failure to consult with Congress before acting) and the mistakes Johnson had made in Vietnam (failure to line up international support, failure to launch the war with overwhelming force, failure to let the generals fight the war).

In the process, however, Bush made mistakes of his own. The chief was the failure to set a clear policy. The U.N. resolution authorized force to drive Iraq out of Kuwait and required Iraq to submit to U.N. inspection teams to insure that Hussein's weapons of mass destruction were destroyed and to pay reparations for the rape of Kuwait. Those policies were clear enough, but Bush had continued to equate Hussein with Hitler and to insist that there would be war crimes trials, which implied a policy of unconditional surrender and the creation of a new government in Iraq. That was an open-ended goal.

On January 17, 1991, an air attack on Iraq and Kuwait by multinational forces, code-named Operation Desert Storm, began. It was massive. Fighter bombers, using so-called "smart" bombs, struck at the presidential palace, the airport, oil refineries, nuclear research reactors, and electrical plants in Baghdad, while B-52s dropped huge numbers of conventional bombs on Hussein's Republican Guard troops in their trenches along the Kuwait–Saudi border, and the U.S. Navy fired more than 100 sea-launched Tomahawk cruise missiles at targets in Iraq.*

---

*It turned out that the "smart" bombs were not as accurate

The next day, Hussein answered. Using surface-to-surface Scud missiles armed with conventional warheads, he bombarded targets in Israel and sent one Scud against the U.S. air base in Dhahran, Saudi Arabia. The missile was destroyed in the air by a U.S. Patriot missile, the first destruction in combat of a ballistic missile. Bush rushed Patriot missiles to Israel to defend against Scuds; Israel did not retaliate against Iraq; Israeli restraint helped the coalition hold. One reason was that the Scud was a purely terrorist weapon, and not a very good one at that. It was inaccurate, slow-flying, and carried only a small amount of explosives. It could do no military damage.

In the following six weeks, the coalition air forces destroyed or incapacitated the Iraqi air force. Iraq defense was woefully ineffective. Flying almost without opposition, the coalition forces destroyed much of Baghdad and rendered the Iraqi army helpless. It was exactly what Bush had said it was going to be, quick, massive, and decisive.

Still Hussein would not give up. He continued to fire off Scud missiles, he continued to predict heavy American casualties in the mother of battles, and he spilled oil from five tankers in Kuwait into the Persian Gulf, creating an oil slick that was 35 miles long and 10 miles wide, containing an estimated 450 million gallons of oil, the largest oil slick in history. But the same day, January 26, 1991, some 80 Iraqi Soviet-built warplanes, most of what was left of the Iraqi air force, flew to Iran, where the pilots were interned and the planes impounded. Hussein's troops in Kuwait had taken heavy casualties; the troops who survived were shell-shocked; the Iraqi army had no way to get reinforcements or supplies to the front lines, no way to communicate, no way to carry out even the smallest reconnaissance mission.

As Hussein's position became more desperate, Bush's

---

as Pentagon publicists said they were. Many of the U.S. military claims were later shown to be exaggerations. As Churchill once said, "Truth is the first casualty of war."

improved. In early February his Administration announced that this tremendous display of America's military might was not going to cost the taxpayers anything.
Saudi Arabia ($16.8 billion), Kuwait ($16 billion), Japan
($10.7 billion), and Germany ($6.6 billion) had pledged
to pay the bill. Nor was the air war over Iraq expensive
in American lives. The anticipated ground battle, however, caused great apprehension, although not to General Schwarzkopf, who knew that he had blinded and
blunted the Iraqi army and could easily outflank the
remaining Iraqi troops in the trenches.

With no air force, a battered and helpless army, and
the failure of the Scud attacks on Israel to rally other
Arab states to his side or to do any serious damage to
the American military machine in the desert, Hussein
offered a compromise solution. On February 15 he announced his willingness to withdraw from Kuwait, but
only on condition that the U.N. withdraw the 12 resolutions on Iraq passed in 1990; these included reparations and U.N. inspection teams in Iraq to insure the
destruction of weapons of mass destruction.

Bush had won his initial objective—Iraq agreed to get
out of Kuwait. But since the crisis began Bush had added
other goals. He denounced the Iraqi peace proposal as
"a cruel hoax, full of unacceptable old conditions and
several new conditions." Hussein then sent his Foreign
Minister, Tariq Aziz, to Moscow to attempt to involve
Gorbachev in the negotiations. Gorbachev, who was in
a desperate situation himself, had been supportive of the
Americans from the start; in return for that support he
had gotten from Bush loans and credits, food, and a
hands-off reaction by the United States toward the pressing problem of the succession of the Baltic States from
the Soviet Union. Now he turned peacemaker. On February 22, 1991, after his meeting with Aziz, Gorbachev
announced that Iraq had accepted Moscow's peace plan.
It called for a phased withdrawal from Kuwait, to be
completed in three weeks, and the recision of the 12
U.N. resolutions on Iraq.

Bush replied that the plan was unacceptable and

warned Hussein to get out of Kuwait by February 23. When he did not, Schwarzkopf launched the ground attack the next day. It was immensely and quickly successful. The mother of all battles never took place; the coalition forces, led by American armed units, Marines and paratroopers, outflanked and destroyed the Iraqi army in 100 hours. Iraqi casualties were in the tens of thousands; coalition casualties were in the dozens.

On February 25, Hussein announced that he had given the order to withdraw from Kuwait. Bush responded by saying that the coalition would "continue to prosecute the war with undiminished intensity" because Iraq still had not accepted the additional UN resolutions. The next day, the retreating Iraqi troops set fire to Kuwait's oil wells. On February 27, Bush declared that "Iraq's army is defeated and Kuwait is liberated." He announced that the coalition would cease hostilities immediately.

That decision came as a shock. With the road to Baghdad open, the expectation was that United States and other coalition troops would occupy the city, take Hussein prisoner, put him on trial and establish a new government. But Bush never intended to assume such responsibilities and risks. American casualties in the 100-hour war had been 79 killed, 213 wounded. American casualties in street fighting in Baghdad could be expected to be much higher and might take weeks, even months, to complete. Bush's astonishing popularity rating (90 percent, the highest ever for any president) would not have survived a protracted war. No U.N. resolution authorized the occupation of Iraq. The Arab partners in the coalition would not have supported a move on Baghdad. In any case, Bush and virtually everyone else anticipated that either the humiliated Iraqi army leaders would overthrow Hussein or that the people would revolt against him. Indeed, Bush encouraged the Iraqi people to do just that.

But the army did not act. Although Iraq accepted all the U.N. resolutions, Hussein found various ways of avoiding their genuine implementation, especially with regard to his nuclear weapon research. Meanwhile, the

Kurds in the north and the Shi'a Muslims in the south revolted. The Kurds wanted a homeland of their own (which would have included parts of Iran, Turkey, and the Soviet Union), while the Shi'a wanted to join with Iran. These prospects were unwelcome to those involved, who feared an independent Kurdistan, a strengthened Iran, and a vacuum in Iraq.

Hussein put down the Kurd and Shi'a revolt with brutal and bloody efficiency. The American-led coalition, which had sprung to the defense of Kuwait, watched as Iraqi helicopter gunships and artillery devastated the rebels. The U.N. embargo against the sale of Iraqi oil continued, as did other economic sanctions, and the United States helped European nations establish refugee camps for the Kurds (nearly 2 million of them were made homeless), but there was no military response.

Within a year of Desert Storm, Baghdad had managed to repair much of the destruction, the rebels were crushed, Iraq was intact, Hussein was apparently more firmly in control than before the war. He was able to frustrate the U.N. inspection teams and even, in his own words in July 1992, "thumb his nose" at President Bush. Middle East peace talks, meanwhile, were as always stalled by Arab and Israeli intransigence.

These developments put the on-going Gulf crisis in a different perspective. In February 1991, the American people had exulted in the triumph of American arms in the desert. There was a feeling of pride and unity in the country not experienced since 1945. Bush had proclaimed, "The specter of Vietnam has been buried forever in the desert sands of the Arabian peninsula," and had declared in private, "By God, we've kicked the Vietnam syndrome once and for all." He had spoken of "a reestablished credibility for the U.S." and had proclaimed a new world order based on the principle of unalterable opposition to aggression.

But over the next year the United States stood supinely aside as Iraq committed acts of aggression against the Kurds and Shi'a and as Serbia committed acts of aggression against Croatia and Bosnia, which made it appear that the United States would act quickly, massively, and decisively to counter aggression when it was directed against an oil-rich state, but not otherwise.

Bush's critics, who had been silenced by the success of Desert Storm, began to speak out. Among the more eloquent were Robert Tucker and David Hendaickson, who wrote that the nation was in the grip of a pathology.

> The essence of that pathology consists of the attitude now taken toward the use of force. We have fastened upon a formula for going to war—in which American casualties are minimized and protracted engagements are avoided—that requires the massive use of American firepower and a speedy withdrawal from the scenes of destruction. . . . Its peculiar vice is that it enables us to go to war with far greater precipitancy than we otherwise might while simultaneously allowing us to walk away from the ruin we create without feeling a commensurate sense of responsibility. It creates an anarchy and calls it peace. In the name of order, it wreaks havoc. It allows us to assume an imperial role without discharging the classic duties of imperial rule. . . . The Panamanian intervention in 1989, though on a much smaller scale, revealed many of the same characteristics.

So the debate over the role of America in a post-Cold War world was not ended by the success of Desert Storm. Would the nation be the world's policeman? If so, how selective would the United States be in implementing a doctrine of no reward for aggression? In putting Vietnam behind it, did the United States embrace the imperial temptation to intervene whenever it saw fit, never otherwise? These questions were begging to be answered in the 1992 Presidential election, but Democratic nominee Bill Clinton hardly brought them up in a campaign that stressed the domestic economy. At the end of 1992, following Clinton's victory in the election, the nation was still groping for a policy to guide its foreign relations in the post-Soviet Union, post–Cold War era.

18

Clinton and Democratic Enlargement

We have put our economic competitiveness at the heart
of our foreign policy.
    BILL CLINTON, 1994 BUDGET MESSAGE TO CONGRESS

Campaigning for the presidency in 1992 as a self-styled
"New Democrat," forty-six-year-old Bill Clinton, a five-
time governor of Arkansas, had articulated three foreign policy initiatives that would confront the next
Commander in Chief: modernizing and restructuring
American military and security capabilities; elevating the
role of economics in international affairs; and promoting democracy abroad. Clinton was running at a time
when America's bedrock values—the rule of law, democracy, and free market economies—appeared to be in
ascendancy worldwide. The image was of newly en-
franchised global citizens bustling about drafting legal
codes, casting votes, and buying stock. The reality was
not quite so rosy. The collapse of the Soviet empire had
left a vacuum equally amenable to being filled by ethnic
animosities and regional conflicts. An even greater
menace was the increased threat of "loose nukes" falling
into the hands of rogue states or black marketeers. So
the Clinton imperatives would play themselves out in an
environment where the end of the Cold War had re-
solved certain international problems but had unleashed others that had not been anticipated, the
knottiest being the precise role the United States should
play as the world's only remaining superpower.
    Clinton possessed no post–Cold War grand design to
unveil while on the campaign trail but, when pressed,
stated his position on several controversial foreign pol-

icy issues, such as the war in Bosnia (pro-air strikes) and China (emphasize human rights). At the same time, Clinton constantly rebuked his main opponent, President George Bush, whom he tagged "the recession President," for paying too much attention to global affairs at the expense of domestic renewal. And he criticized twelve years of Republican supply-side economics, which had resulted in a federal deficit of $290 billion by 1992, the highest in U.S. history. If the Cold War was dominated by foreign policy, Clinton vowed, the post–Cold War period would be dominated by domestic concerns. His campaign strategy emphasizing the domestic economy worked: In a three-way race Clinton was elected forty-second President with only 44 percent of the vote as against 37 percent for Bush and 19 percent for Texas billionaire Ross Perot. But as Clinton soon learned, defeating Bush and Perot was a cakewalk compared to coping with the many international problems that greeted him on Inauguration Day.

Clinton entered the White House with U.S. troops deployed all over the world: In January 1993, Bush had ordered U.S. Marines into Somalia; the U.S. Navy and Coast Guard had begun a quarantine of Haiti; and the U.S. Air Force, which had recently bombed Iraqi radar stations, was preparing for an airlift in Bosnia. Besides these military operations, Clinton faced an array of urgent foreign policy challenges: Russian democracy was in economic crisis; the Bosnian war was at its most brutal and was threatening to spread; North Korea was developing nuclear weapons; the Middle East peace process was at an impasse; thousands of Haitian refugees were fleeing to U.S. shores; and the survival of the North American Free Trade Agreement (NAFTA) was in serious doubt. Clinton, slow out of the gate in confronting these ongoing problems, chaffed at being diverted by them. Three months into his presidency he explicitly complained that "foreign policy is not what I came here to do."

Clinton evidently meant what he said, at least until he became better acquainted with the job description that went along with being President of the United States. Focused on budget issues and health care reform, he made only four foreign policy speeches in his first eight months in office, all stressing continuity with his predecessor's policies. In February 1993 at American University he promoted regional trade pacts; at an April talk to the American Society of Newspaper Editors just days before his summit in Vancouver with Russian President Boris Yeltsin, Clinton offered a modest aid package to Moscow. The following month his appearance aboard the U.S.S. *Theodore Roosevelt* to discuss modernizing the Navy was sidetracked by the media's focus on his proposal to allow gays in the military, and his May 29 commencement address at West Point was chock-full of flag-waving sprinkled with a few generalities about global responsibility and the danger of weapons proliferation. These speeches also made clear that Clinton, a proponent of multilateralism, would always prefer to engage in global police action when the U.N. or NATO was resolutely at America's side. One security issue, however, was too urgent to ignore: The nuclear arsenal of the former Soviet Union had been distributed among four new countries (Russia, Ukraine, Kazakhstan, and Belarus) with few safeguards.

If Clinton deserved credit for any single foreign policy initiative in his first term, it would be for the Administration's efforts to dismantle nuclear weapons stockpiles with the former Soviet Union, a process begun during the Bush administration. Clinton's foreign policy team— led by Secretary of State Warren Christopher, National Security Advisor Anthony Lake, and Secretary of Defense Les Aspin (and his successor, William Perry)—regarded the dismantling program as urgent, because control of the Soviet arsenal of tactical weapons was now scattered among scores of local military commanders rather than centralized in Moscow, as it had been during the Cold War. The Administration's effort culminated in the U.S.-Russian-Ukraine Trilateral Statement and Annex, signed by the presidents of all three countries in Moscow on January 14, 1994, which led to the dismantling of all nuclear weapons in Ukraine. A psychological milestone was reached that same month, when President Clinton signed a landmark agreement with Boris Yeltsin to detarget U.S. and Russian strategic missiles. For the first time since the early 1950s no Russian missiles would be aimed at targets on U.S. soil. (Of course, the missiles still existed and could be retargeted in a matter of minutes.) Using nuclear disarmament, democracy building, and a joint belief in open markets as their common ground, Clinton and Yeltsin began to forge a fruitful relationship based on cautious trust.

News of apparent nuclear dismantling made some analysts edgy. What did it mean to "dismantle" nuclear weapons? Were they destroyed? Could they fall into the hands of rogue nations such as North Korea, Libya, or Iraq? The response by Clinton administration officials to such concerns was to point to an increase in the funding of the International Atomic Energy Commission, a watchdog agency that monitors the development, trafficking, and proliferation of nuclear weapons and materials throughout the world. The U.S. Customs Service and the FBI were also ordered to make the prevention of illicit trafficking of nuclear materials a top priority.

To deal with nuclear proliferation in other areas of the world the Administration relied on some public scolding and mild arm-twisting. In 1993, for instance, the United States protested China's export of ballistic missile parts to Pakistan by blocking the shipment to Beijing of three American-made communications satellites the Chinese planned to launch on their own rockets. China was again chastised in 1994, along with Pakistan, for selling missiles to Libya, as was one of the newly formed Russian republics for selling arms to Iran.

Because nuclear devices as small as a softball could be manufactured without much difficulty, nuclear security and keeping plutonium and uranium out of the hands of potential terrorists also became priorities of the Clinton administration. For example, Operation Sapphire involved airlifting nearly 600 kilograms of highly enriched uranium from Kazakhstan for safe disposal in Oak Ridge, Tennessee. Other global initiatives targeted

improved security at civilian nuclear reactors and prudent management of nuclear wastes. Clinton also made
it clear that unaccounted for nuclear weapons, whether
in the Balkans, the Middle East, or Asia, would be con-
fiscated, shipped to America, and blended down into
low-enriched uranium for use as fuel in commercial nuclear reactors.

The Clinton-Yeltsin nuclear dismantlement effort was
a genuine success. In 1990 Russia and the United States
each had more than 20,000 strategically deployed warheads. By carrying out the revolutionary START I and II
treaties orchestrated by Bush's Secretary of State, James
Baker, the Clinton administration had reduced the total
to about 7,000 by the end of 1996, on the way to an
eventual goal for each country to keep 3,000 warheads,
a significant reduction in nuclear risk but nevertheless
enough nuclear firepower to incinerate hundreds of
millions. By January 1997 Ukraine and Kazakhstan were
nuclear-free zones, and Belarus was on the path to
achieving nuclear disarmament. And no one could
doubt that the Cold War was over when Yeltsin ordered
the last vestiges of Russian troops to evacuate the Baltic
States and Germany.

From the outset of his presidency it was obvious that
U.S. economic interests would be central to Clinton's
foreign policy. Clinton saw his primary goal as President
to make the world safe for U.S. business and its global
system of capital accumulation. Only one other aspect
of foreign policy, besides Russian aid and nuclear reduction, seemed to engage Clinton: global trade policy.
He spoke repeatedly of the need for global integration
and technology sharing, and in July 1993 he spent a
fruitful week in Asia cementing security and trade pacts
with Japan and South Korea. Only six months into his
Administration economic acronyms such as G7, NAFTA,
APEC, and GATT were sprinkled throughout Clinton's
foreign policy pronouncements. As Clinton saw it, the
United States was "like a big corporation competing in
the global marketplace." Many international affairs experts, however, criticized him for confusing a sound

trade policy with a coherent foreign policy. "A foreign economic policy is not a foreign policy, and it is not a national security strategy," cautioned Council on Foreign Relations president Leslie Gelb.

By the late summer of 1993, the criticism of Clinton's foreign policy had mushroomed. House Republicans, conservative Democrats such as Senator Robert Byrd (D-WV), and highly regarded foreign affairs journalists such as the *Washington Post*'s Stephen Rosenfeld and Jim Hoagland all blasted the Clinton administration for over-reliance on the U.N. in Somalia, timidity in Haiti, and fickleness in Bosnia. The general sentiment in Washington was that the President was ill-equipped to serve as Commander in Chief. No one disagreed with Secretary of State Warren Christopher that "foreign policy is always a work in progress," but it seemed to many that Clinton was afflicted by indifference as well as indecision. Republican stalwarts Henry Kissinger and Jeane Kirkpatrick, among others, charged that the President, a foreign policy novice by any standard, had to resort to Band-Aid diplomacy in the absence of a grand design: improvising tactics at each flash point, proposing half remedies that would exacerbate admittedly intractable situations, and treating inaction as tantamount to action—all to protect Clinton's popularity at home. Brent Scowcroft, NSC advisor during the Bush administration, saw the Clinton administration as running "a peripatetic foreign policy at prey to the whims of the latest balance of forces."

For the most part, the critics were right about U.S. foreign policy during Clinton's first year in office: It involved putting out fires, not developing a strategy. But developing a coherent strategy was a tall order in the immediate post–Cold War world. The end of the Cold War meant the loss of a single enemy, the Soviet Union, around which to rally a national and international consensus. Truman himself had no preordained blueprint when he arrived at Potsdam in July 1945; the strategy of containment was nearly two years in the making. An amorphous foreign policy also meshed with Clinton's style of governance. It allowed him the freedom to ma-

neuver as the day's headlines dictated, to be a proponent of Metternich one week and Eleanor Roosevelt the
next. Even though this type of reactive diplomacy was
unsurprising from a politician famous for avoiding being painted into corners, Clinton began to realize that it
would take a larger vision to boost him into the ranks of
presidential greats. America was now the world's only superpower, and that reality demanded that global leadership emanate from the Oval Office. Great foreign policy,
Clinton grew to understand, was not reactive; it created
opportunities.

Unfortunately for Clinton, just as he was gaining
deeper insights into foreign policy his Administration
was sandbagged by a confused Somalia policy he had
inherited from the Bush administration. A reluctant
Clinton proved unwilling to extract those 25,000 U.S.
troops—sent to ensure that emergency food aid was
properly distributed from the drought-ridden African
nation—before disaster struck.

When Clinton took office, the United States was engaged in a humanitarian mission in Somalia, where
350,000 people had recently died of famine and two
million more were threatened with imminent starvation.
Somalian leader Mohammed Farah Aidid had requested
international assistance in ending the famine in his im-
poverished country, and a U.S.-led operation, Restore
Hope, authorized by President Bush, had begun in December 1992. In actuality, Somalia had no functional
government. Rather, this crippled nation served primarily as an anarchistic battleground for rival warlords who
now found it even more profitable to engage in systematic looting and theft of donated humanitarian provisions air-dropped to combat the mass starvation. On the
surface, the operation seemed to be going well, until
events on October 3, 1993, exposed a different reality.
In a botched raid on Mogadishu, eighteen U.S. Army
Rangers were killed by a well-armed clan, and the naked
corpse of a U.S. helicopter pilot being dragged through
the streets was flashed across the world's TV screens.
Five months later, Clinton withdrew all U.S. troops from

Somalia. The tactical responsibility for the debacle largely belonged to the Pentagon, which had ordered vulnerable Black Hawk helicopters to fly over a hostile urban area without either adequate air cover or armored forces on hand to mount a rescue. The strategic failures had to be shared by the Bush and Clinton administrations, as well as the U.N., which had permitted a humanitarian mission to escalate into a counterinsurgency campaign against local militia forces.

The next crisis came closer to home. Haiti's first democratically elected president, Jean-Bertrand Aristide, was ousted in a 1991 military coup, leading to considerable unrest in the country. Two hundred lightly armed U.S. and Canadian peacekeepers were dispatched to Haiti's capital, Port-au-Prince, on the U.S.S. *Harlan County* in October 1993, only to turn back when the ship was met by an angry mob of Haitians waving machetes and yelling, "We are going to make this another Somalia!" Clinton looked weak and indecisive.

The military embarrassments of Somalia and Haiti occurred on the watch of Defense Secretary Les Aspin, a former chairman of the House Armed Services Committee. Aspin had been appointed to the Pentagon not only to manage an orderly reduction in the defense budget but also for his perceived ability to smooth over political tensions as a Capitol Hill veteran. Failing in the latter and in the face of Republican attacks, Aspin resigned; he was replaced by veteran military affairs analyst William Perry. Sharing the blame, Secretary of State Warren Christopher also tendered his resignation, which Clinton, after days of consideration, declined. Instead, Clinton deflected the blame to the confusion engendered by George Bush's multinational "New World Order" approach to the post–Cold War world.

The Administration's very public foreign policy failures unfolded against a backdrop of scandal, right-wing rumormongering, and ordinary partisan attacks, not to mention serious, principled criticism by foreign policy analysts. It was in this chaotic climate that the President sought out his pragmatic, unassuming National Security

Advisor, Anthony Lake, to identify a single "compass" word or concept that would embrace the three foreign policy themes Clinton had articulated on the campaign trail. If "containment" had come to embody the United States Cold War strategy of countering global threats to democracy and open markets, Clinton wanted an equivalent phrase and concept to embody his policy of expanding the community of market democracies.

Lake organized a task force to tackle the assignment. "Democratic engagement" and "democratic expansionism" were the early favorites, until Jeremy Rosner, a speechwriter at the NSC, came up with "enlargement." The word had struck Rosner as a perfect description of the fluid sort of democracy the end of the Cold War had ushered in. After test-marketing it on several colleagues, Rosner brought his suggestion to Lake, who liked it enough to encourage its use in speeches. To Rosner's delight, "enlargement" was pronounced the winner, the most concise term for representing the administration's post–Cold War foreign policy strategy.

Almost immediately Clinton adopted "enlargement" to convey the notion that as free states gained in number and strength, the international order would grow both more prosperous and more secure. In Lake's words, the successor to the strategy of containment would be an enlargement "of the world's free community of market democracies." Lake and Rosner's blueprint focused on four points: (1) "strengthen the community of market democracies"; (2) "foster and consolidate new democracies and market economies where possible"; (3) "counter the aggression and support the liberalization of states hostile to democracy"; and (4) "help democracy and market economies take root in regions of greatest humanitarian concern." The enlargement strategy explicitly rejected the idealist foreign policy view that the United States was duty-bound to promote constitutional democracy and human rights everywhere. For Clinton, a politically viable foreign policy had to be centered upon protecting primary U.S. strategic and economic interests. If, for example,

China's political regime emphasized social order over individual rights, under enlargement America's chief goal then would be to establish a free-market economy and to assume that the rule of law and economic freedom, required for capitalism to flourish, would eventually work their way into China's political system.

Clinton saw enlargement as a corollary of the domino theory: It predicted that once major Communist economies collapsed, it was only a matter of time for the others to fall. Free markets would eventually arise and flourish the world over. As Martin Walker wrote in *The New Yorker,* "Now the age of geopolitics has given way to an age of what might be called geo-economics. The new virility symbols are exports and productivity and growth rates and the great international encounters are the trade pacts of the economic superpowers." Or, as Clinton put it in his 1994 budget message to Congress, "We have put our economic competitiveness at the heart of our foreign policy."

As for the emerging democracies, Clinton believed that if they developed consumption-oriented middle classes with an appetite for American products, world peace and prosperity could become a reality. Therefore, countries with bright economic futures such as Poland, Brazil, Russia, Mexico, and South Korea would be put on the front burner in his Administration; poor, blighted nations, particularly in sub–Saharan Africa and Central America, would be subject to benign neglect. Only if domestic or international public opinion clamored for humanitarian aid would the Administration pay serious attention to such nations. By the same token, the United States would no longer concern itself with the bloody, unprofitable civil and religious wars that raged from Angola through the Caucasus to Kashmir.

For the Clinton administration, economic policy was not only the key to domestic renewal but also the key to global leverage. Under the tutelage of his Secretary of Treasury Robert E. Rubin, Clinton created the National Economic Council, which was to coordinate domestic and foreign economic policies. Commerce Secretary

Ron Brown began traveling the world with Fortune 500 CEOs to promote the need for open markets and open doors for American business; he died in a plane crash on one such mission to Bosnia. U.S. Trade Representative Mickey Kantor noted the new foreign-policy emphasis: "Trade and international economics have joined the foreign policy table. Clinton is the first President to really make the trade bridge between foreign and domestic policy." Never before had increasing exports been viewed as a primary national security problem. "Information, ideas, and money now pulse across the planet at light speed," Lake observed. "This borderless global economy has generated an entrepreneurial boom and a demand for political openness." When asked about the Administration's obsession with economic globalization, Secretary of State Christopher matter-of-factly replied: "I make no apologies for putting economics at the top of our foreign policy agenda." Enlargement encompassed Clinton's worldview that domestic growth was dependent on a foreign policy promoting U.S. exports and global free trade. "For his Administration," political scientist Henry Nau would write in *Trade and Security* (1995), "trade policy is not only the key to U.S. competitiveness and national economic security in a post–Cold War world but also the cutting edge of domestic economic reforms that create high-wage jobs and accelerate changes in technology, education, and public infrastructure."

In July 1994 Clinton attempted to weave his foreign policy themes of enlargement into the so-called En-En document: the *National Security Strategy of Engagement and Enlargement.* At the center of the policy paper is the belief that "the line between our domestic and foreign policies has increasingly disappeared—that we must revitalize our economy if we are able to sustain our military forces, foreign initiatives, and global influence, and that we must engage actively abroad if we are to open foreign markets and create jobs for our people." By the time two subsequent En-En policy papers were released from the White House, in February 1995 and February 1996, domestic renewal had become the linchpin of

U.S. foreign policy. And nowhere was the En-En strategy more relevant than in Russia.

Although Russia remained a nuclear power, U.S. concern shifted from Moscow's military strength to its economic weakness. The irony did not go unnoticed. "The old rules have been turned upside down," analyst Ronald Steel noted in *Temptations of a Superpower* (1995). "Instead of 'containing' the Russians, we now subsidize them." Political concerns over the U.S. budget deficit and a half-century war of words with the Soviets had left Clinton unwilling or unable to explicitly propose a Marshall Plan for Russia. However, his Administration came up with $4.5 billion in bilateral assistance to Yeltsin's government from 1993 to 1996. This aid helped facilitate economic reform in Russia by curbing inflation and stabilizing the ruble. As a result, by 1996 more than 60 percent of Russia's gross domestic product was generated by its private sector. In fact, the Clinton administration's assistance helped Russia privatize more property in less time than any other foreign development venture in history: By September 1996 more than 120,000 Russian enterprises had been transferred to private hands, with foreign trade up 65 percent since 1993. Meanwhile, the United States became Russia's largest foreign investor, with the Export-Import Bank of the United States, the Overseas Private Investment Corporation, and the Trade and Development Agency supporting commercial transactions with Moscow valued at more than $4 billion.

This expansion of the global free market, coupled with Russia's 1995 parliamentary elections and 1996 presidential contest, indicated that democracy had begun to take root there. Clinton used a visit to Russia to reiterate his view that the two were linked: "The political and security partnership between our nations is strengthened by our growing commercial ties. We've worked hard to take down the old barriers to trade and investment." With U.S.-Russian relations normalized for the first time since World War I, the Clinton administration was eager to expedite the export of U.S. goods to Rus-

sia's 150 million consumers. And although Russia had a
long way to go before it caught up with Western European nations, Yeltsin's government had ushered in representative democracy and free-market capitalism by
peaceful revolution—albeit primitive examples of both.

A foreign-policy initiative Clinton linked even more
closely to domestic renwal was the North American Free
Trade Agreement. Recognizing that the U.S. economy
did not stand on its own but was the hub of an ever-
evolving global economy, Clinton managed to forge a bipartisan Congressional coalition to pass NAFTA during
his first year in office, despite intense opposition from
many Democrats. The trade agreement, which allowed
businesses in the United States to form production part-
nerships with Mexico and Canada, was vehemently opposed by many, especially Ross Perot, the AFL-CIO, and
consumer activist Ralph Nader, all of whom perceived
NAFTA as undermining the American labor base. Opponents predicted an increase in U.S. companies sending more work overseas, where wages were lower and
working rules less stringent. Not only would the United
States lose jobs, but tax dollars as well. In Perot's immor-
tal sound bite: "The sucking sound you hear is all the
jobs heading south of the border." Clinton argued the
contrary, insisting that NAFTA would not only save jobs
but also open new markets for U.S. products, by com-
bining 250 million Americans with 90 million Mexicans
and 27 million Canadians into a no-tariff trading bloc
with a combined GNP of some $7 trillion a year. Despite
the frontal assault on NAFTA at home, the House
passed NAFTA by a 234 to 200 vote on November 17,
1993. Clinton's enlargement strategy was taking root.

Following NAFTA's passage, Clinton signed the Uruguay Round Agreement Act of GATT into law in December 1994. The trade agreement lowered tariffs
worldwide by $744 billion over a ten-year period—the
largest international reduction in history. It also created
a new international trade regime called the World Trade
Organization. The Uruguay Round did not bring any
dramatic lowering of U.S. barriers to foreign trade, be-

cause America had been the world's most open market since World War II, but it did help further open foreign markets to U.S. goods, thereby helping to accelerate American exports.

What Clinton liked best about agreements such as NAFTA and GATT was their link to domestic renewal and their emphasis on ensuring that the United States remained the world's largest exporter. The mantra of the Clinton administration was that in the post–Cold War era good trade policy was the *sine qua non* of a sound foreign policy, as a world full of robust, market-based democracies would make the world a safer, richer place. If the Cold War enemy had been Communism, the post–Cold War villain was protectionism, a villain enlargement was designed to overcome.

Aside from risking the split of his own party to force NAFTA and GATT through Congress, Clinton's boldest execution of enlargement occurred in Asia. He convened fifteen heads of state from the Pacific region at an Asia-Pacific Economic Cooperative forum (APEC) in Seattle in 1993 to push for the creation of a giant free trade zone. A year later, at the second APEC summit in Indonesia, its fifteen members signed an accord pledging themselves to develop a free-trading Pacific Rim by 2010. Since 45 percent of the world's foreign currency reserves resided in Asia and 40 percent of all new purchasing power would emanate from the region by the year 2000, Clinton wanted to start ripping down trade barriers as a part of his long-range enlargement strategy.

When trade talks between Tokyo and Washington collapsed in February 1994, Clinton decided it was time to brandish a big stick. For the first time in the history of postwar U.S.-Japanese relations, an American President took a tough stance toward Japan. Privately, U.S. Trade Representative Mickey Kantor began to threaten Tokyo with trade sanctions for violating a 1989 agreement to open its market to American cellular phones. The President supported Kantor's threats publicly: "America for ten years tried thirty different trade agreements," Clinton said in a radio interview on February 17, 1994,

"[A]nd nothing ever happened. . . . [T]he trade deficit just got bigger and bigger. So we're going to try to pursue a much more aggressive policy now which will actually open markets." The threat worked, and some of Japan's markets began to slowly open. Spurred by this initial success, the Clinton administration renegotiated more than twenty individual market access agreements with Japan, resulting in an 85-percent increase in U.S. exports in sectors covered by the new trade pacts.

Clinton's tenure also wrought change in U.S. military agreements with Japan. In the face of a wave of anti-Americanism that rippled through Japan in the wake of the rape of a twelve-year-old girl by G.I.s stationed in Okinawa in 1995, the Clinton administration not only strengthened the U.S.-Japan security alliance but also forced Tokyo to bear 75 percent of the cost of keeping about 100,000 American troops stationed in the Asia Pacific. The new relationship was not one-sided, for the United States upheld some unusual security arrangements with Japan: According to the Japan-American Security Treaty, the United States continued to obligate itself to send troops to defend the Senkakus—eight tiny islets lying between Taiwan and Okinawa—should China, which claims them, ever make a military move to seize them. Concerned about the over-emphasis on economic policy in Asia, Assistant Secretary of Defense Joseph Nye issued an official report known as the *United States Security Strategy for the East Asia-Pacific Region* in February 1995, which recommended that U.S. forces in the Asia-Pacific region not be reduced beyond 100,000 and that bilateral ties in the region be strengthened to create a climate of safety.

The Clinton administration was not without diplomatic successes in other areas of the Asia Pacific. In February 1994 Clinton lifted the U.S. trade embargo on Vietnam, liaison offices were opened in January 1995, and the normalization of diplomatic relations followed six months later. This long-overdue normalization of relations with Vietnam—a decision harshly criticized by the Vietnam Veterans of America organization—not only led to the fullest possible accounting of U.S. POWs and MIAs but also increased U.S. exports to Vietnam to $253 million in 1995, up 47 percent over 1994. With economic help from Washington, both Vietnam and Cambodia were on the path to joining their neighbors South Korea, Thailand, the Philippines, Taiwan, and Indonesia as nations with free-market economies.

Against these encouraging signs in the Pacific weighed the intransigence of China, the one Asian country the Clinton administration proved incapable of dealing with effectively. Despite China's receiving most-favored-nation trading status, U.S.-Chinese relations were constantly unsettled. Even though 40 percent of Chinese exports were sold in the United States, creating a $30 billion annual trade surplus, Beijing seemed unfazed by Washington's demands that China dismantle trade barriers, improve human rights, and stop selling missile and nuclear technology to unstable governments. Secretary of State Warren Christopher tried to raise the issue of human rights during his only trip to Beijing, but was scolded by hard-line Chinese premier Li Peng. In total disregard of world opinion, the Chinese government continued systematically to jail citizens whose only crime was speaking out in favor of democratic reform. Ignoring international pleas, in November 1996 Beijing sentenced Wang Den, a leader of the 1989 Tiananmen Square demonstrations, to eleven years in prison. Worse still, the Chinese secret police staged a "crackdown" in Tibet, arresting dissidents who dared to call for independence. Meanwhile, the Chinese politburo obdurately denied it had sold Pakistan ballistic missiles, in the face of CIA evidence that it had.

By the end of his first term, Clinton found himself in the untenable position of threatening trade sanctions against the Chinese for intellectual property piracy—such as bootlegging Hollywood movies or music CDs—while simultaneously promoting most-favored-nation trading status. In an attempt to bridge the widening gulf between Washington and Beijing, Anthony Lake journeyed to China in September 1996 to initiate a "new understanding" between the two great powers. Clinton himself headed to the Pacific Rim soon after, his first foreign trip following his November 1996 reelection. He met with Chinese president Jiang Zemin in Manila to discuss the recent freezing of North Korea's nuclear weapons development, expanding trade, and finding innovative ways to keep the "new understanding" on track. The meeting yielded no breakthroughs: "Only in the precarious relationship between the United States and China could a meeting that resolves no differences be termed a success by both sides," was a *New York Times* editorial conclusion about the November 1996 meeting.

While the Clinton administration muddled its way through the post–Cold War seas, the Republicans took over both houses of Congress in January 1995. Conservative and moderate Republicans, regardless of personal conviction, stuck to their partisan positions for most of the next two years and followed Speaker of the House Newt Gingrich (R-GA). The shell-shocked minority Democrats, by necessity, rallied around President Clinton. To counter GOP claims that Clinton's foreign policy record was a disaster, the Administration had been trying a new tack: the President as peacemaker. If President Theodore Roosevelt won a Nobel Peace Prize for ending the Russo-Japanese War, Clinton perhaps could do the same by making peace in Bosnia, Haiti, Northern Ireland, or the Middle East.

Washington had traditionally taken the lead in trying to achieve peace in the Middle East ever since hostilities first erupted in 1948. But when Palestinian leader Yasser Arafat and Israeli prime minister Yitzhak Rabin met in Oslo in December 1993 to iron out political differences, Clinton was on the sidelines. The outcome of Oslo, an Israel-Palestinian Declaration of Principles, stipulated the removal of some Israeli troops from Arab towns in the occupied West Bank and granted the Palestinian Authority self-rule by mid-1996. Although the two Middle East leaders signed the declaration at an elaborate White House ceremony on September 13, 1993, the President was more approving spectator than active participant. Compared to the hands-on role Jimmy Carter had played in the Camp David Accords, Clinton was, at best, a genial facilitator, as evidenced by photos of the famous Arafat-Rabin handshake for peace, which showed a smiling Clinton hovering behind the two leaders.

Clinton did try to help Jordan and Israel overcome their differences, clearing the way for the signing of a formal peace treaty in October 1994. He also opened a new dimension of the peace process by organizing economic summits with Middle East leaders at Casablanca, Amman, and Cairo—encouraging and important new steps toward normalizing relations between Israel and its Arab neighbors. Warren Christopher visited Damascus more than twenty times, hoping to forge a peace treaty between Syria and Israel but instead catching criticism in the press for his empty-handed efforts. Yet there were diplomatic successes, including securing a written agreement between Israel and Syria to end Hezbollah attacks on Israel and provide security to civilians on both sides of the Lebanon-Israel border. When Israeli prime minister Yitzhak Rabin was assassinated on November 4, 1995, Clinton himself led a U.S. delegation to Tel Aviv as an unambiguous show of American support, both for Israel and the peace process. "Those who practice terror must not succeed," Clinton announced on a visit to Israel a few months after Rabin's death. "We must root them out, and we will not let them kill the peace."

On the military front, Clinton remained vigilant in dealing with the Middle East's wild card, Saddam Hussein. In October 1994, the Administration dispatched a full reserve of U.S. planes, ships, and ground troops in response to renewed Iraqi military activity at the Kuwait border. Clinton deployed nearly 30,000 U.S. troops to the Gulf during this crisis in the name of preserving peace in the region. Clinton made it clear in his famous "dual containment" speech to the World Jewish Congress in April 1995 that he was not going to let either Teheran or Baghdad destabilize the Middle East: "[Iran and Iraq] harbor terrorists within their borders. They establish and support terrorist base camps in other lands.

They hunger for nuclear and other weapons of mass destruction. Every day, they put innocent civilians in danger and stir up discord among nations. Our policy toward them is simple: They must be contained."

In Northern Ireland, the Clinton administration played a new and vital role in advancing the peace process by insisting that Sinn Fein, the political arm of the Irish Republic Army (IRA), had a rightful place at the bargaining table to determine the future of Ulster. The U.S. State Department issued Sinn Fein leader Gerry Adams an American visa in 1994. The British immediately objected, insisting that Adams was a terrorist. Unmoved by British complaints, Clinton, with domestic political considerations in mind, invited Adams to the White House on St. Patrick's Day in 1995. The visit allowed Adams to travel and raise support in the United States for his cause. The President's initiative led directly to the IRA declaring a unilateral cease-fire in late 1995. Soon thereafter, Clinton visited Belfast and was accorded a euphoric public welcome when he promised U.S. support if the Irish antagonists renounced violence and participated in the peace process. "Only the United States could form a bridge to bring the isolated Republican [IRA] leaders into the mainstream," Irish journalist Conor O'Cleary wrote in *Daring Diplomacy: Clinton's Secret Search for Peace in Ireland.*

President Clinton sent former Senator George Mitchell as his personal representative to the negotiations, and a truce between the British government, the Ulster Defense Association, and the IRA was declared. That cease-fire was broken in April 1996 by renewed IRA bombings in London. Negotiations for a final political solution to the decades-old Northern Ireland dispute began anew in September 1996, with Mitchell again representing the United States. Despite the administration's good intentions, a permanent peace in Northern Ireland proved elusive.

Clinton had better luck in Haiti. After the public relations defeat the administration suffered in October 1993, increased pressure was put on Haiti's military rulers, led by the brutal General Raoul Cedras. Unable to persuade the military to restore the exiled Aristide to power, the U.S. government imposed economic sanctions. When sanctions failed to budge the junta's leaders, Clinton ordered a military invasion of the island in September 1994. The invasion was averted in last-minute negotiations. Clinton's representatives (former President Jimmy Carter, Senator Sam Nunn, and retired General Colin Powell) managed to convince Cedras of the merits of stepping down. If Carter was lionized for his "peace intervention," the Clinton administration was criticized for farming out its foreign policy. To some foreign affairs analysts it also seemed misguided for the United States to be getting mired in such a backwater nation as Haiti. But Clinton weathered the attacks and implemented a policy that proved effective.

Clinton deployed more than 20,000 U.S. troops to Haiti, part of a multinational force (MNF) made up of contingents from thirty nations, to rid the island nation of the military regime and restore the democratically elected Aristide to power. The MNF dismantled the brutal FAd'H (the army of the de facto regime) and F-RAPH (the right-wing paramilitary organization) quickly, making the streets of Port-au-Prince safe in a matter of months. The U.S. government also oversaw the establishment of a new national police academy and trained a new Haitian national police force. More impressive, the United States and the United Nations assisted the Haitian government in conducting three rounds of national elections, culminating in the internationally monitored free and fair election of President René Preval in December 1995, succeeding President Aristide. This was the first democratic transition of power from one president to another in Haiti's history. On March 31, 1995, the thirty-nation multinational force pulled out of Haiti, turning peacekeeping over to the U.N. In a transition ceremony in Port-au-Prince, Clinton could honestly boast that the "mission has been accomplished on schedule" and with "remarkable success."

Another milestone on Clinton's road to peace was a historic moment in arms reduction. On September 25,

1996, the President addressed the U.N. General Assembly and announced that he would sign the Comprehensive Test Ban Treaty (CTBT). Holding the same pen his boyhood hero, President John F. Kennedy, had used to sign a partial test ban treaty in 1963, he joined the leaders of fifty other nations in signing what he called "the longest sought, hardest fought prize in arms control history." If implemented, the CTBT would thwart the development of new generations of dangerous weapons, encourage further reductions in nuclear weapons stockpiles, and spare the environment the shock of further underground nuclear blasts.

It was a post–Cold War moment to savor. After having conducted more than 20,000 nuclear tests on flyspeck Pacific islands and in underground Mojave Desert bunkers, the U.S. government was leading the international effort to ban all nuclear explosions. "This week, in this place, we take a giant step forward," Clinton told the General Assembly as the foreign ministers of the other four acknowledged nuclear powers—Qian Qichen of China, Herve de Charette of France, Yevgeni Primakov of Russia, and Malcolm Rifkind of Great Britain—followed the American's lead and signed the highly publicized treaty. For antinuclear groups Clinton's giant step forward toward a nuclear-free world was cause for celebration: Church bells tolled, rallies were held, and prayers of thanks were uttered the world over. But like many other commendable Clinton administration diplomatic initiatives, once the confetti settled, the herculean task of implementation remained.

In this case the Administration foundered by failing to persuade India, which first began testing nuclear weapons in 1974, to stop. India's representative at the U.N., Prakash Shah, was adamant: Only if *all* existing nuclear weapons were abolished would his country adhere to the test ban, a proposition the United States, for obvious political and military reasons, could not possibly accept. Without India's signature, the treaty was a technical nullity, a semantically absurd Partial Comprehensive Test Ban Treaty that was, critics claimed, little more than a photo-op conveniently orchestrated six weeks before the U.S. presidential election. For the treaty to achieve its objective, Clinton would have to put great economic and political pressure on New Delhi, which was unlikely in an atmosphere in which the Indian government was embracing economic protectionism while it decided whether or not to align itself with the West.

But by far the most serious foreign policy problem Clinton inherited in 1992 was the Balkans. The former Yugoslavia had disintegrated into ethnic battle zones over which three warring factions lay claim: Serbs (Eastern Orthodox), Croatians (Catholic), and Bosnians (Muslim). Sarajevo, which had hosted the 1984 Winter Olympics, was now a killing field. During the Tito era, Yugoslavia had managed to submerge its ethnic and religious animosities, but once the hatred was unleashed, the world was shocked by reports of ethnic cleansing, genocidal acts by Serb troops on Bosnia's civilian population, and atrocities committed by Serbian forces against Bosnians held in detention camps.

Because the slaughter was extensively covered by television, the domestic political debate over what role Washington should play in ending the war threatened to become a foreign policy crisis for the Clinton administration. While Congressional Republicans strongly favored providing arms to the Bosnian Muslims so they could better defend themselves against the Serbs, Clinton steadfastly supported the ineffective multinational U.N. peacekeeping efforts. While the U.N. made some strides—the sustained artillery shelling of Sarajevo's civilian population was sporadically halted and a war crimes tribunal was established—the war continued.

A turning point in the Bosnian war occurred on February 5, 1994, when sixty-eight civilians in Sarajevo died in a mortar attack. This time the Clinton administration called on NATO to protect Bosnian Muslim "safe havens." By April NATO jets were hitting Serb ground targets at Gorazde. Then a Bosnian-Croatian peace agreement was signed, under U.S. prodding, ending the "war within a war" and suspending the second front. But a genuine and lasting ceasefire proved elusive despite the efforts of the U.N., the U.S., the European Union, and NATO. Clinton found himself buffeted between the need to maintain NATO and U.N. credibility, and an unwillingness to commit U.S. troops. In July 1995 the so-called Bosnian Muslim "safe havens" of Srebrenica and Zepa fell—thousands of Muslim civilians were killed. Washington's promise to protect the Bosnian Muslims, not to mention the credibility of NATO, was severely tarnished by the Serbian capture of these towns. Soon after the Croatians, with Bosnian army support, launched a lightning offensive against Bosnian Serbs. In August, NATO air strikes against Bosnian Serb air defenses began in earnest, following a Bosnian Serb attack on Sarajevo. This exertion of NATO military might brought the rivals to the negotiation table. On October 5, a Bosnian cease-fire was announced and hopes of a lasting peace swept the world.

Relying heavily on special envoy and Assistant Secretary of State Richard C. Holbrooke, Clinton immediately called for a peace summit to be held at Wright-Patterson Air Force Base in Dayton, Ohio, far from war-ravaged Bosnia. With Slobodan Milošević representing the Bosnian Serbs and Alija Izetbegović serving as the voice of both the Bosnian government and the Bosnian Croatians, Holbrooke, a tenacious mediator, brokered a peaceful settlement, believing that someday Dayton would become synonymous with Camp David as diplomatic shorthand for successful conflict resolution. The Dayton peace agreement had solved territorial differences and Constitutional questions, while forcing everybody involved to lay down their armaments.

The tenets of the agreement reached at Dayton on November 21 were officially memorialized in the Paris Peace Accord signed December 14 by the presidents of Bosnia, Serbia, and Croatia. That same month Clinton, in the face of staunch opposition, committed American troops to Bosnia as part of a NATO-led multinational force, in an effort to prevent further bloodshed and support the new Dayton peace agreement. Sending in

U.S. troops, Clinton told the nation in a televised address, would signal to other countries that America was not shirking its responsibilities as the world's most powerful nation. Clinton went forward with the deployment, and 20,000 U.S. troops joined 40,000 troops from other NATO and Partnership for Peace countries. The U.S. Congress never officially supported the President's decision to deploy U.S. troops, but it did not try to block it.

From the start the NATO Implementation Force (IFOR) did an exceptional job of maintaining the cease-fire, stopping the widespread killing of civilians, and restoring security to Sarajevo, where people could once again walk the streets in safety. "We stood for peace in Bosnia," Clinton noted in his January 23, 1996, State of the Union address. "Remember the skeletal prisoners, the mass graves, the campaign to rape and torture, the endless lines of refugees, the threat of a spreading war. All these threats, all these horrors have now begun to give way to a promise of peace." Only a few months after the deployment of troops, Clinton deemed the NATO Bosnia mission "a terrific success." Morton I. Abramowitz, president of the Carnegie Endowment for International Peace, jumped on Clinton for gloating: "It's wrong to say something is a success when there was massive ethnic cleansing and two million people [were] displaced." Both Clinton and Abramowitz were right: The slowness in Western response in Bosnia was shameful, but the cease-fire *had* taken hold. Six months after the deployment, with only a few casualties, the Dayton accords had, at least temporarily, brought to a halt the worst fighting in Europe since World War II.

To the surprise of many, NATO was proving to have a viable role in the post–Cold War world. After the Berlin Wall fell, many analysts assumed that with no Soviet threat NATO itself would disintegrate. After all, logic dictated that for a military alliance to exist, it had to have enemies. But the Bosnian NATO mission proved to be a model for cooperative deployments in the burgeoning catchall of "operations other than war." NATO's credibility was enhanced by its performance in Bosnia, and the transatlantic link was suddenly touted as more important than ever. Even France, which had withdrawn from NATO's military structure nearly three decades before, announced that its defense minister would once again join NATO's military committee. Many countries in Europe were anxious to huddle under NATO's security umbrella, even if the alliance had no clear-cut enemy.

With his top three State Department advisors—Richard Holbrooke, Strobe Talbot, and Warren Christopher— strongly behind it, Clinton viewed NATO enlargement as a means toward the larger objective of European integration. If Ronald Reagan was associated with ending the Cold War and George Bush with German reunification, Bill Clinton saw himself as having the potential for leaving a lasting legacy as the President who presided over a united Europe. At the Brussels NATO summit in January 1994, President Clinton first put forth his proposal to "enlarge" the transatlantic military alliance to include the new free-market democracies emerging in Central and Eastern Europe, particularly the Czech Republic, Hungary, and Poland. Encouraged by the United States's lead, the leaders of the NATO countries agreed in principle to a process of NATO enlargement that would, as Clinton put it, "reach to democratic states to our east as part of an evolutionary process."

Clinton also led the way toward creating the alliance's Partnership for Peace (PFP) in 1994, a commitment by NATO's members to an orderly process of enlargement that would admit new members while modernizing and strengthening the organization. "Partnership will serve one of the most important goals in our enlargement strategy," Lake noted, "building a stable environment in which the new democracies and free markets of Eastern and Central Europe and the former U.S.S.R. can flourish." In its early stages the Partnership for Peace proved successful: In Bosnia, for example, soldiers from more than a dozen "partner" states joined with U.S. and NATO troops, and Hungary actually became the largest staging ground for American troops serving in Bosnia. "PFP is not just 'defense by other means' but 'democracy by other means,'" wrote Secretary of Defense William Perry in the November–December 1996 issue of *Foreign Affairs,* "and it is helping turn George Marshall's dream of a democratic and unified Europe into a reality."

Clinton made an important speech on NATO enlargement on October 22, 1996, in Detroit. He called for admitting the first of the former Warsaw Pact nations in 1999, a year that would mark NATO's fiftieth anniversary as well as the tenth anniversary of the fall of the Berlin Wall. "If we fail to seize this historic opportunity to build a new NATO—if we allow the Iron Curtain to be replaced by a veil of influence—we will pay a higher price later," the President asserted. (Although Clinton did not identify the nations to be admitted, nor would he until July 1997, it was widely assumed that the first round would include Hungary, the Czech Republic, and Poland.) He went on to urge Russia to reconsider its opposition to NATO expansion on the grounds that it would "advance the security of everyone."

The Republicans tried to score some political points from the Detroit speech, delivered, as it was, in the midst of the 1996 presidential campaign. His opponent, Bob Dole, cited it as evidence of Clinton's "election-year conversion" to NATO enlargement. Questioning Clinton's bona fides, Dole charged that Clinton had "been dragging his feet since 1993," and during one of the nationwide campaign debates accused the President of pursuing a "photo-op foreign policy." For all Dole's criticism, there was no substantive difference over NATO enlargement between the two candidates, according to European analysts: "Republicans are trying to score points by saying Clinton's not moving fast enough, but from the European perspective, it's been the Americans pushing this idea from the start," noted Philip Gordon, a senior analyst with the International Institute for Strategic Studies in London. He pointed out that it was Clinton who had announced in January 1994 that it was not a question of *whether* NATO would enlarge, but of *when.* In the end, the lack of a sharp difference over NATO's future rendered it a nonissue in the 1996 campaign.

There may have been a general consensus in the United States and Europe for NATO enlargement, but, not surprisingly, Moscow fretted, arguing that since the military alliance was a hostile Cold War creation, the ultimate post–Cold War aim of an expanded NATO was to isolate Russia from the West. Although resigned to the fact that the first round of NATO enlargement would occur, Moscow became intent on making sure that there was no second round. It remained to be seen how fully Moscow trusted Clinton's assertion in the Detroit speech that "NATO enlargement is not directed against anyone. I know that some in Russia still look at NATO through a Cold War prism, but I ask them to look again. We are building a new NATO just as they are building a new Russia."

If Republicans were not bestowing passing grades to the Clinton administration as the 1996 presidential campaign hit full stride, attention turned to the voters' assessment. A *New York Times*/CBS poll taken during the home stretch of the campaign found that Clinton's foreign policy approval rating was a solid 53 percent. The *Times*'s political analyst, R. W. Apple, Jr., concluded that Clinton had clearly "escaped any significant damage from crises overseas." Apple went further, arguing that the polls revealed how little foreign policy had to do with Bill Clinton's reelection, because the voters were focused on the economy, as they had been in 1992. If the voters failed to make the connection between foreign policy and domestic policy, Apple should have. From the start, Clinton viewed domestic renewal as linked to foreign policy, especially from foreign trade issues. From 1993 to 1996 more than a million new export-related jobs were created and the strength of the dollar increased, largely because of trade policy. In his 1997 farewell address, passing the torch to his successor Madeline Albright, Secretary of State Warren Christopher would boast: "Thanks to over 200 new market agreements we have created 1.6 million American jobs." One of Christopher's predecessors, John Foster Dulles, had often been accused of "pactomania" for engineering so many security treaties; the Clinton administration was becoming the "pactomaniacs" of free trade.

Republicans tried to shift the campaign debate from Clinton's obviously successful trade policy to what they saw as deficiencies in the military and security aspects of Clinton's foreign policy. They pointed to the President's failure to revitalize the national missile defense program and his sending U.S. soldiers to fight for the U.N. flag. They also argued that he was too weak with Russia and too slow on NATO enlargement. Worst of all, he had no grand design. Republican political strategists William Kristol and Robert Kagan attacked Clinton's enlargement strategy in the July–August 1996 issue of *Foreign Affairs*. In an elegiac burst of romantic militarism, they called for a "heroic" foreign policy based on "elevated patriotism" that "educate[s]" the citizenry "about the virtues of militarism" and shuns "cowardice and dishonor" in favor of "destroy[ing] many of the world's monsters." Other Republicans would also fault the Clinton administration for failing to develop a grand design, although in less florid terms. "My biggest criticism is that this Administration lacks a conceptual framework to shape the world going into the next century and [to] explain what threatens that vision," Senator John McCain (R-AZ) complained about Clinton during the 1996 election campaign. "Without that global strategy, we keep getting ourselves involved in peripheral matters such as Northern Ireland and Haiti."

Clinton's foreign policy also received flak from the Democratic side. Proponents of the U.N. faulted him for humiliating the organization by not spearheading the drive to pay America's bills and scapegoating U.N. Secretary-General Boutros Boutros-Ghali over Somalia and Bosnia. "Instead of defending the U.N. as the most logical instrument for peaceful settlement of Third World crisis in a chaotic post–Cold War world," *Los Angeles Times* U.N. correspondent Stanley Meisler griped, "the Clinton administration has chosen to berate the organization as unwise (in Somalia), cowardly (in Bosnia), and inept (in its bureaucracy)." Blaming the Adminis-

tration for allowing the U.N. to teeter on the brink of
bankruptcy, U.N. advocates chastised Clinton for allowing FDR's world organization to become another unem-
powered League of Nations.

Clinton was also denounced by the left for his indifference to the global environment. Liberals were hard-
pressed to understand how a President who professed
concern with peace, mediation, nuclear arms reduction,
abolition of chemical wapons, and the universal removal
of land mines virtually abandoned any leadership role
in developing global environmental policies. Clinton
might have talked the talk at a 1995 Earth Day rally in
Maryland—"Our natural security must be seen as a part
of our national security"—but he consistently failed to
walk the walk. Why a country as powerful as the United
States did not take the lead in curbing the world's
pollution was deemed by global environmentalists as un-
conscionable. Vice-President Al Gore, in his 1992 bestseller *Earth in the Balance,* sounded the environmental
alarm bells loud and clear. But once in office, Clinton-
Gore buckled under, partially over political concerns of
being labeled "Green." With powerful corporations lob-
bying against both domestic and international environmental regulations, the Administration was silent,
particularly because of its own guiding principle of economic enlargement. Without its own environmental
moral compass, the Administration was scarcely in a position to move America's corporate citizens toward becoming responsible global citizens, especially when the
compass readings were distorted by the lodestone of a
domestic and foreign policy of economic growth *über
alles.*

Critics on both sides dismissed Clinton as an amateur
juggler when it came to foreign policy, and they were
half right. While Clinton got off to a rocky start, he
eventually developed into an able practitioner of Band-
Aid diplomacy, demonstrating the flexibility necessary
to deal with such troubled areas as Haiti, Bosnia, the
Persian Gulf, North Korea, and the Taiwan Straits. At
least one observer regarded what many analysts saw as a

major flaw in Clinton's foreign policy, the lack of strategic vision, as a major stength: "U.S. foreign policy has been increasingly successfully precisely because Bill Clinton has refused to embrace chimerical visions," Jacob Heilbrun observed in a November 1996 *New Republic.* "As a result, he has skillfully piloted the U.S. through a sea of new world disorder."

Whatever the current world hot spot, free trade remained the core of Clinton's foreign policy, the heart of enlargement. When Clinton went to Madrid in December 1995 to create a new transatlantic agenda with European Union leaders, he was merely continuing a half century of U.S. efforts to economically integrate North America and Western Europe. While Reagan was chiefly responsible for engineering the trade pact with Canada and Bush brought Mexico into the NAFTA framework, it was Clinton who most fully realized that in the post–Cold War world democracy could be built through free trade as well as through ballot boxes. "The elegance of the Clinton strategy was that the Pacific, the European, and Western Hemisphere blocs should all have one thing in common: Clinton's America was locking itself steadily into the heart of each one," Martin Walker observed.

Clinton emphasized enlargement over gunboat diplomacy, preferring to help American industry flourish abroad over dispatching Marines to quell civil unrest in a nation of marginal consequence to U.S. interests. "With our help, the forces of reform in Europe's newly free nations have laid the foundations of democracy," Clinton claimed. "We've helped them to develop successful market economies, and now are moving from aid to trade and investment." *New York Times* columnist Thomas L. Friedman captured the heart of Clinton's enlargement doctrine on December 8, 1996: "No two countries that both have a McDonald's have ever fought a war against each other." In the Clinton worldview, it is GATT, NAFTA, APEC, the Summit of the Americas, the World Trade Organization, and the Free Trade Agreement of the Americas that will forward Washington's

global agenda far into the next century while promoting
domestic renewal.

Some critics of Clinton foreign policy strategy saw his
emphasis on economics as narrow, short-term and su-
perficial. Former Secretary of State Lawrence Eagle-
burger complained that there was little "hard strategic
thinking about how we want to see the world in the first
part of the next century," implying that the President
could not treat economic growth in a vacuum, as if it existed in a different realm than political and military considerations. These critics might say of the Clinton
mind-set what Dean Acheson said of John Foster Dulles,
his fierce ideological opponent—he was "a single-
minded concentrator."

Clinton was not without a defense to such charges.
Martin Walker argued that by adopting the strategy of
democratic enlargement Clinton had become the leading architect of a new world order, the free-trade leader
who "abandoned the militarized slogans of the past to
the commercial realities of the future." With U.S. defense spending still at 235 billion annually, the United
States clearly was heading into the next millennium as
both the world's largest military *and* economic power.
And as America prepared for the next millenium,
democracy was sweeping the globe. In 1974 only thirty-
nine countries—one in four of the world's independent
countries—were democratic. By the end of Clinton's
first term, 117 countries—nearly two of every four independent nations—held democratic elections to choose
their leaders.

Of course, all was not smooth sailing on the Clinton
foreign policy front. With China ignoring Clinton's economic and human rights demands, U.S. troops still stationed in Bosnia, environmental degredation rampant,
and international terrorism always a threat, the world
was still an unstable place no matter how many McDonald's Golden Arches dotted the planet. As Clinton began
his second term, no one would claim that he had
wrought a global utopia of free-market democracies, but
he had made genuine progress.

Suggestions for Further Reading

A good overview of American policy in the past forty years is the sprightly and informative *American Foreign Policy: A History* (1977) by Thomas Paterson, J. Garry Clifford, and Kenneth Hagan. A thorough and judicious recent interpretation is Warren I. Cohen's *America in the Age of Soviet Power* (1993), a volume in the Cambridge History of American Foreign Relations. John Lewis Gaddis's *We Now Know: Rethinking Cold War History* (1997) is a useful analysis of recent international events. For a witty, perceptive history of the American experience of the Cold War, from Truman's creation of the CIA to Reagan's creation of SDI to the disintegration of the Soviet Union, see H. W. Brands's *The Devil We Knew* (1993). There are a number of good general histories of the Cold War, although unfortunately most tend to begin in 1945. An exception is D. F. Flemming's *The Cold War and Its Origins, 1917–1960* (1961), a comprehensive two-volume study that, although poorly organized, is vigorous in its criticism of American policy. A better balanced treatment is Walter LaFeber's *America, Russia, and the Cold War, 7th Edition* (1993). Louis Halle's *The Cold War as History* (1967) attempts with some success to view with detachment, and has been described as the confessions of a former Cold War Warrior. For a thoughtful, under-appreciated appraisal see Martin Walker's *The Cold War: A History* (1993). Henry Kissinger's *Diplomacy* (1994) is full of important Cold War insights and is surprisingly easy to read. One of the first critical accounts of America's Cold War policies is *The Tragedy of American Diplomacy* (1962) by William A. Williams. Herbert S. Dinerstein looks at events from the Russian point of view in *Fifty Years of Soviet Foreign Policy* (1968). A good general survey of the personalities involved is Lloyd Gardner's *Architects of Illusion: Men and Ideas in American Foreign Policy* (1970). The best book ever written on U.S. Cold War policymaking is Walter Isaacson and Evan Thomas, *The Wise Men* (1986), a group portrait of Dean Acheson, George Kennan, Averell Harriman, Robert Lovett, Charles Bohlen, and John McCloy. On the CIA be sure to read Robert M. Gates, *From the Shadows* (1996), an indispensable slice of Cold War history. The best scholarly analysis of covert operations since the Second World War is John Prados's *President's Secret Wars* (1986). McGeorge Bundy, *Danger and Survival* (1988), is a history of nuclear weapons, their political use and misuse, and their impact on superpower relations. For this section, as well as those that follow, the interested student should consult the excellent bibliographies in the already cited works of Gaddis and LaFeber.

World War II

The literature on American policy in World War II is staggering in scope. One happy result is that there are a number of excellent, engaging, interpretative works, such as Robert Dallek's *Franklin D. Roosevelt and American Foreign Policy, 1932–45*, (1979), Robert A. Divine's *Roosevelt and World War II* (1969), Kent Robert Greenfield's *American Strategy in World War II: A Reconsideration* (1963), which is stronger on the military than on foreign policy, John L. Snell's *Illusion and Necessity: The Diplomacy During the Second World War* (1963), and Gaddis Smith's *American Diplomacy During the Second World War* (1965). Eric Larrabee's *Commander-in-Chief: Franklin Delano Roosevelt, His Lieutenants, and Their War* (1987) is a wonderful illustration of FDR's grand strategy in action. *The Supreme Commander: The War Years of Dwight D. Eisenhower* (1970) and *D-Day: June 6, 1944* (1994) by Stephen E. Ambrose are detailed accounts of American military policy in Europe. Paul Fussell's *Wartime: Understanding and Behavior in the Second World War* (1989) is a masterful psychological analysis of war. The newly revised *Atomic Diplomacy* (1985), by Gar Alperovitz, examines the motives behind the use of the atomic bomb. Although long, detailed, and somewhat dated, Robert E. Sherwood's *Roosevelt and Hopkins: An Intimate History* (1950) is still very much worth reading. The standard work for wartime diplomacy is Herbert Feis, *Churchill, Roosevelt, Stalin: The War They Waged and the Peace They Sought* (1957), which is almost an official history. For a forthright revisionist account, highly critical of American policy, consult Gabriel Kolko, *The Politics of War: The World and the United States Foreign Policy, 1943–1945* (1968). Volume three of Forrest C. Pogue's biography of George Marshall, *Organizer of Victory: 1943–1945* (1973), is a magnificent book about the man who was at the center of the whirlwind for the last two years of the war. John Keegan's *The Second World War* (1989) is the best of the one-volume histories of the conflict. A book that cannot be put down, once begun, and that as a bonus has many insights into the politics of the use of the atomic bomb, is *Enola Gay* (1977), by Gordon Thomas and Max Witt, and is the story of the bomb from its inception to the first shock wave over Hiroshima. David Eisenhower's *Eisenhower at War* (1987) is a detailed and argumentative work that concentrates on Ike's relations with the Russians. Townsend Hoopes and Douglas Brinkley's *FDR and the Creation of the U.N.* (1997) offers a comprehensive overview of postwar planning from the Atlantic Charter to the San Francisco Conference.

The Truman Years

There have been a number of outstanding books on the early Cold War, particularly Herbert Feis's *From Trust to Terror: The Onset of the Cold War, 1945–1950* (1970), John Lewis Gaddis's *The United States and the Origins of the Cold War, 1941–1947* (1972), Melvyn P. Leffler's *A Preponderance of Power* (1992), and Daniel Yergin's *Shattered Peace: The Origins of the Cold War and the National Security State*

(1977). Truman's own two-volume *Memoirs* (1955), and those of Dean Acheson, *Present at the Creation* (1969), provide a comprehensive official view. David McCullough's *Truman* (1992) and Alonzo Hamby's *Man of the People: A Life of Harry S Truman* (1995) are both first-rate biographies. George Kennan's *Memoirs, 1925–1950* (1967) is a joy to read, not only because of Kennan's matchless style but also because he is somewhat detached, admits to mistakes, and examines the assumptions on which policy was based. There are a number of solid academic studies of Kennan, including Walter Hixson, *George F. Kennan: Cold War Iconclast* (1989) and Anders Stephenason, *Kennan and the Art of Foreign Policy* (1989). Another important memoir, particularly with respect to the creation of Israel, is Clark Clifford's *Counsel to the President* (1991). Townsend Hoopes and Douglas Brinkley, *Driven Patriot: The Life and Times of James Forrestal* (1992), is an important account of America's first Secretary of Defense. *The Forrestal Diaries* (1951) edited by Walter Millis and *Private Papers* (1952) by Arthur H. Vandenberg are other important sources. Joseph M. Jones's *The Fifteen Weeks* (1955) examines in detail, but uncritically, the events leading to the Truman Doctrine and the Marshall Plan. Michael Hogan's *The Marshall Plan* (1987) is a model scholarly study. Bruce Kuniholm's *The Origins of the Cold War in the Near East: Great Power Conflict and Diplomacy in Iran, Turkey, and Greece* (1980) is a landmark work. There have been a number of good books on Truman's China policy, but the best is Nancy B. Tucker's *Patterns in the Dust* (1983). H. W. Brands's *The Specter of Neutralism* (1989) evaluates the emergence of the Third World between 1945 and 1950. Bruce Cumming's two-volume *The Origins of the Korean War* (1981–90) is remarkable in its judicious detail and keen insight. David Ree's *Korea: The Limited War* (1964) is a good general treatment of the conflict. The most balanced popular account is Burton Kaufman, *The Korean War* (1987). Max Hastings's *The Korean War* (1987) is a superb battlefield history. *N.A.T.O.: The Entangling Alliance* (1962) by Robert E. Osgood and *N.A.T.O. and the United States* (1998) by Lawrence

S. Kaplan are model studies. Forrest Pogue's fourth and concluding volume, *Marshall: Statesman, 1945–1959* (1989), is indispensable to any study of the Truman administration's foreign policy. A scathing denunciation of that policy, from a Marxist perspective, is Joyce and Gabriel Kolko's *The Limits of Power* (1972). Robert James Maddox has blasted the revisionists' work, especially that of William A. Williams and Gabriel Kolko, in his controversial *The New Left and the Origins of the Cold War* (1973). Michael S. Sherry's *The Rise of American Airpower: The Creation of Armageddon* (1987) is an outstanding study of the role of the atomic bomb in the early Cold War. Paul Boyer, *By the Bomb's Early Light* (1985), covers the impact of the bomb on American life in general. Richard Rhodes has written two first-rate studies of U.S. nuclear policy: *The Making of the Atomic Bomb* (1986) and *Dark Sun: The Making of the Hydrogen Bomb* (1995).

The Eisenhower Years

Eisenhower's memoirs, *The White House Years: A Personal Account* (two volumes, 1963 and 1965), are primarily concerned with foreign policy. For a comprehensive and critical view, see Stephen E. Ambrose, *Eisenhower: The President* (1984). Samuel P. Huntington's *The Common Defense: Strategic Programs in National Politics* (1961), a truly outstanding work, is essential to any study of Eisenhower's (and Truman's) military policy. There was a multitude of critics of the New Look; perhaps the most important was Maxwell Taylor's *The Uncertain Trumpet* (1959). Herman Finer's *Dulles Over Suez* (1964) is a critical account of the secretary of state's role in the 1956 crisis. The best book on the crisis is *Suez 1956* (1989), edited by W. Roger Louis and Roger Owen. The most searing attack on Eisenhower's policy toward Castro is William A. Williams, *The United States, Cuba and Castro* (1962). Theodore Draper's *Castro's Revolution* (1962) expressed the view that Castro betrayed the revolution.

Stephen G. Rabe's *Eisenhower and Latin America* (1988) is the best book on hemispheric affairs in the 1950s. A good biography of Ike is Pete Lyon, *Eisenhower: Portrait of the Hero* (1974). Herbert Parmet's *Eisenhower and the American Crusades* (1972) is a solid account of Ike's years in office. Richard A. Melanson and David Mayers have edited an important collection of revisionist essays in *Reevaluating Eisenhower* (1987). The politics of oil is explored by Burton Kaufman in *The Oil Cartel Case* (1978) and Daniel Yergin in *The Prize: The Epic Quest for Oil: Money and Power* (1991). Walter McDougall, *The Heavens and the Earth: The Politics of the Space Age* (1985), is a fascinating account of the relationship between the space race and international politics. Michael Beschloss, *Mayday* (1986), is an insightful and fast-paced narrative of the U-2 incident. Gordon H. Chang, *Friends and Enemies: The United States, China and the Soviet Union, 1948–1972* (1990), while good on the entire period it covers, is especially recommended for its treatment of the Eisenhower administration's relations with China.

Kennedy and Johnson

The best books on JFK's foreign policy are *Kennedy's Quest for Victory* (1989), edited by Thomas G. Paterson, and *The Crisis Years* (1991) by Michael Beschloss. An excellent recent biography of JFK's White House Years is Richard Reeves, *Kennedy* (1993). A previous biography—Herbert Parmet's *J.F.K.* (1983)—is also worthwhile. Arthur M. Schlesinger, Jr.'s *A Thousand Days: John F. Kennedy in the White House* (1965) and Theodore Sorenson's *Kennedy* (1965) are accounts by insiders who are fully devoted to the memory of the late president. Schlesinger writes more about foreign affairs than Sorenson does. Christopher Matthews's splendid study *Kennedy and Nixon* (1996) is a must-read for any one interested in U.S. political history. For evaluations of the Berlin Crisis see Douglas Brinkley, *Dean Acheson: The Cold War Years, 1953–1971* (1992), and Robert Slusser,

The Berlin Crisis of 1961 (1973). The Pentagon mindset during the Kennedy–Johnson years is ably explored in Deborah Shapley's *Promise and Power: The Life and Times of Robert McNamara* (1993). Philip Geyelin, *Lyndon B. Johnson and the World* (1966), and Rowland Evans and Robert Novak, *Lyndon B. Johnson: The Exercise of Power* (1966), are also good. Elie Abel's *The Missile Crisis* (1966) is a first-rate account by a professional journalist; part of the inside story is told by Robert F. Kennedy in his *Thirteen Days: A Memoir of the Cuban Missile Crisis* (1966). The most accurate recent accounts of the Cuban crisis are *The Cuban Missile Crisis Revisited* (1992), edited by James Nathan, and *Eyeball to Eyeball: The Inside Story of the Cuban Missile Crisis* (1991) by Dino A. Brugioni. A groundbreaking recent study—based on Soviet archives—is Aleksandar Fursenko and Timothy Naftali's *"One Hell of a Gamble": Kruschev, Castro, and Kennedy 1958–1964* (1997). The literature on Vietnam is overwhelming and still growing. David Halberstam's *The Best and the Brightest* (1972) is sprightly reading. All of Bernard Fall's books are good; students should begin with the collection of his articles, *Vietnam Witness, 1953–1966* (1966). Stanley Karnow's *Vietnam* (1984; revised 1997) is now the standard one-volume account of both the French and American wars in Indochina. Townsend Hoopes, *The Limits of Intervention* (1969), is an exceptionally good memoir by a key participant in the crucial decision to halt the bombing of North Vietnam. Robert W. Tucker's *Nation or Empire?* (1968) is an excellent essay. David Kraslow and Stuart Loory, in *The Secret Search for Peace in Vietnam* (1968), give the details of Hanoi's peace moves and Washington's reactions. Johnson's own memoirs, *From the Vantage Point* (1971), are rather dull and uninformative. Philip Caputo's *A Rumor of War* (1978) is the exact opposite, an autobiography that skillfully captures the mood of the time and the war as it was. Larry Berman's two Vietnam War books *Planning a Tragedy* (1982) and *Lyndon Johnson's War* (1989), are essential to understanding Washington policymaking. Peter Braestrup's *Big Story* (1977) is a detailed, excellent analysis of press coverage of the 1968 Tet offensive. For biographies of Vietnam War dissenters, see James A. Bill's *George Ball* (1997), David DiLeo's *George Ball, Vietnam, and the Rethinking of Containment* (1991), and Randall Woods's *Fulbright* (1995). Of all the many books on Vietnam, the most accessible and balanced remains George C. Herring's *American's Longest War* (second edition, 1986).

The Nixon Years

Begin with Nixon's own memoirs, *RN* (1981), the most revealing of any presidential memoirs. Kissinger's *White House Years* (1979) and *Years of Upheaval* (1982) are massive in both size and ego. Monumental in scope, they are witty, detailed, frequently self-serving, highly quotable, often informative, never dull, sometimes brilliant—in short, rather like the amazing Dr. Kissinger himself. Walter Isaacson's Pulitzer Prize–winning *Kissinger* (1992) is well-written, balanced, and highly recommended. Stephen E. Ambrose, *Nixon: The Triumph of a Politician* (1989), extensively covers Nixon in Vietnam, the opening to China, and détente. Herbert Parmet's *Nixon and His America* (1990) is a solid interpretive study. Michael Herr, *Dispatches* (1977), is on the list of must-reads about Vietnam; it is an impressionistic look at Vietnam in the late sixties, with an emphasis on how the war was fought. Frank Snepp's *Decent Interval* (1978) is well described by its subtitle: *An Insider's Account on Saigon's Indecent End Told by the CIA's Chief Strategy Analyst in Vietnam*. Nguyen Tien Hung and Jerrold Schecter, *The Palace File* (1987), tells the story of American-Vietnamese relations in the Nixon/Ford years. Likewise, John Robert Greene's *The Limits of Power* (1992) is a well-written look at the foreign policy approaches of Nixon/Ford. William Colby's *Lost Victory* (1989) is a firsthand account of the CIA's activities in Vietnam and an analysis of why victory was not achieved.

Gerald Ford's *A Time to Heal* (1979) at times sophomoric, is an underappreciated presidential memoir with a good chapter on the Helsinki Accords. Seymor M. Hersh, *The Price of Power: Kissinger in the Nixon White House* (1983), is a scathing attack on both Kissinger and Nixon. An unabashed defense of Nixon can be found in C. C. Sulzberger's *The World of Richard Nixon* (1987). Far better balanced and much more thoroughly researched and developed is Raymond Garthoff's *Détente and Confrontation: American-Soviet Relations from Nixon to Reagan* (1985). Daunting in size (1,147 pages), it is a treasure, perhaps the best book on American foreign policy we have ever read, and it is ideal for students searching for term paper information. Robert Litwak's *Détente and the Nixon Doctrine* (1984) documents the conflicting sides of U.S.-Soviet détente. Gerald Smith's *Doubletalk* (1980) is a colorful insider's account of SALT I. William Hyland, *Mortal Rivals: Superpower Relations from Nixon to Reagan* (1987), is also a useful study.

The Middle East and Africa

General histories that cover both areas well include James Nathan and James Oliver, *United States Foreign Policy and World Order* (1978), which is especially strong on the relationship between foreign policy and domestic politics, and Stewart C. Easton, *World History Since 1954* (1968), a comprehensive review. Books on Kissinger abound; he is a fascinating subject, irresistible to many authors, including Matti Golan, whose *The Secret Conversations of Henry Kissinger: Step-by-Step Diplomacy in the Middle East* (1976) caused a sensation when it appeared and remains invaluable. G. Warren Nutter's *Kissinger's Grand Design* (1975) is a thoughtful denunciation of détente and Kissinger's Middle East policy. Gil Carl Alroy's *The Kissinger Experience: American Policy in the Middle East* (1975) is a bitter criticism of Kissinger for his supposed abandonment of his own people, the Jews. Much more balanced and trustworthy is Edward Sheehan, *The Arabs, Israelis, and Kissinger* (1976), a detailed account of Kissinger and the Yom Kippur War. The best overview of America in the Middle East can be found in Thomas L. Friedman's *From Beirut to Jerusalem* (1989), a brilliant analysis of Israeli-Arab relations.

A good background for U.S.-African relations is Thomas J. Noer's *Cold War and Black Liberation* (1985); another excellent concise account is Roland Oliver and J. D. Fage, *A Short History of Africa* (1969). Vernon McKay's *African Diplomacy* (1966) is a collection of essays on emerging Africa by various African scholars; so is Yassin El-Ayouty and Hugh Brooks, *African and International Organization* (1974). For Kennedy's African policy, see Richard Mahoney *JFK: Ordeal in Africa* (1983). Anthony Lake's *The Tar Baby Option* (1976) is a classic account of U.S.-Rhodesian policy. Kwame Nkrumah's *Neo-Colonialism: The Last Stage of Imperialism* (1965), the book that made Lyndon Johnson furious, is an African account of how economics works in Africa. John Stockwell's *In Search of Enemies: A CIA Story* (1978) is the memoir of CIA Chief of the Angola Task Force; Stockwell had second thoughts about what he was doing, resigned from the CIA, and published a book about his experiences, in what had become a relatively common practice for disgruntled ex-CIA agents.

The best raw source on the CIA and its impact on foreign policy is in government publications, especially hearings, and most especially the various volumes of the Church Committee Hearings (the "Senate Select Committee to Study Governmental Operations With Respect to Intelligence Activities"). Published in 1976, the volumes contain a history of the CIA and testimony from dozens of ex- and current agents and their bosses about various operations dating back to 1948. One entire volume is devoted to "Alleged Assassination Plots Involving Foreign Leaders." Another government document that is most helpful in understanding American policy in Africa is NSSM 39, published as *The Kissinger Study of Southern Africa*, edited and with an excellent introduction by Mohamed A. El-Khawas and Barry Cohen (1976).

Carter and Reagan

Zbigniew Brzezinski's memoirs, *Power and Principles* (1985) portions of which appeared in 1982, were the first insider's account of the Carter administration to appear. They revealed his frequent policy differences with Secretary of State Vance. Carter's own White House memoirs, *Keeping Faith* (1983), are disappointing overall, but outstanding on his greatest triumph, the Camp David accords. Gaddis Smith's *Morality, Reason and Power* (1986) is the single best book on Carter's foreign policy. A serious study of Carter's Middle East Diplomacy is William B. Quandt's *Camp David* (1986). The event of the Carter years that has attracted the most attention is, of course, the Iranian revolution and the hostage crisis, which has produced a number of excellent books. First among them is Barry Rubin, *Paved with Good Intentions: The American Experience and Iran* (1981), a masterful study that is indispensable. Nearly as good is John Stempel, *Inside the Iranian Revolution* (1981), by the former Deputy Chief of Political Section of the American Embassy in Teheran. A *New York Times* team of reporters led by Robert McFadden published *No Hiding Place: Inside Report of the Hostage Crisis* (1981), which provides extensive, excellent coverage. Michael Leeden and William Lewis, *Debacle: The American Failure in Iran* (1981), is a useful short summary. William H. Sullivan's *Mission to Iran* (1981) is a candid report by the last American ambassador to Iran. Former NSC hand Gary Sick's *All Fall Down* (1985) and *October Surprise* (1991) both controversially recount America's tragic encounter with Iran from an insider's perspective. James Bill's *The Eagle and the Lion: The Tragedy of Iranian-American Relations* (1988) is outstanding. Strobe Talbott, *Endgame: The Inside Story of Salt II* (1979), is a fascinating account of the intricate nature of arms talks. Wayne S. Smith, *The Closest of Ene-*

mies: A Personal and Diplomatic Account of U.S.-Cuban Relations Since 1957 (1987), written by a Foreign Service career officer, is critical of American reliance on covert operations rather than on diplomacy. Robert A. Pastor's *Whirlpool* (1992) offers a brilliant analysis of U.S. foreign policy toward Latin American and the Caribbean during the Carter, Reagan, and Bush presidencies. T. Carothers's *In the Name of Democracy* (1991) is another important interpretive study of U.S. policy toward Latin American in the Reagan years. An interesting defense of Reagan's Nicaragua policy is Robert Kagan's *A Twilight Struggle* (1996). Lou Cannon, *Reagan* (1981), and Bill Boyarsky, *Ronald Reagan* (1982), are solid early studies. Michael Schaller's *Reckoning with Reagan* (1992) is a valuable brief analytical primer. Mark Hertsgaard, *On Bended Knee: The Press and the Reagan Presidency* (1988), is a fascinating account of the way the Reagan administration managed the news, especially the bad news on foreign policy misadventures. John Dumbrell's *American Foreign Policy* (1997) offers a shrewd analysis of the Reagan doctrine. An indispensable memoir of the Reagan years is George P. Shultz's *Turmoil and Triumph* (1993). By contrast Reagan's *An American Life* (1990) is disappointing.

Bush

The Bush administration has produced two first-rate memoirs: James A. Baker, *The Politics of Diplomacy* (1995), and Colin Powell, *My American Journey* (1995). There are a number of books on Desert Storm. Among the best are Jean Edward Smith, *George Bush's War* (1992), which is very critical of the former President, and Norman Friedman, *Desert Victory* (1992), which strongly supports Bush's policies. L. Freedman and E. Karsh's *The Gulf Conflict, 1990–1991* (1994) is also worth consulting. The history of U.S.–Iraqi relations during the Reagan–Bush years is best understood through reading Bruce Jentleson's *With Friends Like These* (1994). Investigative journalist Bob Woodward's

The Commanders (1991) is full of Gulf War gossip and plucky analysis.

Robert Tucker and David Hendrickson, *The Imperial Temptation* (1992), is a thoughtful and disturbing look at the new world order and America's purpose. *The End of the Cold War: Its Meaning and Implications* (1992), edited by Michael Hogan, is a timely collection of essays from some of the leading diplomatic historians in the United States and Europe. It discusses such important issues as the origins of the Cold War, its ideological and geopolitical sources, the cost of the conflict, and the future world order. A brilliant recounting of the collapse of the Soviet Empire is David Remmick's *Lenin's Tomb* (1993). Raymond L. Garthoff's *The Great Transition* (1994) is the best study of U.S.-Soviet relations at the end of the Cold War.

For Gorbachev, consult Zhores Medvedov's *Gorbachev* (1986), a balanced biography of a leading Soviet dissident. Zbigniew Brzezinski, *The Grand Failure: The Birth and Death of Communism in the Twentieth Century* (1989), written by Carter's national security adviser on the eve of the demise of Communism in Eastern Europe, is challenging, thought-provoking, and solid. For a wide-ranging discussion of the end of the Cold War, consult the Summer 1989 issue of *The National Interest* which contains Francis Fukuyama's article, "The End of the History?" and responses by six critics. Michael Beschloss and Strobe Talbott, *At the Highest Levels* (1992), is a fast-paced account of Gorbachev's relationship with Reagan and Bush. A highly recommended critique of post–Cold War democracy building is Tony Smith's *America's Mission* (1994).

Clinton

The best critique of Clinton's first-term foreign policy is Martin Walker's *The President We Deserve* (1996). A fair early appraisal of Clinton's diplomacy is Larry Berman and Emily O. Goldman's "Clinton's Foreign Policy at

Midterm" in *The Clinton Presidency* (1996), edited by Colin Campbell and Bert A. Rockman. A good survey of Clinton's trade efforts is William A. Orme, Jr.'s *Understanding NAFTA* (1996). Elizabeth Drew's *The Clinton Presidency* (1994) is a smart, trenchant look at our forty-second president's leadership style. Ronald Steel's *Temptations of a Superpower* (1995) is a provocative study on how to avoid the excesses of the Cold War in a post–Cold War world. Michael Parenti's *Against Empire* (1995) is a devastating critique of Clinton's globalization efforts. Douglas Brinkley's "Democratic Enlargement: The Clinton Doctrine" in *Foreign Policy* (Spring 1997) is a positive examination of NSC Advisor Anthony Lake's attempts at creating a post–Cold War grand strategy. Warren Christopher explains his foreign policy vision in "America's Leadership, America's Opportunity" in *Foreign Policy* (Spring 1995). William J. Perry summarized Clinton's military strategy record in "Defense in an Age of Hope" in *Foreign Affairs* (Nov./Dec. 1996). By contrast, a fairly critical appraisal is *Clinton and Post–Cold War Defense* (1996), edited by Stephen J. Cimbala. Much has been written about the West's failure in Bosnia but the two most accessible studies are David Rieff's *Slaughterhouse* (1995) and Roy Gutman's *Genocide* (1993). Yet by bringing NATO into the Balkans the Clinton administration was able to stabilize the region. The best explanation of Clinton's successful Bosnia policy is Richard Holbrooke's "Annals of Diplomacy: The Road to Sarajevo" published in *The New Yorker* (October 21 and 28, 1996).

For a powerful polemic against NATO expansion read Michael Mandelbaum's *Dawn at Peace in Europe* (1996). The case for NATO expansion is taken up in Thomas Blood and Bruce Henderson, *State of the Union: A Report on President Clinton's First Four Years in Office* (1996). A positive review of the administration's attempts to bring peace to Northern Ireland is Conor O'Cleary's *Daring Diplomacy* (1996). Before leaving his post as NSC Advisor Lake had compiled a massive fact book (known as the blue book) titled "Clinton Administration Foreign and Security Policy" (September 30, 1996). It offers the most ardent defense of Clinton global strategies available.

For instant yet thoughtful analysis of the state of the world, students should go to *Current History*, published monthly during the academic year, and containing articles on current developments by leading scholars. *Current History* is also invaluable for its section "The Month in Review: Country by Country, Day by Day," which provides one-sentence summaries of the important events around the world. *The Washington Post* "Weekly Edition" is a reliable guide to U.S. policymaking abroad. And any serious student of diplomacy should also acquire the four-volume *Encyclopedia of U.S. Foreign Relations* (1997), edited by Bruce Jentleson and Thomas G. Paterson. For Washington insider information reading *National Journal* is a must. We urge students who wish to study foreign policy in greater depth to join The Society for Historians of American Foreign Relations (SHAFR) in order to receive its quarterly journal, *Diplomatic History*, with its many outstanding articles, ideal for use in preparing term papers, and its superb book review section. The pertinent articles in two contemporary journals—*Foreign Affairs* and *Foreign Policy*—are always, without exception, essential reading.

Index